LIVING-ROOM

LIVING-ROOM MATSUNAGA-SAN

5

Keiko Iwashita

MATSUNAGA-SAN

LIVING-ROOM

Contents

Story

Family circumstances have wrested Meeko from an ordinary family life to her uncle's boarding house, where her unrequited feelings for her housemate Matsunaga-san only grow with each passing day. When she is visiting her grandma over the summer, a drunk Matsunaga calls her and tells her he misses her, sending her over the moon with joy. However, Meeko finds herself in the wrong place at the wrong time, and now Matsunaga-san is convinced she's dating Ryo-kun! With Ryo-kun's help, they resolve the misunderstanding, and as the last summer days slip away, Matsunaga-san promises her they'll go to Kitneyland together... But what secrets lie in Matsunaga-san's past? And will he find out she kissed him when he was sick?!

MATSUNAGA-SAN

Characters

Boarding House

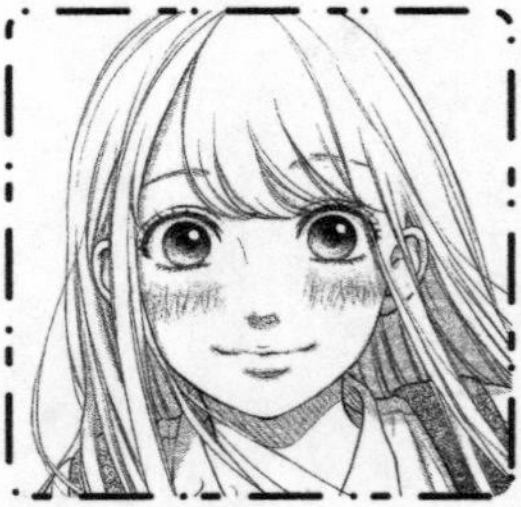

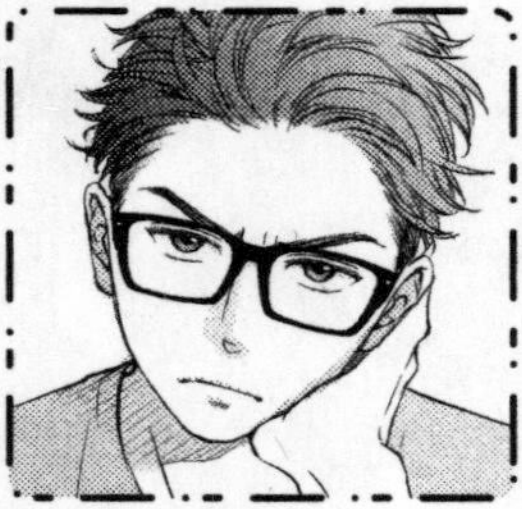

Miko Sonoda

A 17-year-old high school girl.
Only knows how to cook curry.
Pining for Matsunaga-san.

Jun Matsunaga

A designer who works from home.
28 years old.
Sharp-tongued but caring.

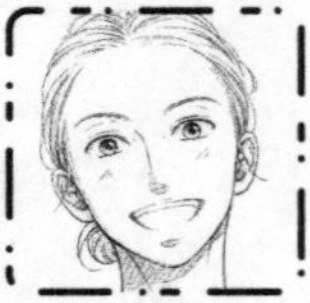

Kentaro Suzuki
A bartender.
Girl-crazy (?)

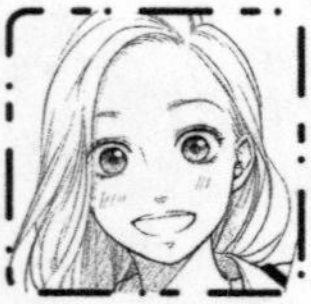

Asako Onuki
A nail artist.
Like a big sister.

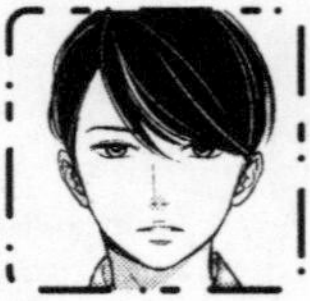

Ryo Hojo
A quiet college student.
Doesn't have a girlfriend.

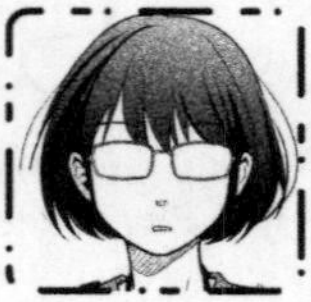

Akane Hattori
An enigma.
Actually has a boyfriend.

School

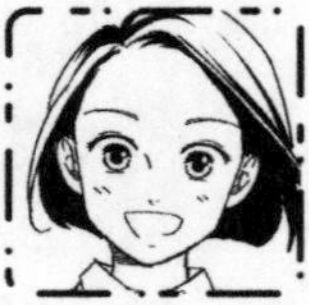

Ricchan
Meeko's friend.

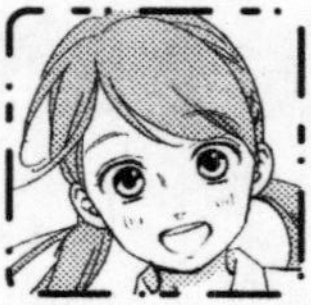

Maho
Meeko's friend.

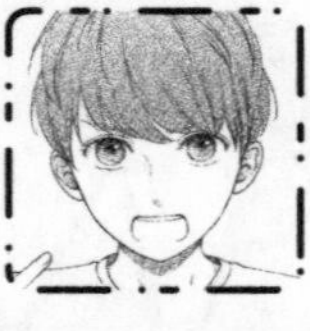

Natsumi Kobayashi
Meeko's homeroom teacher.

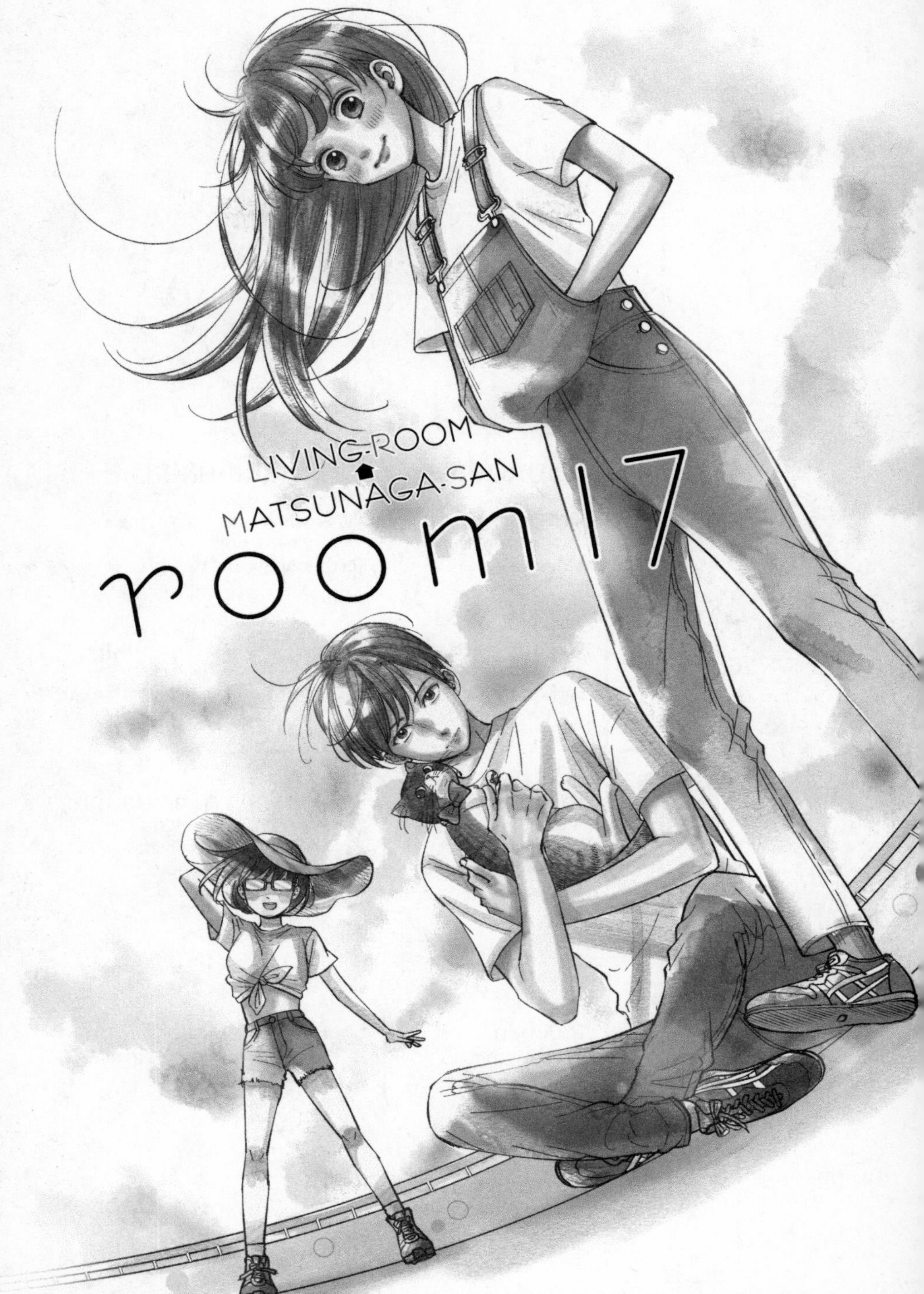
LIVING-ROOM MATSUNAGA-SAN
room 17

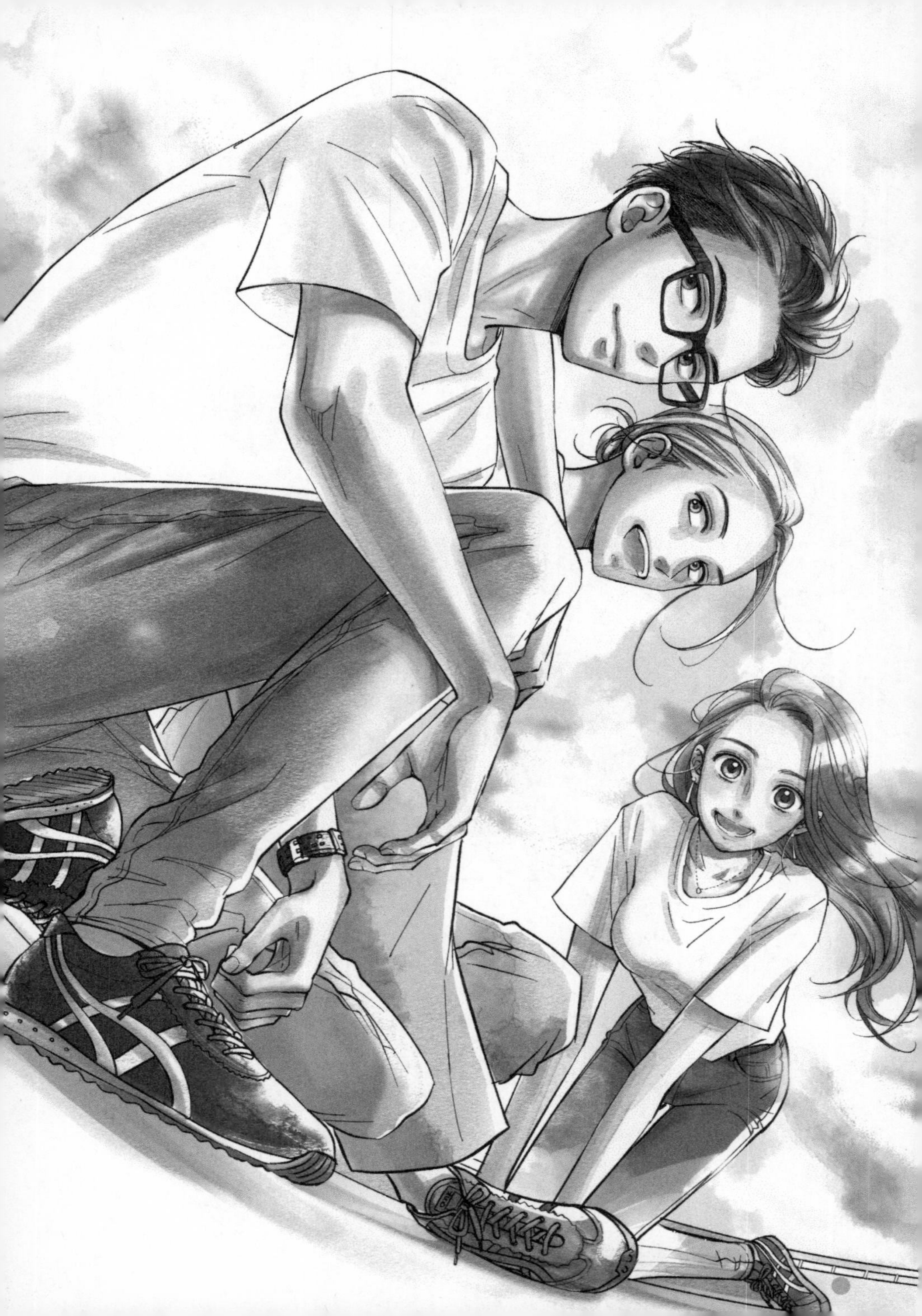

FOREWORD

THANKS SO MUCH FOR READING
LIVING-ROOM MATSUNAGA-SAN!

VOLUME 5 IS THE FIRST TIME I'VE EVER MADE THE
COVER FEATURE.

YOU KNOW, WHEN I FIRST STARTED THIS SERIES, I DIDN'T REALLY
HAVE ANY DELUSIONS OF GRANDEUR OR ANYTHING—I JUST WANTED
TO PUT OUT THE BEST STORY I COULD, CHAPTER BY CHAPTER.
BUT NOW, SEEING ALL MY READERS' FEEDBACK...I'VE STARTED
TO FEEL LIKE...**I'LL MAKE ALL YOUR DREAMS COME TRUE!!**

I WANT TO REPAY EVERYONE FOR THEIR SUPPORT BY FULFILLING
THIS DREAM, LITTLE BY LITTLE.

AND NOW I PRESENT TO YOU: VOLUME 5!!

I HOPE YOU LOOK FORWARD TO DIGGING DEEPER INTO THE MIS-
ADVENTURES OF LOVESICK CURRY GIRL MEEKO AND IDIOT HOTHEAD
MATSUNAGA-SAN... THANK YOU ALL SO MUCH!!

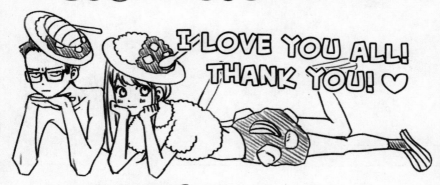

I LOVE YOU ALL!
THANK YOU! ♡

☆ SPECIAL THANKS ☆

TO MY EDITOR, KITAHARA; EVERYONE IN THE DESSERT
MAGAZINE EDITORIAL DEPARTMENT; MY ASSISTANTS, EI
AND SAKATA; THE DESIGNERS; EVERYONE AT THE PRINTER;
MY FRIENDS AND FAMILY; EVERYONE AT SUNAZUKA CAFÉ
WHO PUT UP WITH ALL MY QUESTIONS...

AND ALL MY READERS! REALLY, THANK YOU ALL SO MUCH!!

I LOVE YOU ALL! THANK YOU

2018.11.13

KEIKO IWASHITA

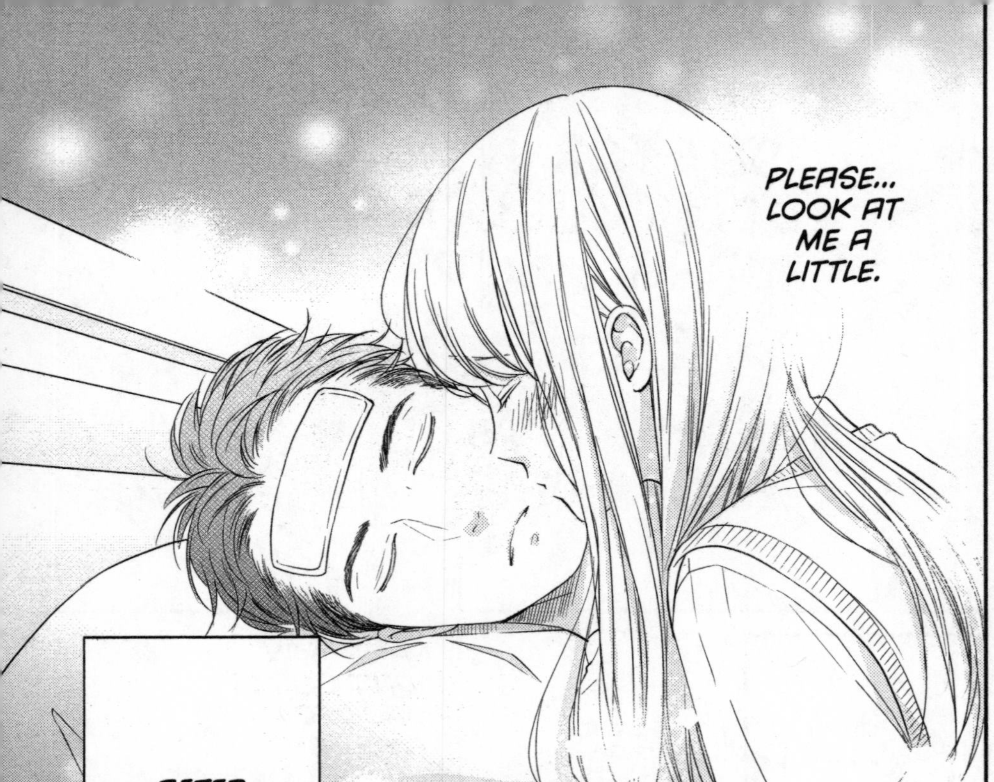
PLEASE... LOOK AT ME A LITTLE.
AFTER THAT...

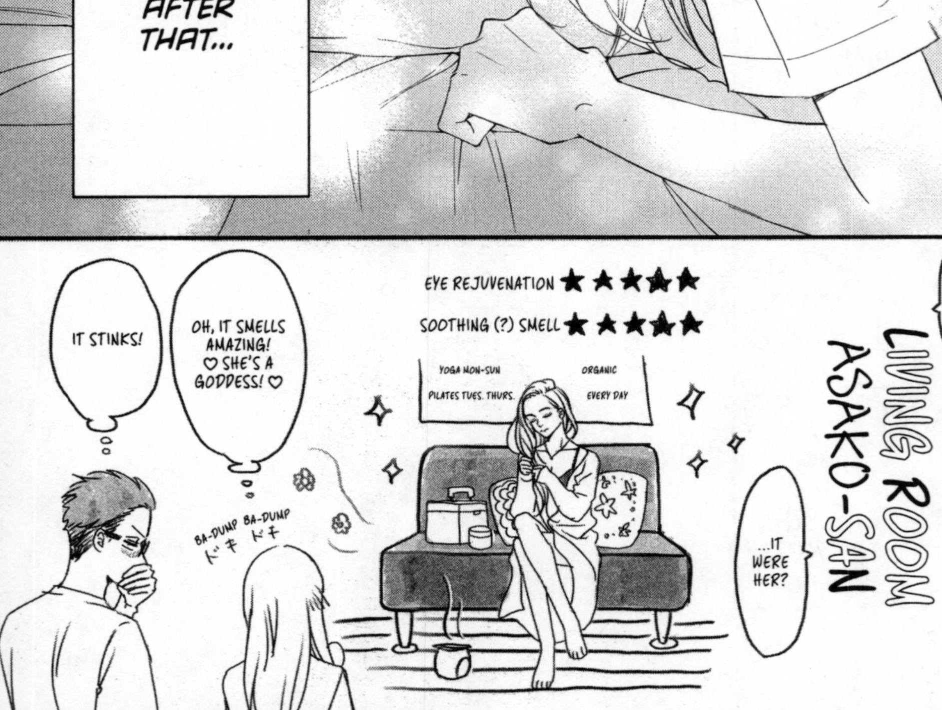
WHAT IF...
LIVING ROOM ASAKO-SAN
...IT WERE HER?
EYE REJUVENATION ★★★★★
SOOTHING (?) SMELL ★★★★★
YOGA MON-SUN
ORGANIC
PILATES TUES. THURS.
EVERY DAY
OH, IT SMELLS AMAZING! ♡ SHE'S A GODDESS! ♡
IT STINKS!
BA-DUMP BA-DUMP
ドキ ドキ

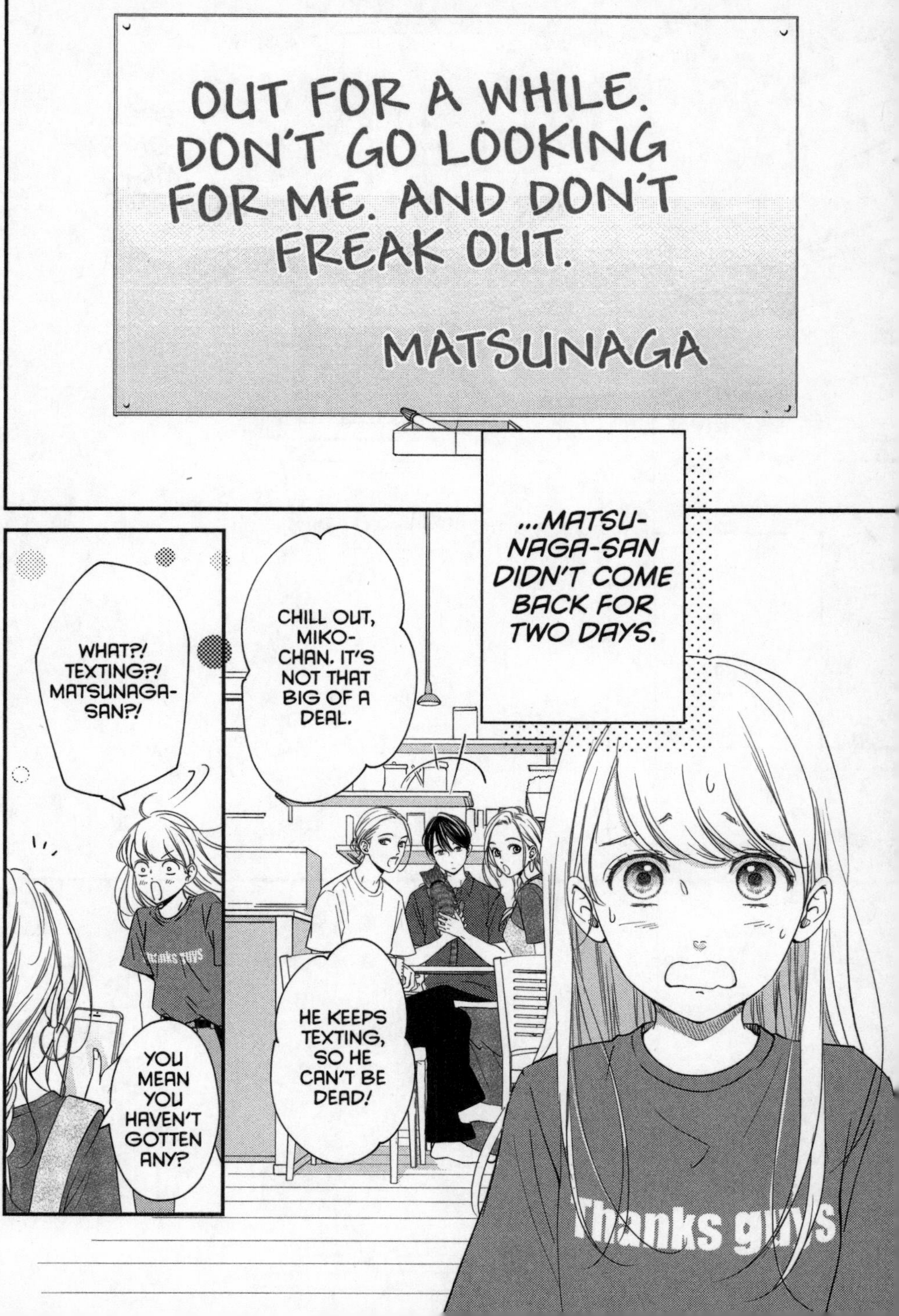
OUT FOR A WHILE. DON'T GO LOOKING FOR ME. AND DON'T FREAK OUT.
MATSUNAGA
...MATSU-NAGA-SAN DIDN'T COME BACK FOR TWO DAYS.
CHILL OUT, MIKO-CHAN. IT'S NOT THAT BIG OF A DEAL.
HE KEEPS TEXTING, SO HE CAN'T BE DEAD!
WHAT?! TEXTING?! MATSUNAGA-SAN?!
YOU MEAN YOU HAVEN'T GOTTEN ANY?
Thanks guys

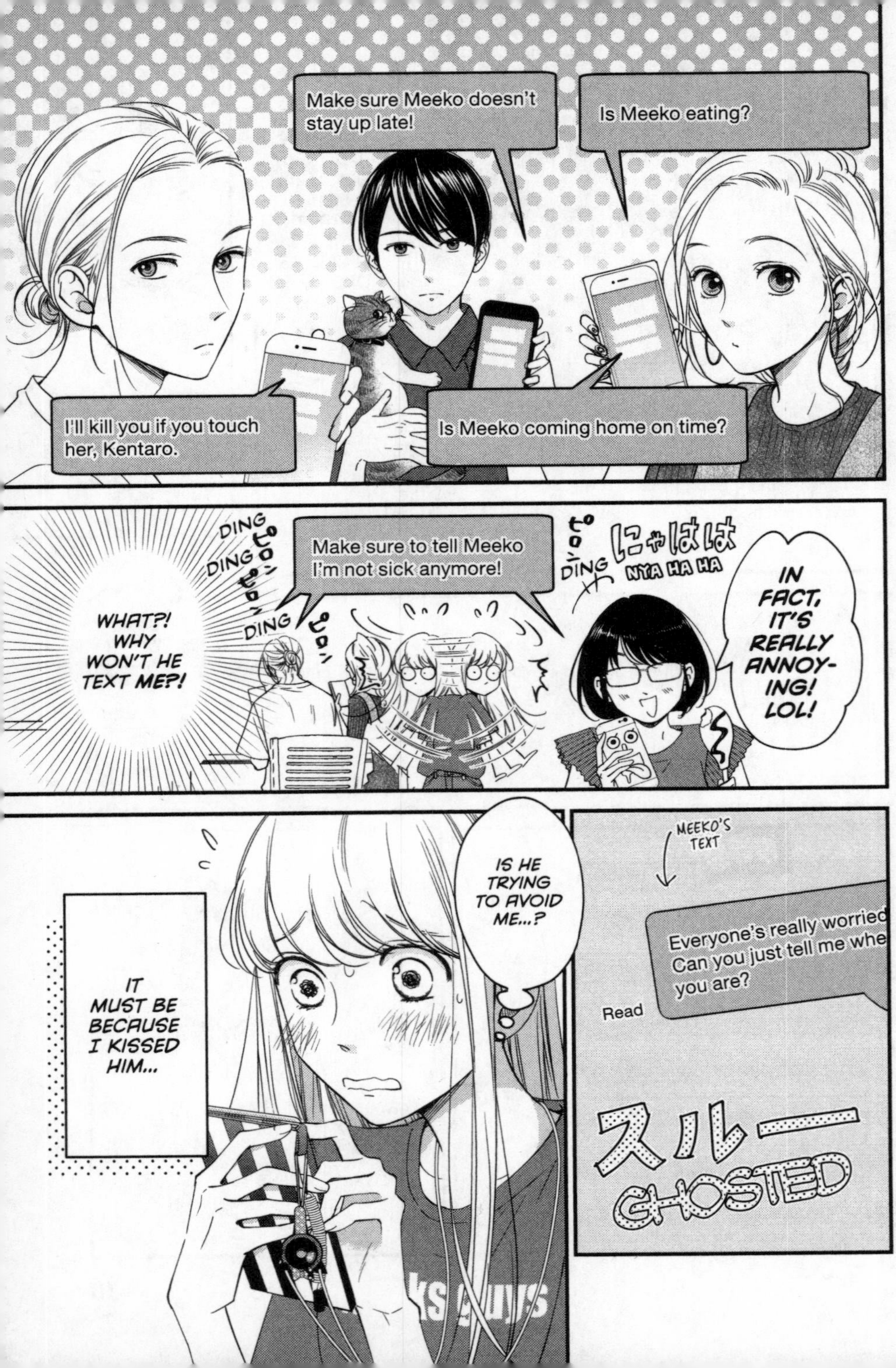
Is Meeko eating?
Make sure Meeko doesn't stay up late!
Is Meeko coming home on time?
I'll kill you if you touch her, Kentaro.
IN FACT, IT'S REALLY ANNOYING! LOL!
にゃはは
NYA HA HA
ピロン
DING
Make sure to tell Meeko I'm not sick anymore!
DING ピロン
DING ピロン
DING ピロン
WHAT?! WHY WON'T HE TEXT ME?!
MEEKO'S TEXT
Everyone's really worried
Can you just tell me whe
you are?
Read
スルー
GHOSTED
IS HE TRYING TO AVOID ME...?
IT MUST BE BECAUSE I KISSED HIM...

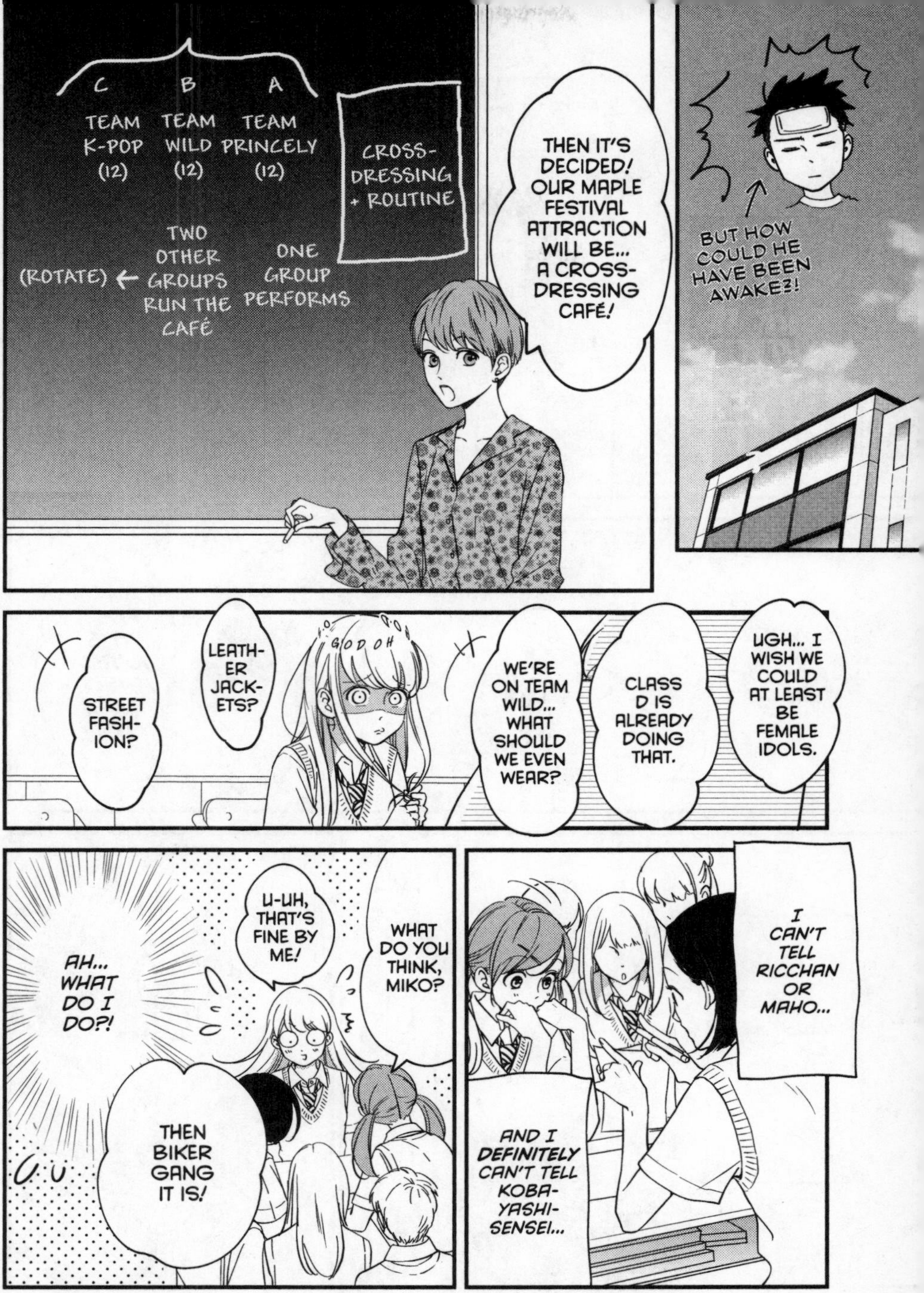
BUT HOW COULD HE HAVE BEEN AWAKE?!
C B A
TEAM K-POP (12) TEAM WILD (12) TEAM PRINCELY (12)
CROSS-DRESSING + ROUTINE
(ROTATE) ← TWO OTHER GROUPS RUN THE CAFÉ
ONE GROUP PERFORMS
THEN IT'S DECIDED! OUR MAPLE FESTIVAL ATTRACTION WILL BE... A CROSS-DRESSING CAFÉ!
UGH... I WISH WE COULD AT LEAST BE FEMALE IDOLS.
CLASS D IS ALREADY DOING THAT.
WE'RE ON TEAM WILD... WHAT SHOULD WE EVEN WEAR?
GOD OH
LEATH-ER JACK-ETS?
STREET FASH-ION?
I CAN'T TELL RICCHAN OR MAHO...
AND I DEFINITELY CAN'T TELL KOBA-YASHI-SENSEI...
WHAT DO YOU THINK, MIKO?
U-UH, THAT'S FINE BY ME!
AH... WHAT DO I DO?!
THEN BIKER GANG IT IS!

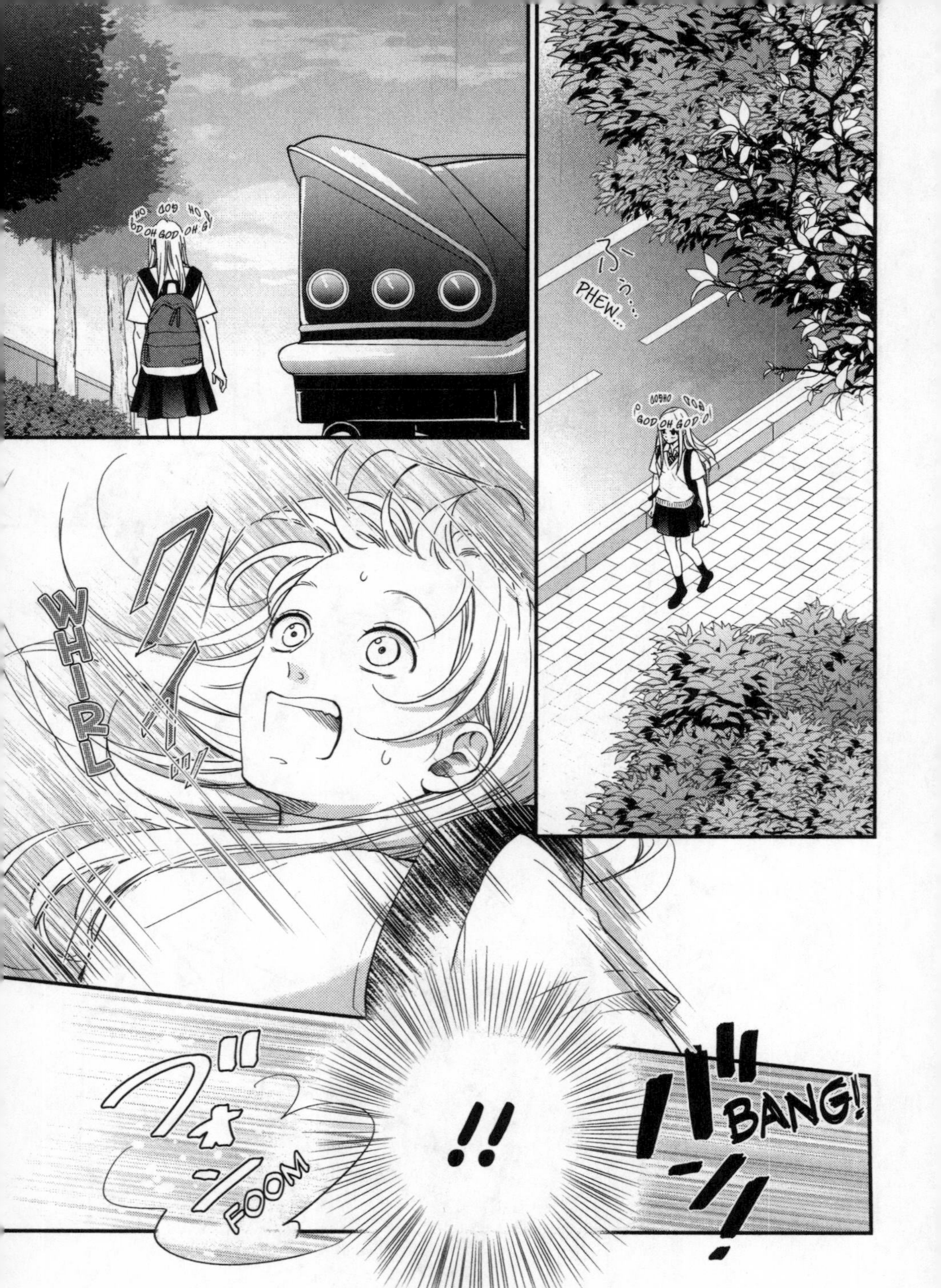
PHEW...
GOD OH GOD O
GOD OH GOD OH G!
WHIRL
BANG!
!!
FOOM

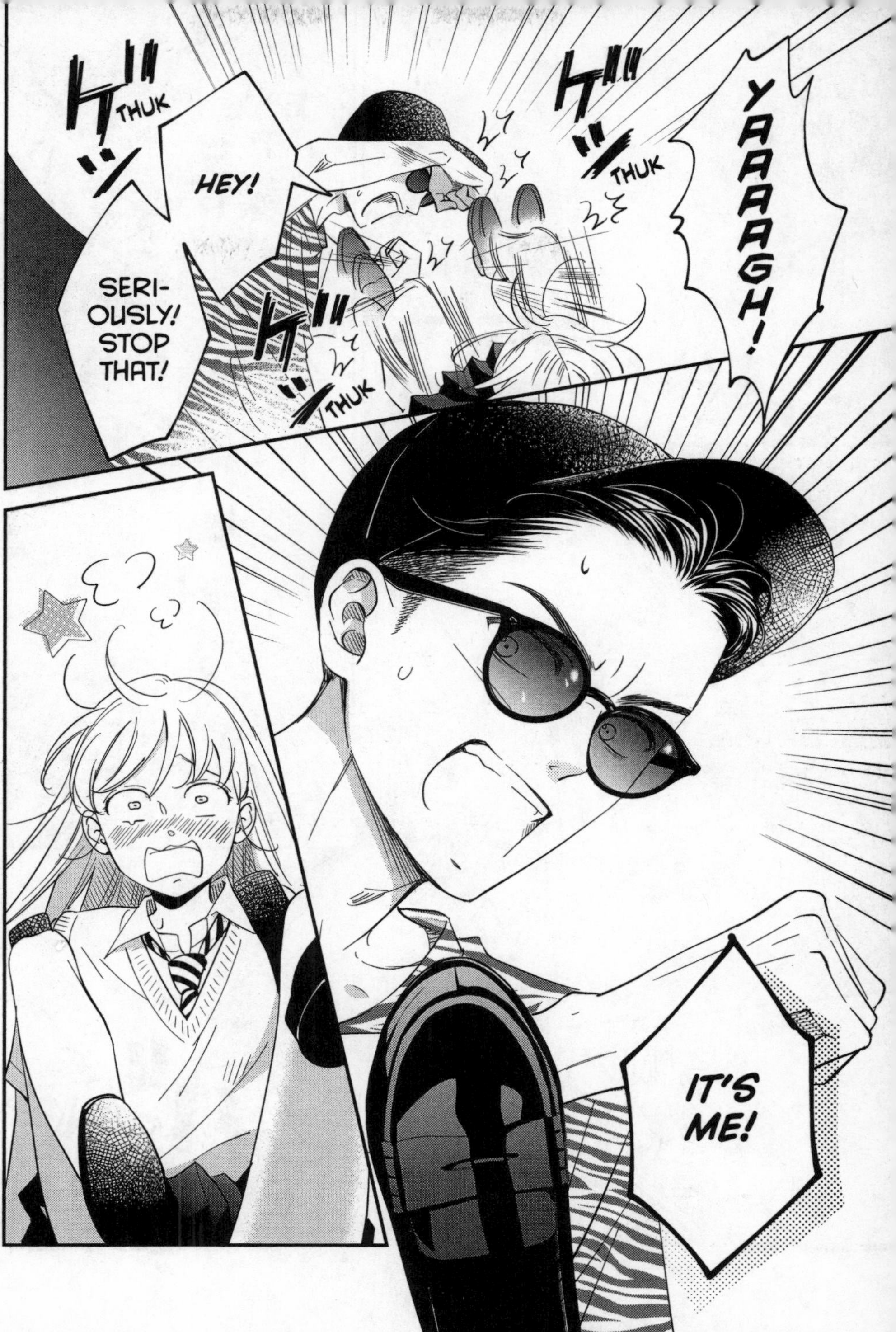
YAAAAAGH!
THUK
THUK
HEY!
SERI-
OUSLY!
STOP
THAT!
THUK
IT'S
ME!

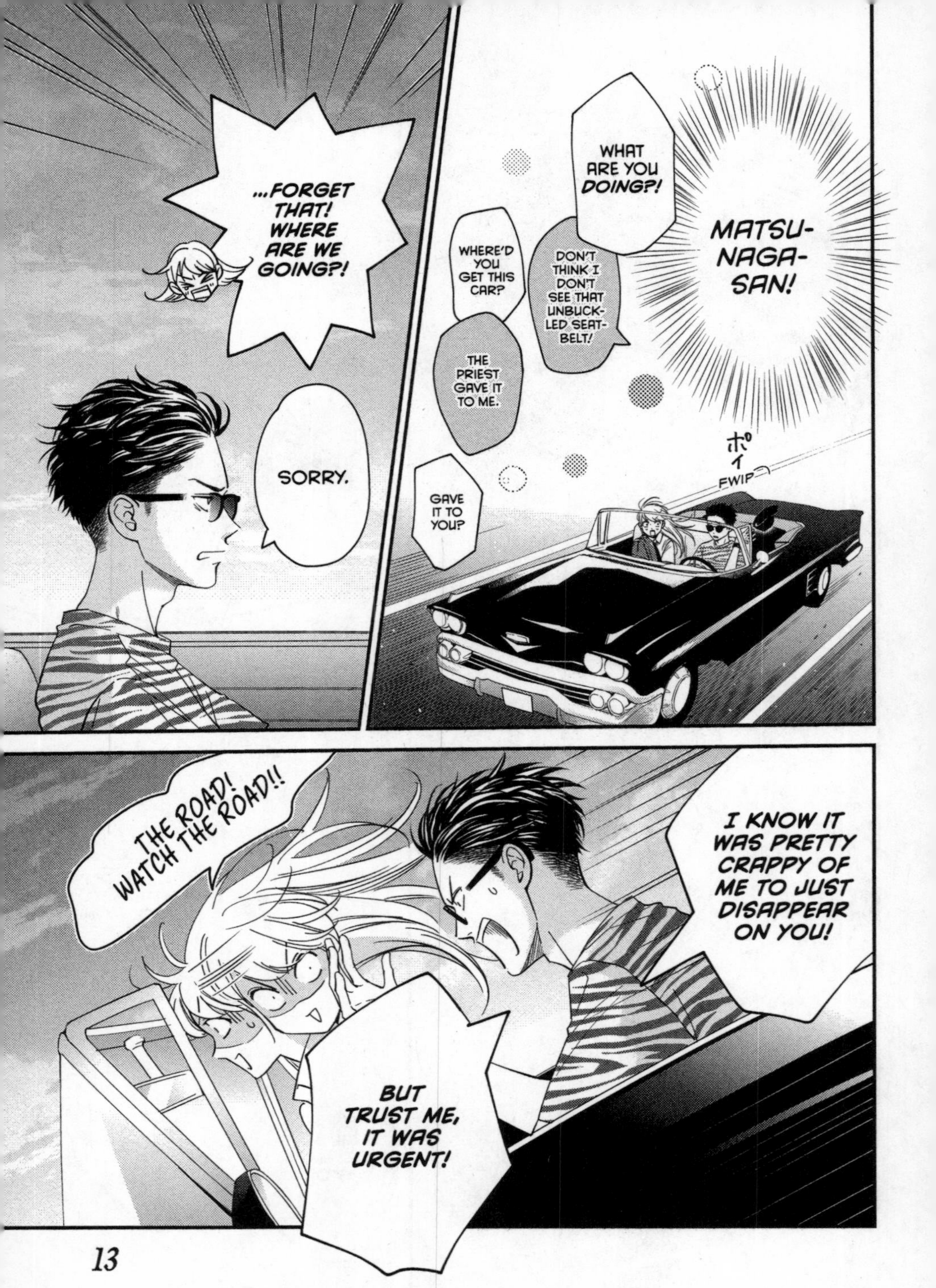
MATSU-NAGA-SAN!
WHAT ARE YOU DOING?!
DON'T THINK I DON'T SEE THAT UNBUCK-LED SEAT-BELT!
WHERE'D YOU GET THIS CAR?
THE PRIEST GAVE IT TO ME.
GAVE IT TO YOU?
ポイ
FWIP
...FORGET THAT! WHERE ARE WE GOING?!
SORRY.
I KNOW IT WAS PRETTY CRAPPY OF ME TO JUST DISAPPEAR ON YOU!
THE ROAD! WATCH THE ROAD!!
BUT TRUST ME, IT WAS URGENT!

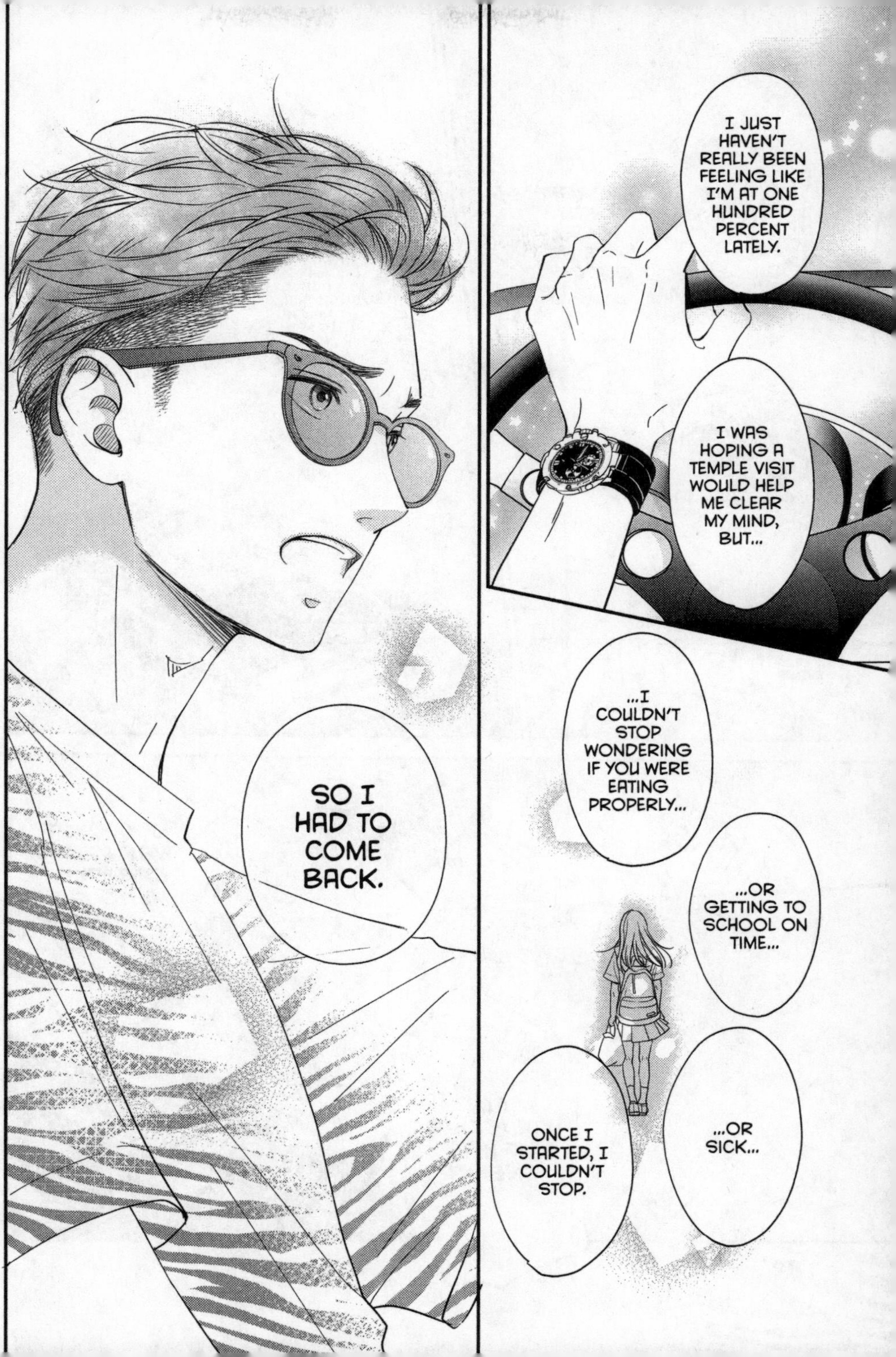

I JUST HAVEN'T REALLY BEEN FEELING LIKE I'M AT ONE HUNDRED PERCENT LATELY.
I WAS HOPING A TEMPLE VISIT WOULD HELP ME CLEAR MY MIND, BUT...
...I COULDN'T STOP WONDERING IF YOU WERE EATING PROPERLY...
...OR GETTING TO SCHOOL ON TIME...
...OR SICK...
ONCE I STARTED, I COULDN'T STOP.
SO I HAD TO COME BACK.

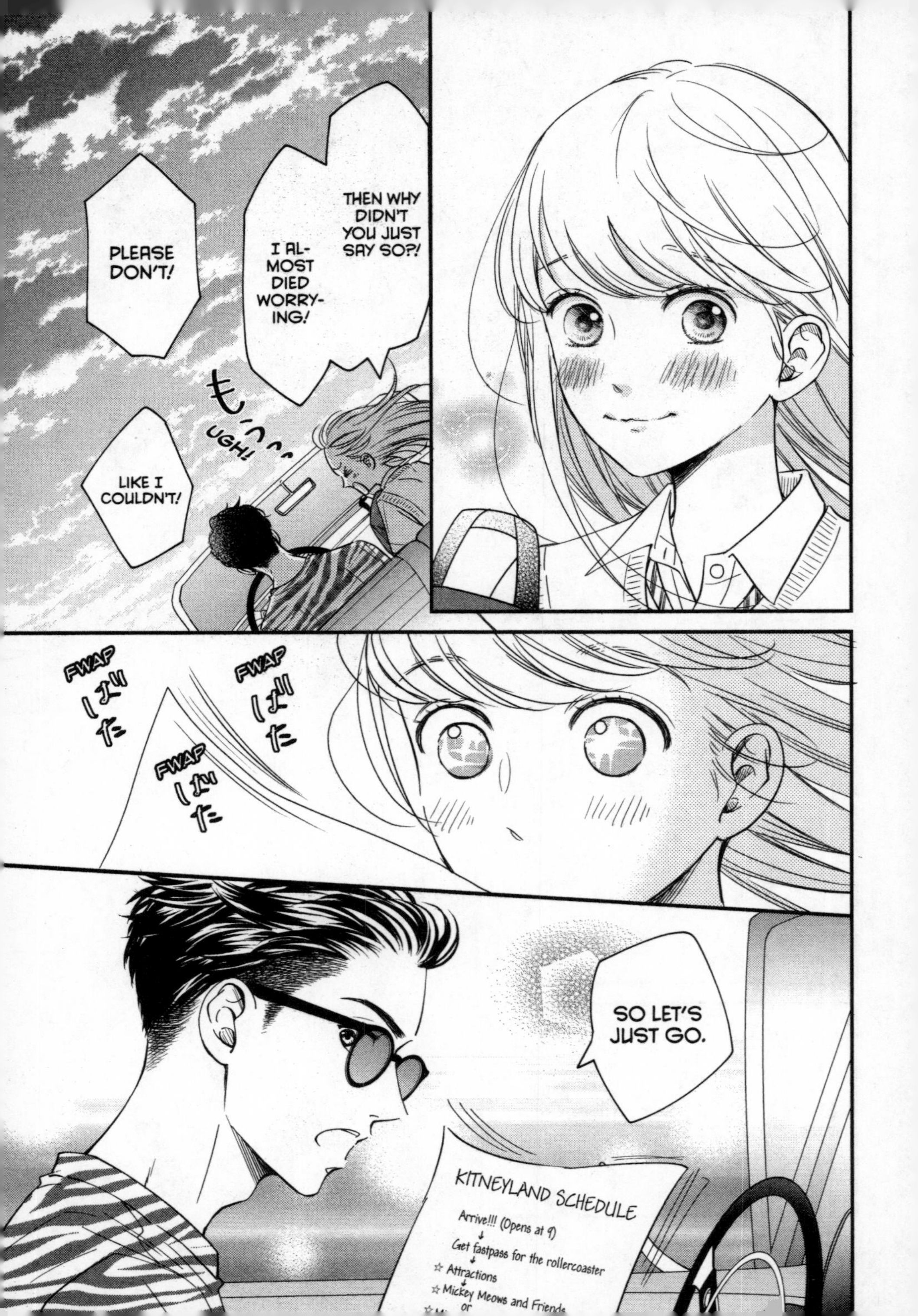
THEN WHY DIDN'T YOU JUST SAY SO?!
I AL-MOST DIED WORRY-ING!
PLEASE DON'T!
UGH!
LIKE I COULDN'T!
FWAP
FWAP
FWAP
SO LET'S JUST GO.
KITNEYLAND SCHEDULE
Arrive!!! (Opens at 9)
Get fastpass for the rollercoaster
☆ Attractions
☆ Mickey Meows and Friends

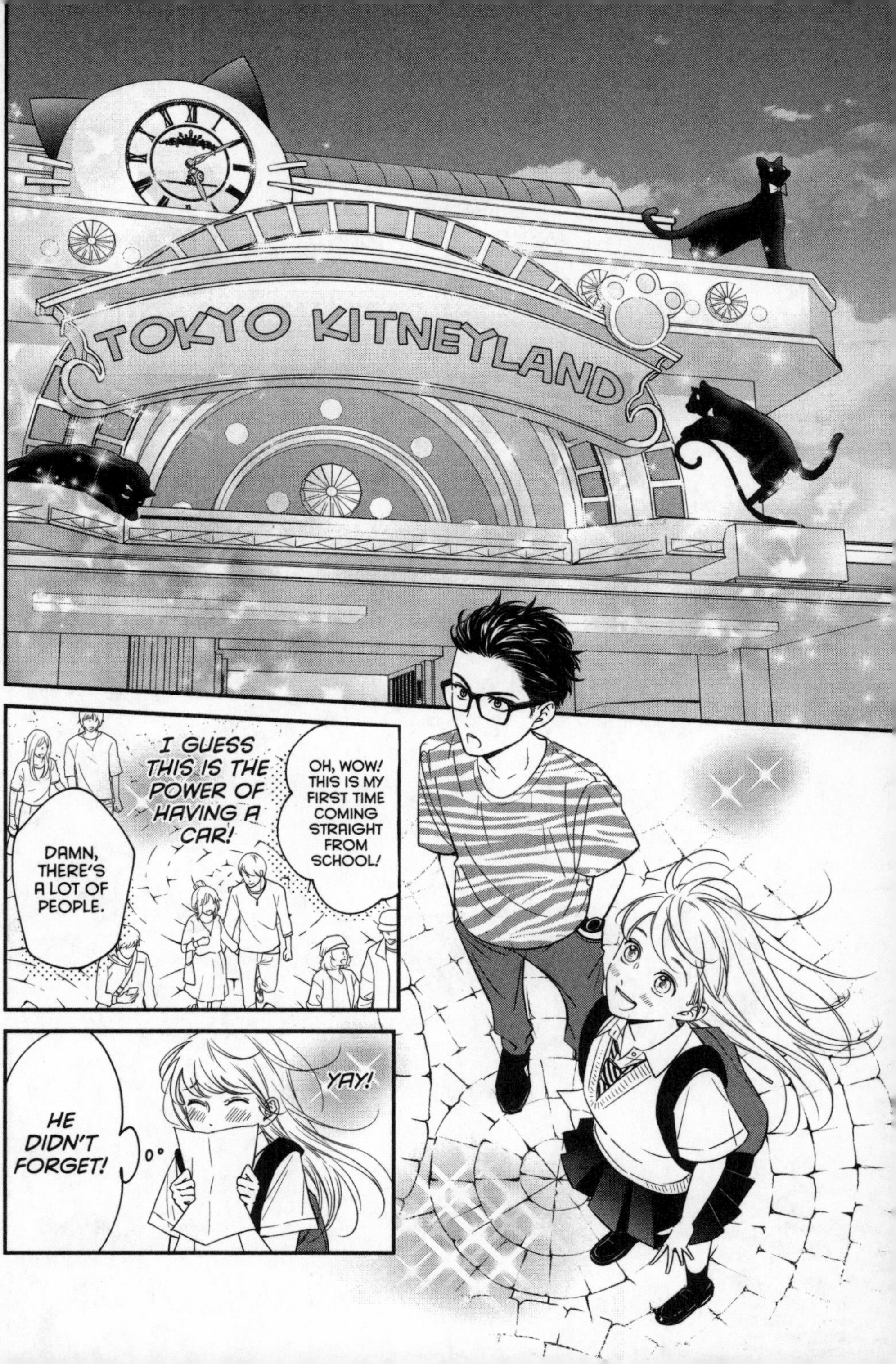
TOKYO KITNEYLAND
OH, WOW! THIS IS MY FIRST TIME COMING STRAIGHT FROM SCHOOL!
I GUESS THIS IS THE POWER OF HAVING A CAR!
DAMN, THERE'S A LOT OF PEOPLE.
YAY!
HE DIDN'T FORGET!

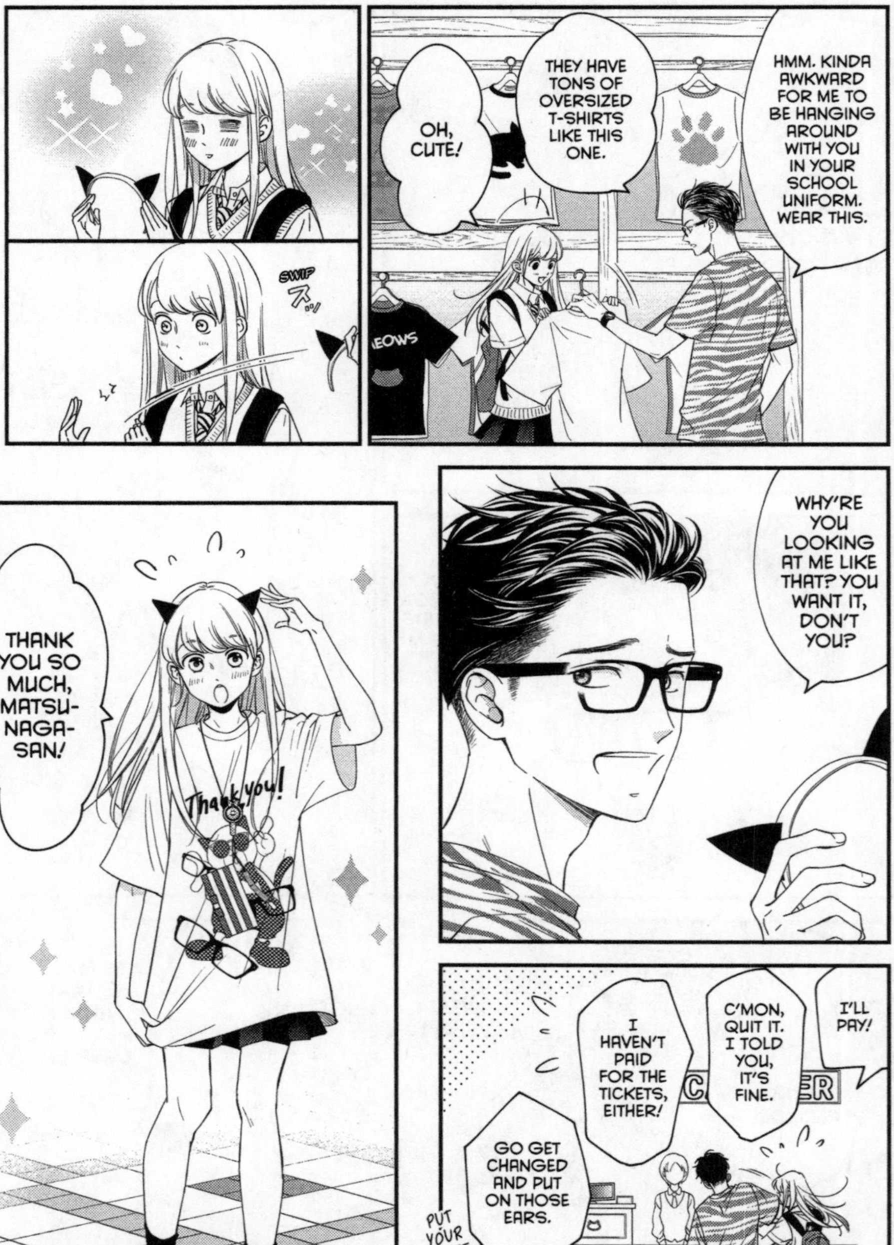
HMM. KINDA AWKWARD FOR ME TO BE HANGING AROUND WITH YOU IN YOUR SCHOOL UNIFORM. WEAR THIS.
THEY HAVE TONS OF OVERSIZED T-SHIRTS LIKE THIS ONE.
OH, CUTE!
SWIP
WHY'RE YOU LOOKING AT ME LIKE THAT? YOU WANT IT, DON'T YOU?
I'LL PAY!
C'MON, QUIT IT. I TOLD YOU, IT'S FINE.
I HAVEN'T PAID FOR THE TICKETS, EITHER!
GO GET CHANGED AND PUT ON THOSE EARS.
PUT YOUR STUFF AWAY, TOO.
THANK YOU SO MUCH, MATSUNAGA-SAN!
Thank you!

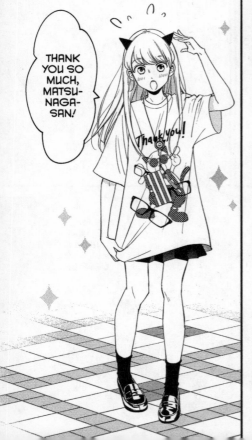

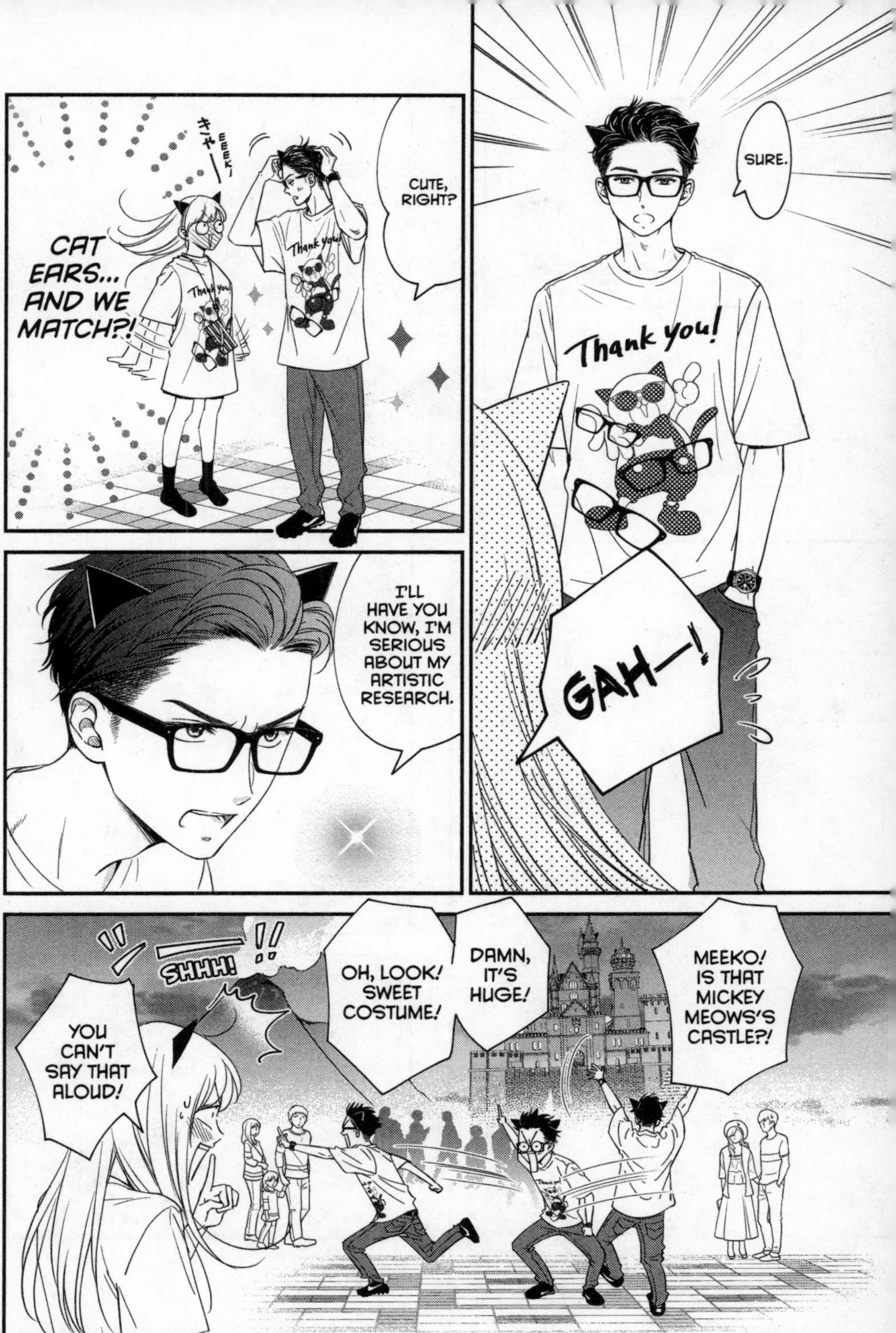
SURE.
GAH—!
CUTE, RIGHT?
キャー
EEEK!
CAT EARS... AND WE MATCH?!
I'LL HAVE YOU KNOW, I'M SERIOUS ABOUT MY ARTISTIC RESEARCH.
MEEKO! IS THAT MICKEY MEOWS'S CASTLE?!
DAMN, IT'S HUGE!
OH, LOOK! SWEET COSTUME!
!! ——— !!
SHHH!
YOU CAN'T SAY THAT ALOUD!

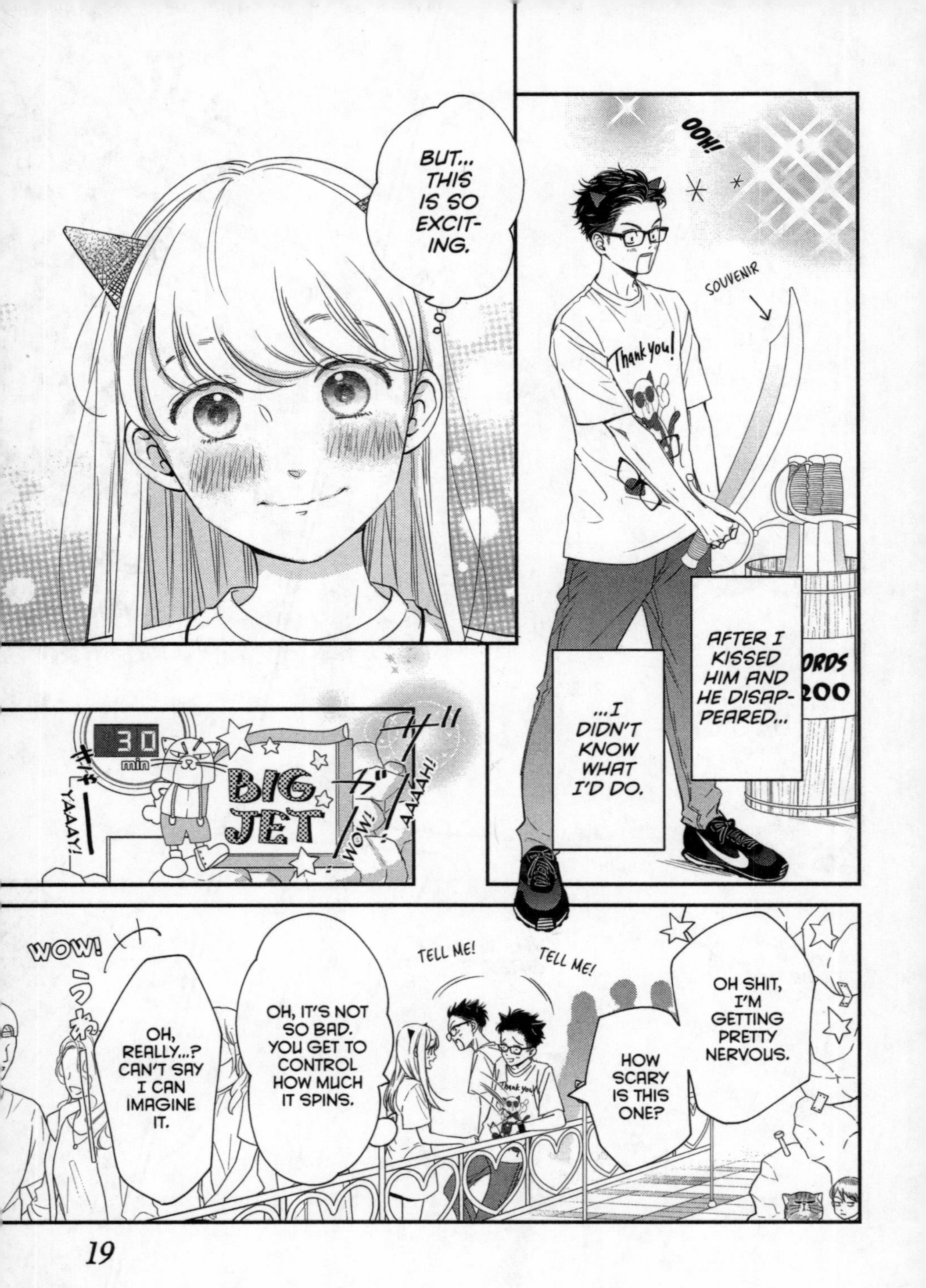
OOH!
SOUVENIR
Thank you!
AFTER I KISSED HIM AND HE DISAPPEARED...
...I DIDN'T KNOW WHAT I'D DO.
BUT... THIS IS SO EXCITING.
AAAAAH!
WOW!
BIG JET
30 min
YAAAY!
OH SHIT, I'M GETTING PRETTY NERVOUS.
HOW SCARY IS THIS ONE?
TELL ME!
TELL ME!
OH, IT'S NOT SO BAD. YOU GET TO CONTROL HOW MUCH IT SPINS.
OH, REALLY...? CAN'T SAY I CAN IMAGINE IT.
WOW!

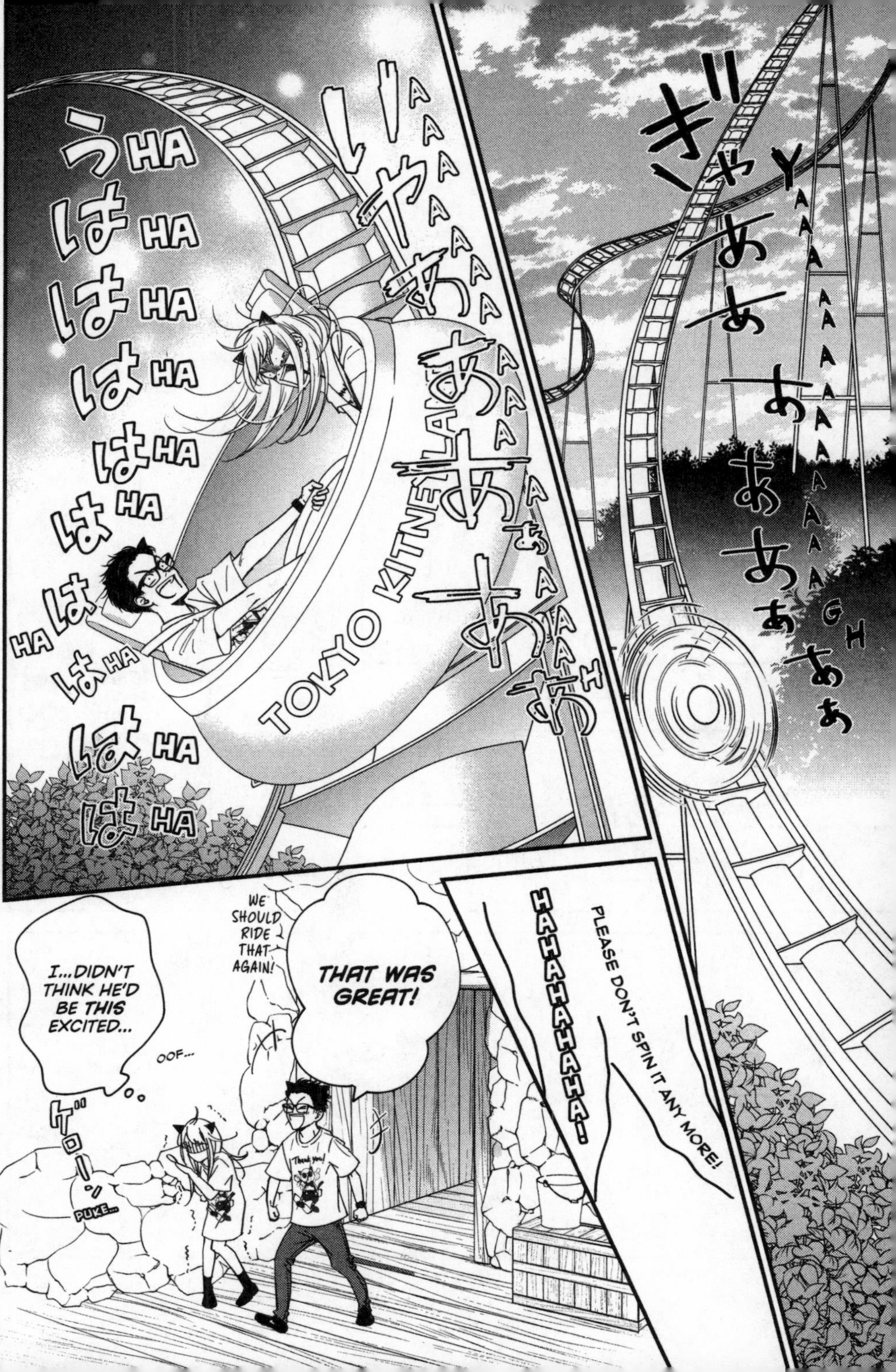

ぎゃあああああああ
YAAAAAAAAAAAAGH
いやああああああ
AAAAAAAAAAAAAAAAAH
うはははははははは
HA HA HA HA HA HA HA HA HA HA
TOKYO KITNE
HAHAHAHAHAHA!
PLEASE DON'T SPIN IT ANY MORE!
THAT WAS GREAT!
WE SHOULD RIDE THAT AGAIN!
I...DIDN'T THINK HE'D BE THIS EXCITED...
OOF...
ゲローー
PUKE...

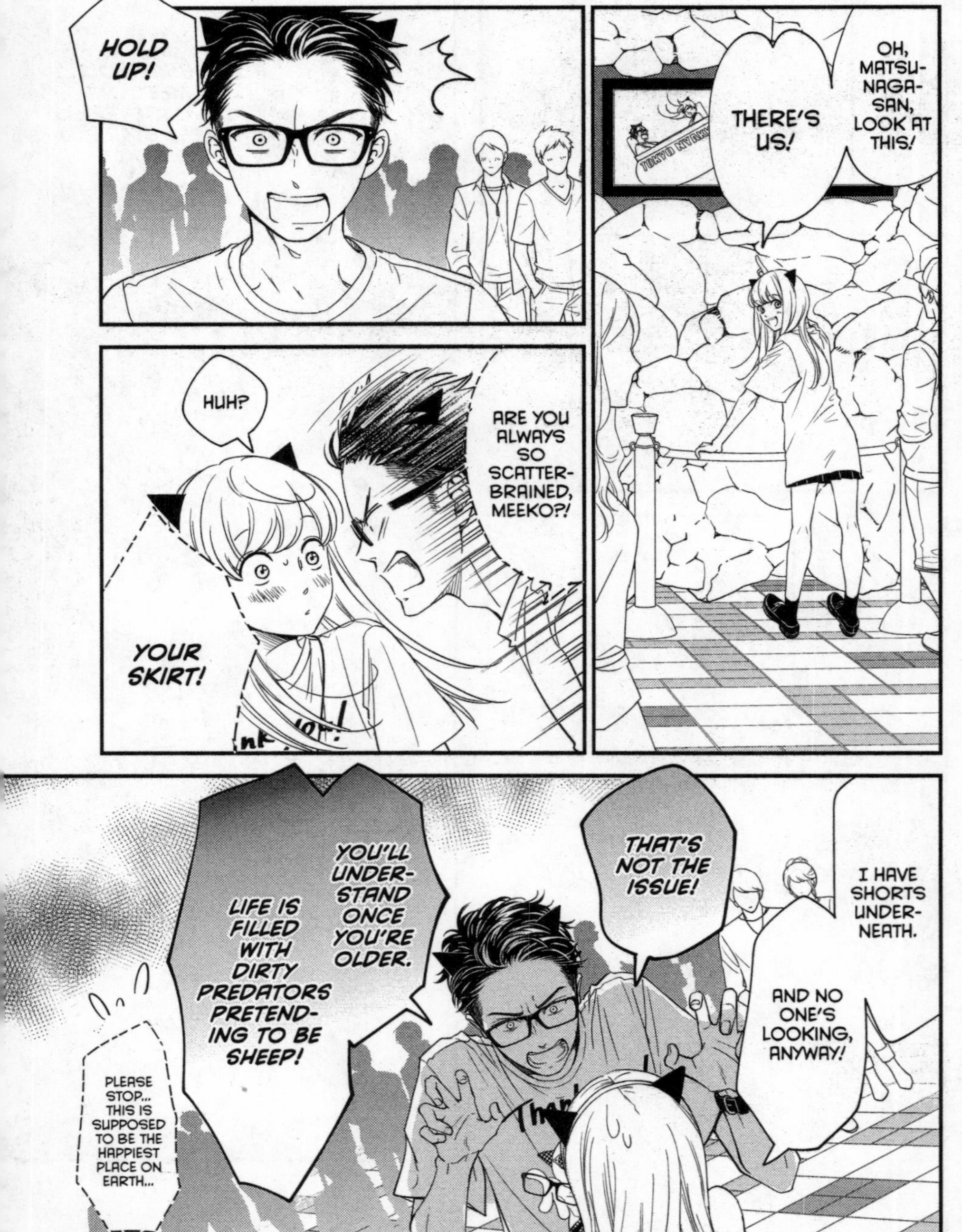
OH, MATSU-NAGA-SAN, LOOK AT THIS!
THERE'S US!
HOLD UP!
ARE YOU ALWAYS SO SCATTER-BRAINED, MEEKO?!
HUH?
YOUR SKIRT!
I HAVE SHORTS UNDER-NEATH.
AND NO ONE'S LOOKING, ANYWAY!
THAT'S NOT THE ISSUE!
YOU'LL UNDER-STAND ONCE YOU'RE OLDER.
LIFE IS FILLED WITH DIRTY PREDATORS PRETEND-ING TO BE SHEEP!
PLEASE STOP... THIS IS SUPPOSED TO BE THE HAPPIEST PLACE ON EARTH...

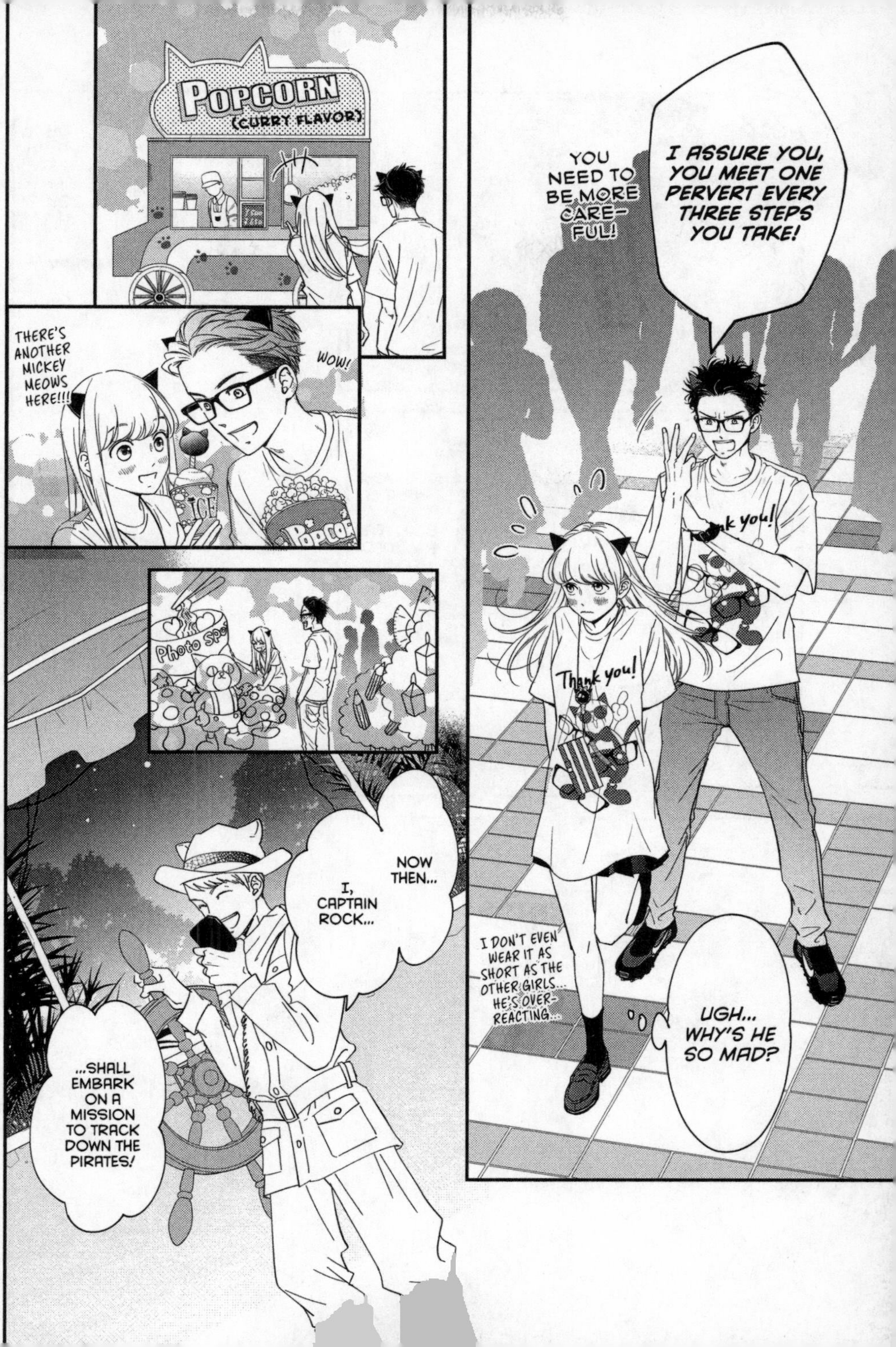
I ASSURE YOU, YOU MEET ONE PERVERT EVERY THREE STEPS YOU TAKE!
YOU NEED TO BE MORE CARE-FUL!
Thank you!
Thank you!
UGH... WHY'S HE SO MAD?
I DON'T EVEN WEAR IT AS SHORT AS THE OTHER GIRLS... HE'S OVER-REACTING...
POPCORN
(CURRY FLAVOR)
WOW!
THERE'S ANOTHER MICKEY MEOWS HERE!!!
ICE
Photo Spot
NOW THEN...
I, CAPTAIN ROCK...
...SHALL EMBARK ON A MISSION TO TRACK DOWN THE PIRATES!

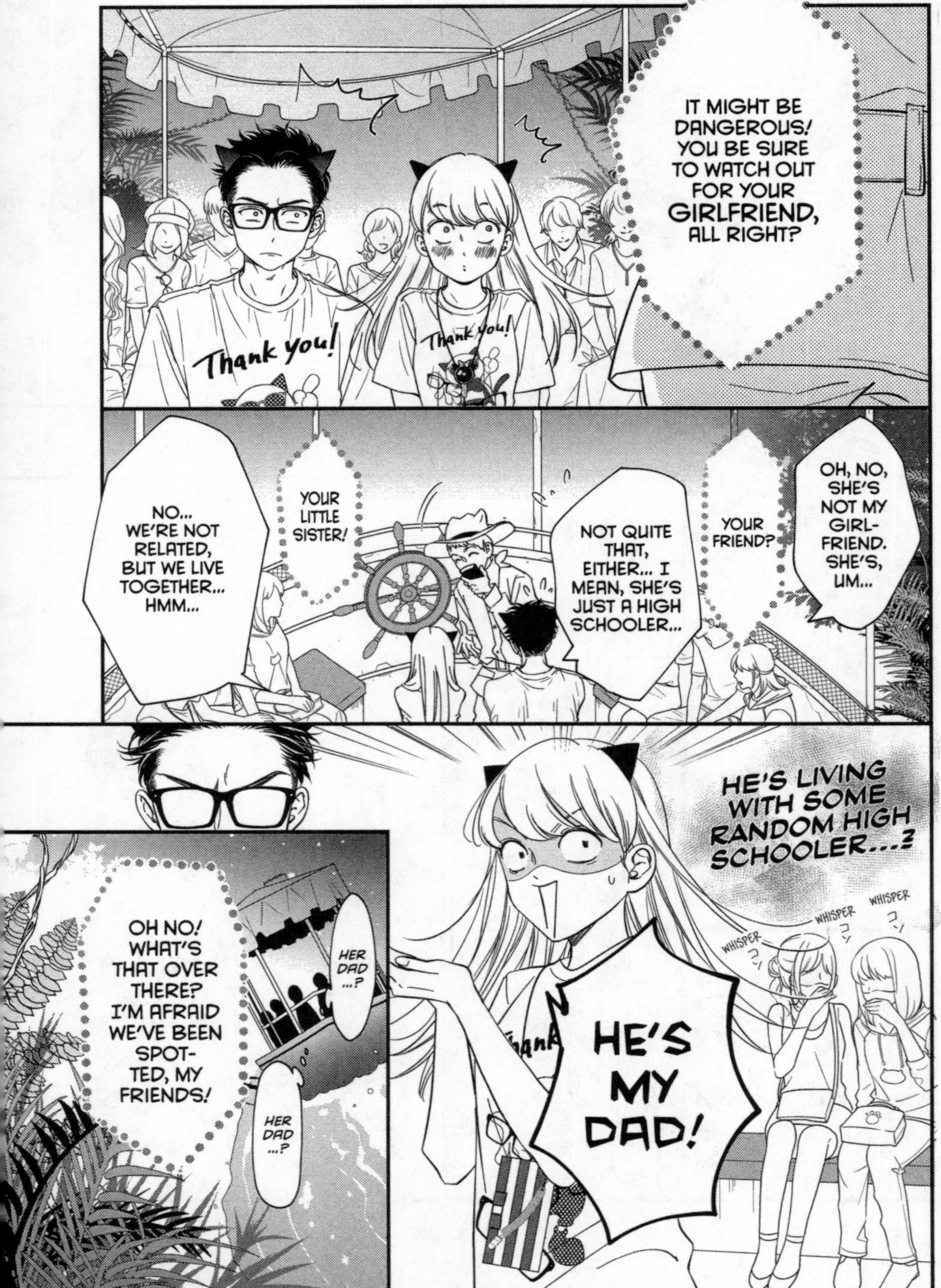
IT MIGHT BE DANGEROUS! YOU BE SURE TO WATCH OUT FOR YOUR GIRLFRIEND, ALL RIGHT?
Thank you!
Thank you!
OH, NO, SHE'S NOT MY GIRL-FRIEND. SHE'S, UM...
YOUR FRIEND?
NOT QUITE THAT, EITHER... I MEAN, SHE'S JUST A HIGH SCHOOLER...
YOUR LITTLE SISTER!
NO... WE'RE NOT RELATED, BUT WE LIVE TOGETHER... HMM...
HE'S LIVING WITH SOME RANDOM HIGH SCHOOLER...?
WHISPER
WHISPER
WHISPER
HE'S MY DAD!
HER DAD...?
HER DAD...?
OH NO! WHAT'S THAT OVER THERE? I'M AFRAID WE'VE BEEN SPOT-TED, MY FRIENDS!

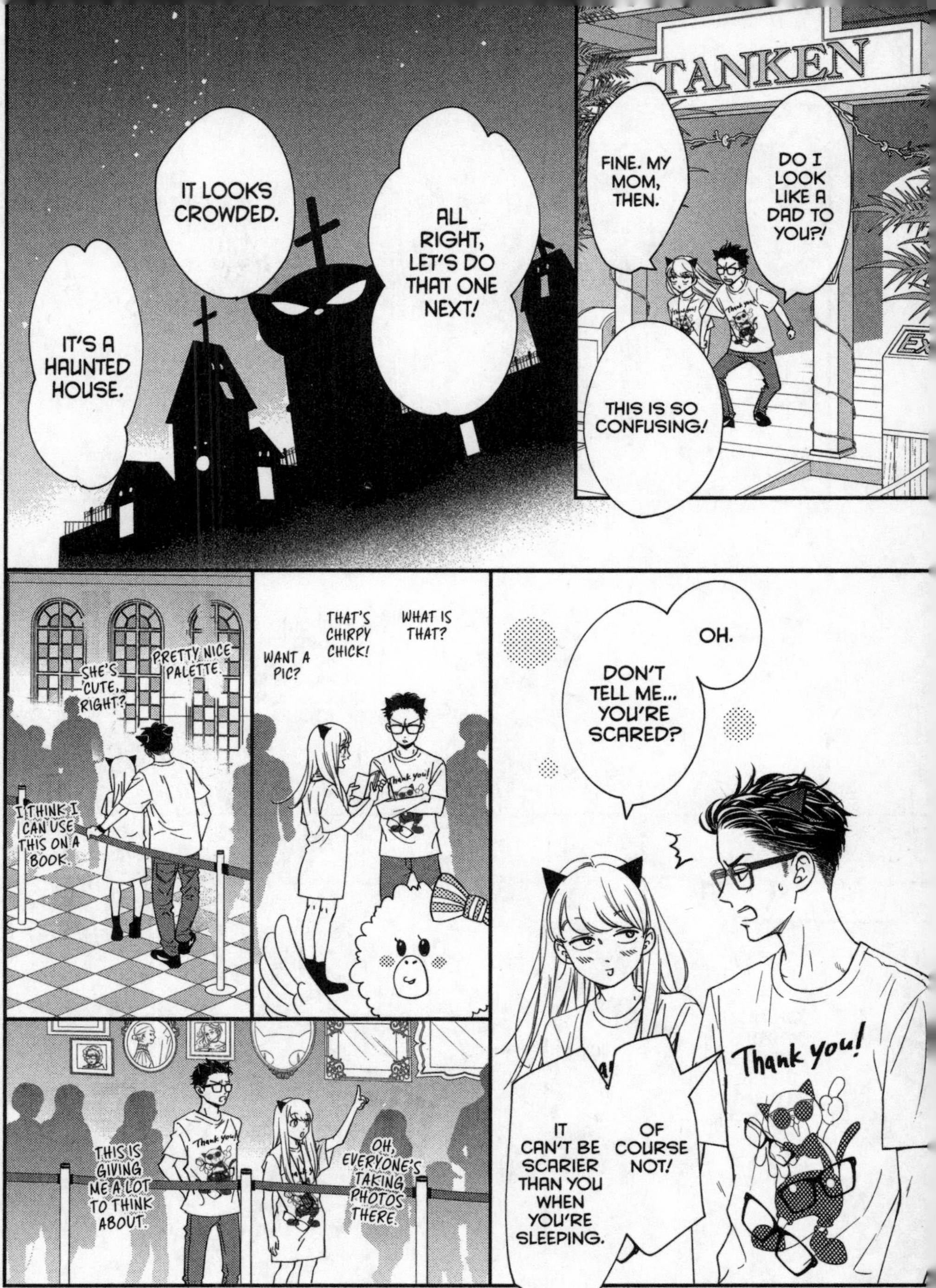
TANKEN
DO I LOOK LIKE A DAD TO YOU?!
FINE. MY MOM, THEN.
THIS IS SO CONFUSING!
ALL RIGHT, LET'S DO THAT ONE NEXT!
IT LOOKS CROWDED.
IT'S A HAUNTED HOUSE.
OH.
DON'T TELL ME... YOU'RE SCARED?
Thank you!
OF COURSE NOT!
IT CAN'T BE SCARIER THAN YOU WHEN YOU'RE SLEEPING.
WHAT IS THAT?
THAT'S CHIRPY CHICK!
WANT A PIC?
PRETTY NICE PALETTE.
SHE'S CUTE, RIGHT?
I THINK I CAN USE THIS ON A BOOK.
OH, EVERYONE'S TAKING PHOTOS THERE.
THIS IS GIVING ME A LOT TO THINK ABOUT.

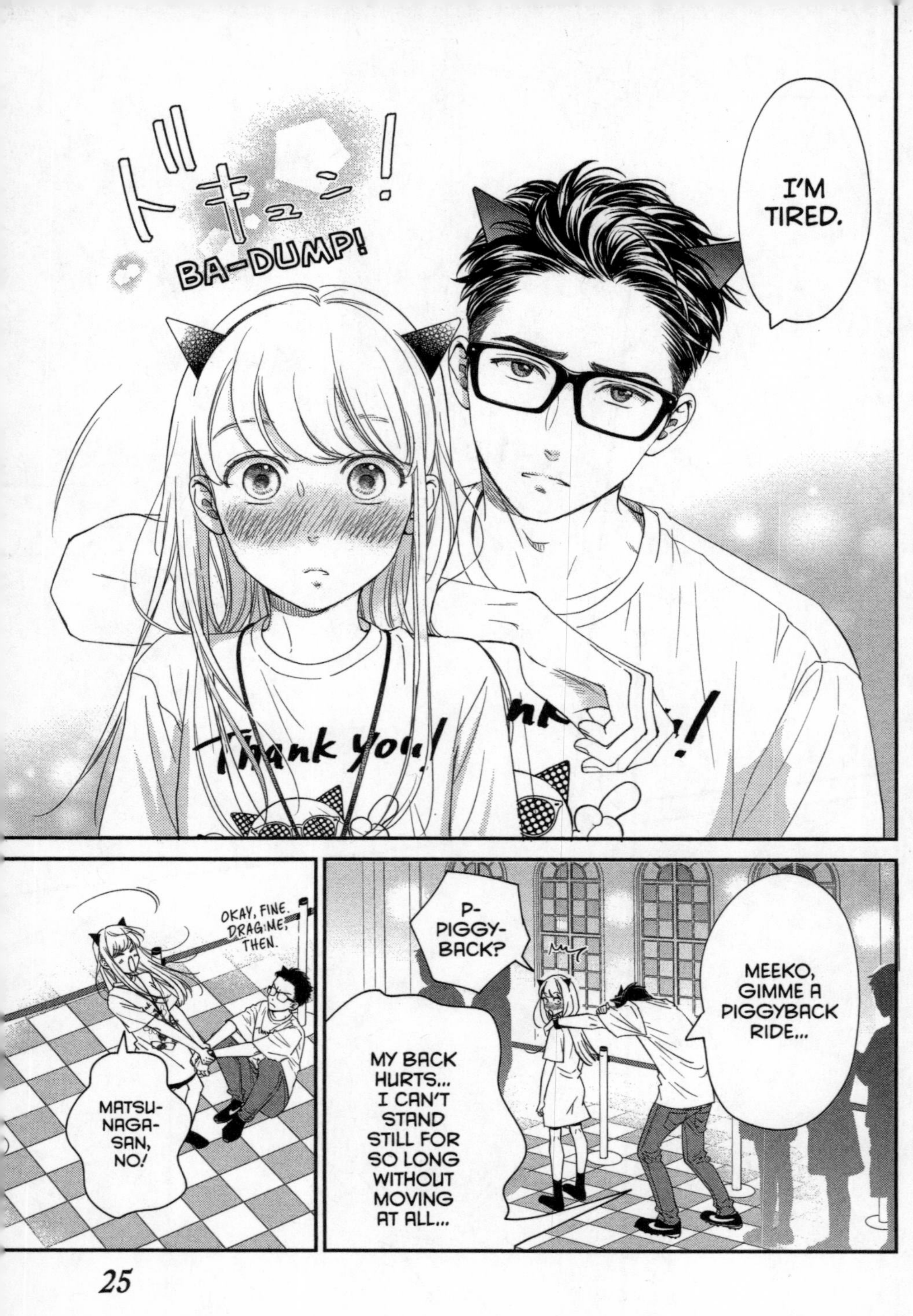
I'M TIRED.
ドキューン!
BA-DUMP!
MEEKO, GIMME A PIGGYBACK RIDE...
P-PIGGYBACK?
MY BACK HURTS... I CAN'T STAND STILL FOR SO LONG WITHOUT MOVING AT ALL...
OKAY, FINE. DRAG ME, THEN.
MATSUNAGA-SAN, NO!

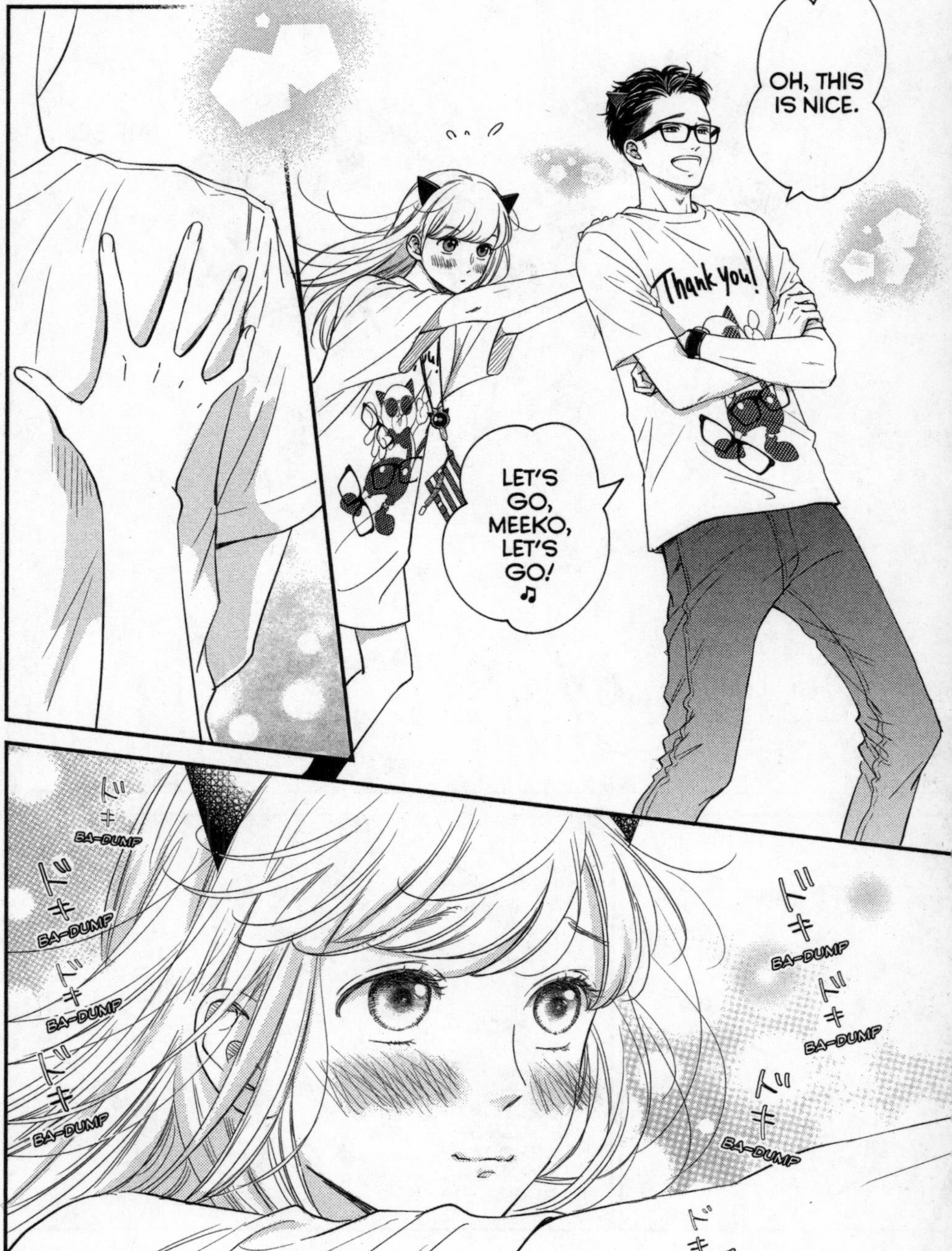
OH, THIS IS NICE.
Thank you!
LET'S GO, MEEKO, LET'S GO! ♫
ドキ
BA-DUMP
ドキ
BA-DUMP
ドキ
BA-DUMP
ドキ
BA-DUMP
ドキ
BA-DUMP
ドキ
BA-DUMP
ドキ
BA-DUMP
ドキ
BA-DUMP

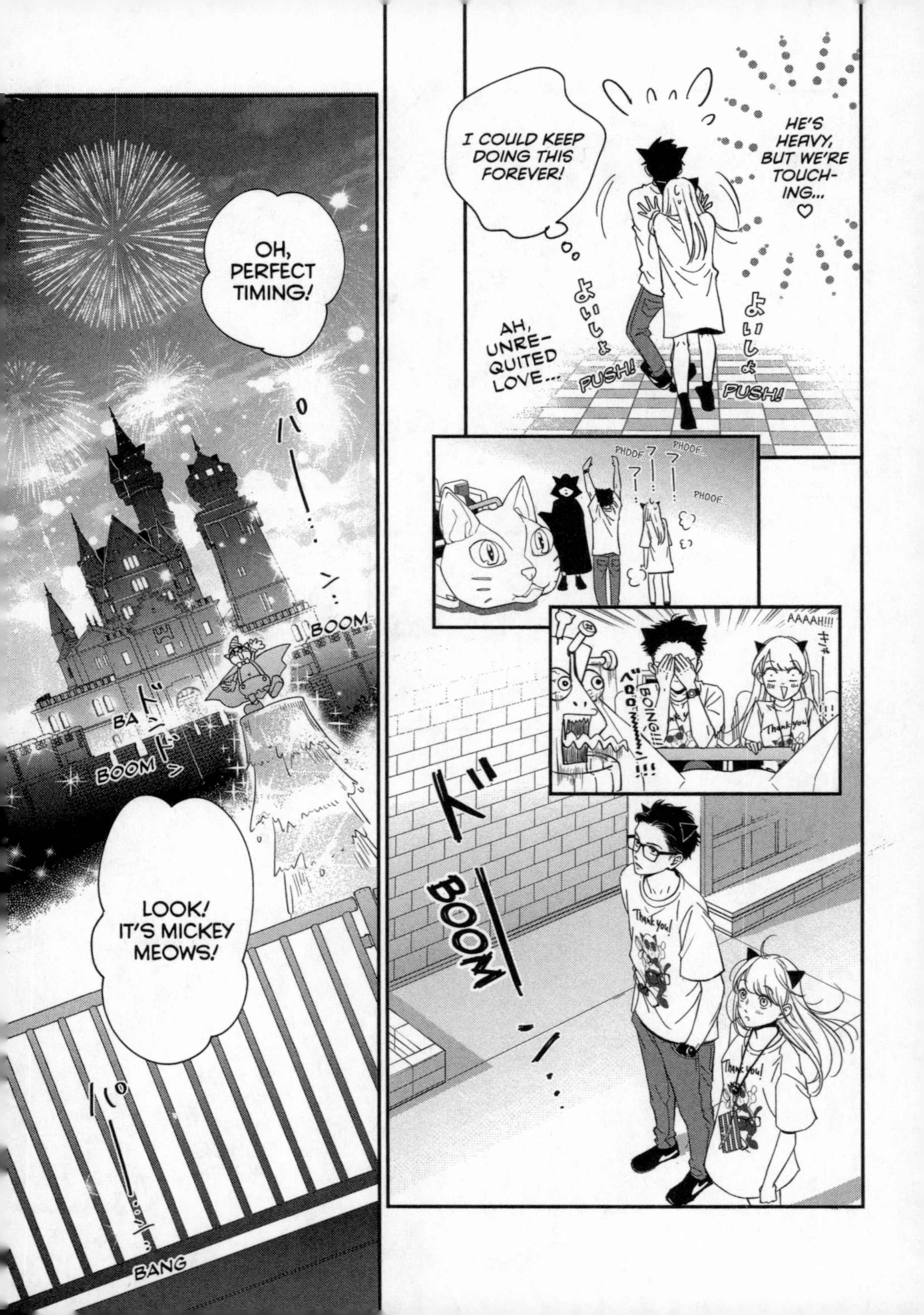
HE'S HEAVY, BUT WE'RE TOUCHING... ♡
I COULD KEEP DOING THIS FOREVER!
よいしょ
PUSH!
よいしょ
PUSH!
AH, UNREQUITED LOVE...
PHOOF...
フー...
PHOOF...
フー...
PHOOF...
AAAAH!!!
キャー!!!
BOING!!!
BOOM
OH, PERFECT TIMING!
パーン...
BOOM
BA
BOOM
LOOK! IT'S MICKEY MEOWS!
パーン...
BANG

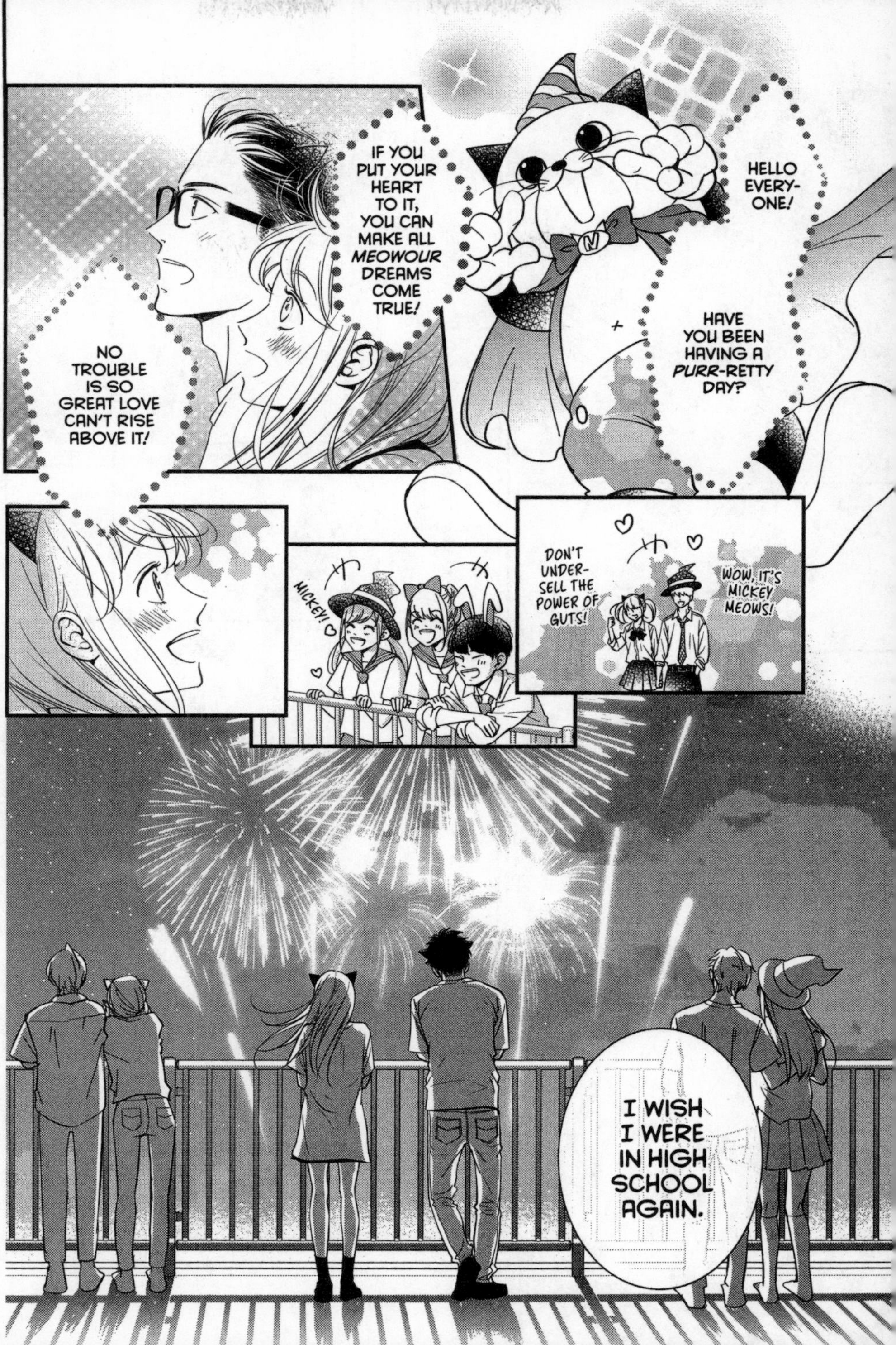
HELLO EVERY-ONE!
HAVE YOU BEEN HAVING A *PURR*-RETTY DAY?
IF YOU PUT YOUR HEART TO IT, YOU CAN MAKE ALL *MEOWOUR* DREAMS COME TRUE!
NO TROUBLE IS SO GREAT LOVE CAN'T RISE ABOVE IT!
WOW, IT'S MICKEY MEOWS!
DON'T UNDER-SELL THE POWER OF GUTS!
MICKEY!
I WISH I WERE IN HIGH SCHOOL AGAIN.

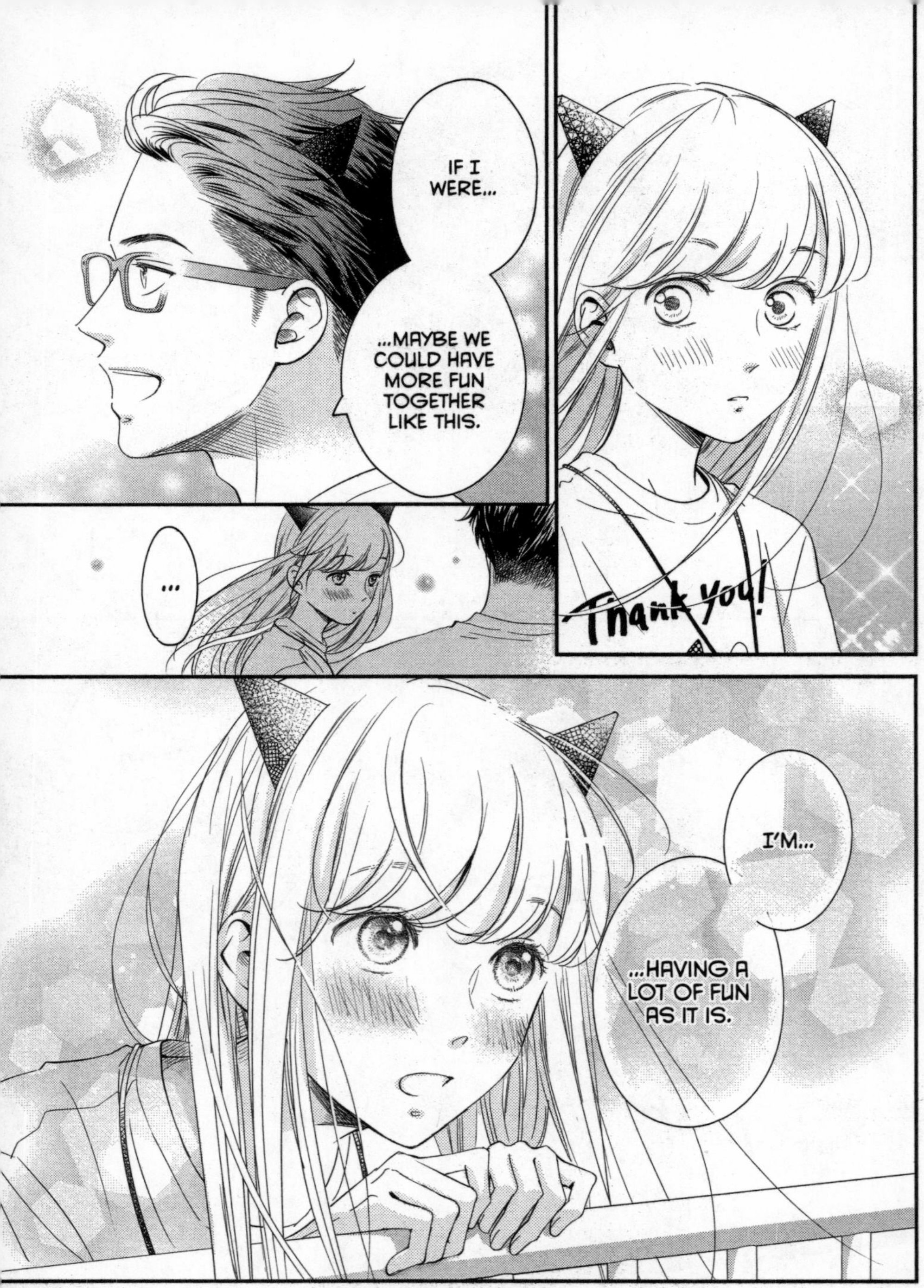
Thank you!
IF I WERE...
...MAYBE WE COULD HAVE MORE FUN TOGETHER LIKE THIS.
...
I'M...
...HAVING A LOT OF FUN AS IT IS.

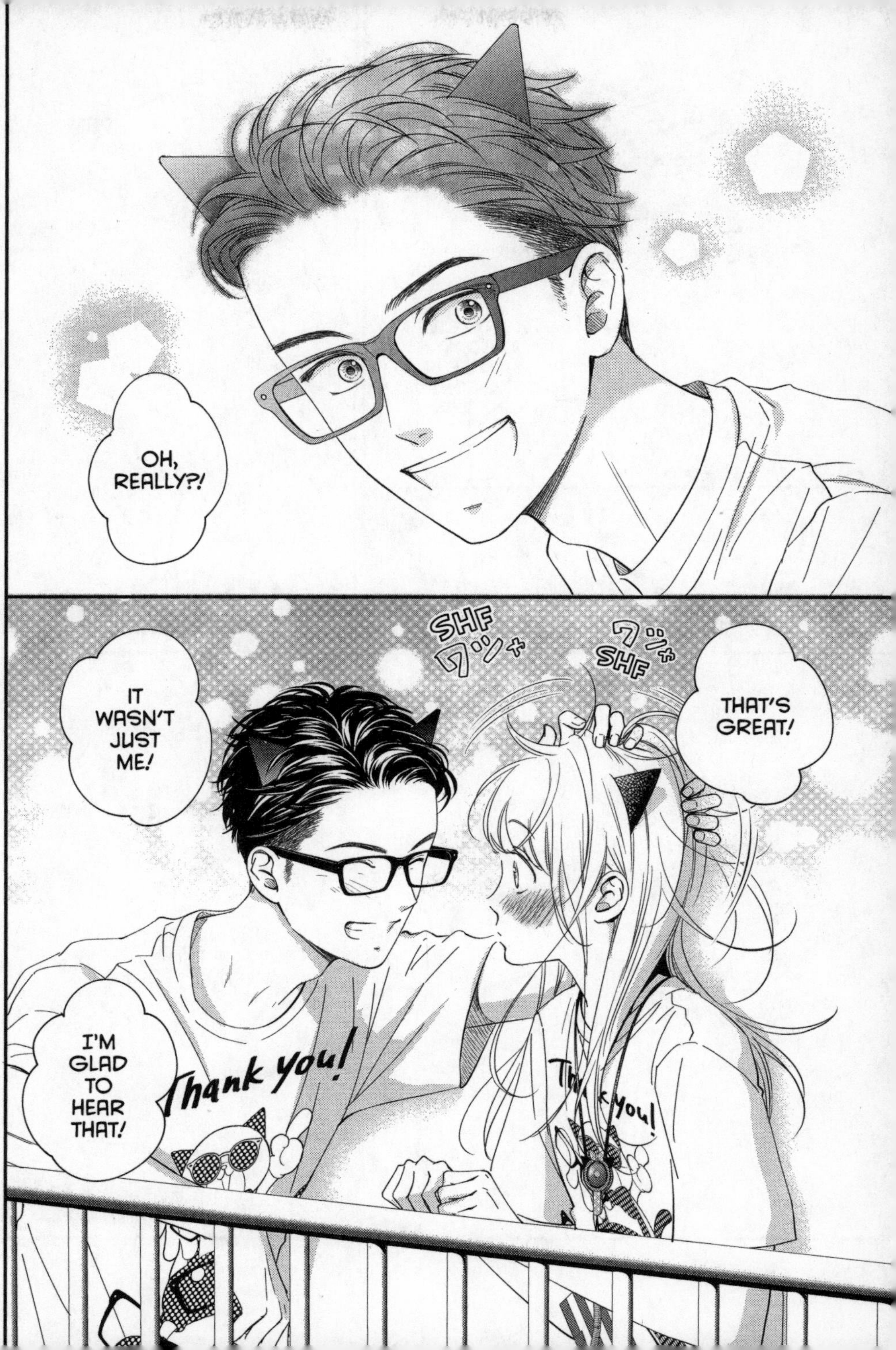
OH, REALLY?!
SHF ワシャ
THAT'S GREAT!
SHF ワシャ
IT WASN'T JUST ME!
I'M GLAD TO HEAR THAT!
Thank you!
Thank you!

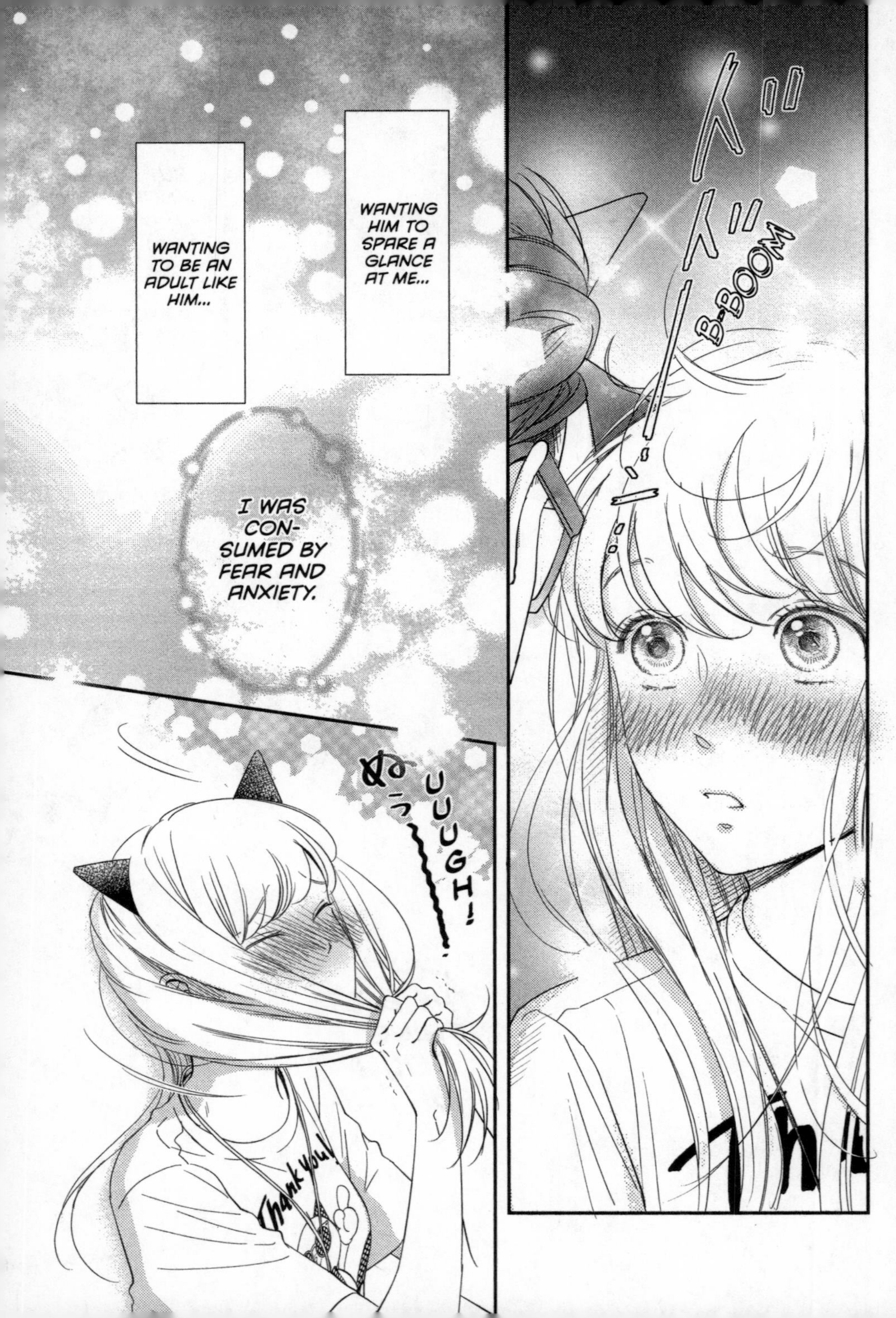
B-BOOM
WANTING HIM TO SPARE A GLANCE AT ME...
WANTING TO BE AN ADULT LIKE HIM...
I WAS CON-SUMED BY FEAR AND ANXIETY.
UUUGH!
Thank you!

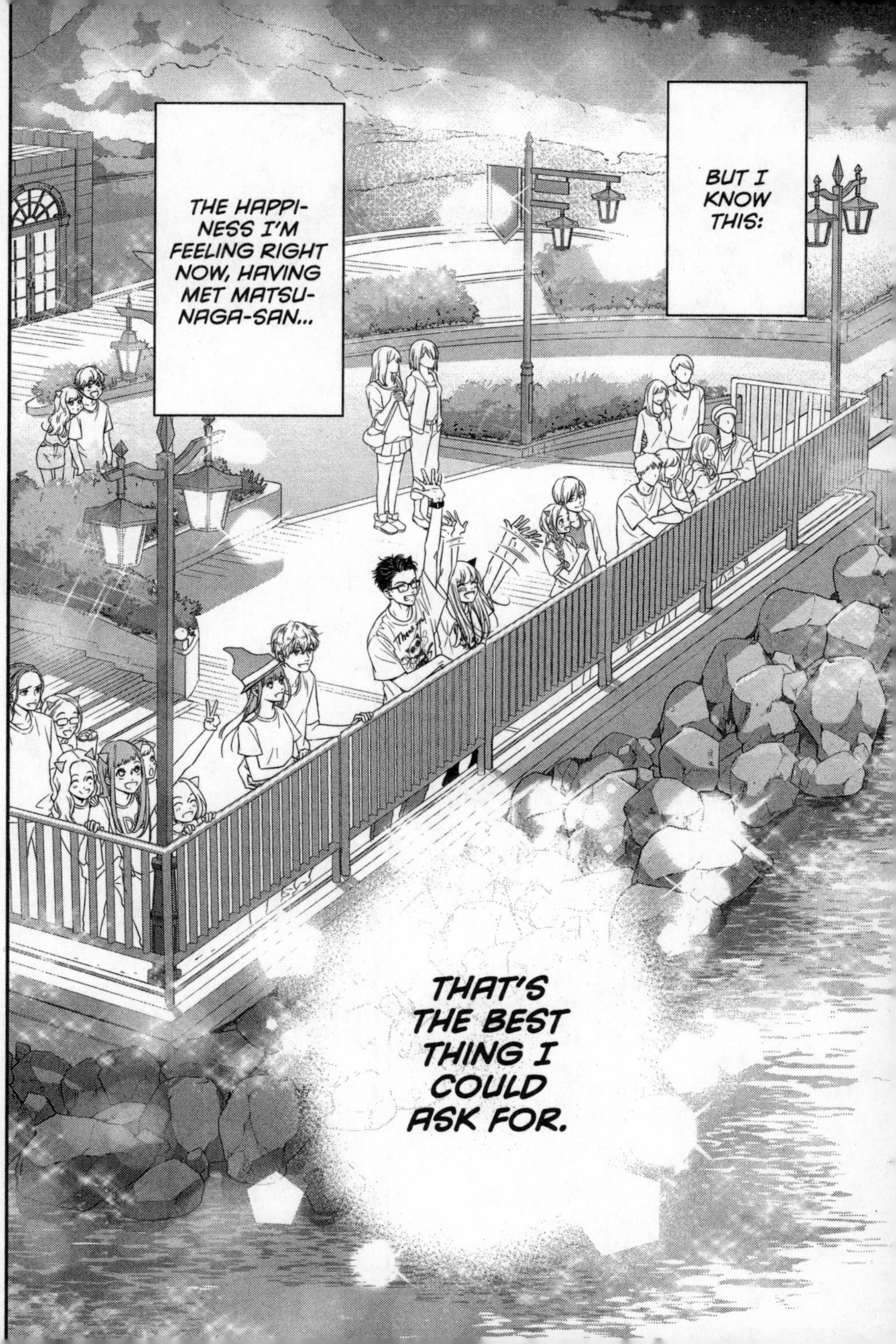
BUT I KNOW THIS:
THE HAPPI-NESS I'M FEELING RIGHT NOW, HAVING MET MATSU-NAGA-SAN...
THAT'S THE BEST THING I COULD ASK FOR.

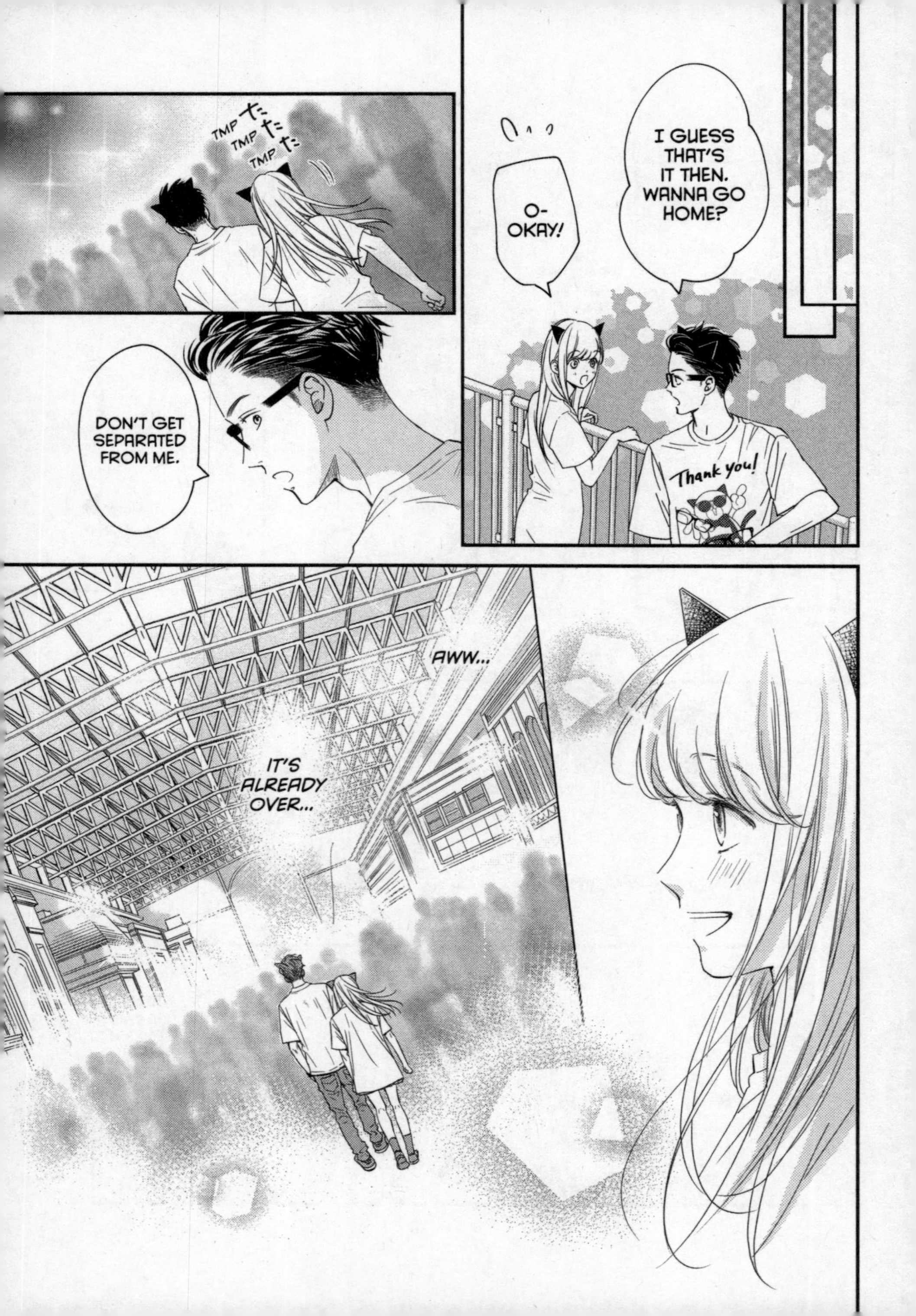
I GUESS THAT'S IT THEN. WANNA GO HOME?
O-OKAY!
TMP た
TMP た
TMP た
DON'T GET SEPARATED FROM ME.
AWW...
IT'S ALREADY OVER...

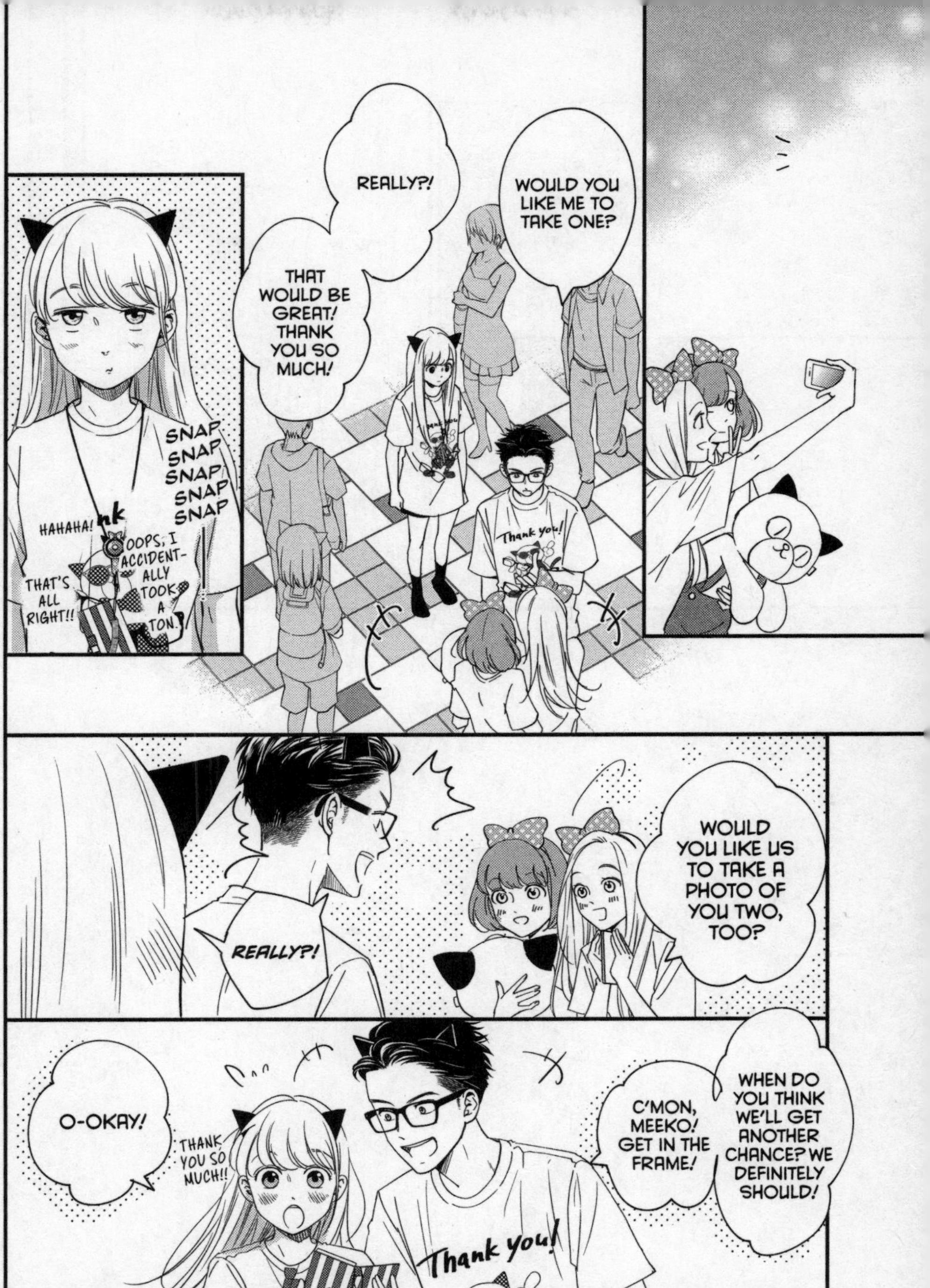
WOULD YOU LIKE ME TO TAKE ONE?
REALLY?!
THAT WOULD BE GREAT! THANK YOU SO MUCH!
SNAP SNAP SNAP SNAP SNAP
OOPS, I ACCIDENT-ALLY TOOK A TON.
HAHAHA!
THAT'S ALL RIGHT!!
WOULD YOU LIKE US TO TAKE A PHOTO OF YOU TWO, TOO?
REALLY?!
WHEN DO YOU THINK WE'LL GET ANOTHER CHANCE? WE DEFINITELY SHOULD!
C'MON, MEEKO! GET IN THE FRAME!
THANK YOU SO MUCH!!
O-OKAY!
Thank you!

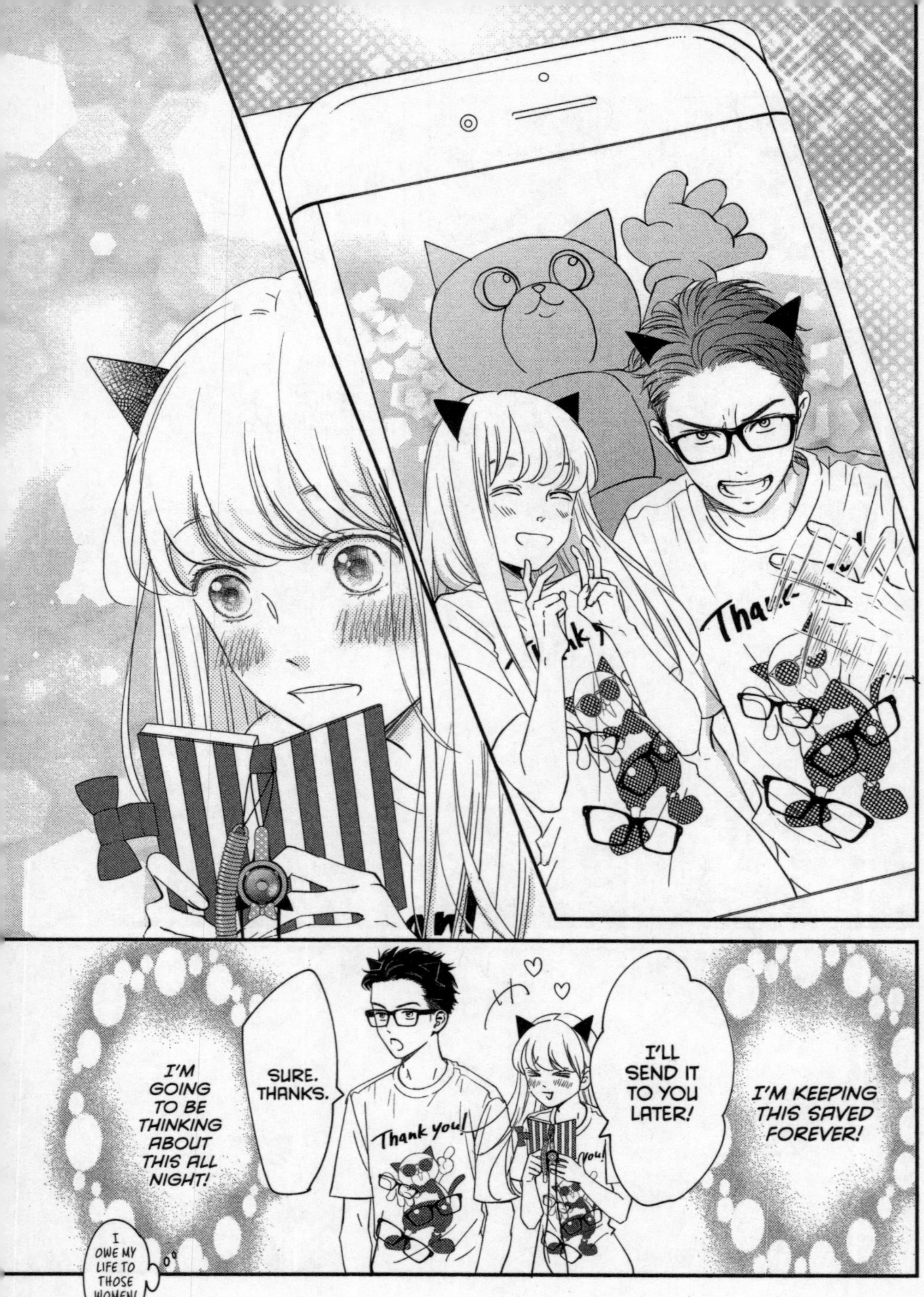

I'M KEEPING THIS SAVED FOREVER!
I'LL SEND IT TO YOU LATER!
Thank you!
SURE. THANKS.
I'M GOING TO BE THINKING ABOUT THIS ALL NIGHT!
I OWE MY LIFE TO THOSE WOMEN! ♡

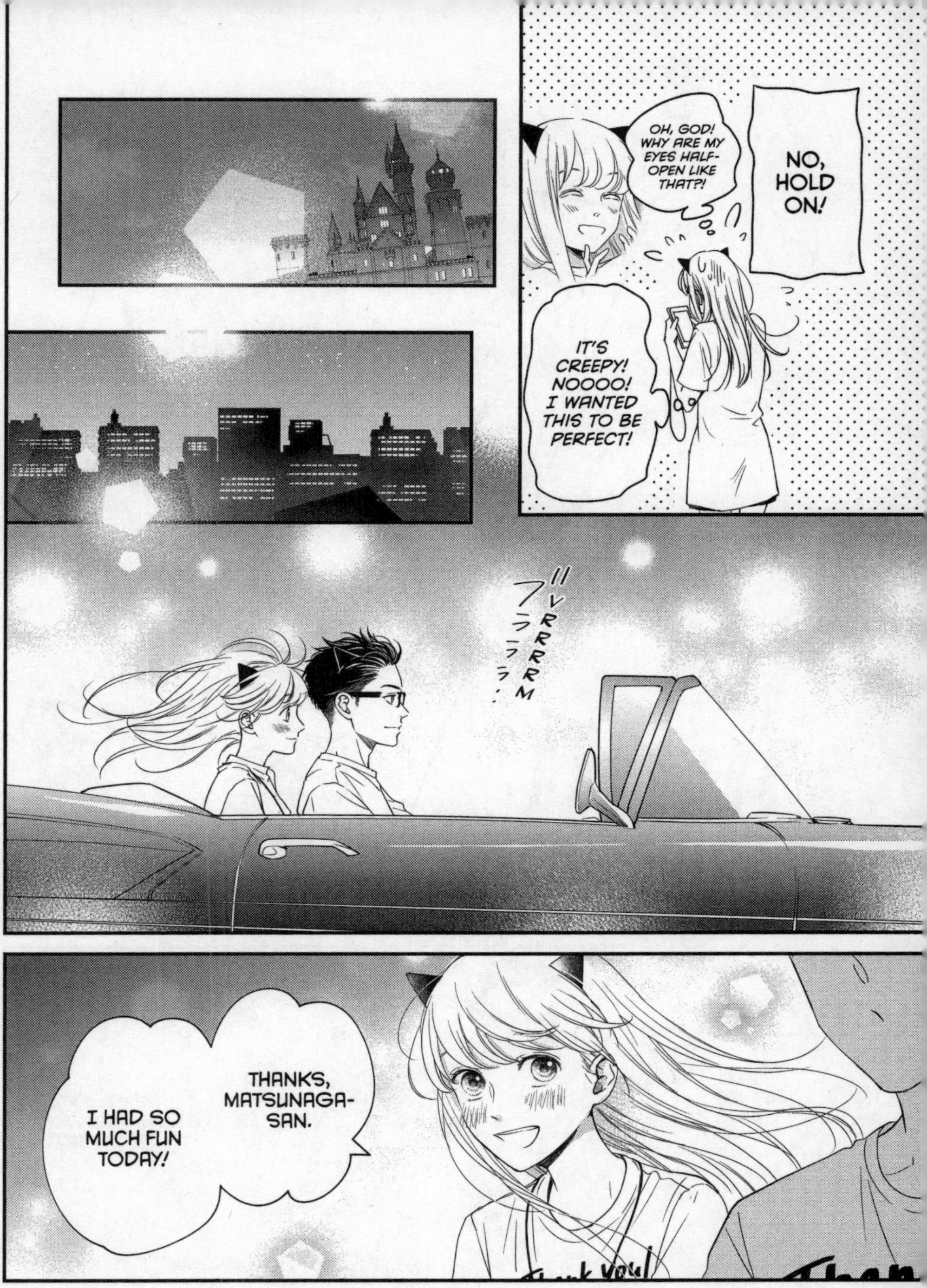
NO, HOLD ON!
OH, GOD! WHY ARE MY EYES HALF-OPEN LIKE THAT?!
IT'S CREEPY! NOOOO! I WANTED THIS TO BE PERFECT!
VRRRRM
THANKS, MATSUNAGA-SAN.
I HAD SO MUCH FUN TODAY!

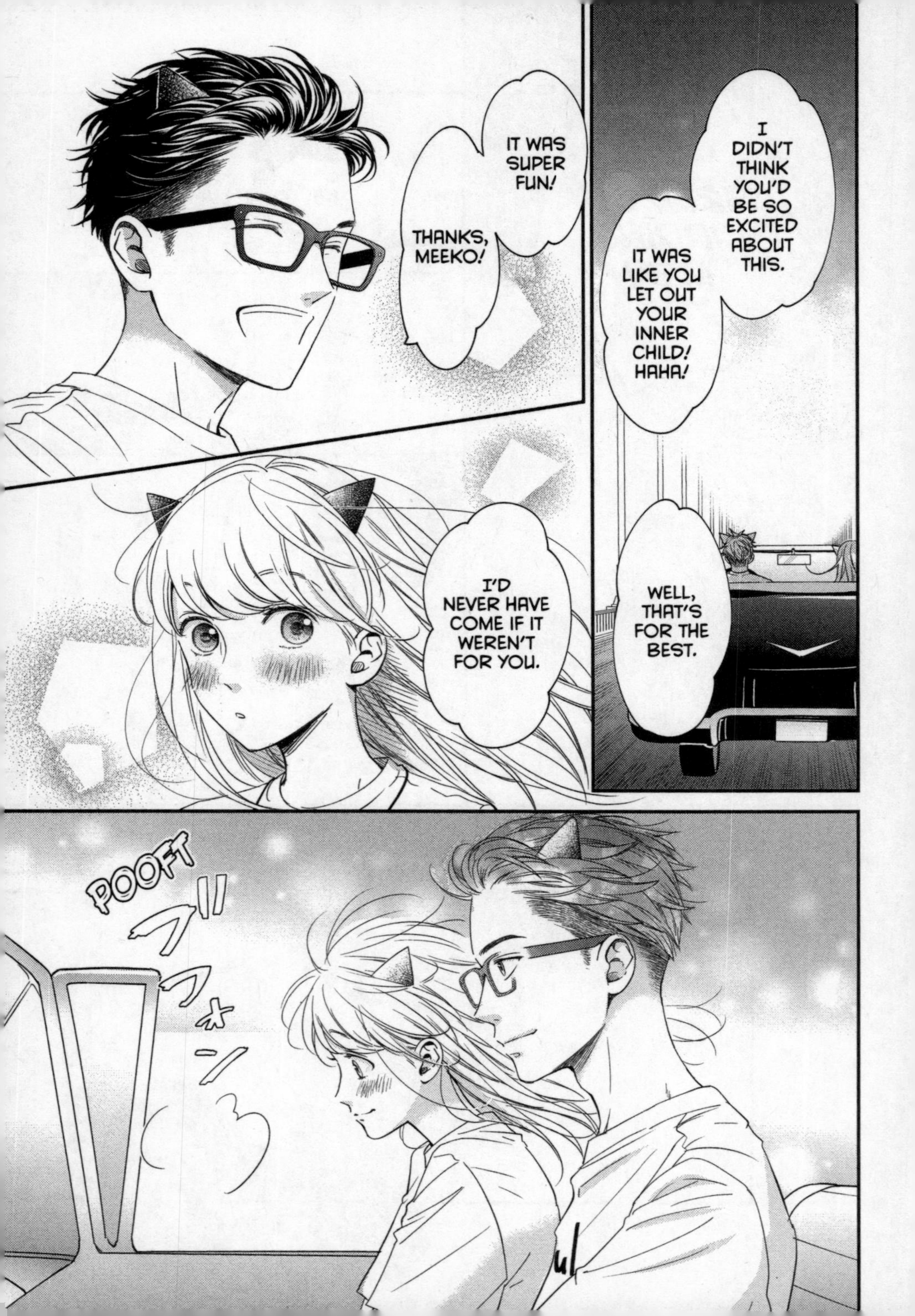
I DIDN'T THINK YOU'D BE SO EXCITED ABOUT THIS.
IT WAS LIKE YOU LET OUT YOUR INNER CHILD! HAHA!
WELL, THAT'S FOR THE BEST.
IT WAS SUPER FUN!
THANKS, MEEKO!
I'D NEVER HAVE COME IF IT WEREN'T FOR YOU.
POOFT

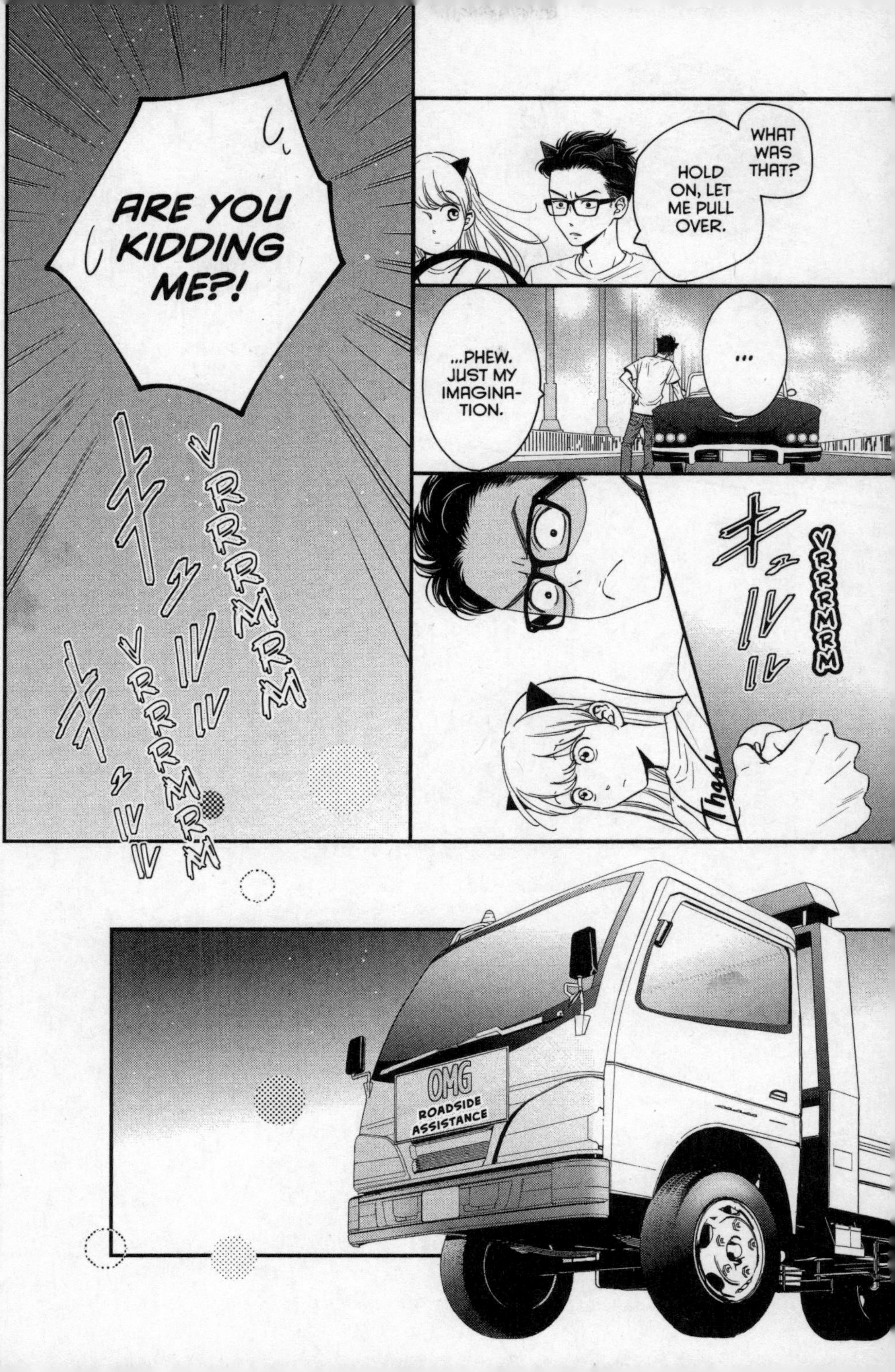
WHAT WAS THAT?
HOLD ON, LET ME PULL OVER.
...
...PHEW. JUST MY IMAGINATION.
VRRRMRM
ARE YOU KIDDING ME?!
VRRRMRM
VRRRMRM
OMG
ROADSIDE ASSISTANCE

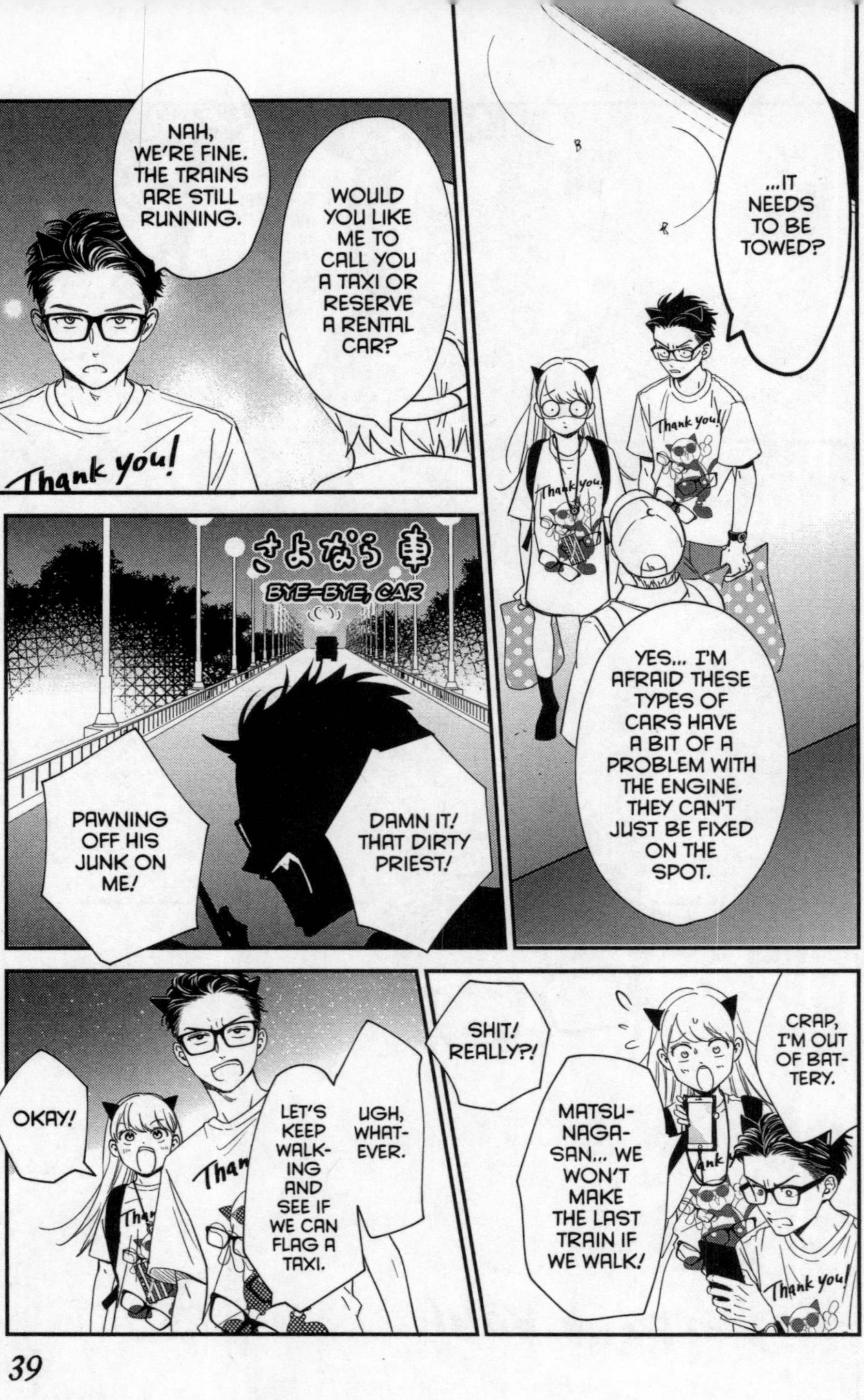

...IT NEEDS TO BE TOWED?
YES... I'M AFRAID THESE TYPES OF CARS HAVE A BIT OF A PROBLEM WITH THE ENGINE. THEY CAN'T JUST BE FIXED ON THE SPOT.
WOULD YOU LIKE ME TO CALL YOU A TAXI OR RESERVE A RENTAL CAR?
NAH, WE'RE FINE. THE TRAINS ARE STILL RUNNING.
Thank you!
さよなら車
BYE-BYE, CAR
DAMN IT! THAT DIRTY PRIEST!
PAWNING OFF HIS JUNK ON ME!
CRAP, I'M OUT OF BAT-TERY.
MATSU-NAGA-SAN... WE WON'T MAKE THE LAST TRAIN IF WE WALK!
SHIT! REALLY?!
UGH, WHAT-EVER.
LET'S KEEP WALK-ING AND SEE IF WE CAN FLAG A TAXI.
OKAY!

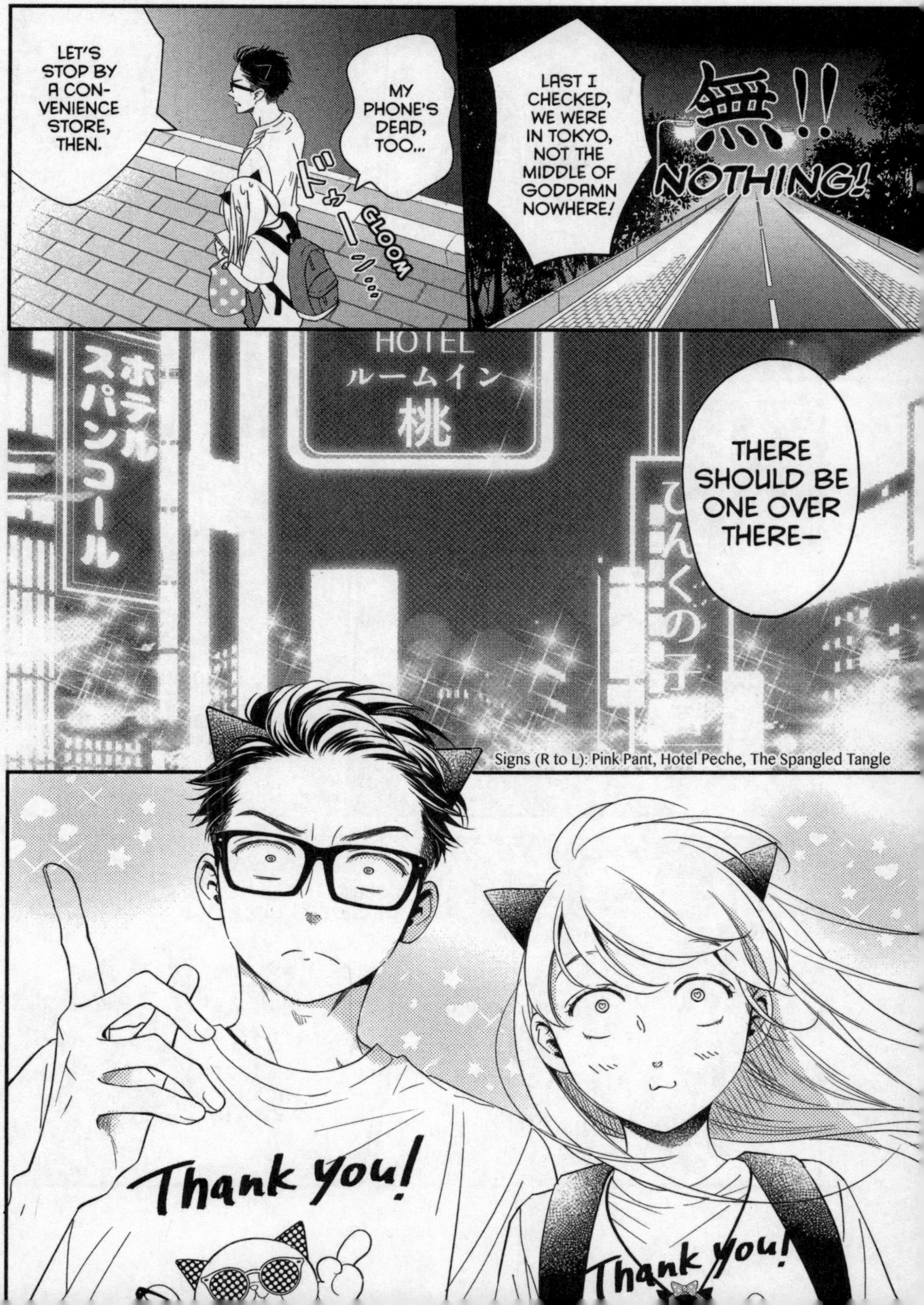
LAST I CHECKED, WE WERE IN TOKYO, NOT THE MIDDLE OF GODDAMN NOWHERE!
無!!
NOTHING!
MY PHONE'S DEAD, TOO...
GLOOM
LET'S STOP BY A CONVENIENCE STORE, THEN.
HOTEL
ルームイン
桃
ホテル
スパンコール
THERE SHOULD BE ONE OVER THERE—
Signs (R to L): Pink Pant, Hotel Peche, The Spangled Tangle
Thank you!
Thank you!

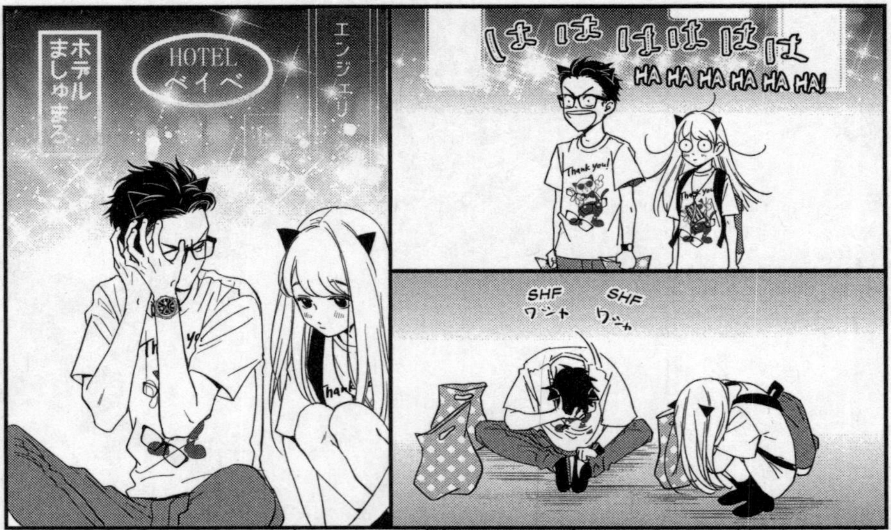
はははははは
HA HA HA HA HA HA!
SHF
SHF
ワシャ
ワシャ
ホテル
ましゅまろ
HOTEL
ベイベ
エンジェリ

Signs (R to L): Cherub's Nest, Hotel Bebe, Mellow Mallow Hotel

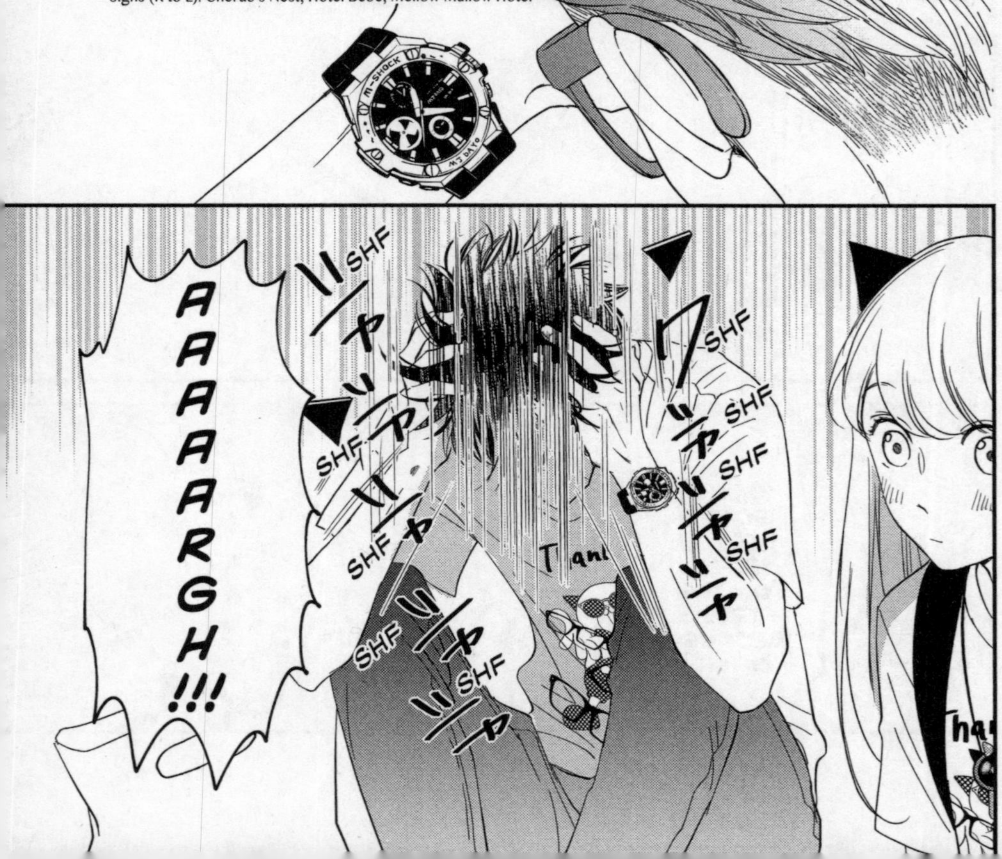
M-SHOCK
ワシャ SHF SHF SHF SHF ワシャ
ワシャ SHF ワシャ SHF ワシャ SHF ワシャ SHF ワシャ SHF
AAAAAAAARGH!!!

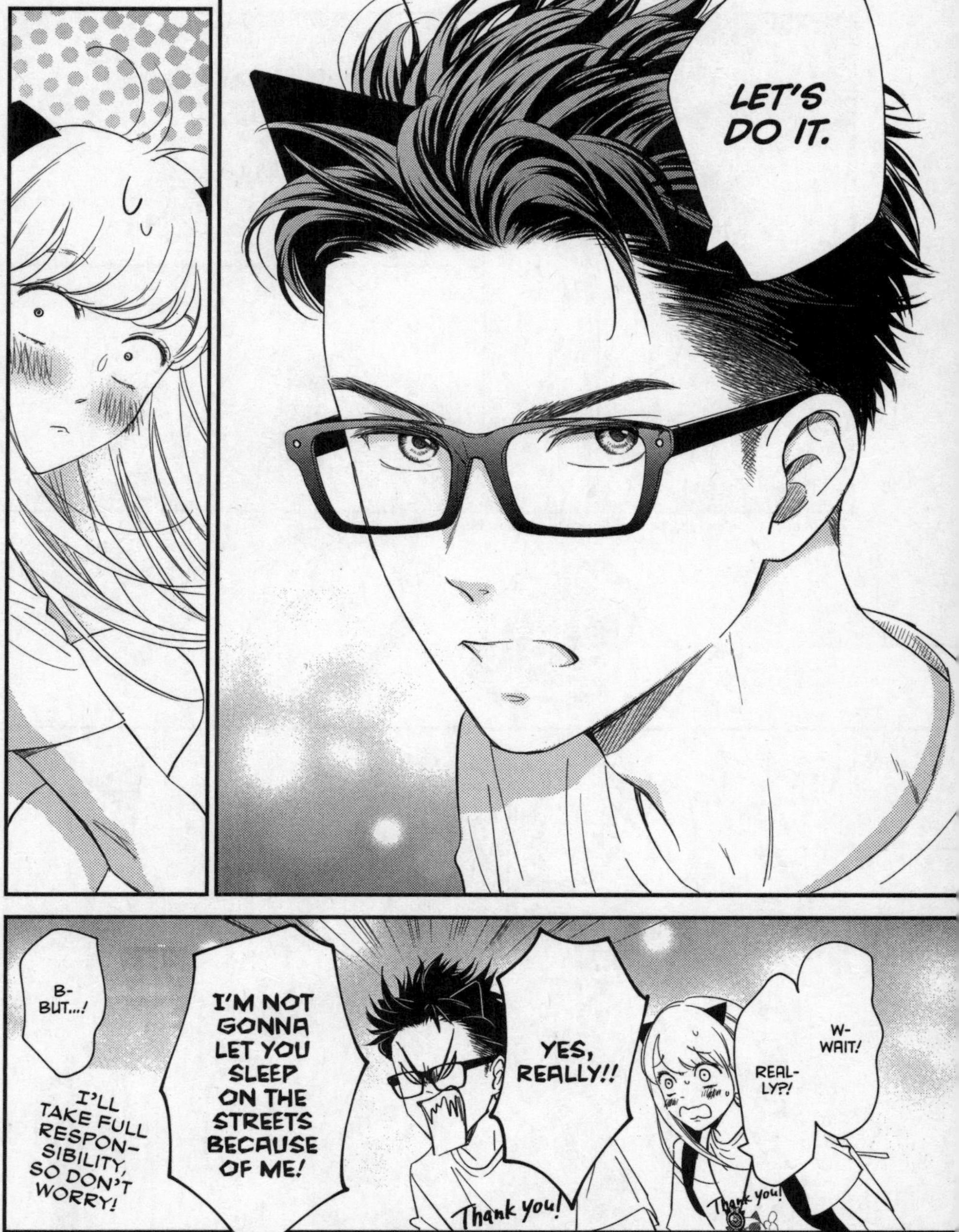
LET'S DO IT.
W-WAIT!
REAL-LY?!
YES, REALLY!!
I'M NOT GONNA LET YOU SLEEP ON THE STREETS BECAUSE OF ME!
B-BUT...!
I'LL TAKE FULL RESPON-SIBILITY, SO DON'T WORRY!
Thank you!
Thank you!

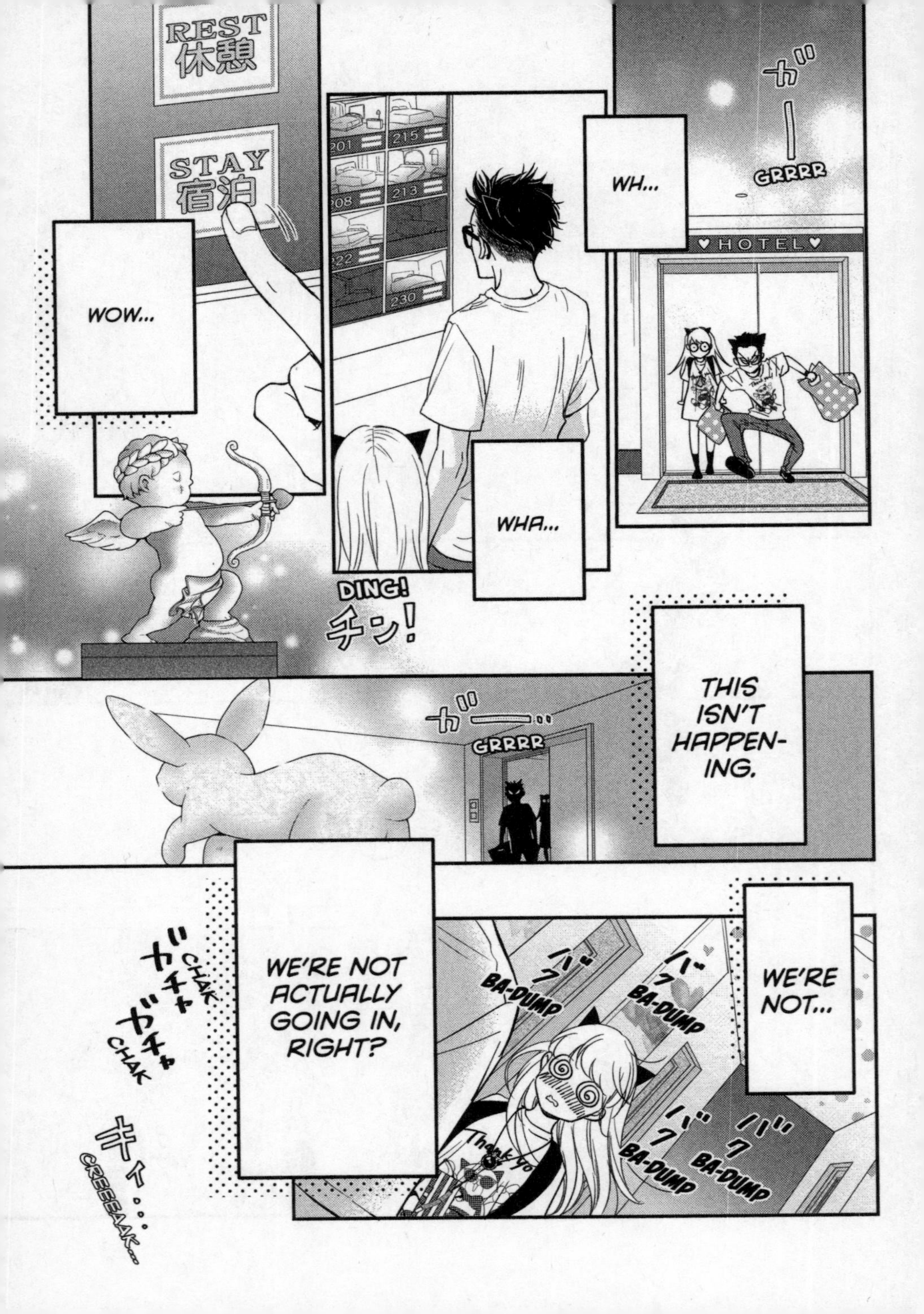
ガー
GRRRR
♥HOTEL♥
WH...
WHA...
REST 休憩
STAY 宿泊
WOW...
DING!
チン!
THIS ISN'T HAPPEN-ING.
ガー
GRRRR
WE'RE NOT...
バク
BA-DUMP
バク
BA-DUMP
バク
BA-DUMP
バク
BA-DUMP
WE'RE NOT ACTUALLY GOING IN, RIGHT?
ガチャ
CHAK
ガチャ
CHAK
キィ…
CREEEAAK...

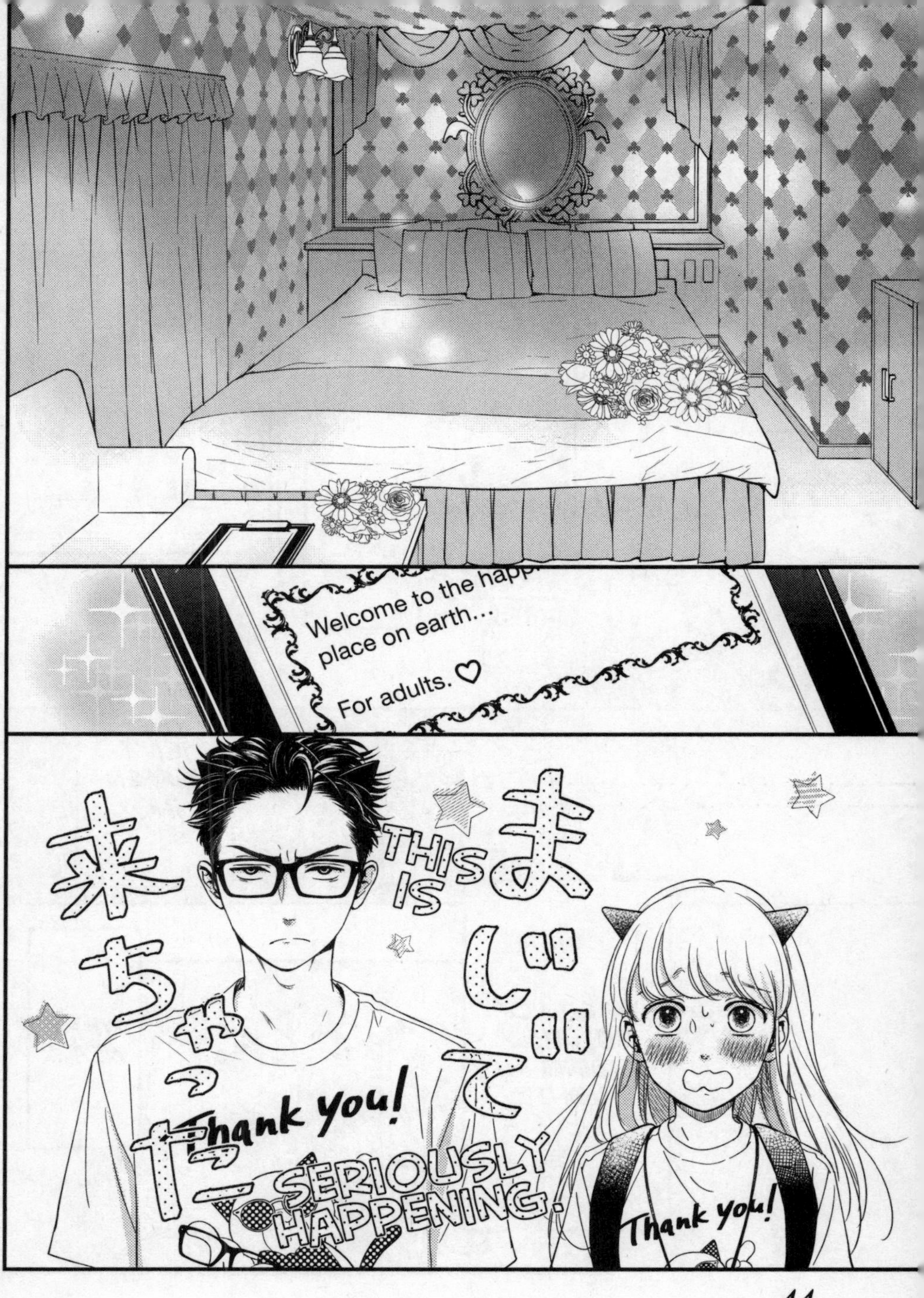
Welcome to the happ
place on earth...
For adults. ♡
まじ
来ちゃってー
THIS IS SERIOUSLY HAPPENING.
Thank you!
Thank you!

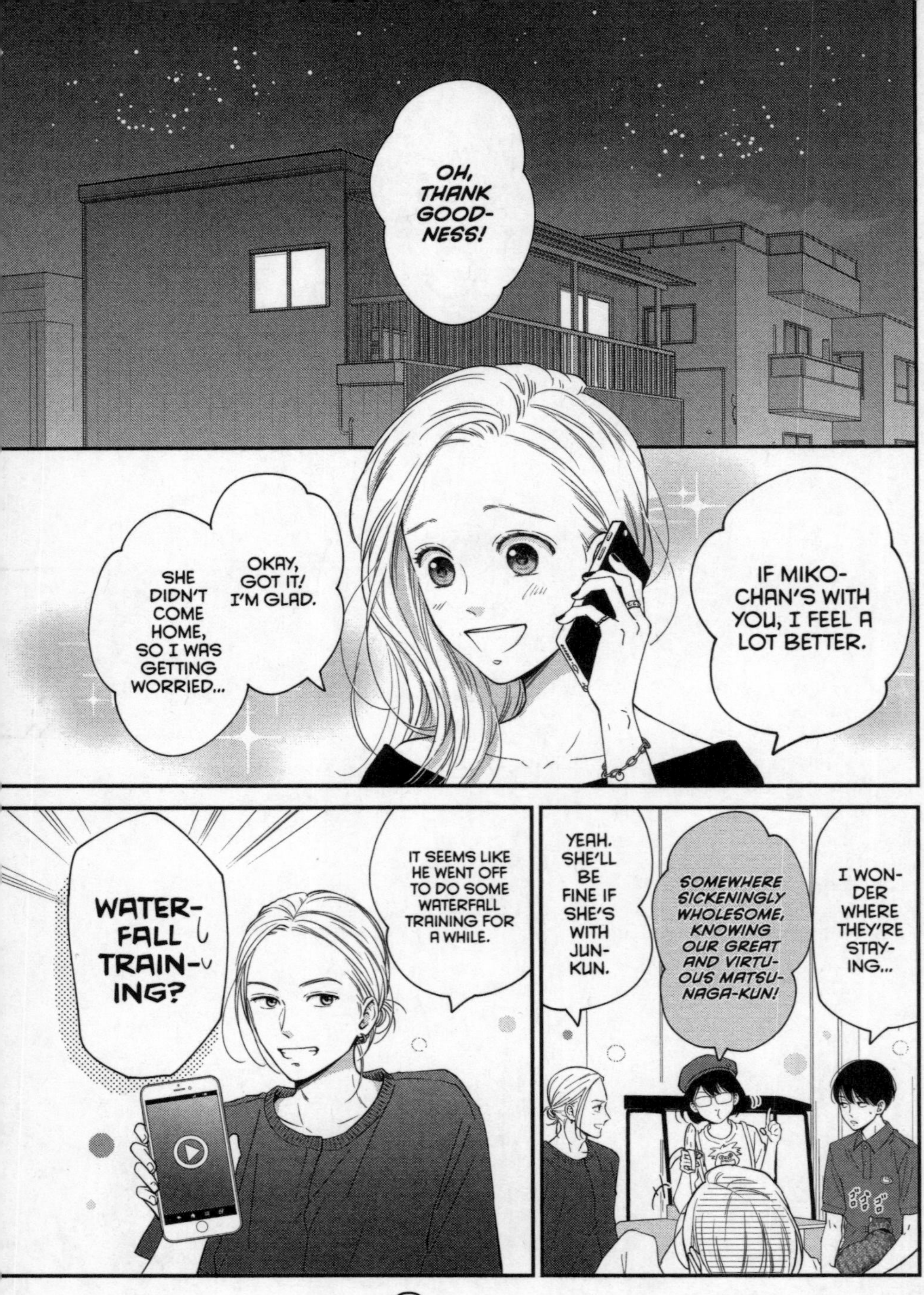
OH, THANK GOODNESS!
IF MIKO-CHAN'S WITH YOU, I FEEL A LOT BETTER.
OKAY, GOT IT! I'M GLAD.
SHE DIDN'T COME HOME, SO I WAS GETTING WORRIED...
I WONDER WHERE THEY'RE STAYING...
SOMEWHERE SICKENINGLY WHOLESOME, KNOWING OUR GREAT AND VIRTUOUS MATSUNAGA-KUN!
YEAH. SHE'LL BE FINE IF SHE'S WITH JUN-KUN.
IT SEEMS LIKE HE WENT OFF TO DO SOME WATERFALL TRAINING FOR A WHILE.
WATERFALL TRAINING?

room 18

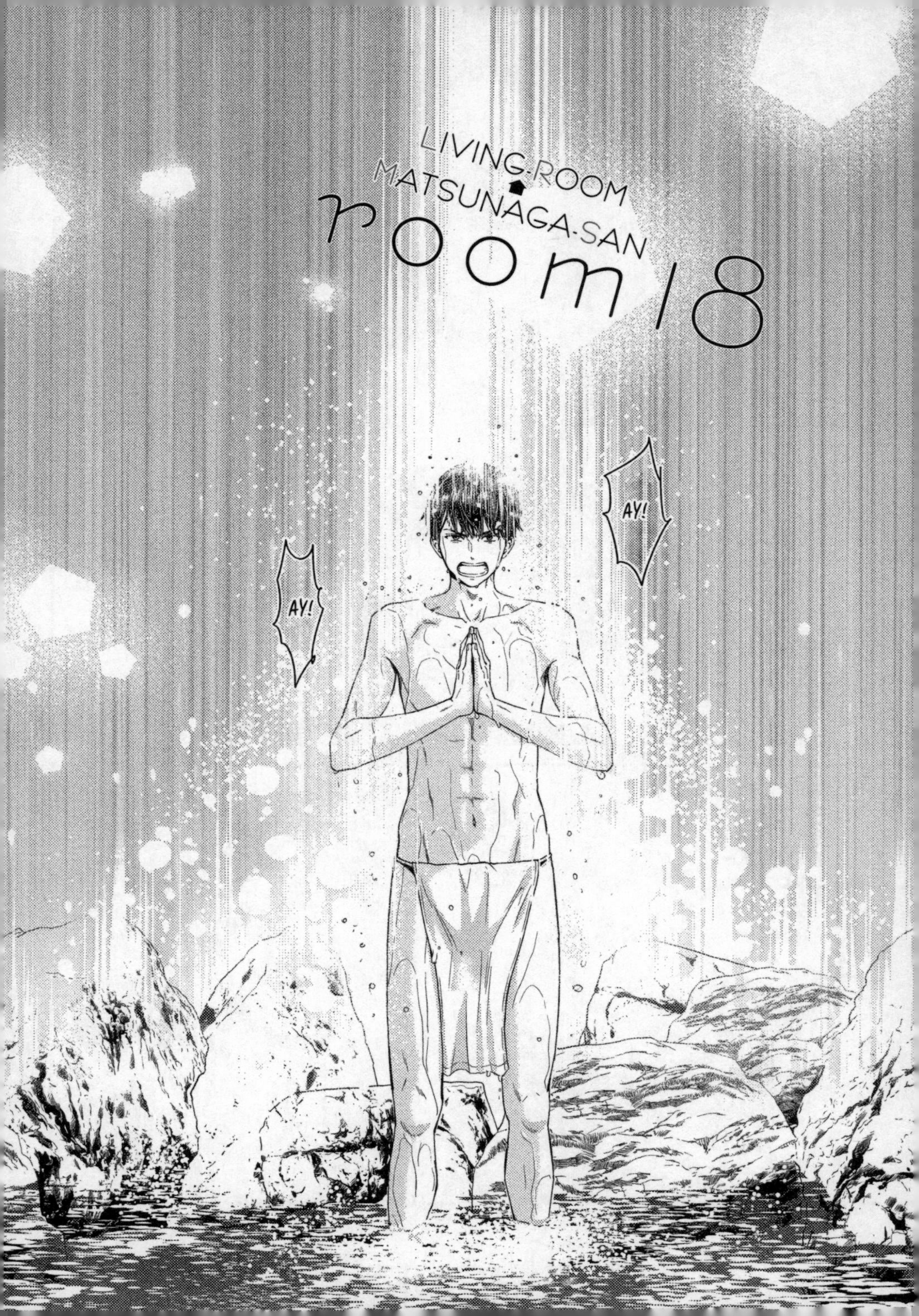
LIVING ROOM
MATSUNAGA-SAN
room 18
AY!
AY!

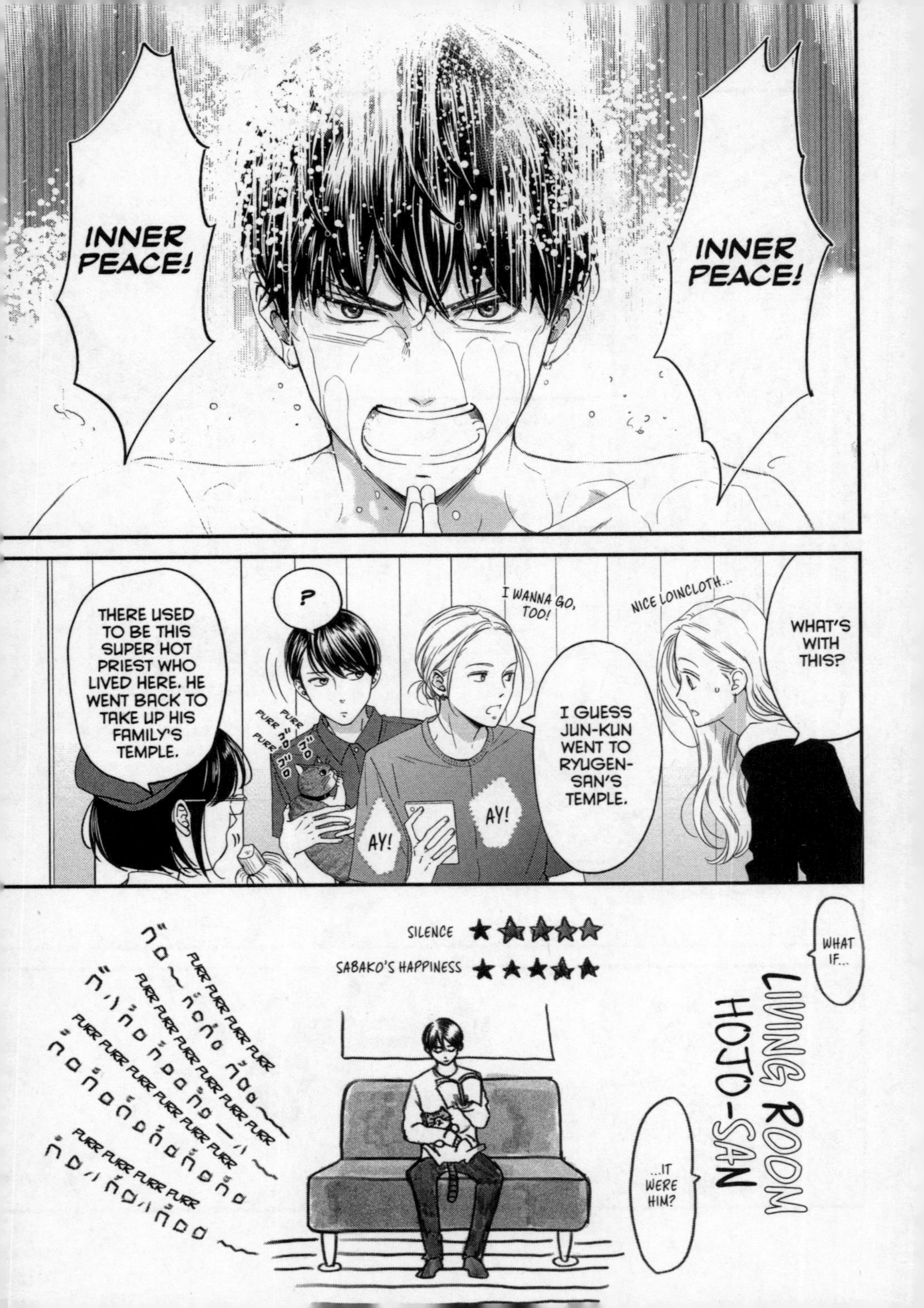
INNER PEACE!
INNER PEACE!
WHAT'S WITH THIS?
NICE LOINCLOTH...
I GUESS JUN-KUN WENT TO RYUGEN-SAN'S TEMPLE.
AY!
AY!
I WANNA GO, TOO!
?
PURR PURR PURR
THERE USED TO BE THIS SUPER HOT PRIEST WHO LIVED HERE. HE WENT BACK TO TAKE UP HIS FAMILY'S TEMPLE.
WHAT IF...
...IT WERE HIM?
LIVING ROOM HOJO-SAN
SILENCE
SABAKO'S HAPPINESS
PURR PURR PURR PURR
PURR PURR PURR PURR PURR
PURR PURR PURR PURR
PURR PURR PURR PURR

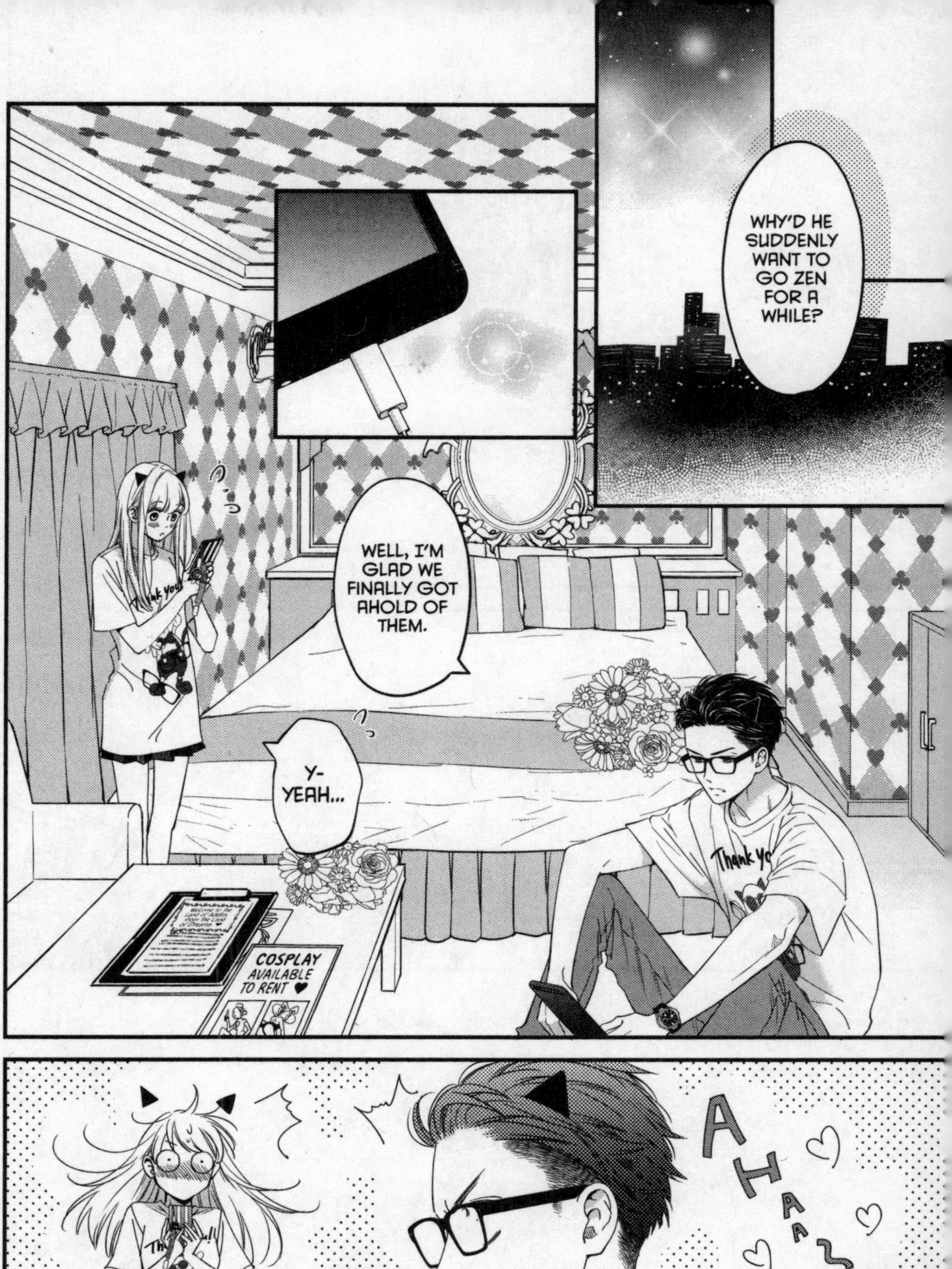
WHY'D HE SUDDENLY WANT TO GO ZEN FOR A WHILE?
WELL, I'M GLAD WE FINALLY GOT AHOLD OF THEM.
Y-YEAH...
COSPLAY AVAILABLE TO RENT ♥

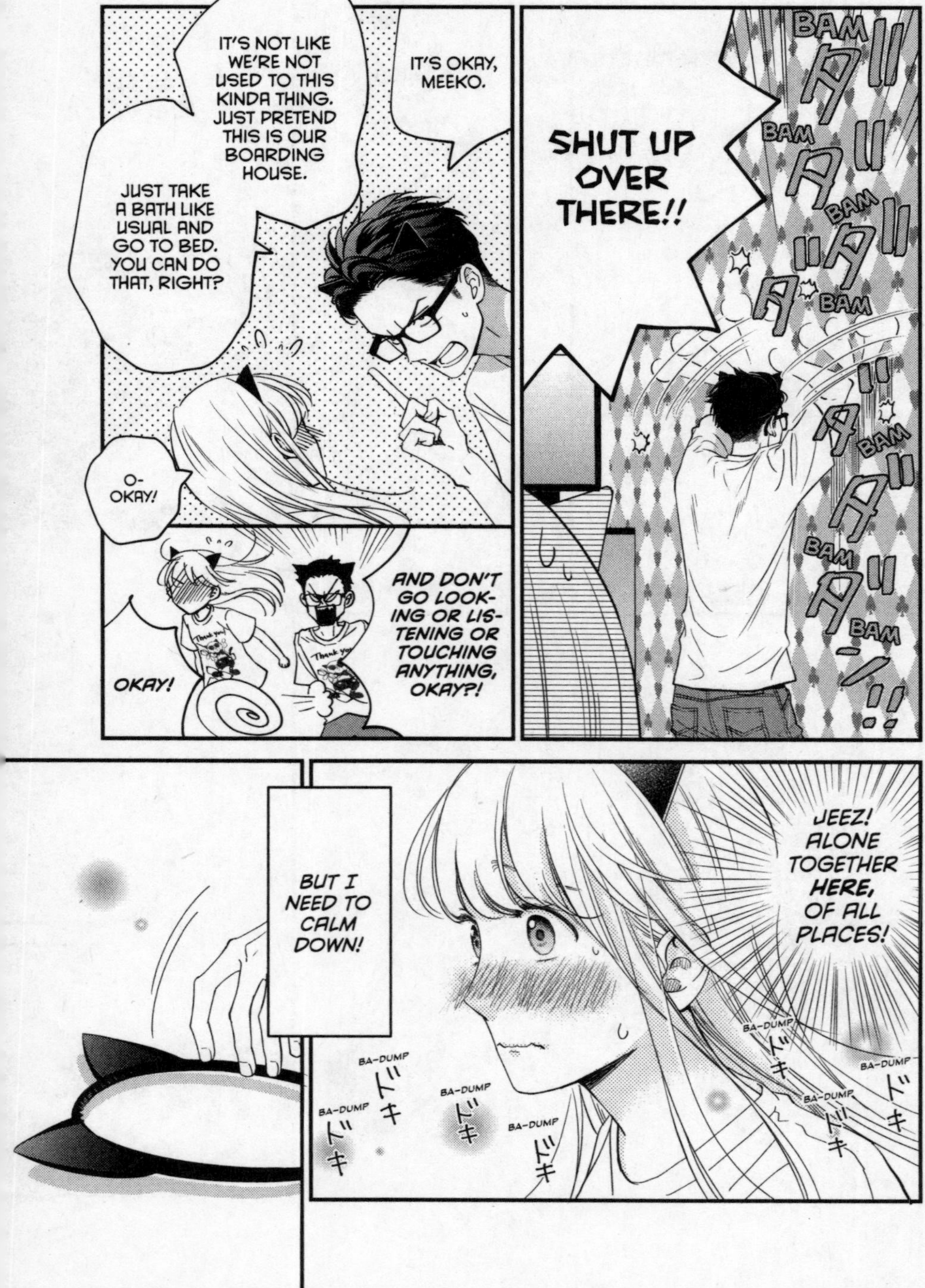
BAM
BAM
BAM
BAM
BAM
BAM
BAM
SHUT UP OVER THERE!!
IT'S OKAY, MEEKO.
IT'S NOT LIKE WE'RE NOT USED TO THIS KINDA THING. JUST PRETEND THIS IS OUR BOARDING HOUSE.
JUST TAKE A BATH LIKE USUAL AND GO TO BED. YOU CAN DO THAT, RIGHT?
O-OKAY!
AND DON'T GO LOOKING OR LISTENING OR TOUCHING ANYTHING, OKAY?!
OKAY!
JEEZ! ALONE TOGETHER HERE, OF ALL PLACES!
BA-DUMP
BA-DUMP
BA-DUMP
BUT I NEED TO CALM DOWN!
BA-DUMP
BA-DUMP
BA-DUMP
BA-DUMP

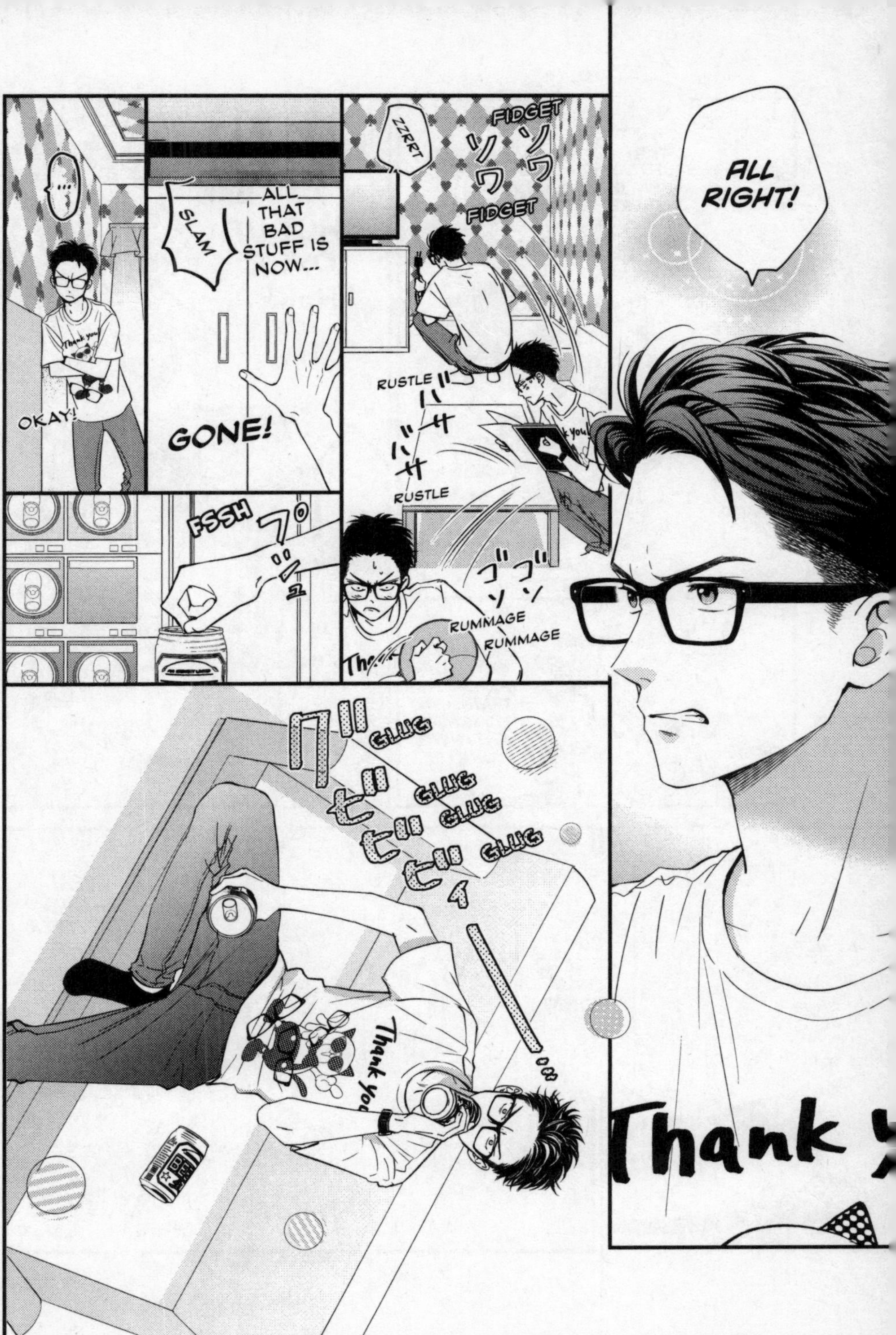
ALL RIGHT!
Thank y
ZZRRT
FIDGET
ソワソワ
FIDGET
RUSTLE
バサバサ
RUSTLE
ゴソゴソ
RUMMAGE
RUMMAGE
SLAM
ALL THAT BAD STUFF IS NOW...
GONE!
...
OKAY!
FSSH
プシュ
GLUG
GLUG
GLUG
GLUG
Thank you

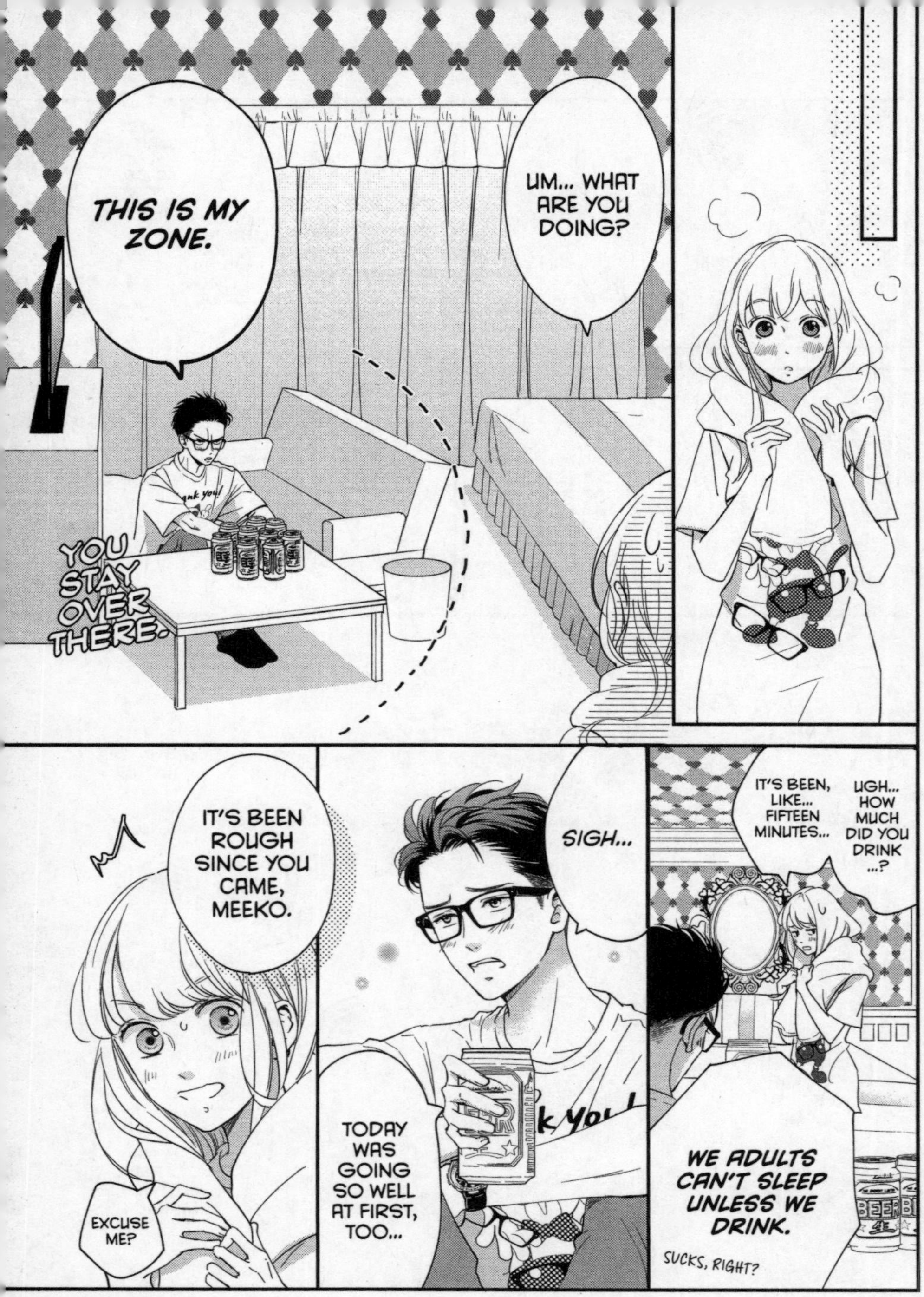
UM... WHAT ARE YOU DOING?
THIS IS MY ZONE.
YOU STAY OVER THERE.
UGH... HOW MUCH DID YOU DRINK ...?
IT'S BEEN, LIKE... FIFTEEN MINUTES...
WE ADULTS CAN'T SLEEP UNLESS WE DRINK.
SUCKS, RIGHT?
SIGH...
TODAY WAS GOING SO WELL AT FIRST, TOO...
IT'S BEEN ROUGH SINCE YOU CAME, MEEKO.
EXCUSE ME?

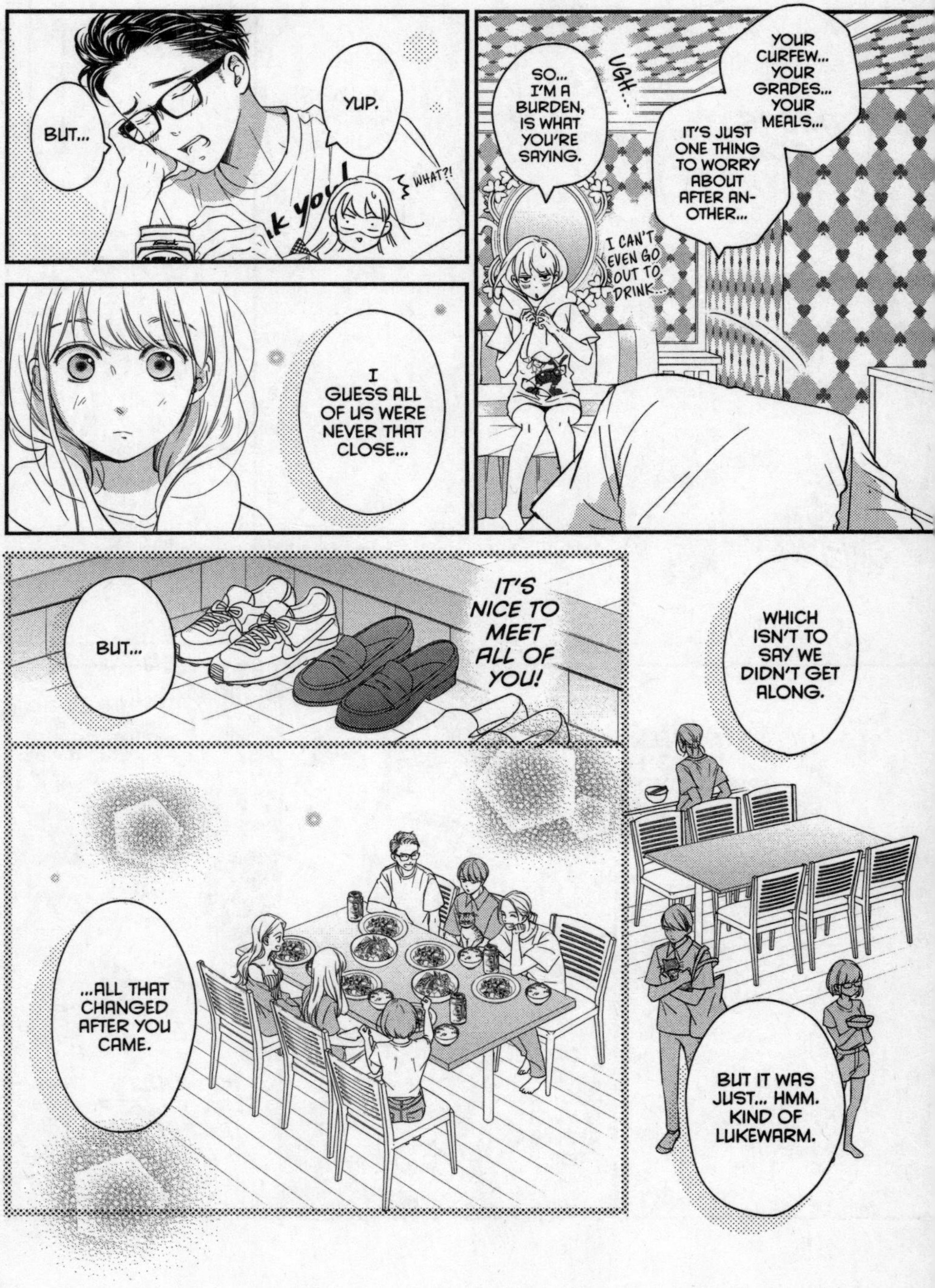
YOUR CURFEW... YOUR GRADES... YOUR MEALS...
IT'S JUST ONE THING TO WORRY ABOUT AFTER AN-OTHER...
UGH...
SO... I'M A BURDEN, IS WHAT YOU'RE SAYING.
I CAN'T EVEN GO OUT TO DRINK...
YUP.
WHAT?!
BUT...
I GUESS ALL OF US WERE NEVER THAT CLOSE...
WHICH ISN'T TO SAY WE DIDN'T GET ALONG.
BUT IT WAS JUST... HMM. KIND OF LUKEWARM.
IT'S NICE TO MEET ALL OF YOU!
BUT...
...ALL THAT CHANGED AFTER YOU CAME.

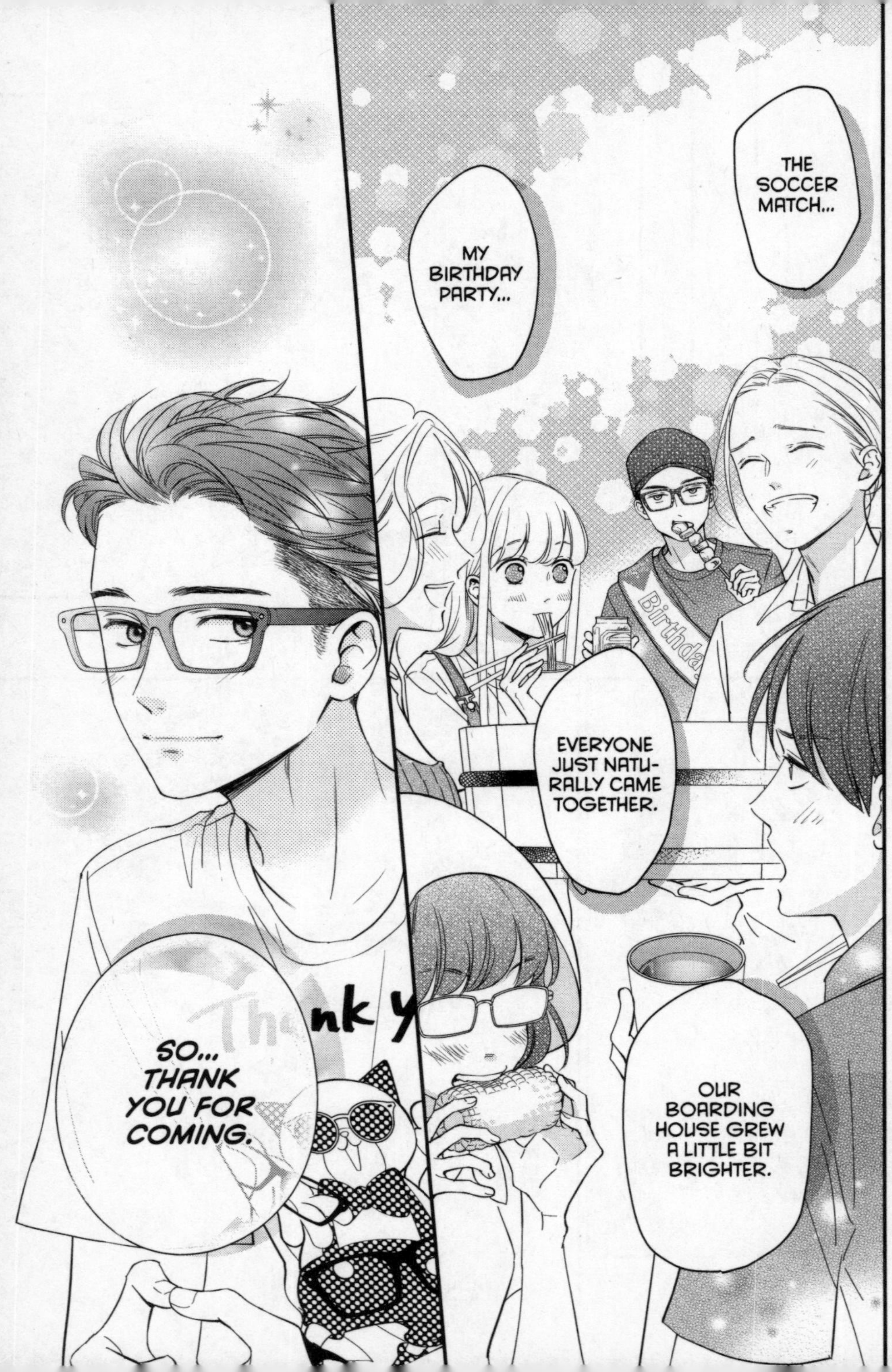
THE SOCCER MATCH...
MY BIRTHDAY PARTY...
EVERYONE JUST NATU-RALLY CAME TOGETHER.
OUR BOARDING HOUSE GREW A LITTLE BIT BRIGHTER.
SO... THANK YOU FOR COMING.

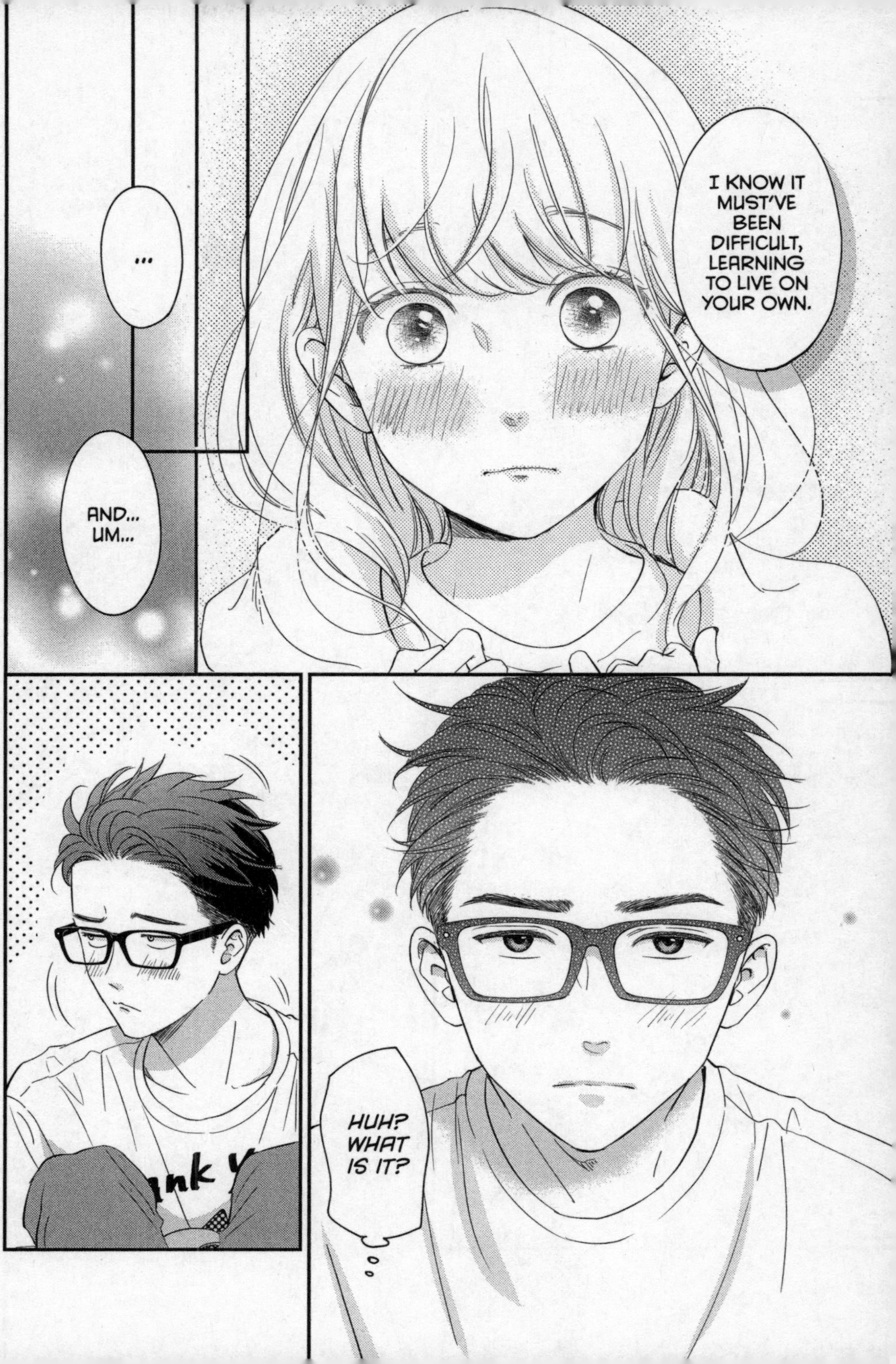
I KNOW IT MUST'VE BEEN DIFFICULT, LEARNING TO LIVE ON YOUR OWN.
...
AND... UM...
HUH? WHAT IS IT?

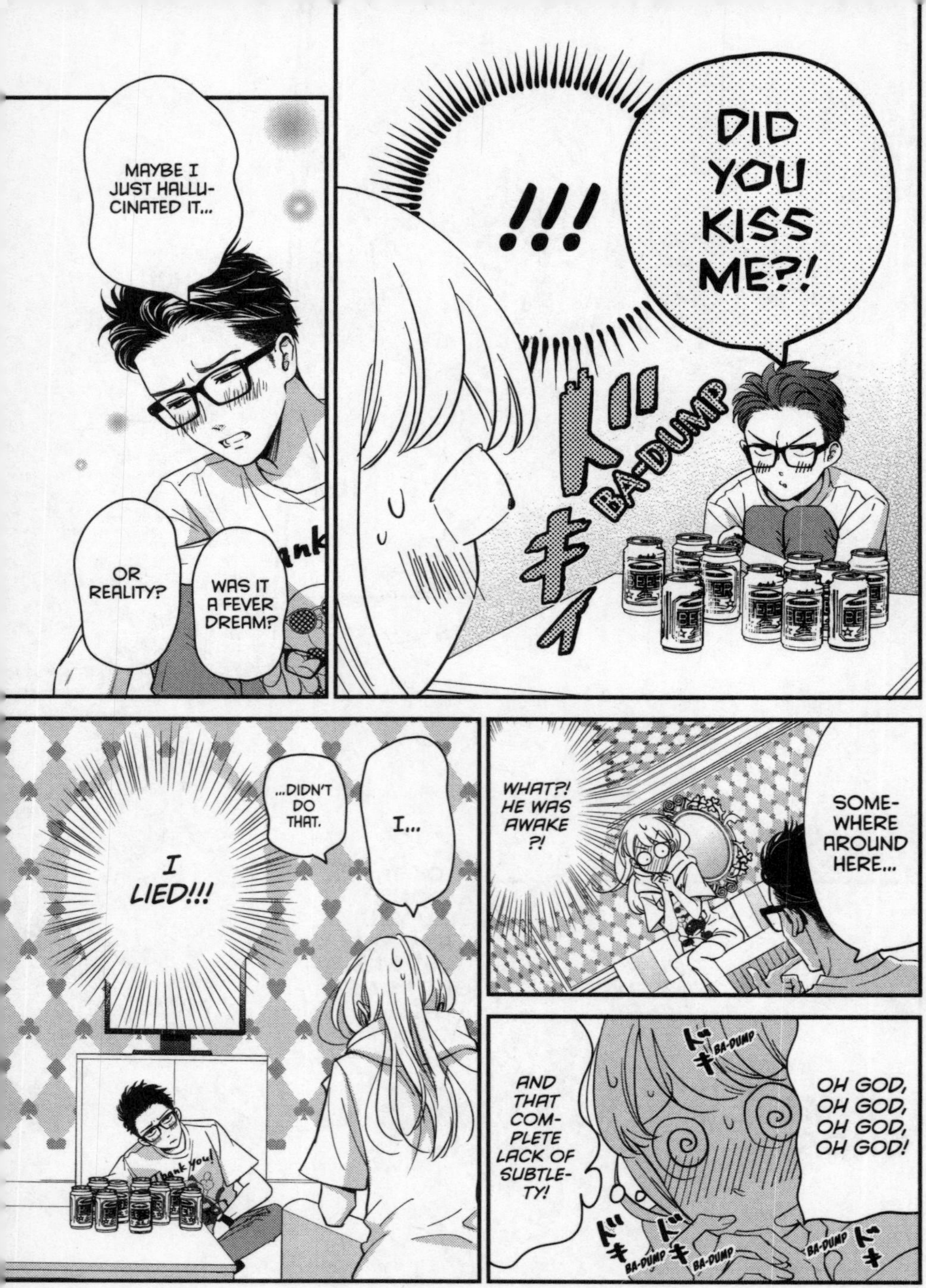
DID YOU KISS ME?!
!!!
BA-DUMP
MAYBE I JUST HALLU-CINATED IT...
WAS IT A FEVER DREAM?
OR REALITY?
SOME-WHERE AROUND HERE...
WHAT?! HE WAS AWAKE?!
OH GOD, OH GOD, OH GOD, OH GOD!
AND THAT COM-PLETE LACK OF SUBTLE-TY!
BA-DUMP
BA-DUMP
BA-DUMP
BA-DUMP
I...
...DIDN'T DO THAT.
I LIED!!!

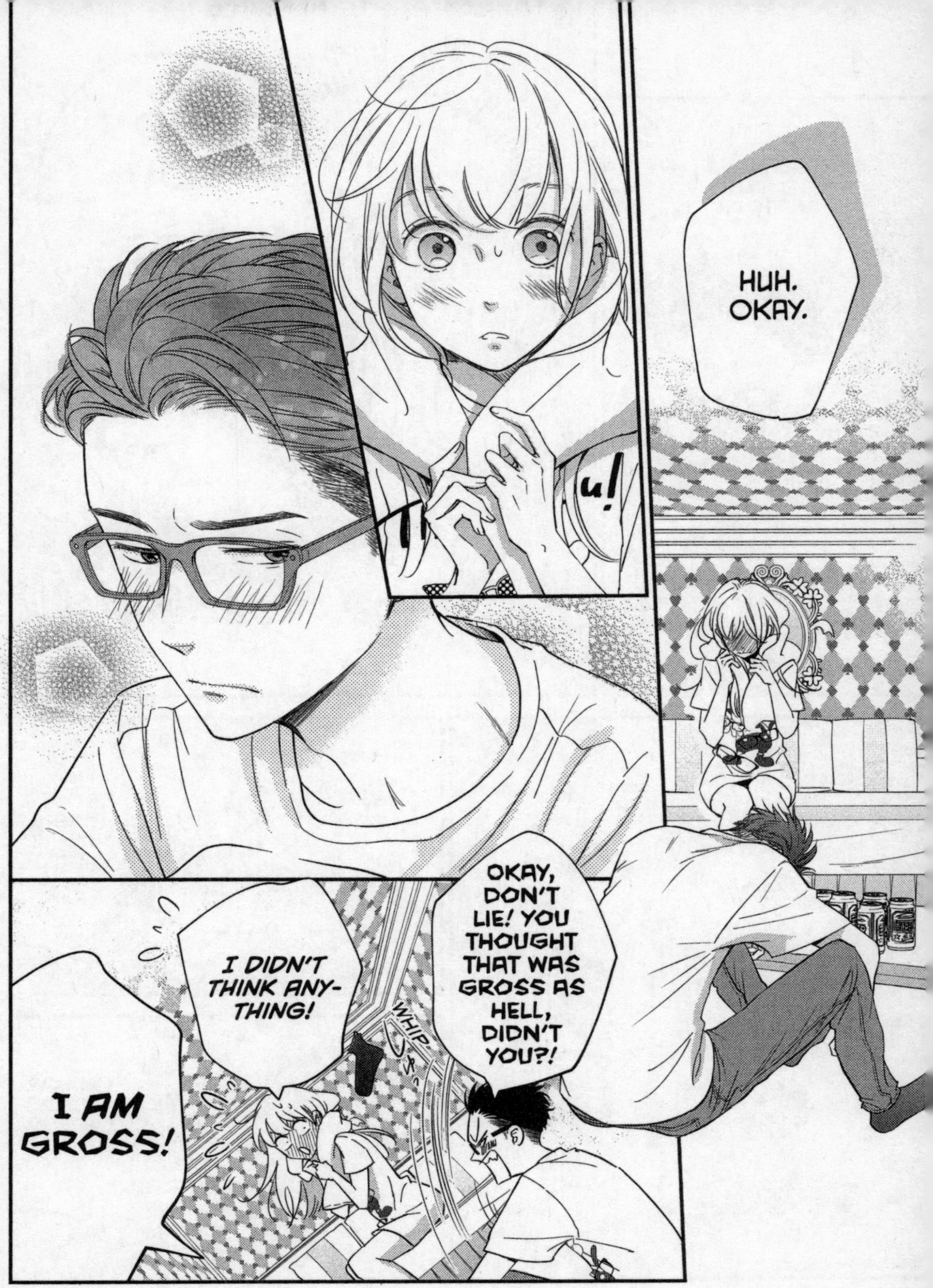
HUH. OKAY.
OKAY, DON'T LIE! YOU THOUGHT THAT WAS GROSS AS HELL, DIDN'T YOU?!
I DIDN'T THINK ANY-THING!
WHIP
I AM GROSS!

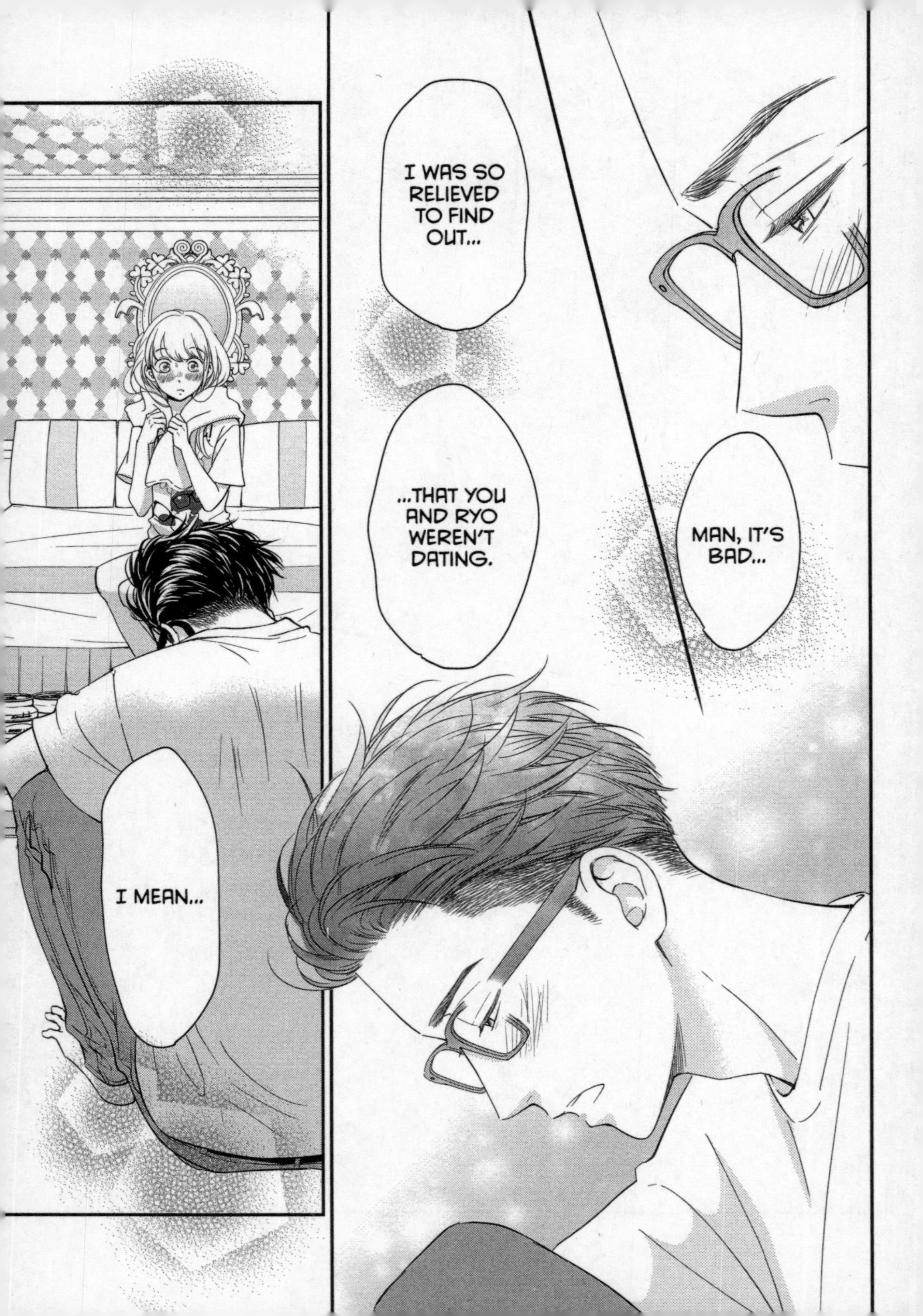
I WAS SO RELIEVED TO FIND OUT...
...THAT YOU AND RYO WEREN'T DATING.
MAN, IT'S BAD...
I MEAN...

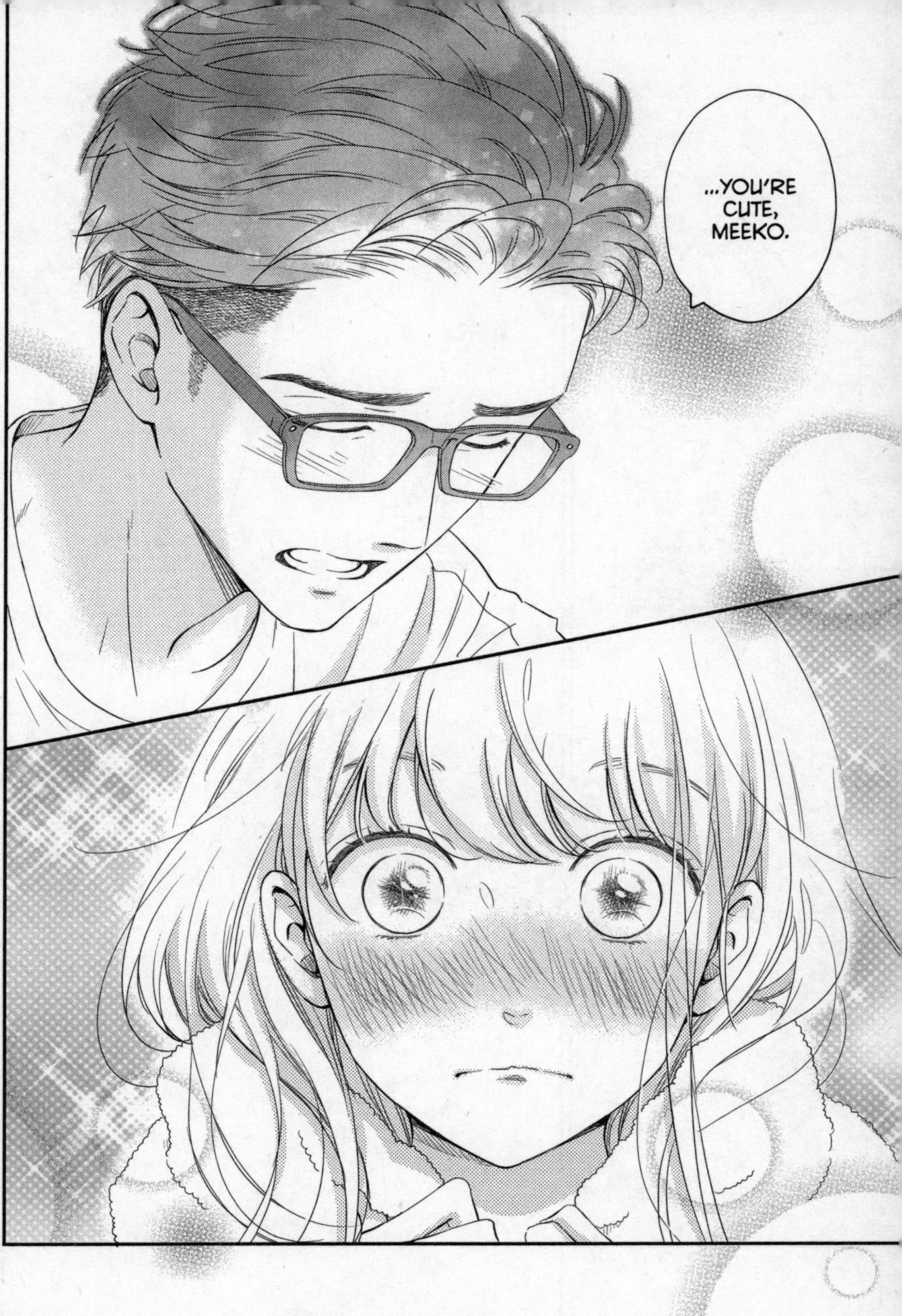
...YOU'RE CUTE, MEEKO.

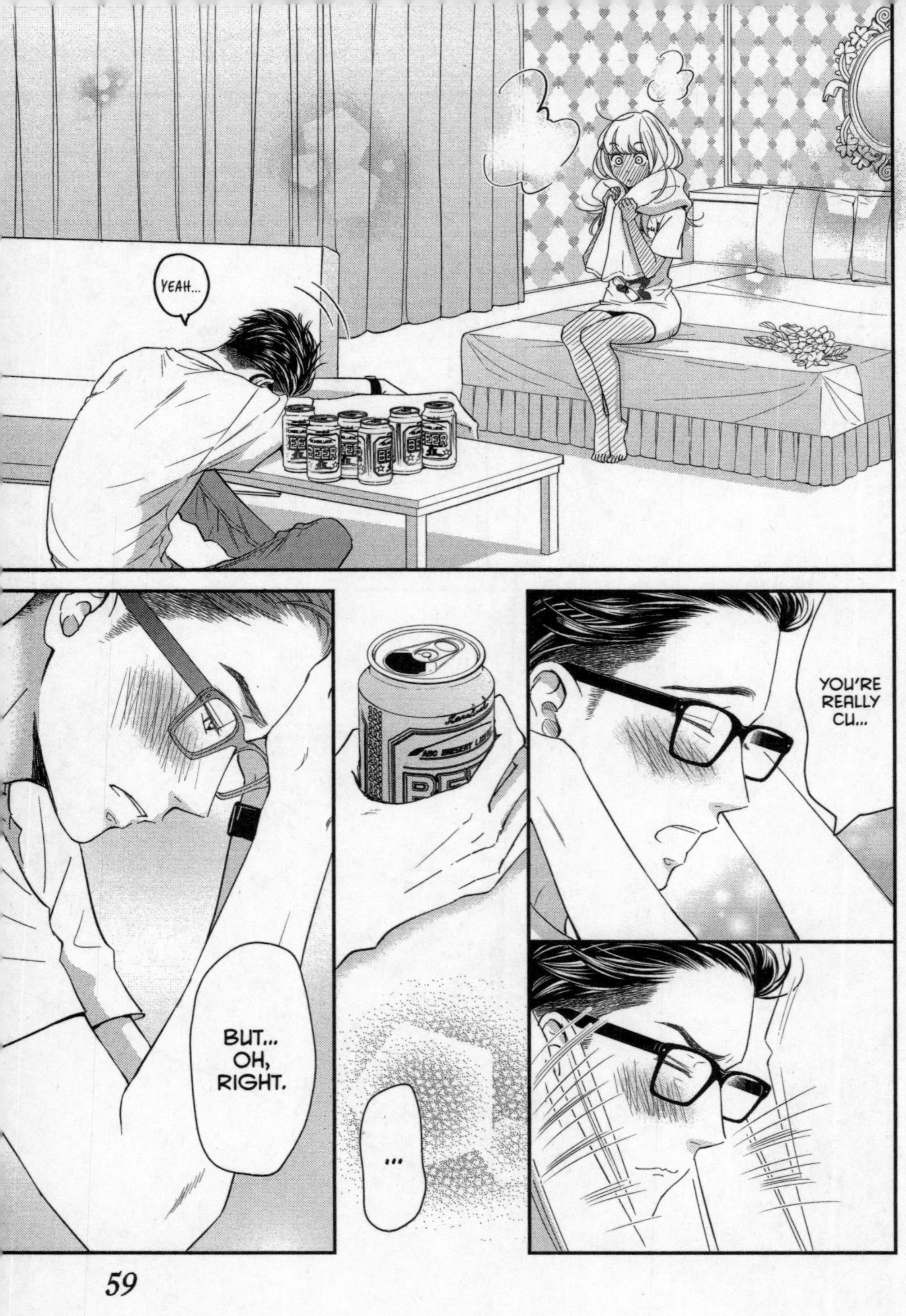
YEAH...
YOU'RE REALLY CU...
...
BUT... OH, RIGHT.

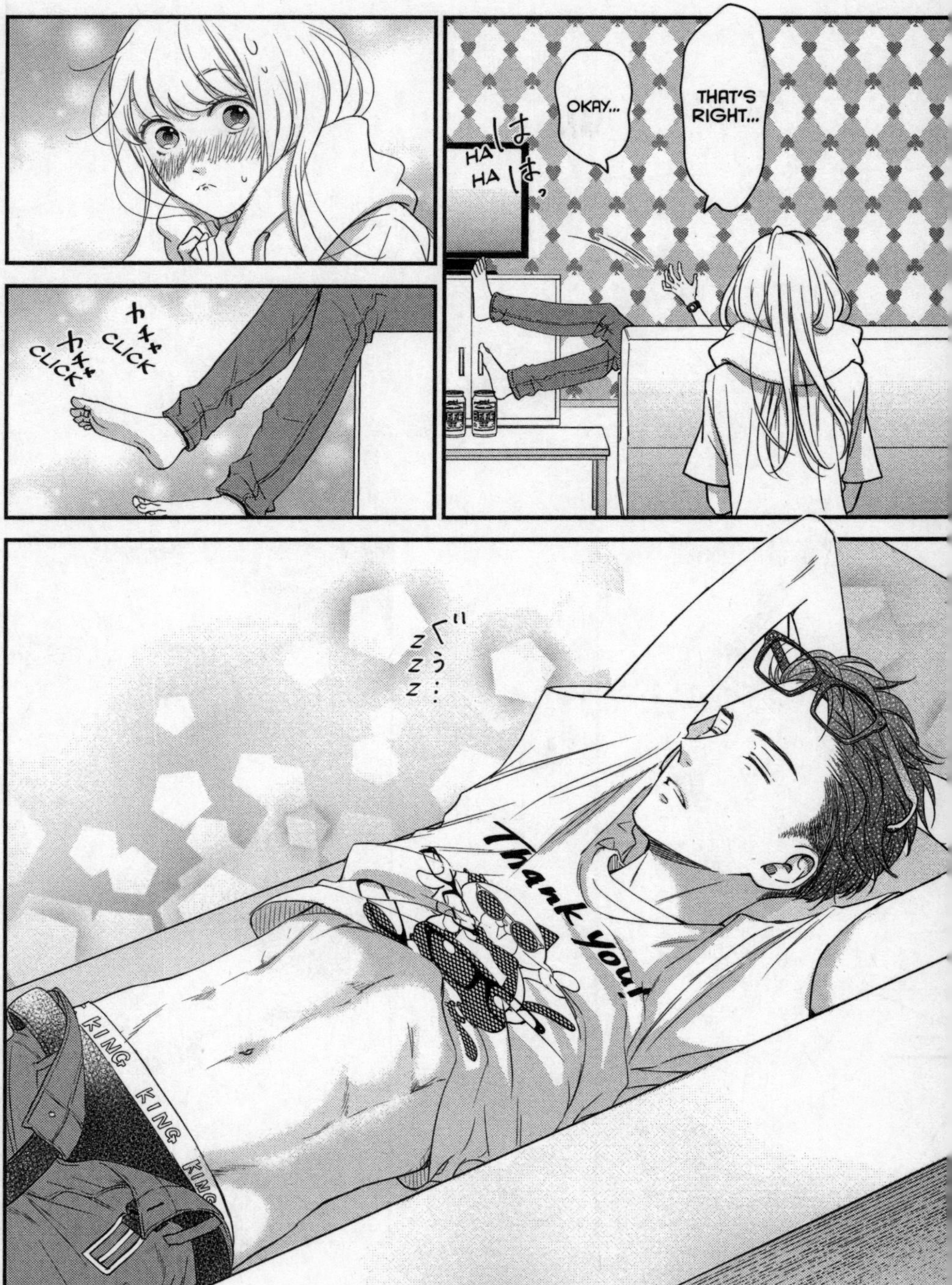
THAT'S RIGHT...
OKAY...
はは HA
はっ HA
カチャ CLICK
カチャ CLICK
ぐぅ… ZZZ
Thank you!
KING KING KING

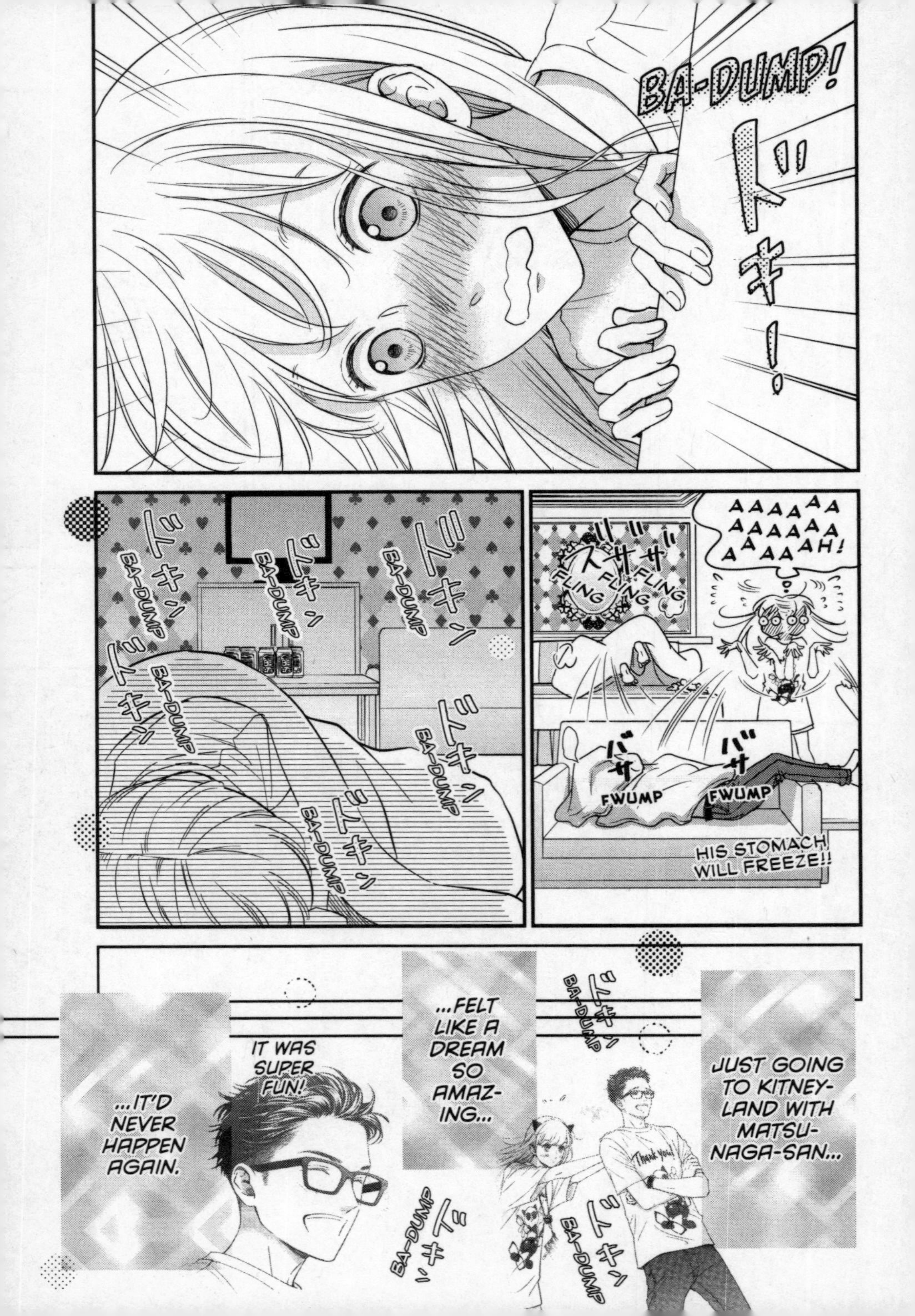
BA-DUMP!
AAAAAA AAAAAA AAAAAH!
FLING FLING FLING
FWUMP FWUMP
HIS STOMACH WILL FREEZE!!
BA-DUMP
BA-DUMP
BA-DUMP
BA-DUMP
BA-DUMP
JUST GOING TO KITNEY-LAND WITH MATSU-NAGA-SAN...
BA-DUMP
...FELT LIKE A DREAM SO AMAZ-ING...
BA-DUMP
BA-DUMP
IT WAS SUPER FUN!
...IT'D NEVER HAPPEN AGAIN.

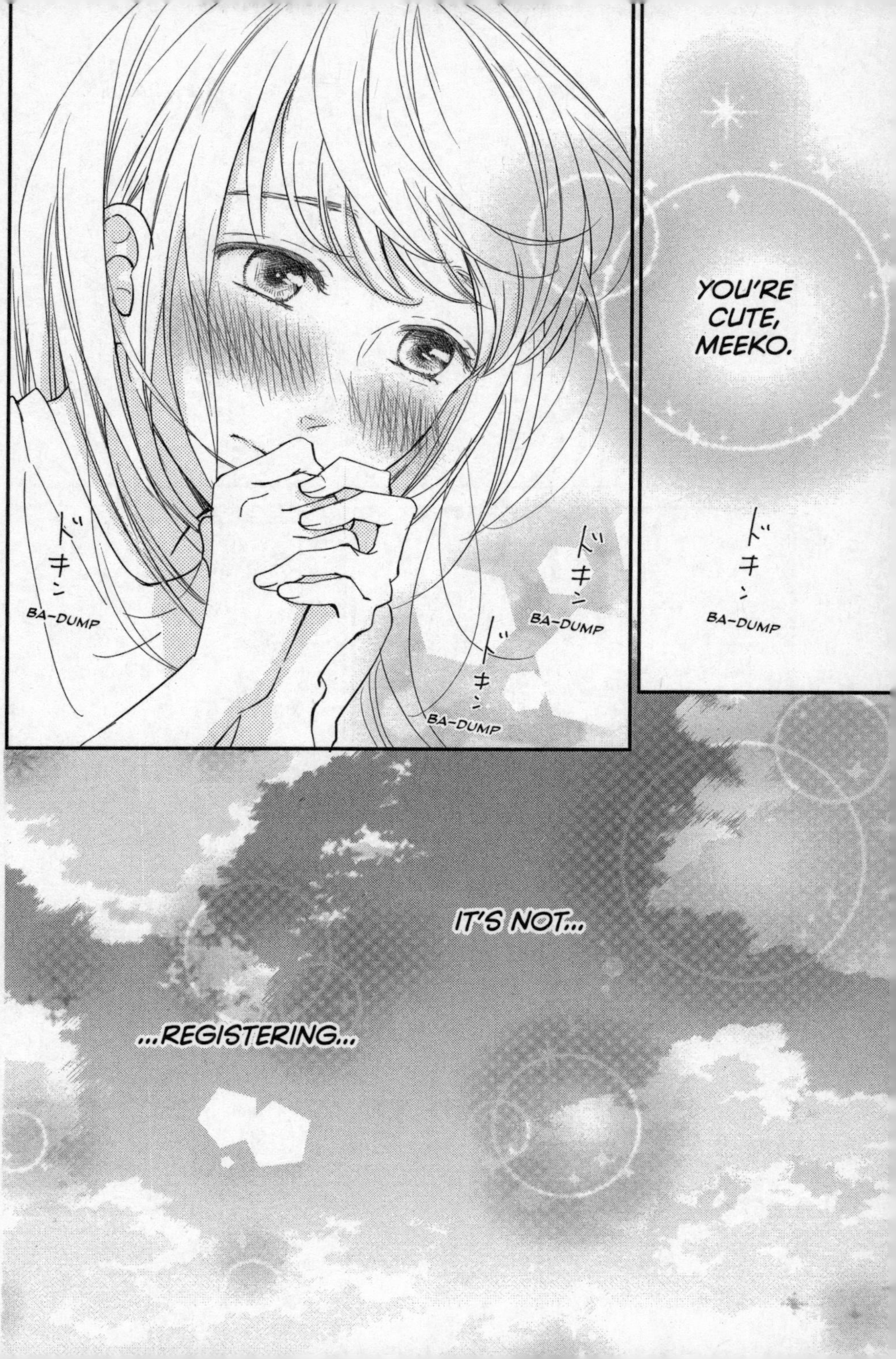
YOU'RE CUTE, MEEKO.
ドキン
BA-DUMP
ドキン
BA-DUMP
ドキン
BA-DUMP
ドキン
BA-DUMP
IT'S NOT...
...REGISTERING...

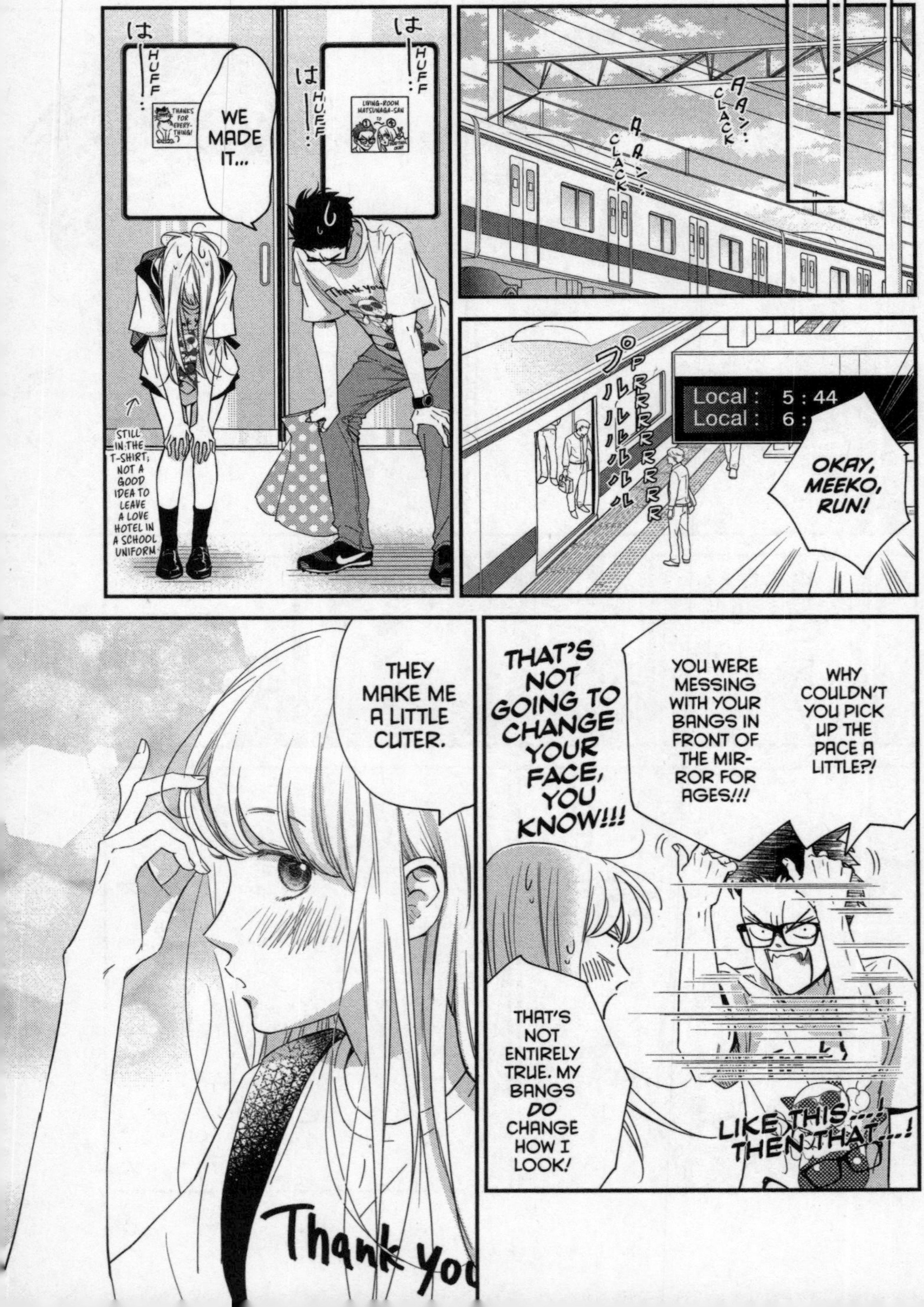
CLACK
CLACK
プルルルル
PRRRRRRRR
Local : 5 : 44
Local : 6 :
OKAY, MEEKO, RUN!
は HUFF…
は HUFF…!
は HUFF…!
WE MADE IT…
THANKS FOR EVERY-THING!
LIVING-ROOM MATSUNAGA-SAN
STILL IN THE T-SHIRT; NOT A GOOD IDEA TO LEAVE A LOVE HOTEL IN A SCHOOL UNIFORM
WHY COULDN'T YOU PICK UP THE PACE A LITTLE?!
YOU WERE MESSING WITH YOUR BANGS IN FRONT OF THE MIR-ROR FOR AGES!!!
THAT'S NOT GOING TO CHANGE YOUR FACE, YOU KNOW!!!
THAT'S NOT ENTIRELY TRUE. MY BANGS *DO* CHANGE HOW I LOOK!
LIKE THIS…! THEN THAT…!
THEY MAKE ME A LITTLE CUTER.
Thank you

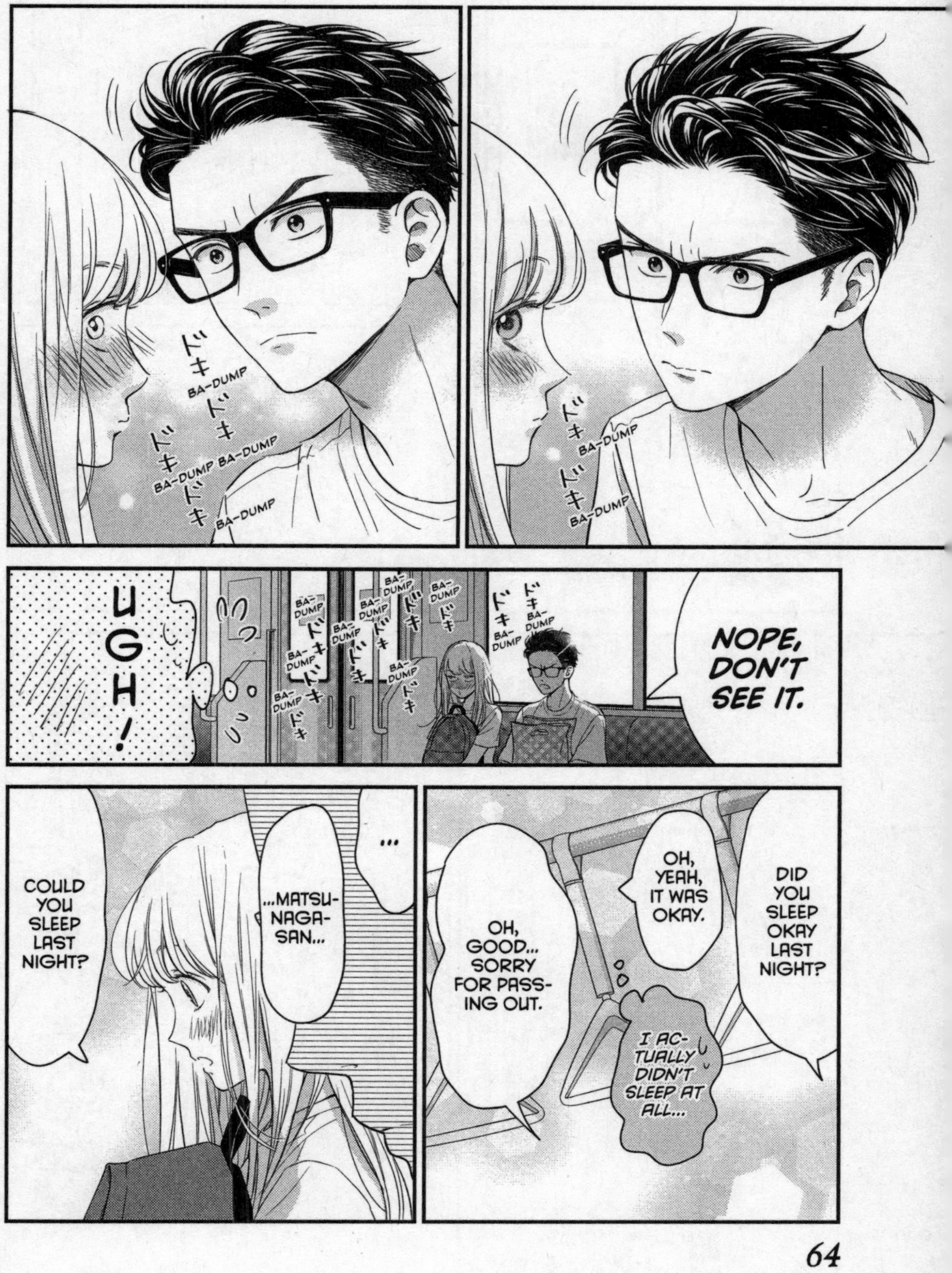
ドキ BA-DUMP
ドキ BA-DUMP
ドキ BA-DUMP
ドキ BA-DUMP
ドキ BA-DUMP
ドキ BA-DUMP
NOPE, DON'T SEE IT.
ドキ BA-DUMP
ドキ BA-DUMP
ドキ BA-DUMP
ドキ BA-DUMP
ドキ BA-DUMP
ドキ BA-DUMP
ドキ BA-DUMP
ドキ BA-DUMP
UGH!
DID YOU SLEEP OKAY LAST NIGHT?
OH, YEAH, IT WAS OKAY.
I ACTUALLY DIDN'T SLEEP AT ALL...
OH, GOOD... SORRY FOR PASSING OUT.
...
...MATSUNAGA-SAN...
COULD YOU SLEEP LAST NIGHT?

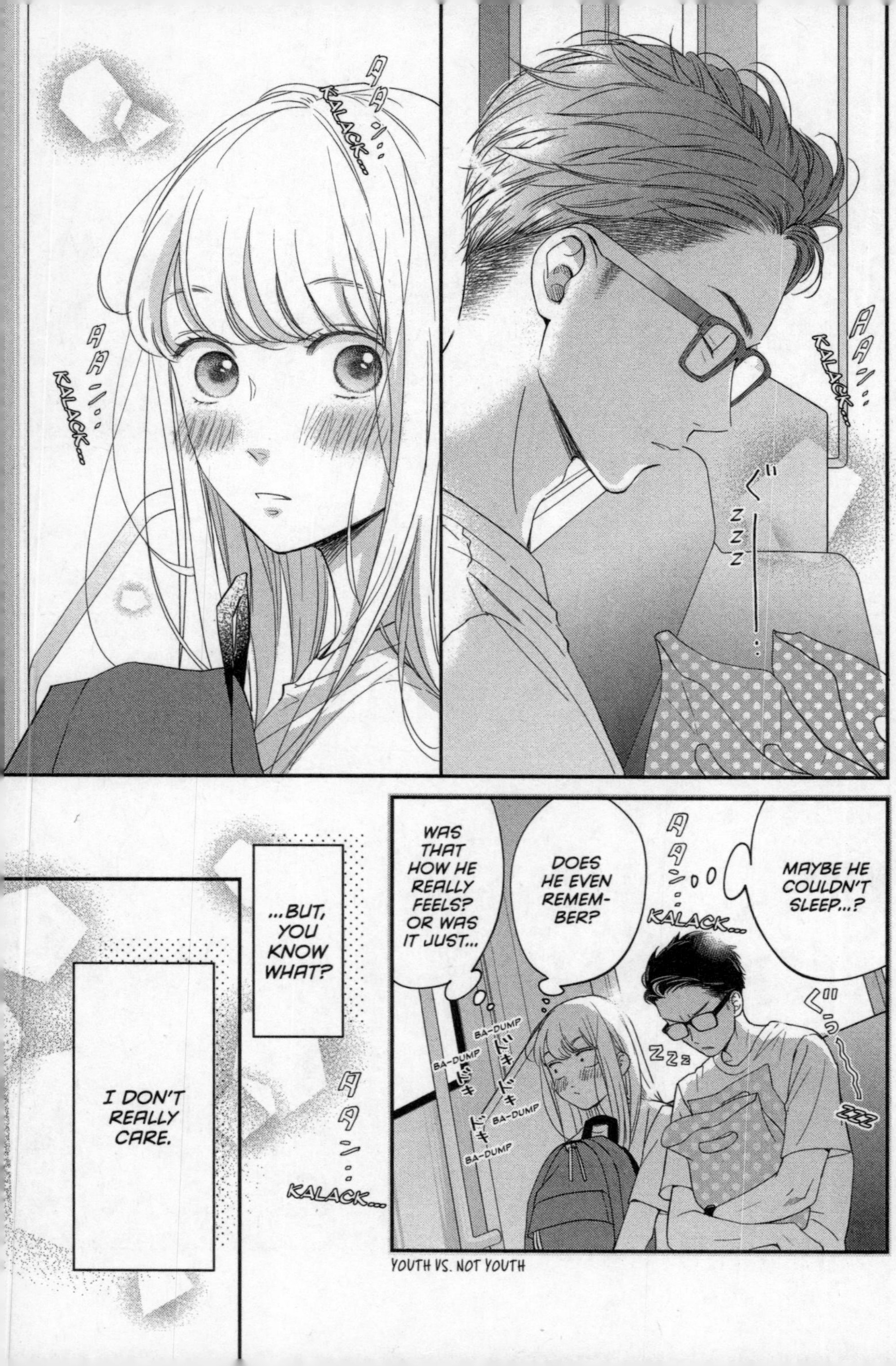
KALACK...
ZZZ
KALACK...
KALACK...
KALACK...
MAYBE HE COULDN'T SLEEP...?
ZZZ
ZZZ
KALACK...
DOES HE EVEN REMEMBER?
WAS THAT HOW HE REALLY FEELS? OR WAS IT JUST...
BA-DUMP
BA-DUMP
BA-DUMP
BA-DUMP
...BUT, YOU KNOW WHAT?
KALACK...
I DON'T REALLY CARE.

YOUTH VS. NOT YOUTH

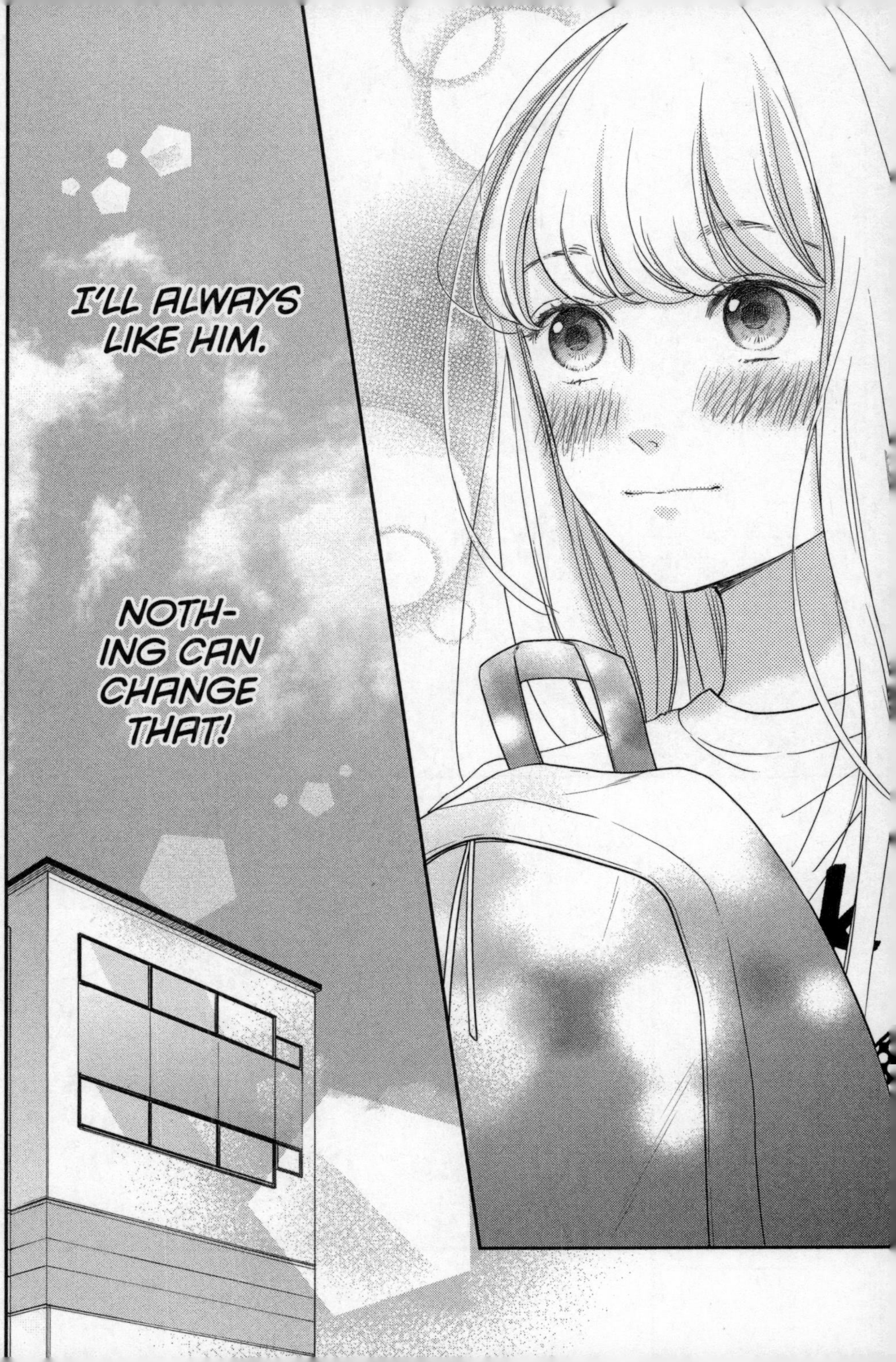
I'LL ALWAYS LIKE HIM.
NOTH-ING CAN CHANGE THAT!

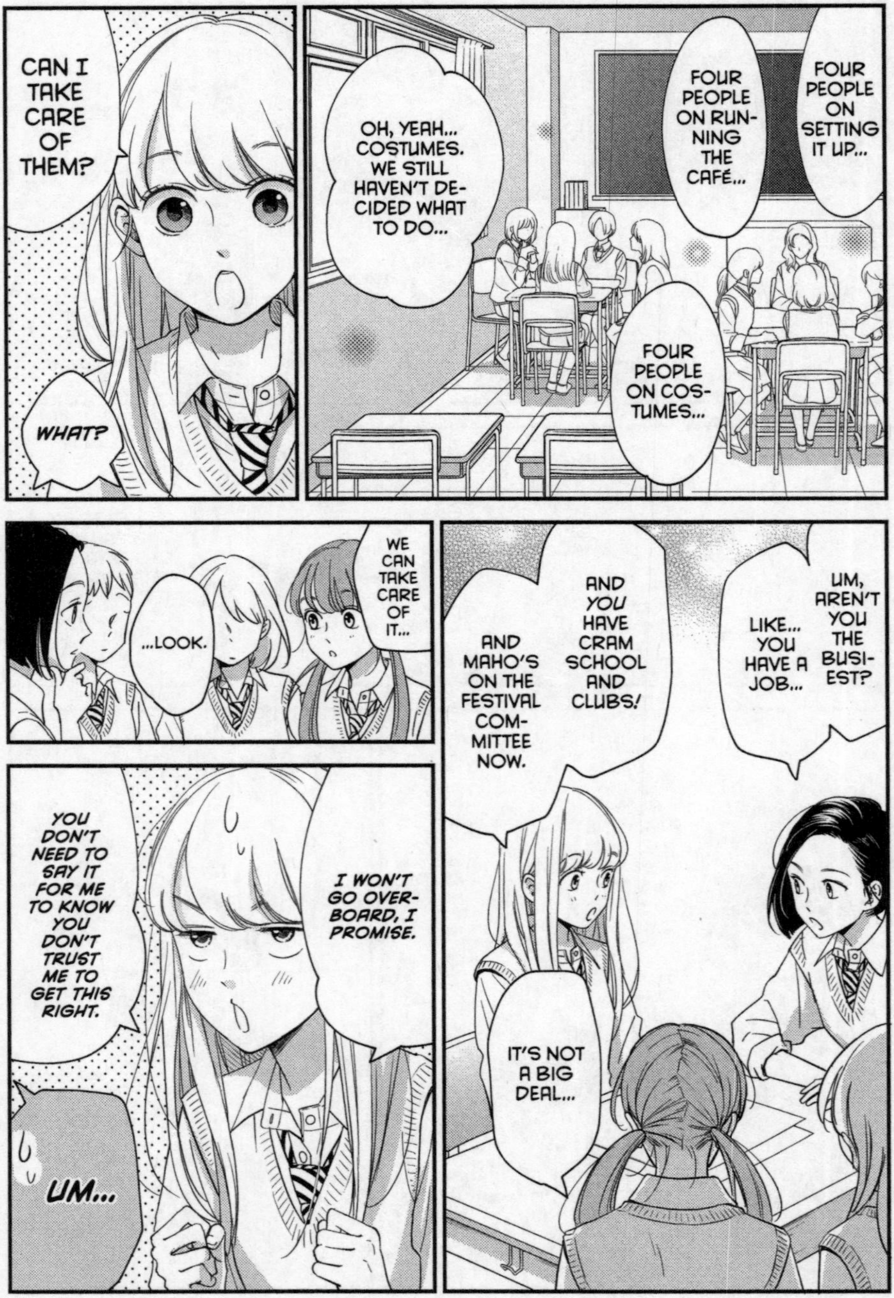
FOUR PEOPLE ON SETTING IT UP...
FOUR PEOPLE ON RUNNING THE CAFÉ...
FOUR PEOPLE ON COSTUMES...
OH, YEAH... COSTUMES. WE STILL HAVEN'T DECIDED WHAT TO DO...
CAN I TAKE CARE OF THEM?
WHAT?
UM, AREN'T YOU THE BUSIEST?
LIKE... YOU HAVE A JOB...
AND YOU HAVE CRAM SCHOOL AND CLUBS!
AND MAHO'S ON THE FESTIVAL COMMITTEE NOW.
IT'S NOT A BIG DEAL...
WE CAN TAKE CARE OF IT...
...LOOK.
I WON'T GO OVERBOARD, I PROMISE.
YOU DON'T NEED TO SAY IT FOR ME TO KNOW YOU DON'T TRUST ME TO GET THIS RIGHT.
UM...

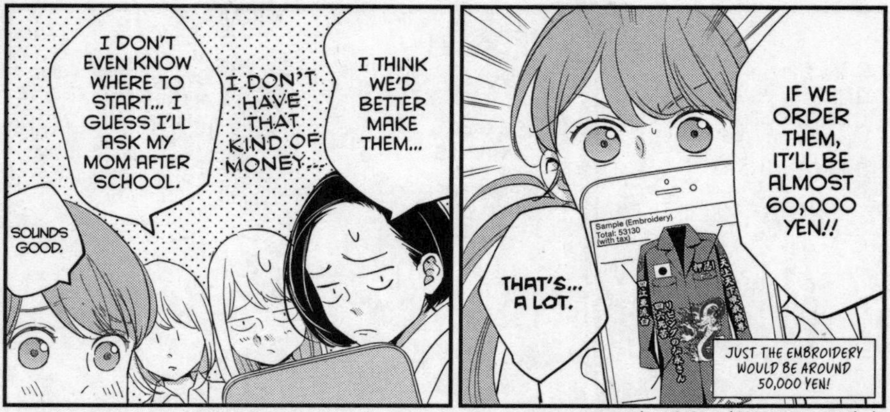
IF WE ORDER THEM, IT'LL BE ALMOST 60,000 YEN!!
Sample (Embroidery) Total: 53130 (with tax)
THAT'S... A LOT.
JUST THE EMBROIDERY WOULD BE AROUND 50,000 YEN!
I THINK WE'D BETTER MAKE THEM...
I DON'T HAVE THAT KIND OF MONEY...
I DON'T EVEN KNOW WHERE TO START... I GUESS I'LL ASK MY MOM AFTER SCHOOL.
SOUNDS GOOD.

*About $600 and $500 USD respectively.

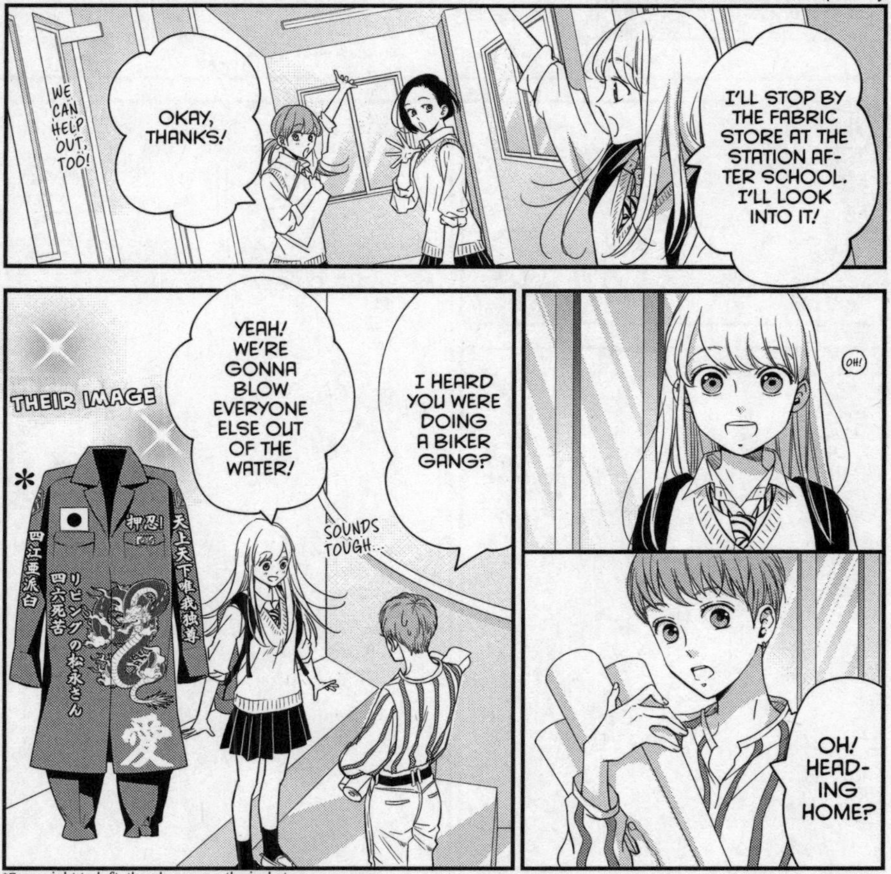
I'LL STOP BY THE FABRIC STORE AT THE STATION AFTER SCHOOL. I'LL LOOK INTO IT!
OKAY, THANKS!
WE CAN HELP OUT, TOO!
OH!
OH! HEADING HOME?
I HEARD YOU WERE DOING A BIKER GANG?
YEAH! WE'RE GONNA BLOW EVERYONE ELSE OUT OF THE WATER!
SOUNDS TOUGH...
THEIR IMAGE
*
天上天下唯我独尊
押忍!
リビングの松永さん
四六死苦
四江亜派白
愛

*From right to left, the phrases on the jacket say:
I am my own lord through the heavens and the earth.
Hey!
Thanks for reading Living-Room Matsunaga-san!
Boarding House

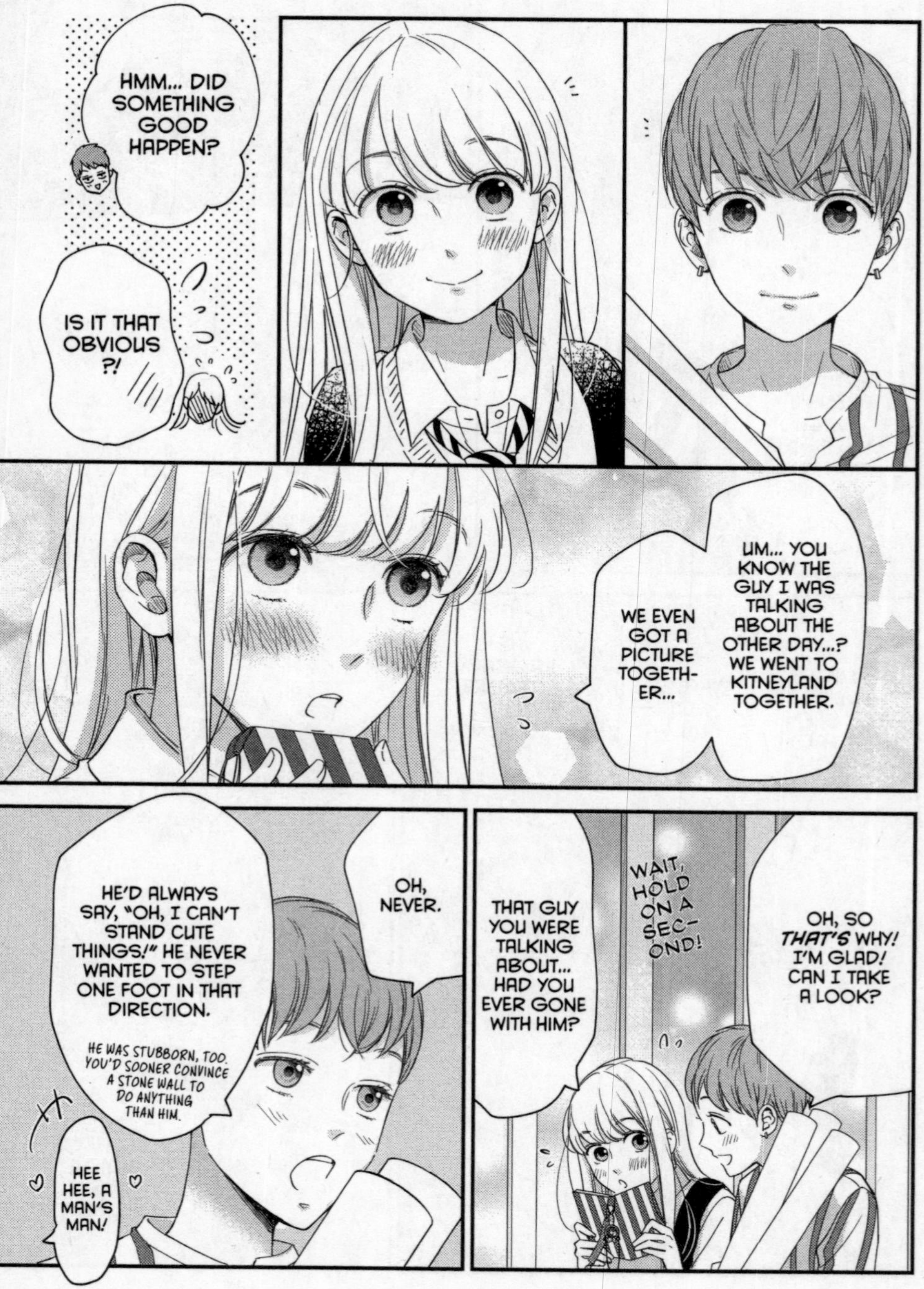
HMM... DID SOMETHING GOOD HAPPEN?
IS IT THAT OBVIOUS?!
UM... YOU KNOW THE GUY I WAS TALKING ABOUT THE OTHER DAY...? WE WENT TO KITNEYLAND TOGETHER.
WE EVEN GOT A PICTURE TOGETH-ER...
OH, SO *THAT'S* WHY! I'M GLAD! CAN I TAKE A LOOK?
WAIT, HOLD ON A SEC-OND!
THAT GUY YOU WERE TALKING ABOUT... HAD YOU EVER GONE WITH HIM?
OH, NEVER.
HE'D ALWAYS SAY, "OH, I CAN'T STAND CUTE THINGS!" HE NEVER WANTED TO STEP ONE FOOT IN THAT DIRECTION.
HE WAS STUBBORN, TOO. YOU'D SOONER CONVINCE A STONE WALL TO DO ANYTHING THAN HIM.
HEE HEE, A MAN'S MAN!

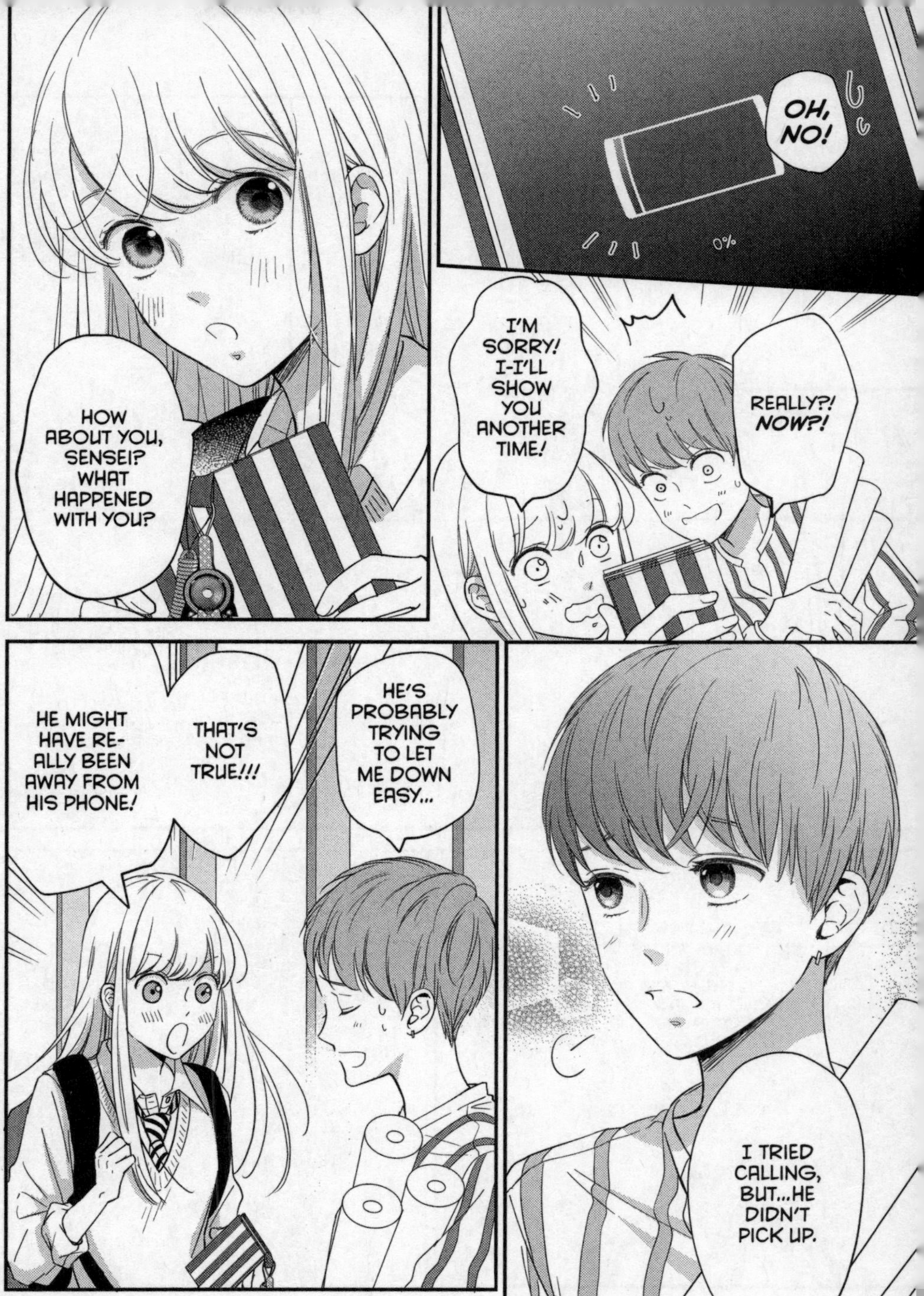
OH, NO!
0%
REALLY?! NOW?!
I'M SORRY! I-I'LL SHOW YOU ANOTHER TIME!
HOW ABOUT YOU, SENSEI? WHAT HAPPENED WITH YOU?
I TRIED CALLING, BUT...HE DIDN'T PICK UP.
HE'S PROBABLY TRYING TO LET ME DOWN EASY...
THAT'S NOT TRUE!!!
HE MIGHT HAVE RE-ALLY BEEN AWAY FROM HIS PHONE!

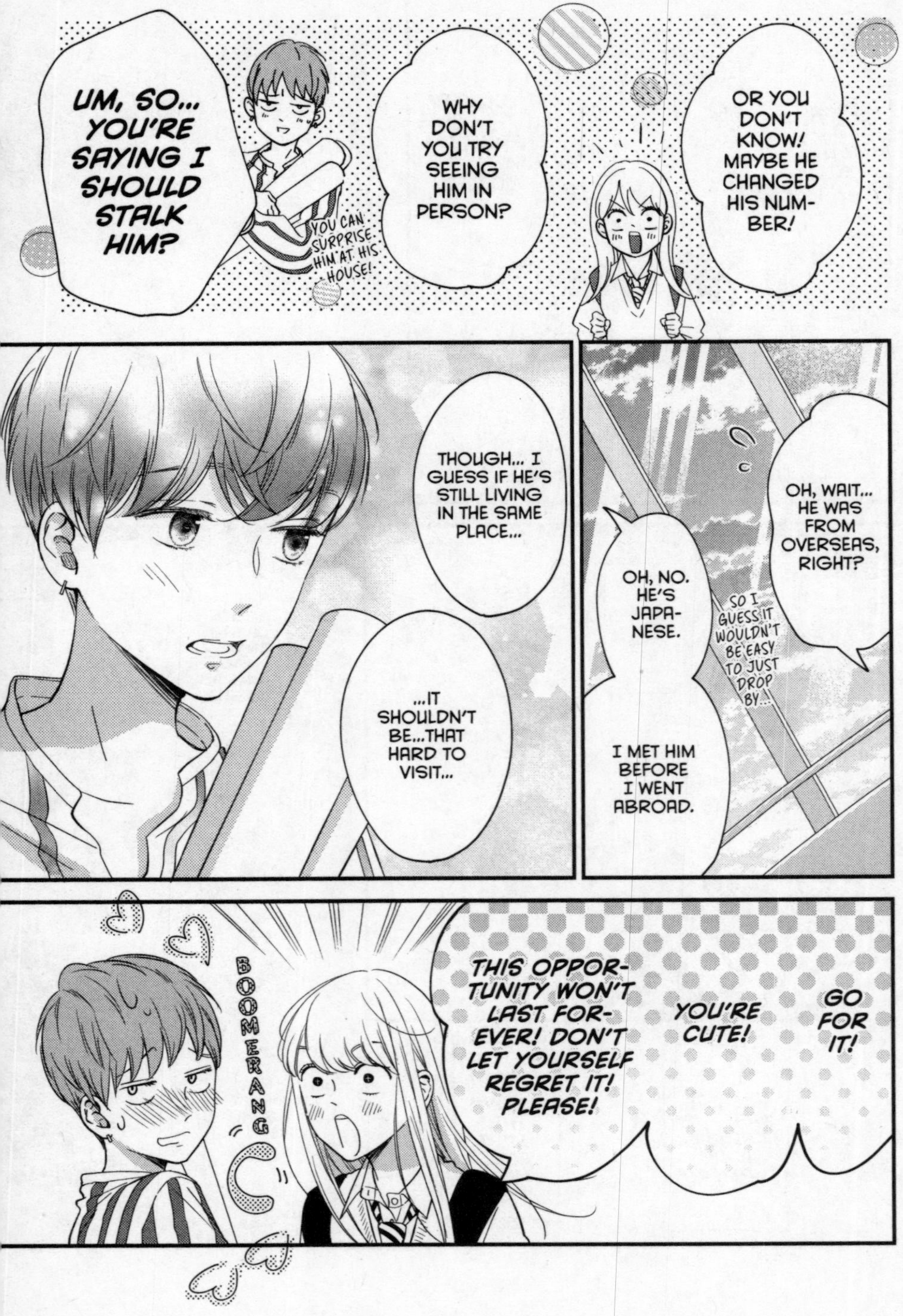
OR YOU DON'T KNOW! MAYBE HE CHANGED HIS NUMBER!
WHY DON'T YOU TRY SEEING HIM IN PERSON?
YOU CAN SURPRISE HIM AT HIS HOUSE!
UM, SO... YOU'RE SAYING I SHOULD STALK HIM?
OH, WAIT... HE WAS FROM OVERSEAS, RIGHT?
SO I GUESS IT WOULDN'T BE EASY TO JUST DROP BY...
OH, NO. HE'S JAPANESE.
I MET HIM BEFORE I WENT ABROAD.
THOUGH... I GUESS IF HE'S STILL LIVING IN THE SAME PLACE...
...IT SHOULDN'T BE...THAT HARD TO VISIT...
GO FOR IT!
YOU'RE CUTE!
THIS OPPORTUNITY WON'T LAST FOREVER! DON'T LET YOURSELF REGRET IT! PLEASE!
BOOMERANG

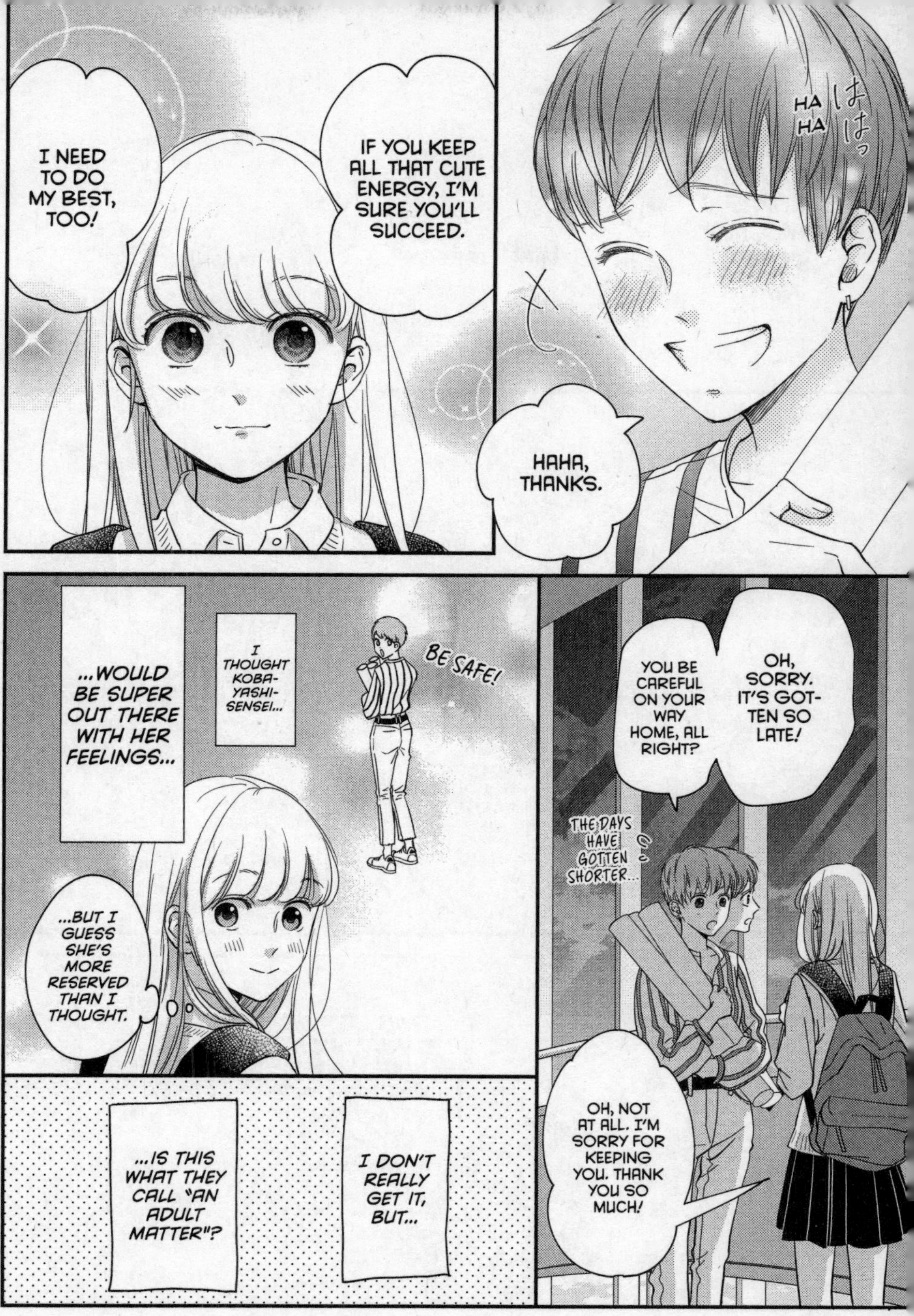
HA HA
はは
HAHA, THANKS.
IF YOU KEEP ALL THAT CUTE ENERGY, I'M SURE YOU'LL SUCCEED.
I NEED TO DO MY BEST, TOO!
OH, SORRY. IT'S GOTTEN SO LATE!
YOU BE CAREFUL ON YOUR WAY HOME, ALL RIGHT?
THE DAYS HAVE GOTTEN SHORTER...
OH, NOT AT ALL. I'M SORRY FOR KEEPING YOU. THANK YOU SO MUCH!
BE SAFE!
I THOUGHT KOBAYASHI-SENSEI...
...WOULD BE SUPER OUT THERE WITH HER FEELINGS...
...BUT I GUESS SHE'S MORE RESERVED THAN I THOUGHT.
I DON'T REALLY GET IT, BUT...
...IS THIS WHAT THEY CALL "AN ADULT MATTER"?

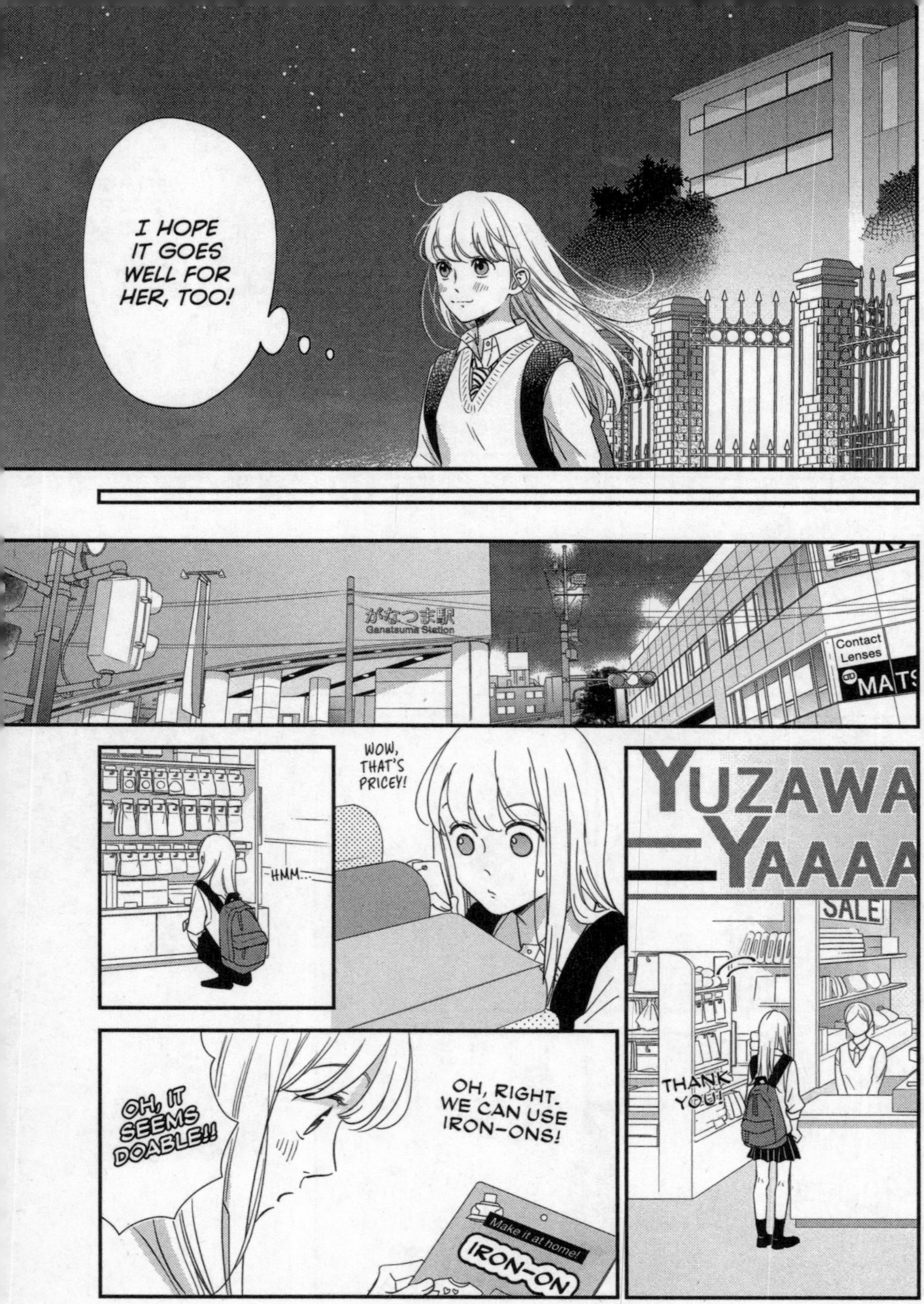
I HOPE IT GOES WELL FOR HER, TOO!
がなつま駅
Ganatsuma Station
Contact Lenses
MATS
YUZAWA
YAAAA
SALE
THANK YOU!
WOW, THAT'S PRICEY!
HMM...
OH, RIGHT. WE CAN USE IRON-ONS!
Make it at home!
IRON-ON
OH, IT SEEMS DOABLE!!

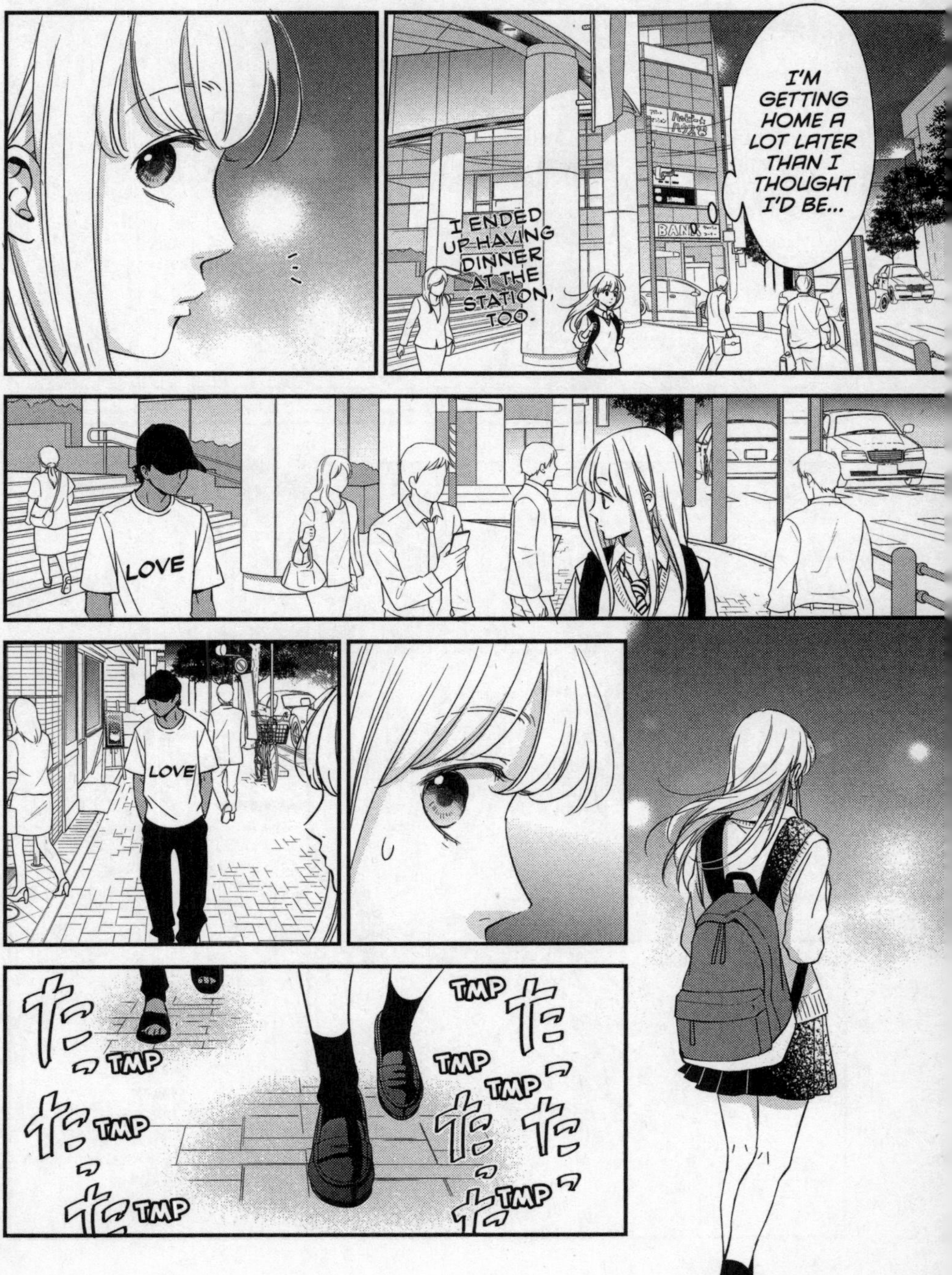

I'M GETTING HOME A LOT LATER THAN I THOUGHT I'D BE...
I ENDED UP HAVING DINNER AT THE STATION, TOO.
LOVE
LOVE
TMP
TMP
TMP
TMP
TMP
TMP

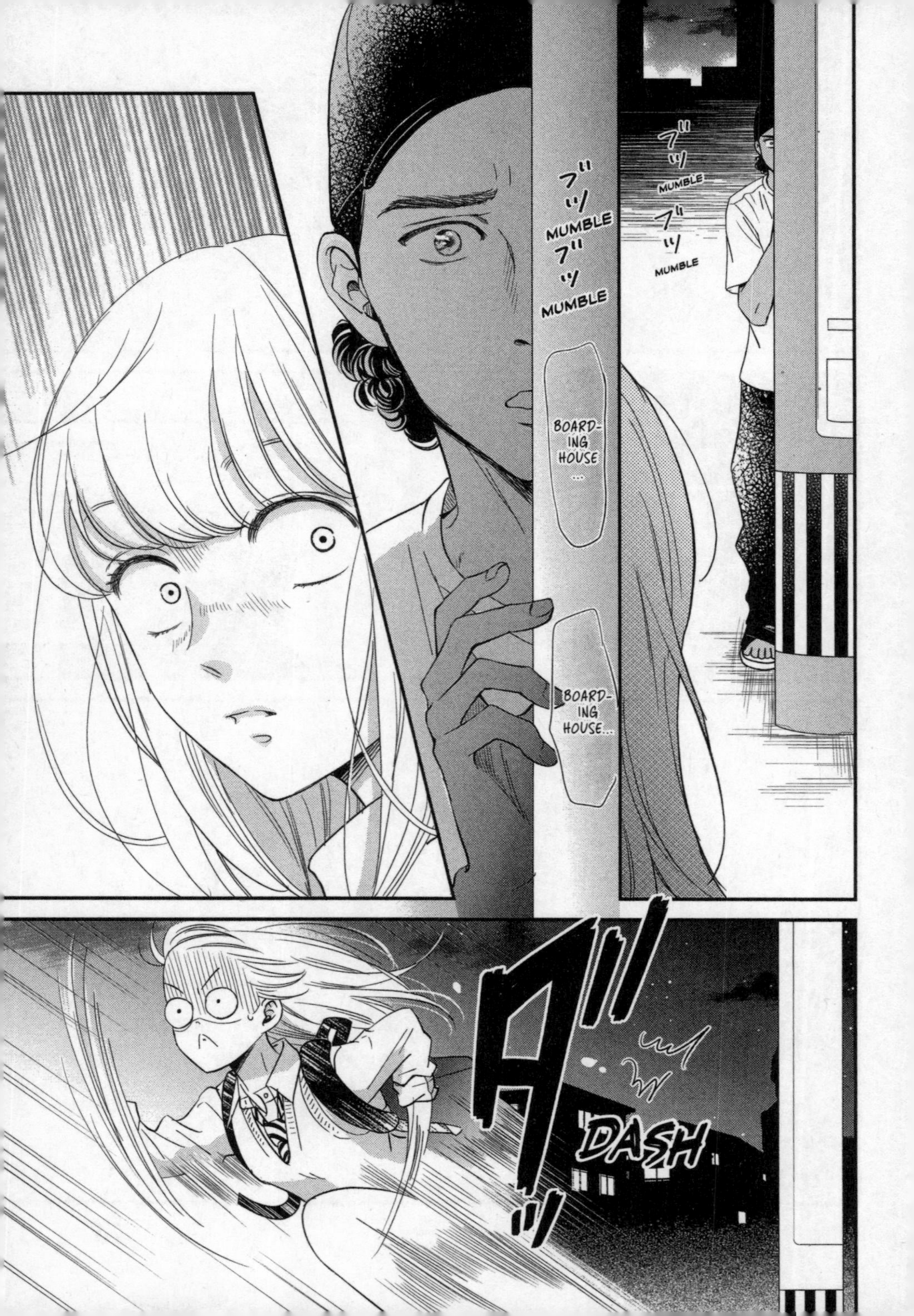

ブツ
MUMBLE
ブツ
MUMBLE
ブツ
MUMBLE
ブツ
MUMBLE
BOARDING-HOUSE...
BOARDING-HOUSE...
ダッ
DASH

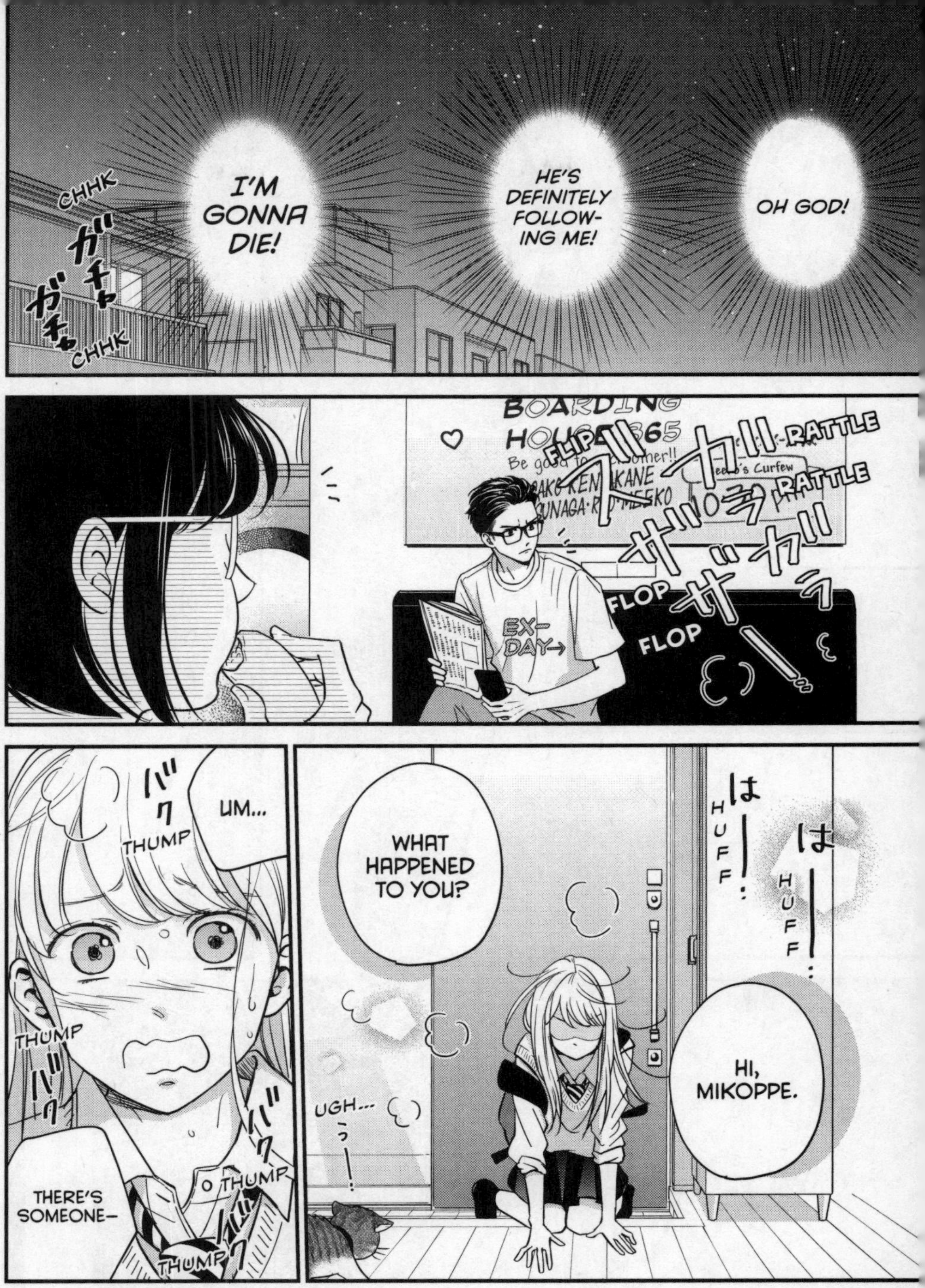
OH GOD!
HE'S DEFINITELY FOLLOWING ME!
I'M GONNA DIE!
CHHK
ガチャ
ガチャ
CHHK
BOARDING HOUSE 365
Be good to ...comer!!
...'s Curfew
FLIP
RATTLE
RATTLE
FLOP
FLOP
HI, MIKOPPE.
は–!
HUFF
は–!
HUFF
WHAT HAPPENED TO YOU?
UGH...
う–!
UM...
バク
THUMP
THUMP
バク
バク
THUMP
THUMP
THERE'S SOMEONE–

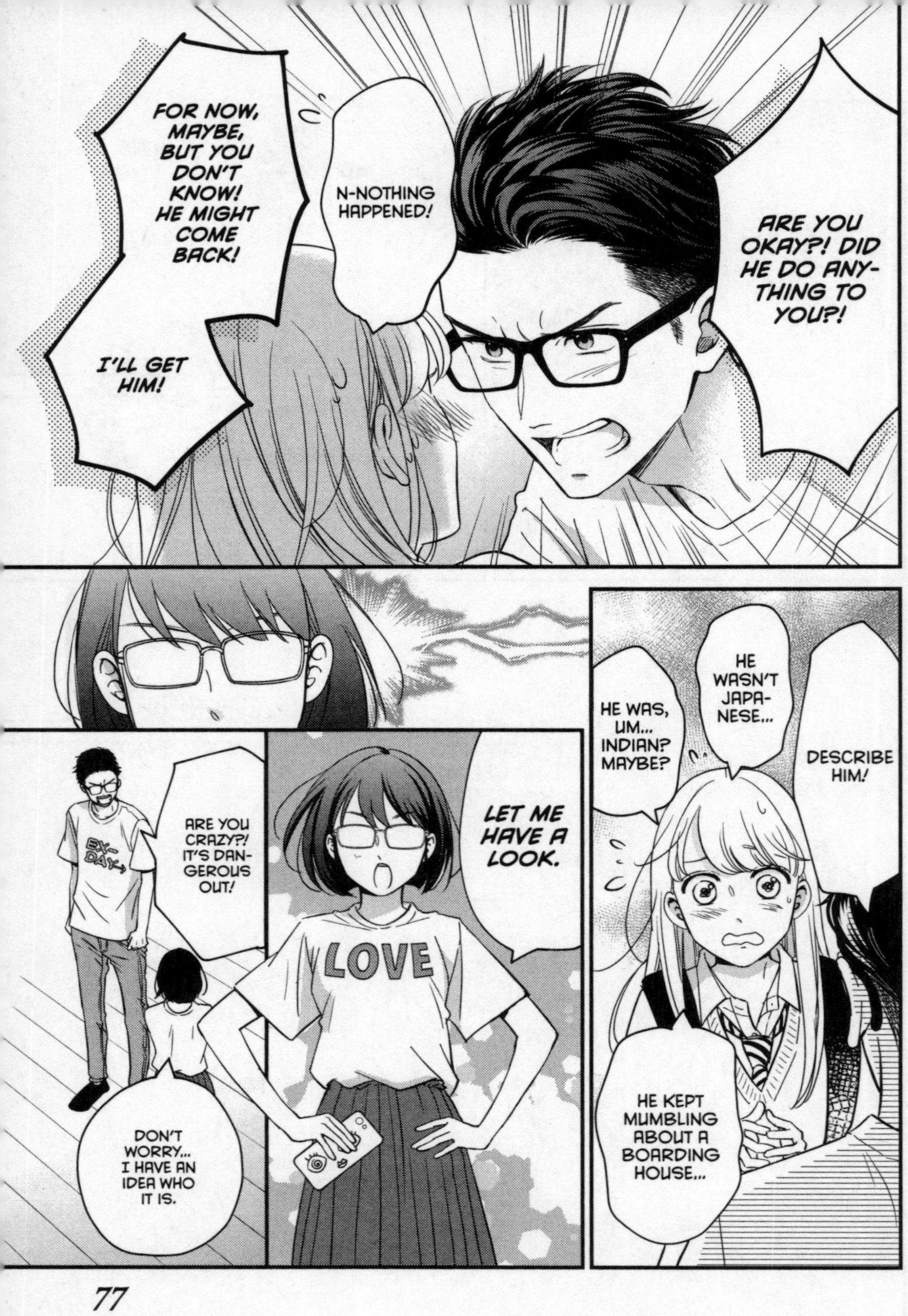
ARE YOU OKAY?! DID HE DO ANYTHING TO YOU?!
N-NOTHING HAPPENED!
FOR NOW, MAYBE, BUT YOU DON'T KNOW! HE MIGHT COME BACK!
I'LL GET HIM!
DESCRIBE HIM!
HE WASN'T JAPANESE...
HE WAS, UM... INDIAN? MAYBE?
HE KEPT MUMBLING ABOUT A BOARDING HOUSE...
LET ME HAVE A LOOK.
ARE YOU CRAZY?! IT'S DANGEROUS OUT!
DON'T WORRY... I HAVE AN IDEA WHO IT IS.

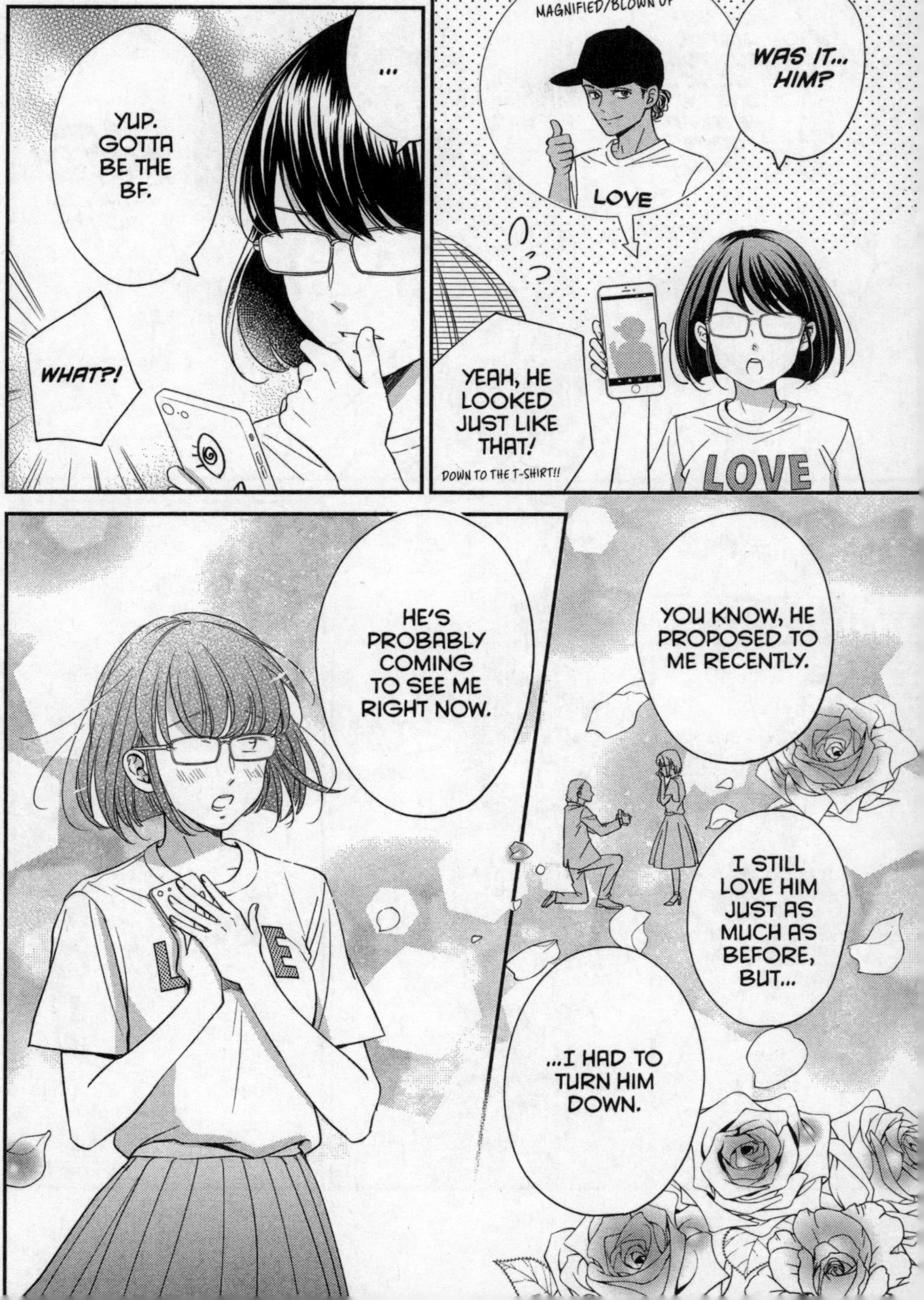
WAS IT... HIM?
MAGNIFIED/BLOWN UP
LOVE
YEAH, HE LOOKED JUST LIKE THAT!
DOWN TO THE T-SHIRT!!
LOVE
...
YUP. GOTTA BE THE BF.
WHAT?!
YOU KNOW, HE PROPOSED TO ME RECENTLY.
I STILL LOVE HIM JUST AS MUCH AS BEFORE, BUT...
...I HAD TO TURN HIM DOWN.
HE'S PROBABLY COMING TO SEE ME RIGHT NOW.

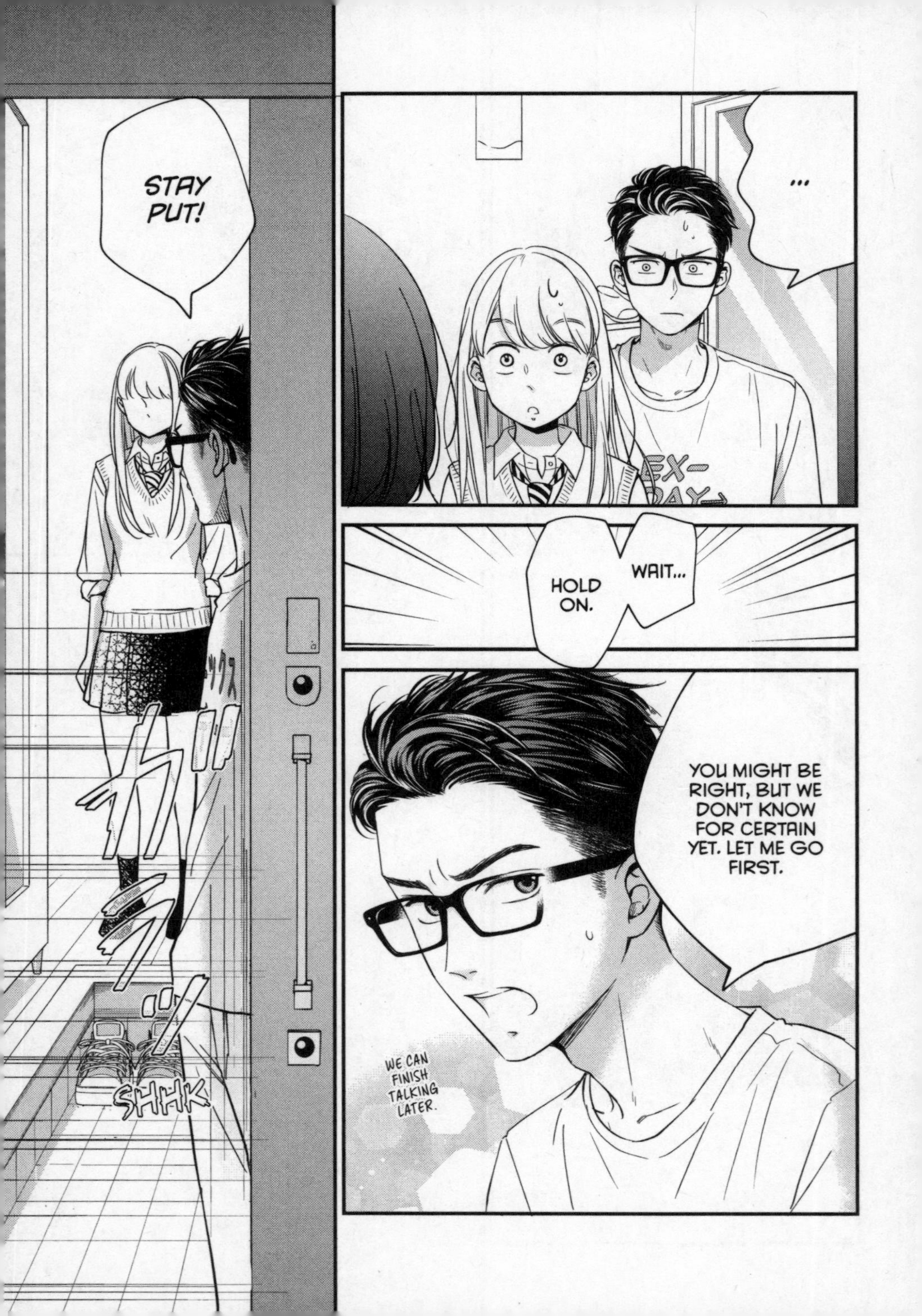
...
WAIT...
HOLD ON.
YOU MIGHT BE RIGHT, BUT WE DON'T KNOW FOR CERTAIN YET. LET ME GO FIRST.
WE CAN FINISH TALKING LATER.
STAY PUT!
SHHK

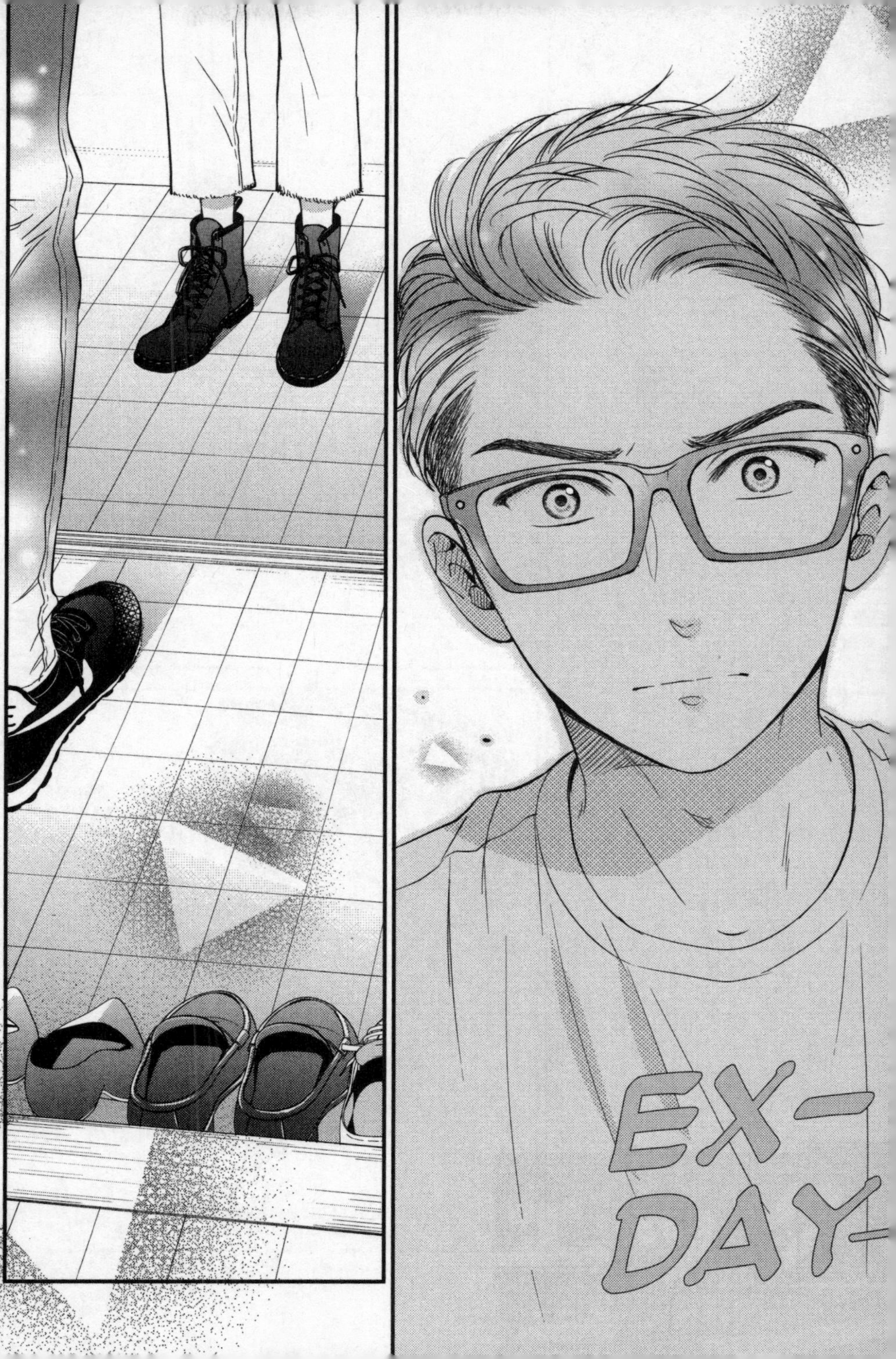
EX-
DAY-

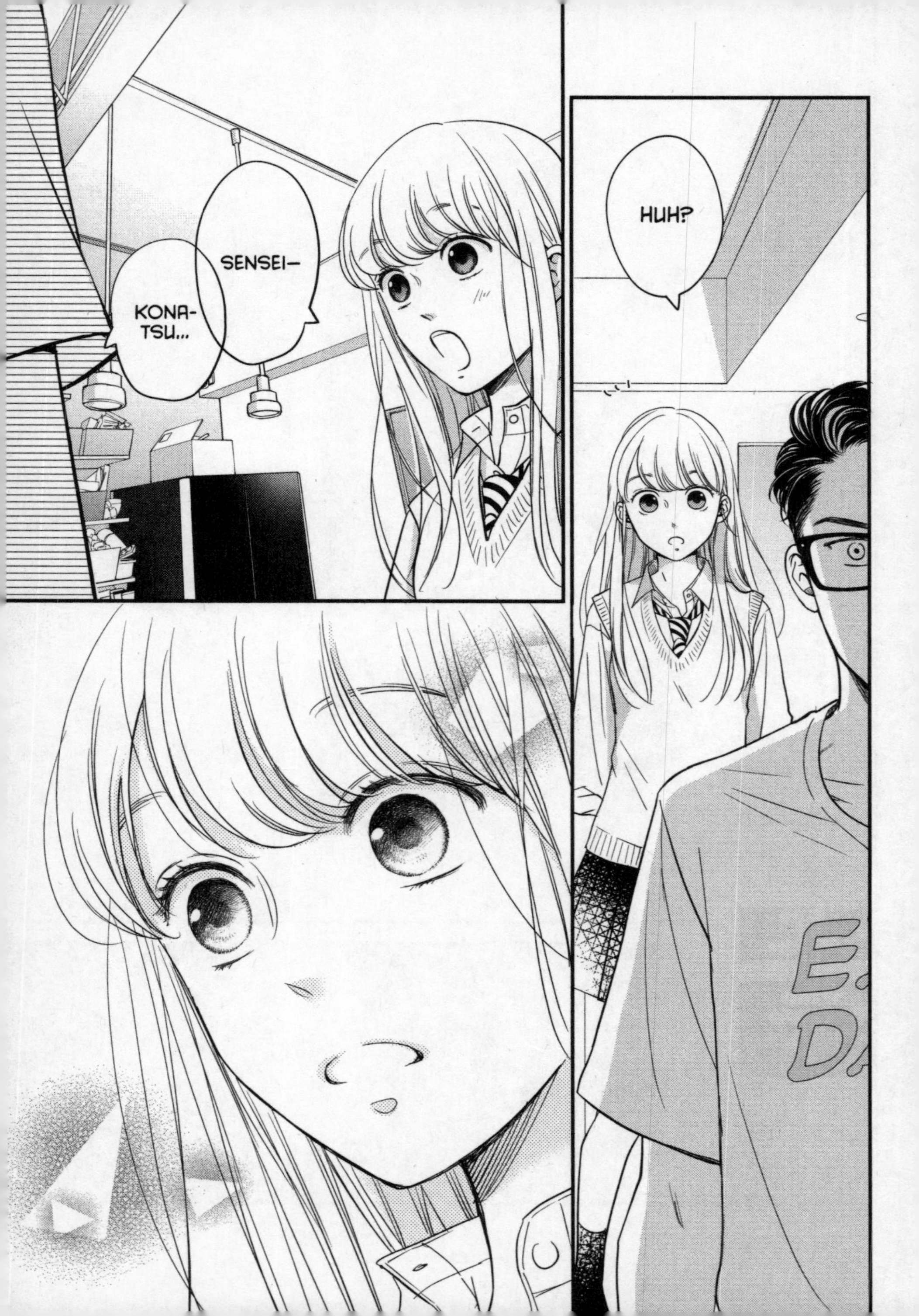
HUH?
SENSEI-
KONA-TSU...

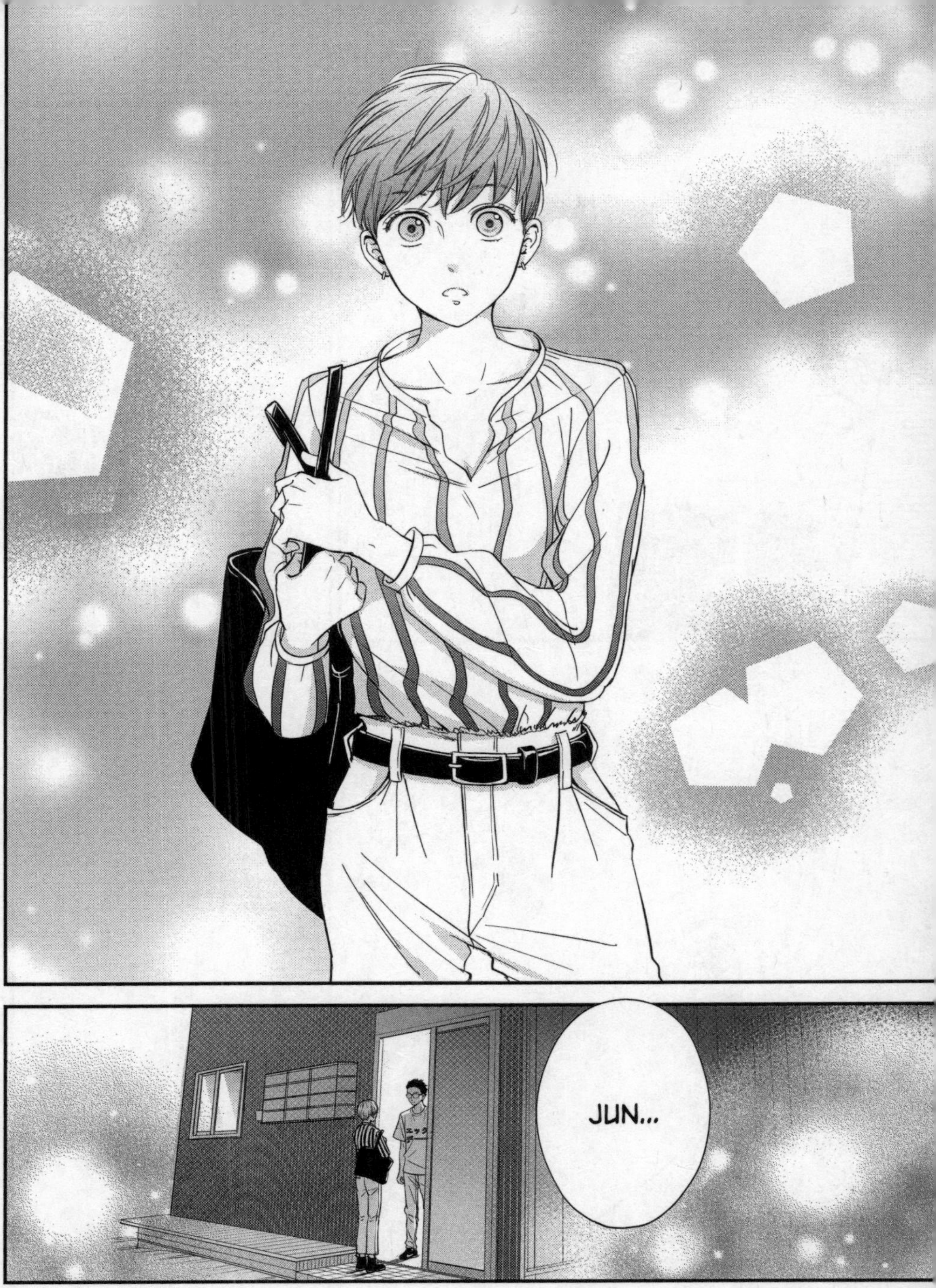
JUN...

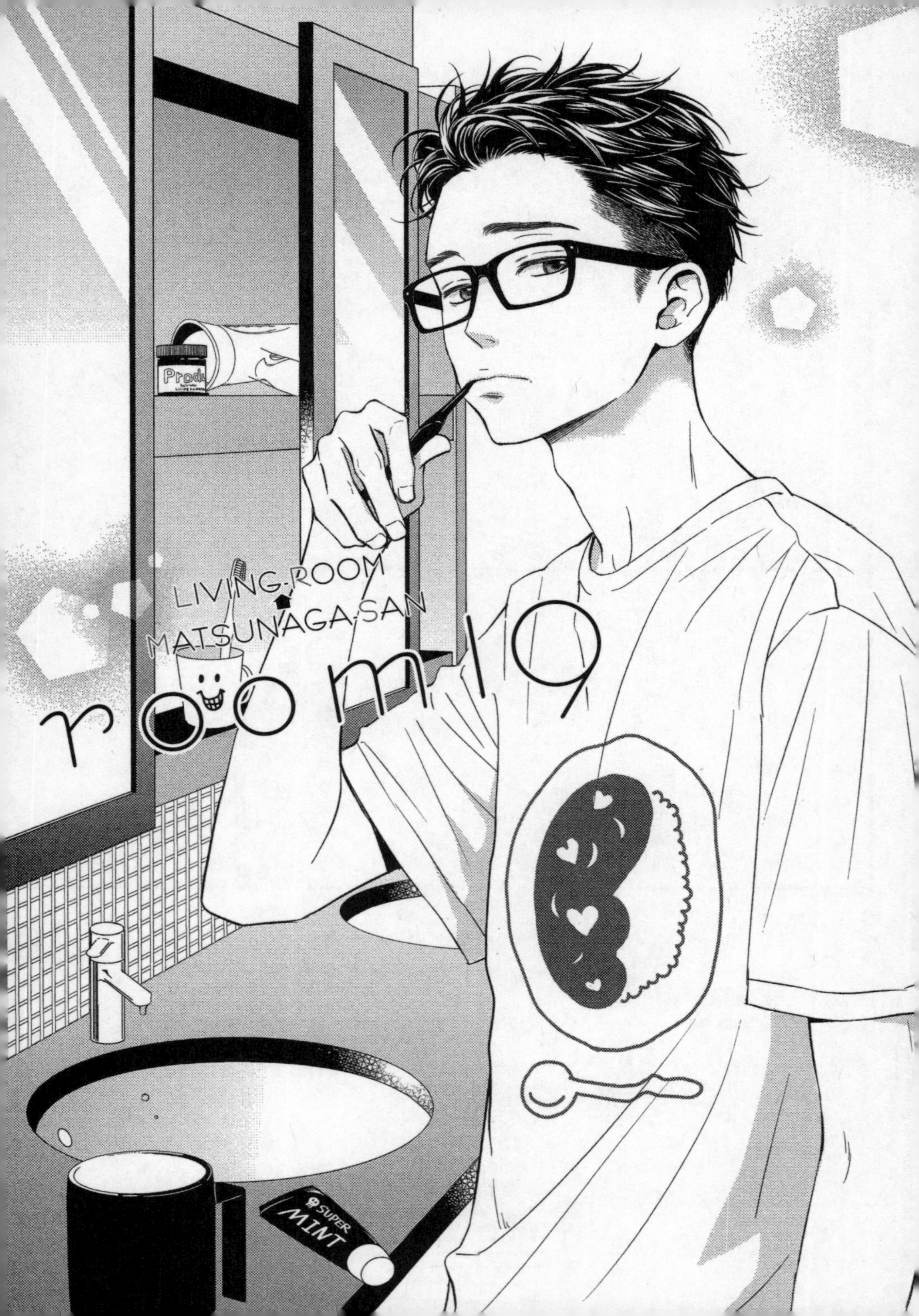
LIVING-ROOM
MATSUNAGA-SAN
room 19
SUPER MINT

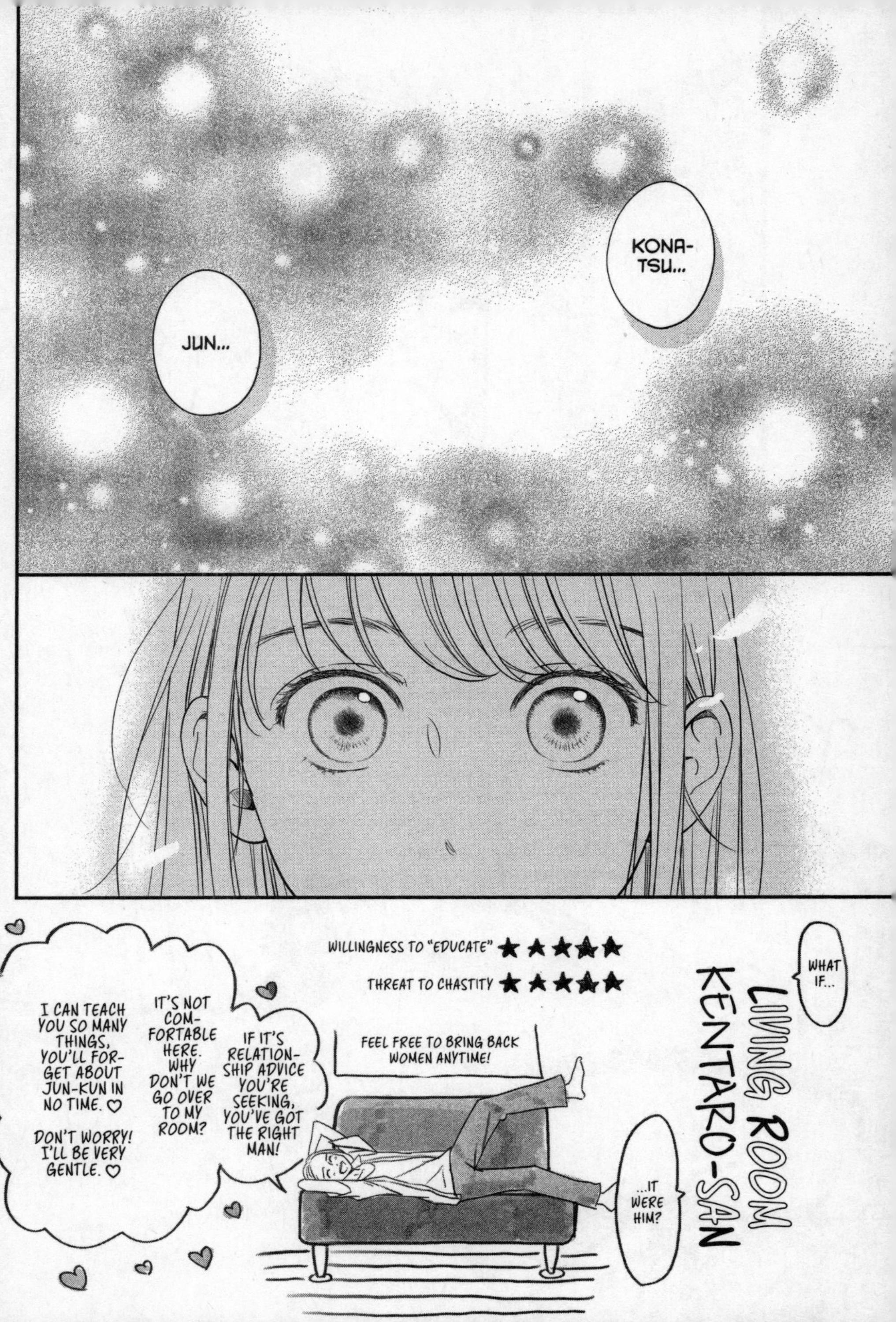
KONA-TSU...
JUN...
WHAT IF...
LIVING ROOM KENTARO-SAN
...IT WERE HIM?
WILLINGNESS TO "EDUCATE" ★★★★★
THREAT TO CHASTITY ★★★★★
FEEL FREE TO BRING BACK WOMEN ANYTIME!
IF IT'S RELATION-SHIP ADVICE YOU'RE SEEKING, YOU'VE GOT THE RIGHT MAN!
IT'S NOT COM-FORTABLE HERE. WHY DON'T WE GO OVER TO MY ROOM?
I CAN TEACH YOU SO MANY THINGS, YOU'LL FOR-GET ABOUT JUN-KUN IN NO TIME. ♡
DON'T WORRY! I'LL BE VERY GENTLE. ♡

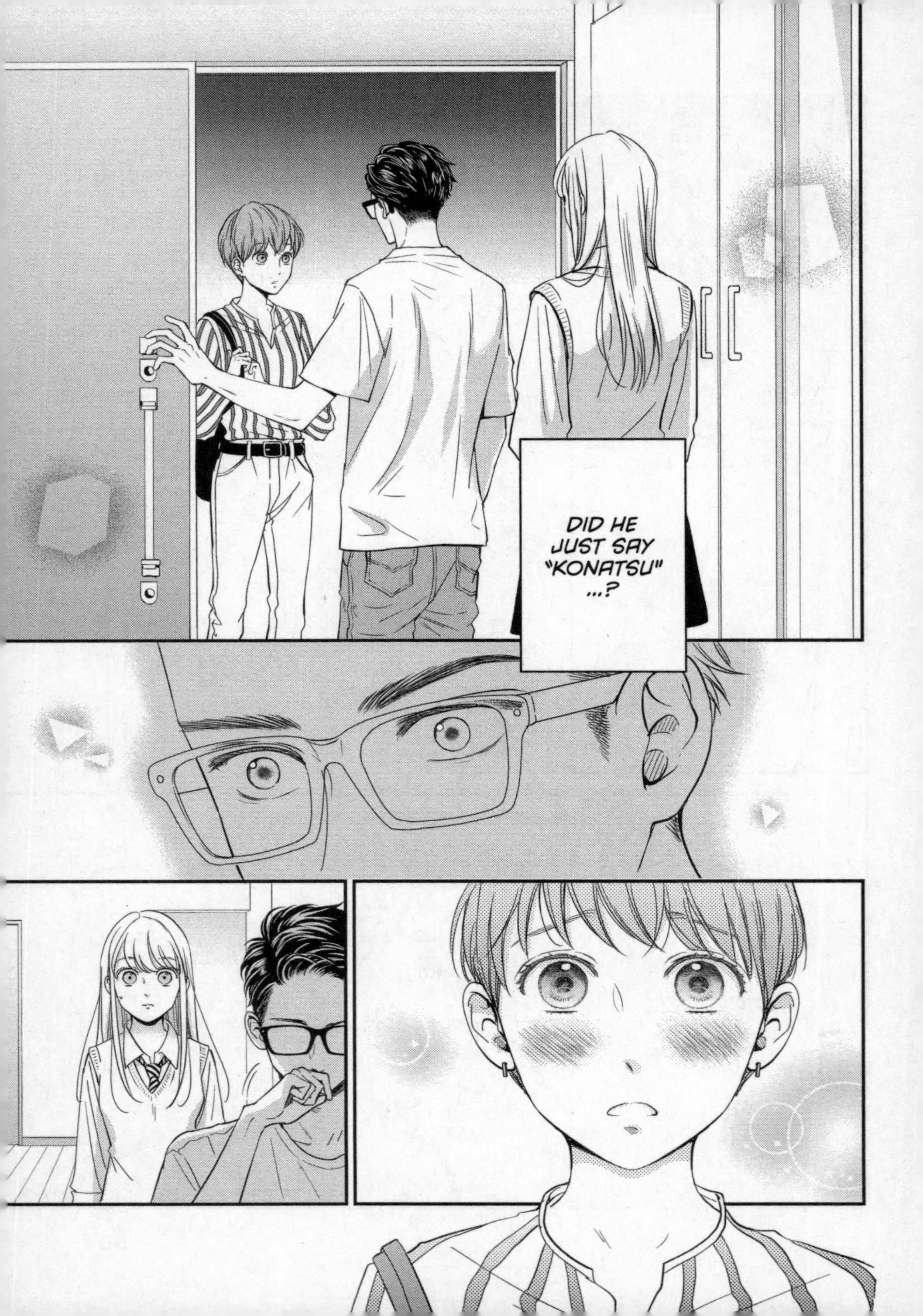
DID HE JUST SAY "KONATSU" ...?

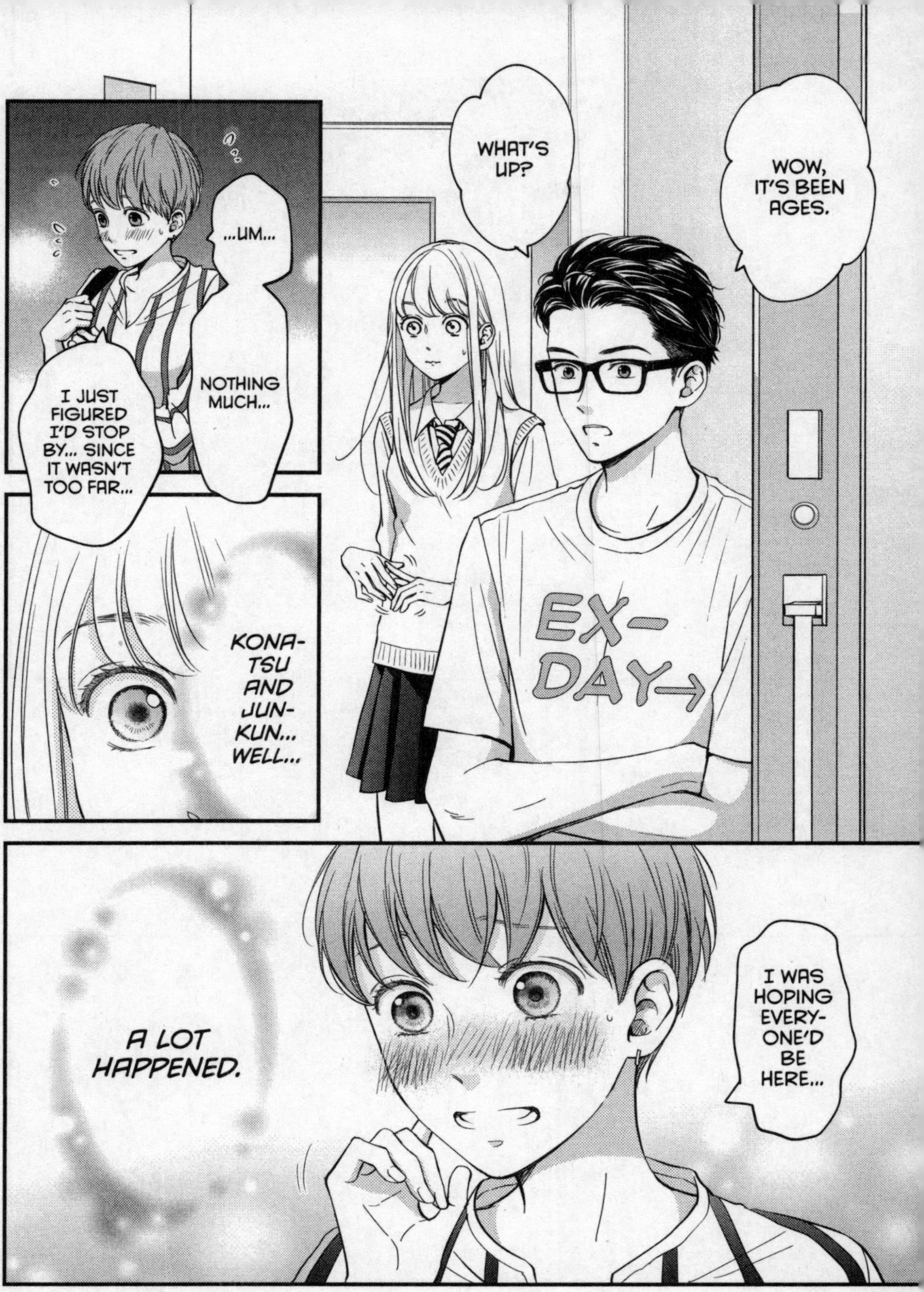
WOW, IT'S BEEN AGES.
WHAT'S UP?
EX-DAY→
...UM...
NOTHING MUCH...
I JUST FIGURED I'D STOP BY... SINCE IT WASN'T TOO FAR...
KONA-TSU AND JUN-KUN... WELL...
I WAS HOPING EVERY-ONE'D BE HERE...
A LOT HAPPENED.

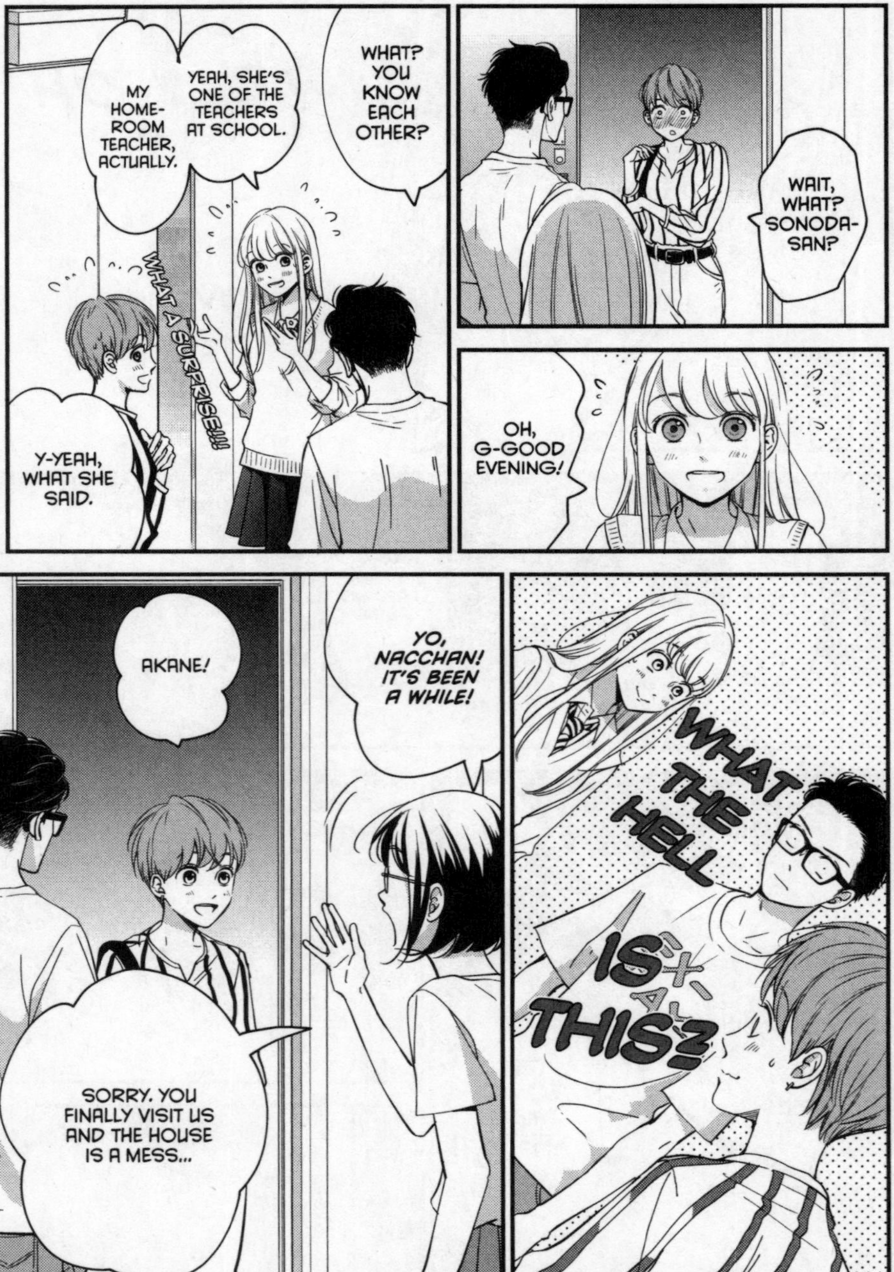
WAIT, WHAT? SONODA-SAN?
OH, G-GOOD EVENING!
WHAT? YOU KNOW EACH OTHER?
YEAH, SHE'S ONE OF THE TEACHERS AT SCHOOL.
MY HOME-ROOM TEACHER, ACTUALLY.
WHAT A SURPRISE!!!
Y-YEAH, WHAT SHE SAID.
WHAT THE HELL IS THIS?
YO, NACCHAN! IT'S BEEN A WHILE!
AKANE!
SORRY. YOU FINALLY VISIT US AND THE HOUSE IS A MESS...

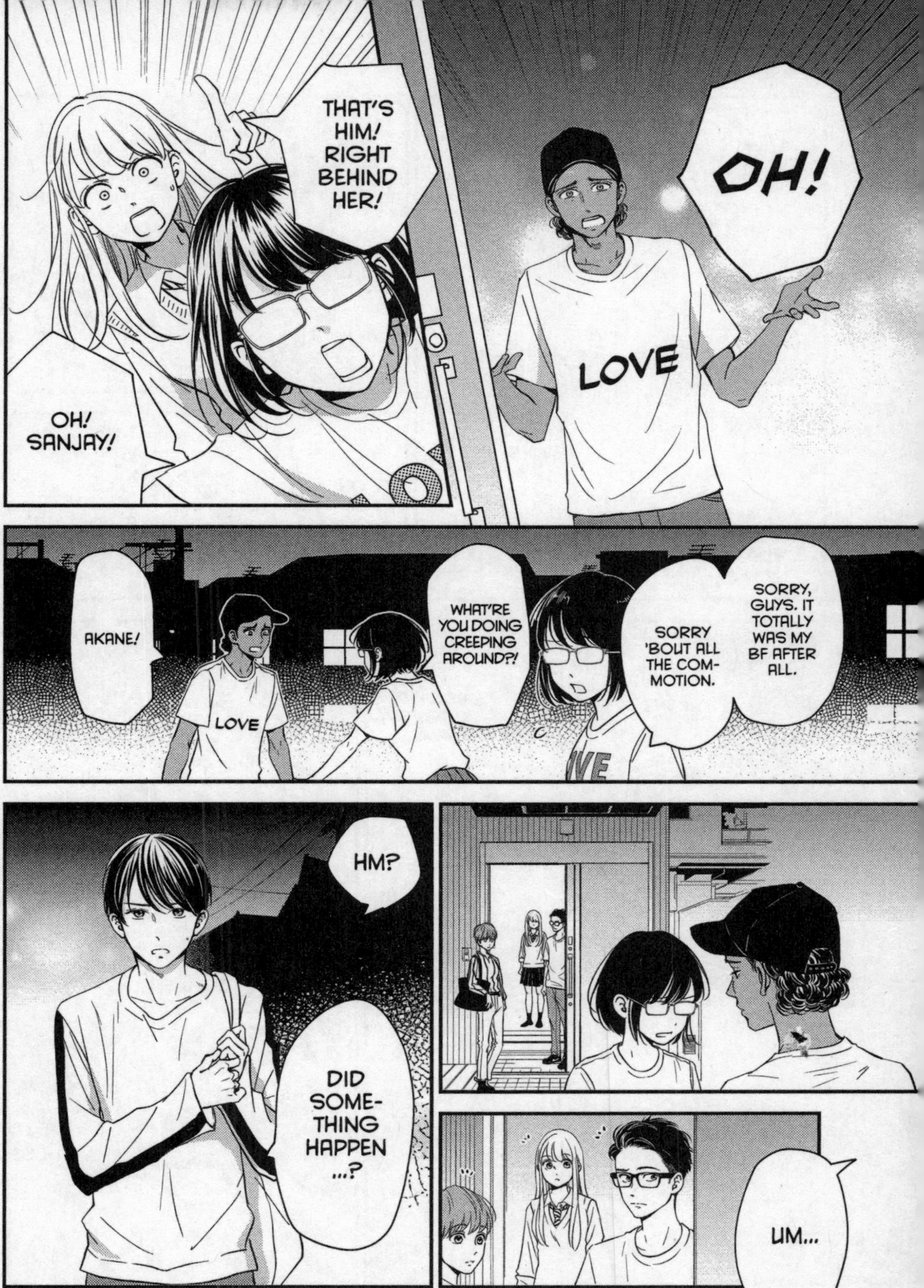
OH!
THAT'S HIM! RIGHT BEHIND HER!
OH! SANJAY!
SORRY, GUYS. IT TOTALLY WAS MY BF AFTER ALL.
SORRY 'BOUT ALL THE COM-MOTION.
WHAT'RE YOU DOING CREEPING AROUND?!
AKANE!
UM...
HM?
DID SOME-THING HAPPEN ...?

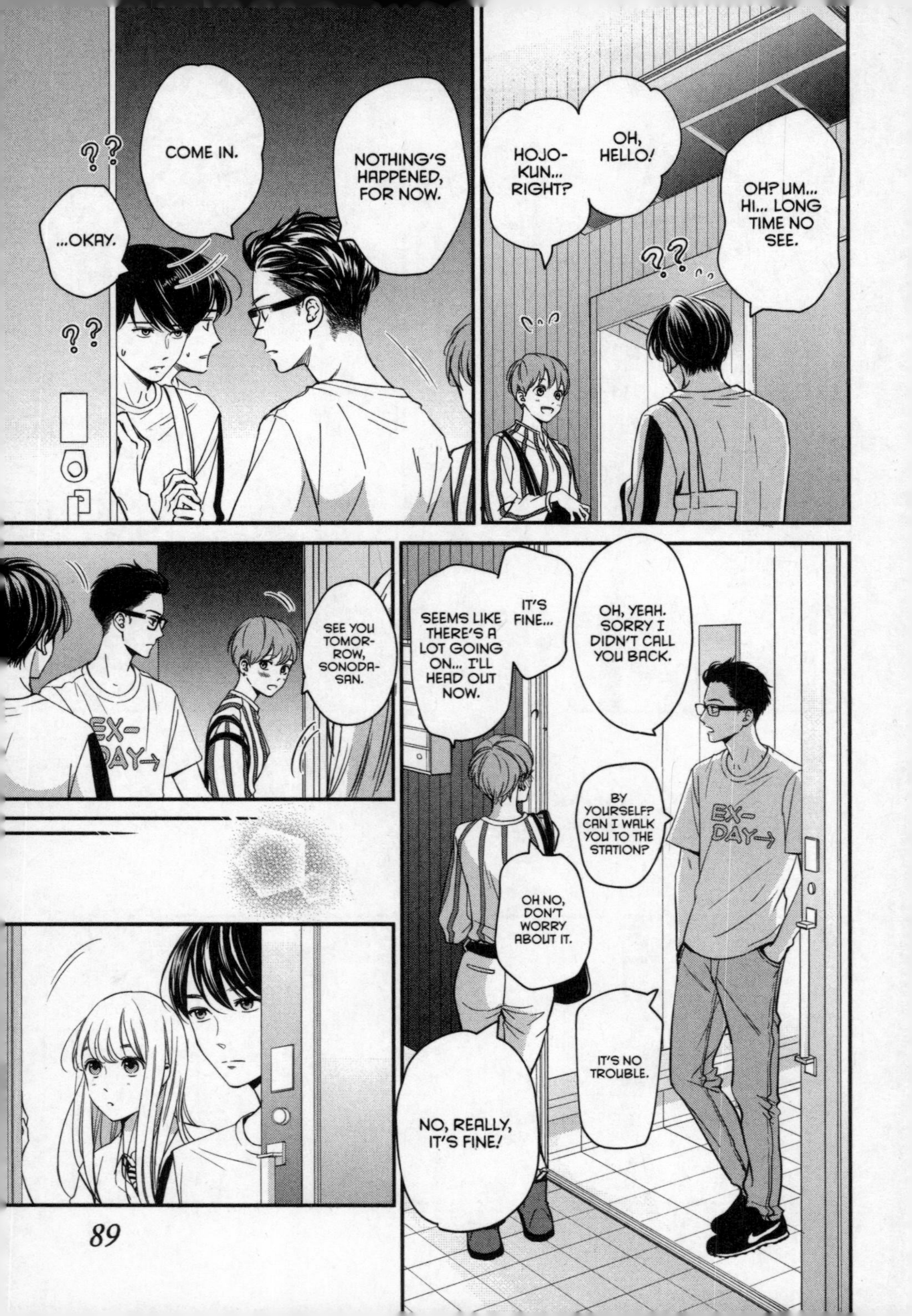
OH, HELLO!
HOJO-KUN... RIGHT?
OH? UM... HI... LONG TIME NO SEE.
??
NOTHING'S HAPPENED, FOR NOW.
COME IN.
??
...OKAY.
??
OH, YEAH. SORRY I DIDN'T CALL YOU BACK.
IT'S FINE...
SEEMS LIKE THERE'S A LOT GOING ON... I'LL HEAD OUT NOW.
BY YOURSELF? CAN I WALK YOU TO THE STATION?
OH NO, DON'T WORRY ABOUT IT.
IT'S NO TROUBLE.
NO, REALLY, IT'S FINE!
EX-DAY→
SEE YOU TOMORROW, SONODA-SAN.
EX-DAY→

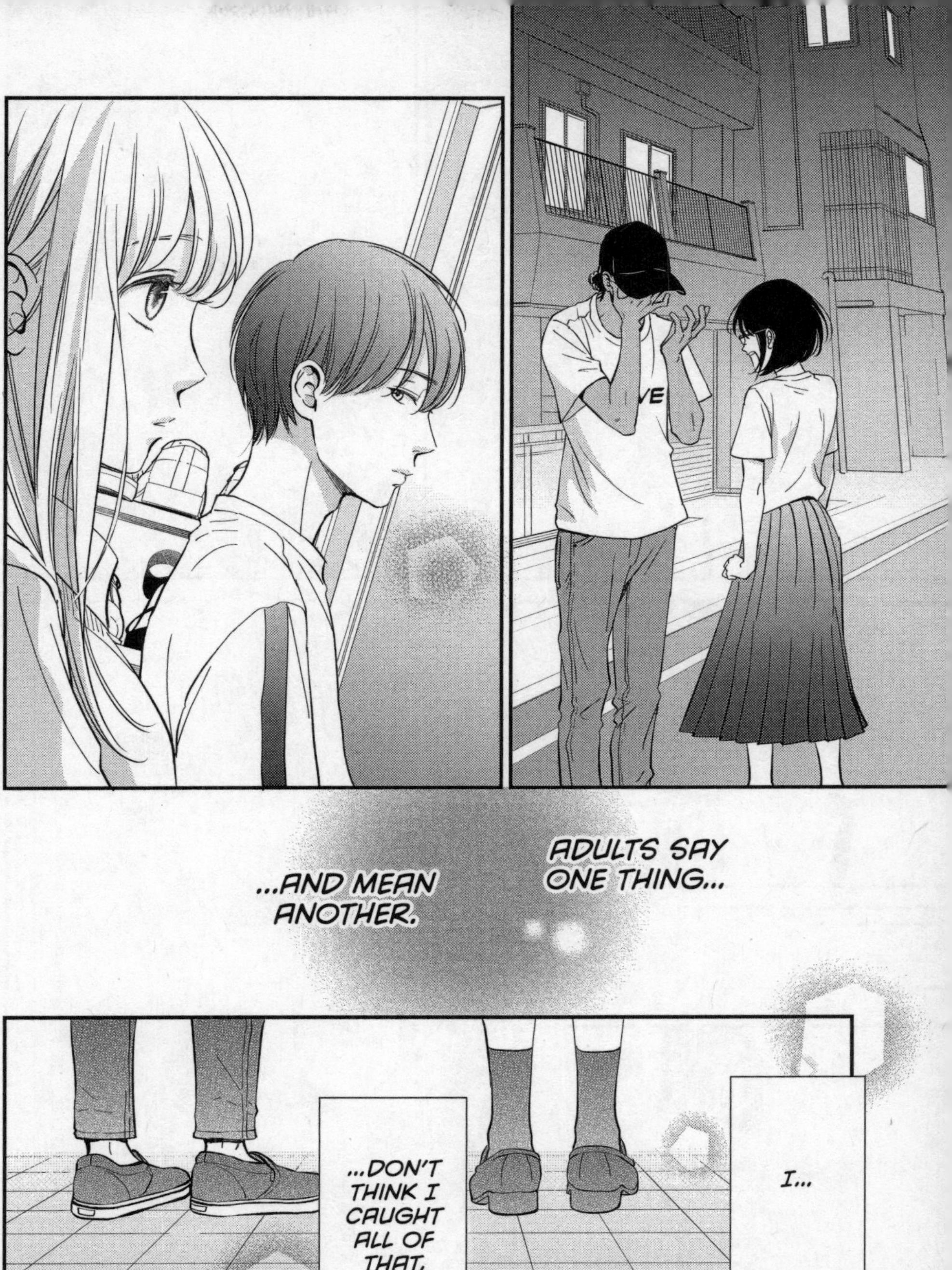
ADULTS SAY ONE THING...
...AND MEAN ANOTHER.
I...
...DON'T THINK I CAUGHT ALL OF THAT, BUT...

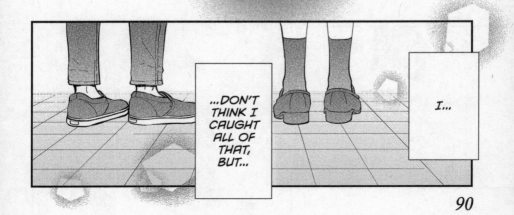

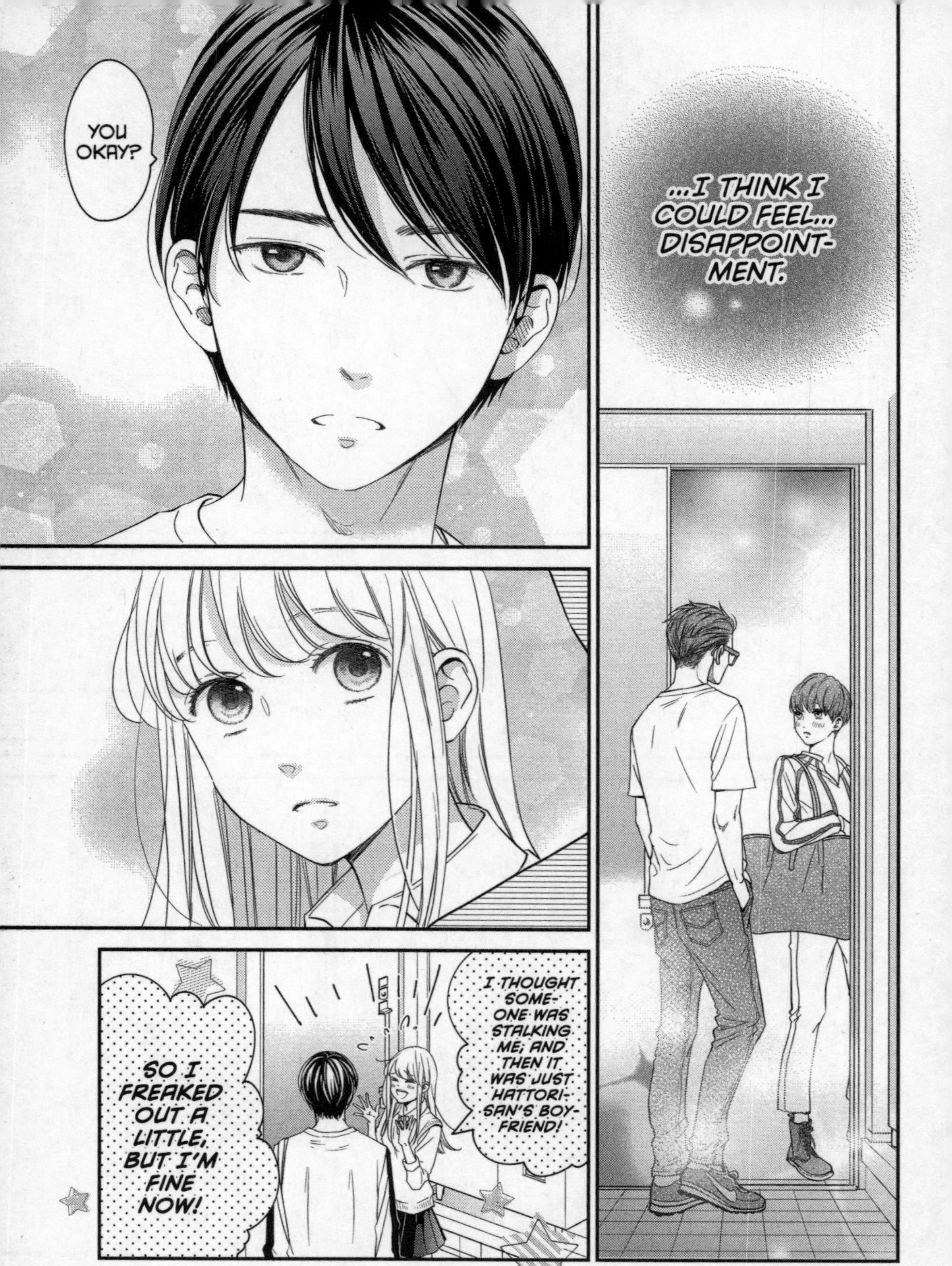
...I THINK I COULD FEEL... DISAPPOINTMENT.
YOU OKAY?
I THOUGHT SOMEONE WAS STALKING ME, AND THEN IT WAS JUST HATTORI-SAN'S BOYFRIEND!
SO I FREAKED OUT A LITTLE, BUT I'M FINE NOW!

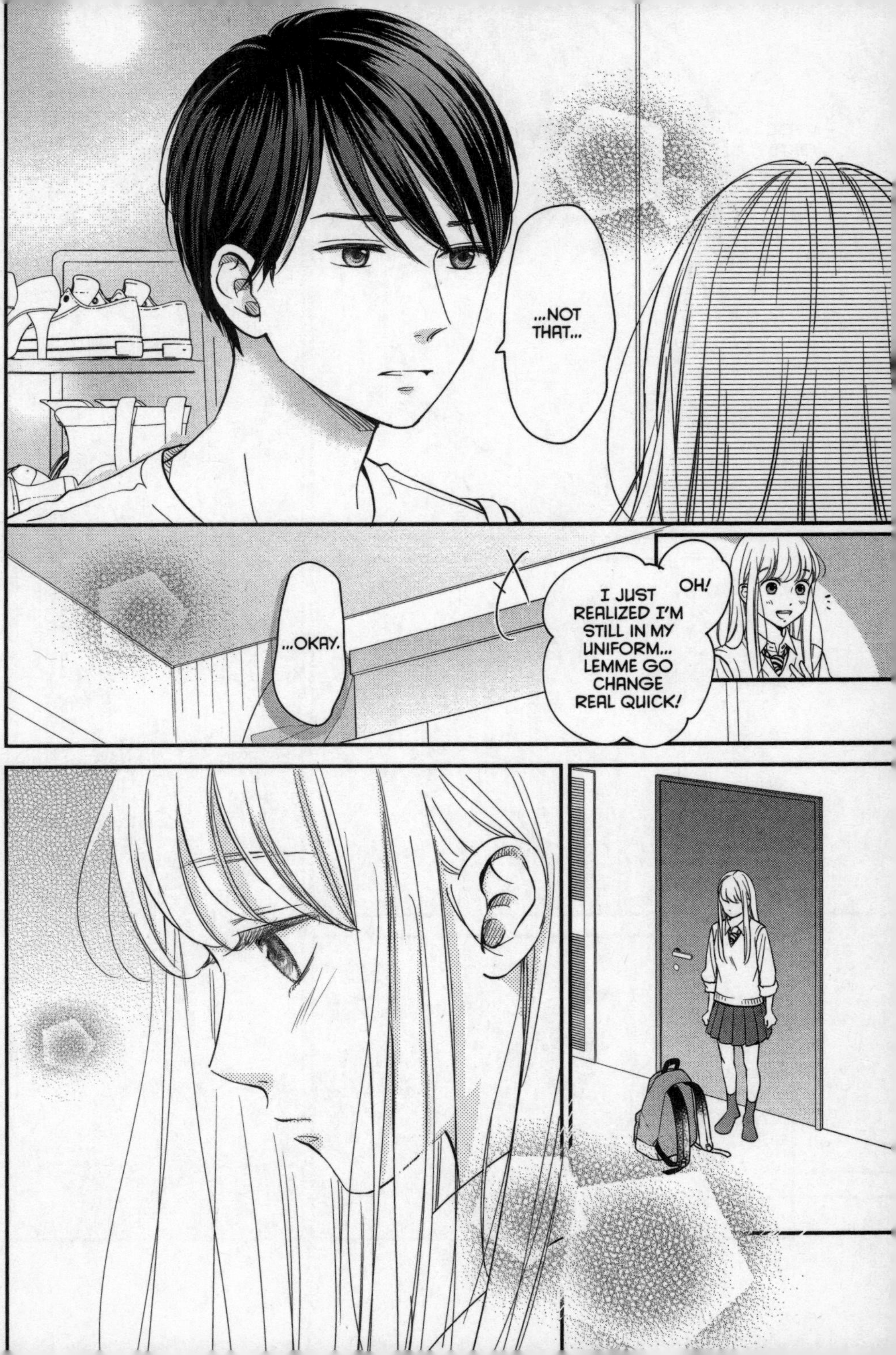
...NOT THAT...
OH! I JUST REALIZED I'M STILL IN MY UNIFORM... LEMME GO CHANGE REAL QUICK!
...OKAY.

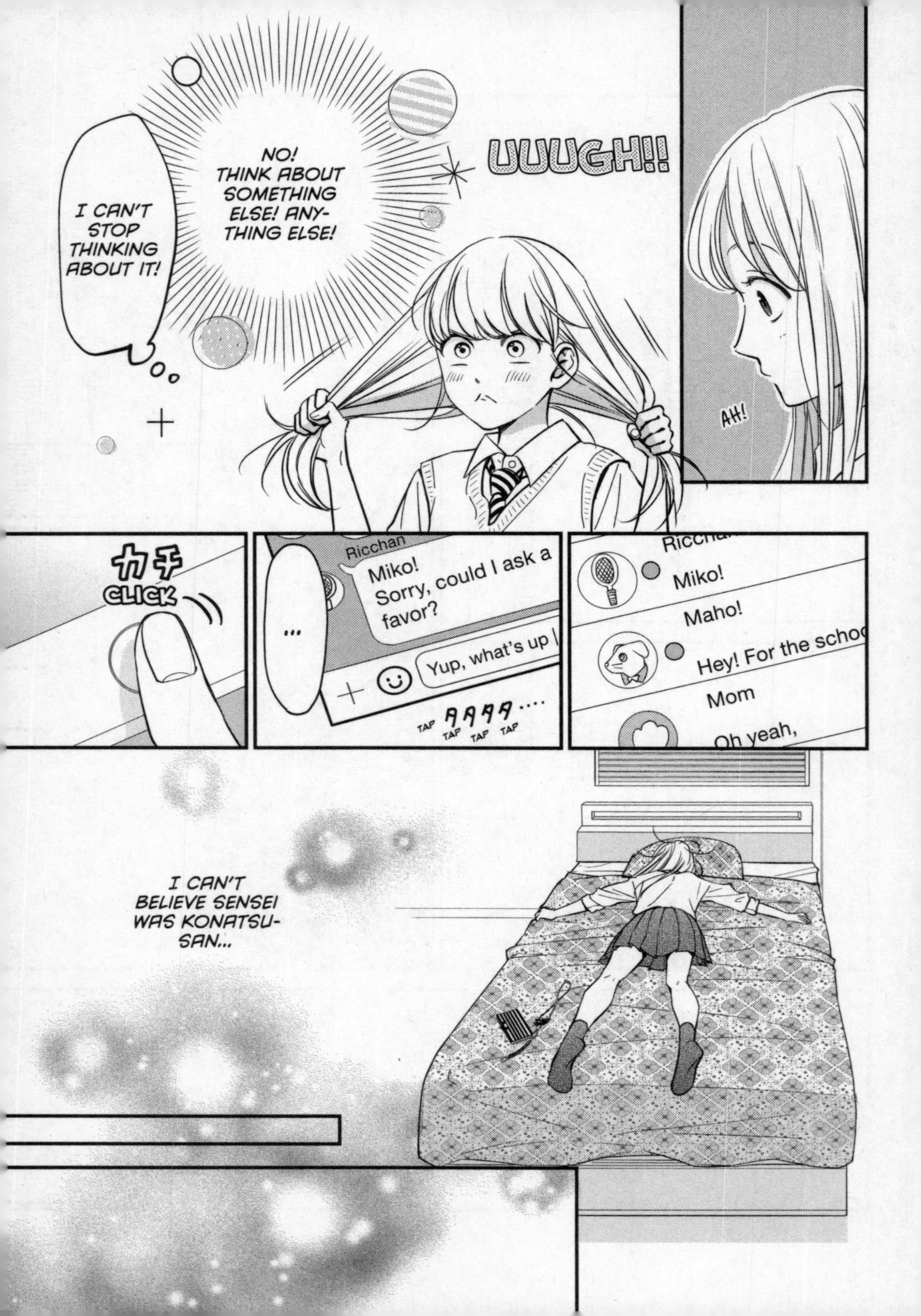
AH!
UUUGH!!
NO! THINK ABOUT SOMETHING ELSE! ANY-THING ELSE!
I CAN'T STOP THINKING ABOUT IT!
Miko!
Maho!
Hey! For the scho
Mom
Oh yeah,
Ricchan
Miko! Sorry, could I ask a favor?
...
Yup, what's up
タタタタ....
TAP TAP TAP TAP
カチ
CLICK
I CAN'T BELIEVE SENSEI WAS KONATSU-SAN...

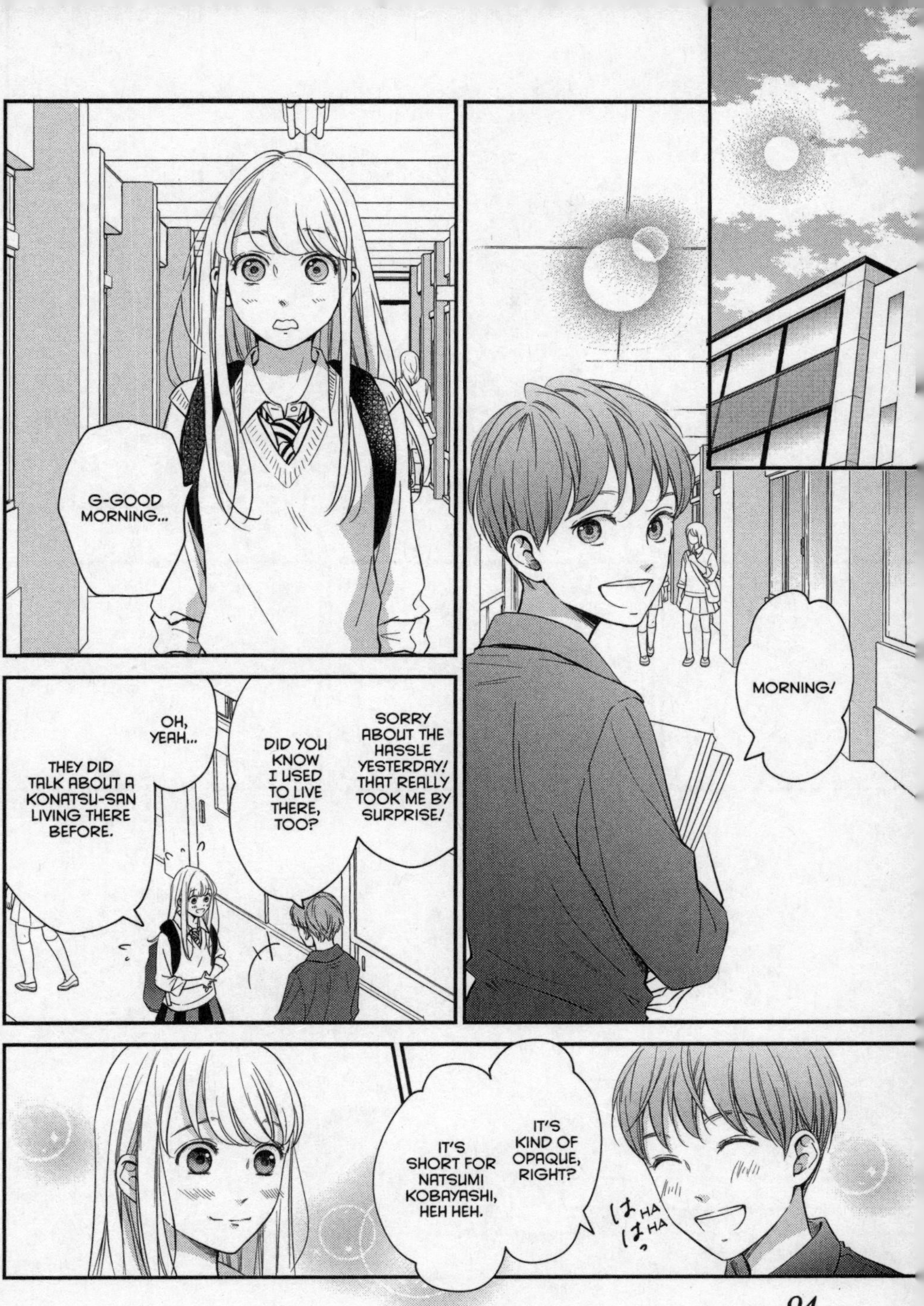
MORNING!
G-GOOD MORNING...
SORRY ABOUT THE HASSLE YESTERDAY! THAT REALLY TOOK ME BY SURPRISE!
DID YOU KNOW I USED TO LIVE THERE, TOO?
OH, YEAH...
THEY DID TALK ABOUT A KONATSU-SAN LIVING THERE BEFORE.
IT'S KIND OF OPAQUE, RIGHT?
IT'S SHORT FOR NATSUMI KOBAYASHI, HEH HEH.
ははっ HA HA

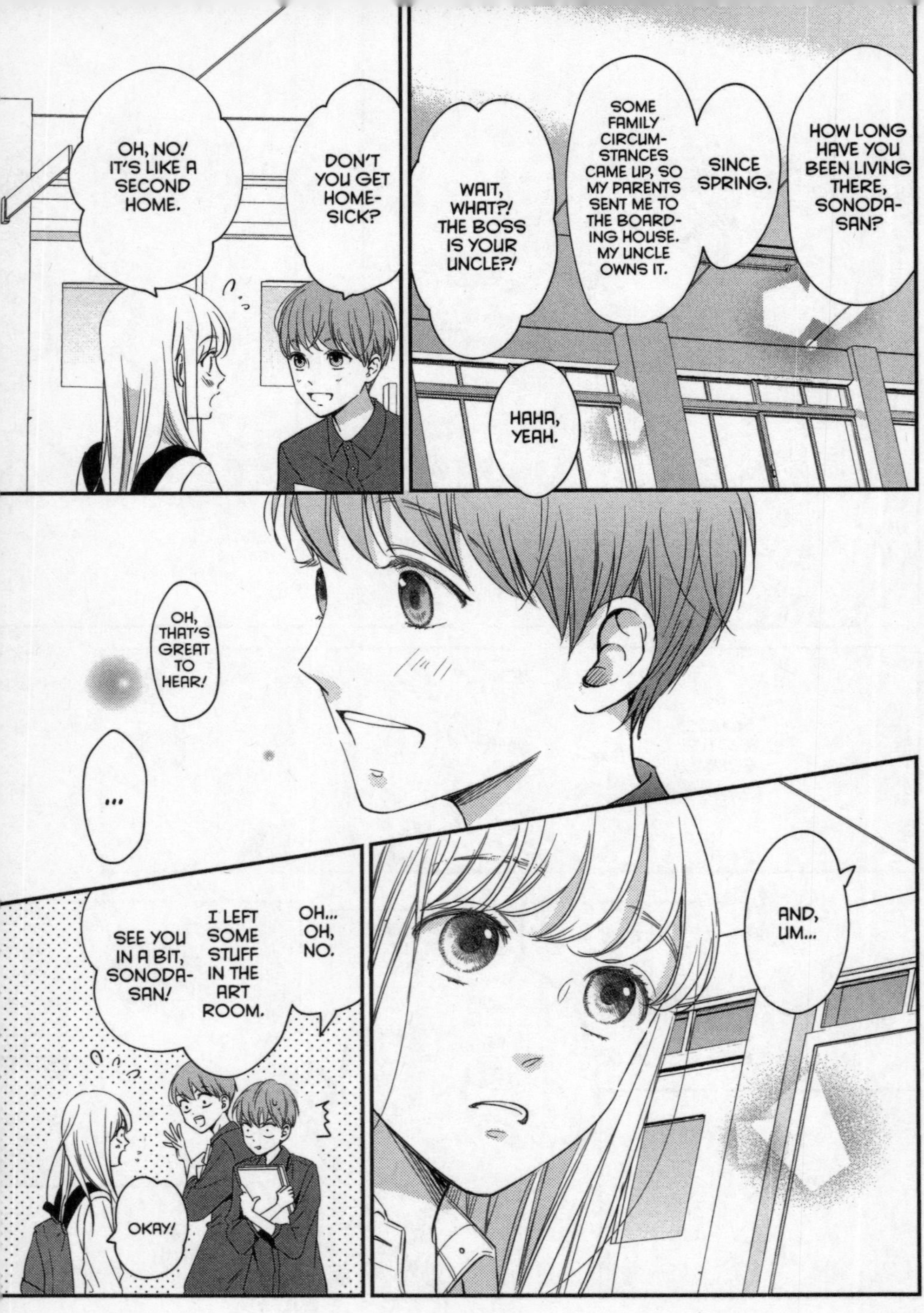
HOW LONG HAVE YOU BEEN LIVING THERE, SONODA-SAN?
SINCE SPRING.
SOME FAMILY CIRCUMSTANCES CAME UP, SO MY PARENTS SENT ME TO THE BOARDING HOUSE. MY UNCLE OWNS IT.
WAIT, WHAT?! THE BOSS IS YOUR UNCLE?!
HAHA, YEAH.
DON'T YOU GET HOMESICK?
OH, NO! IT'S LIKE A SECOND HOME.
OH, THAT'S GREAT TO HEAR!
...
AND, UM...
OH... OH, NO.
I LEFT SOME STUFF IN THE ART ROOM.
SEE YOU IN A BIT, SONODA-SAN!
OKAY!

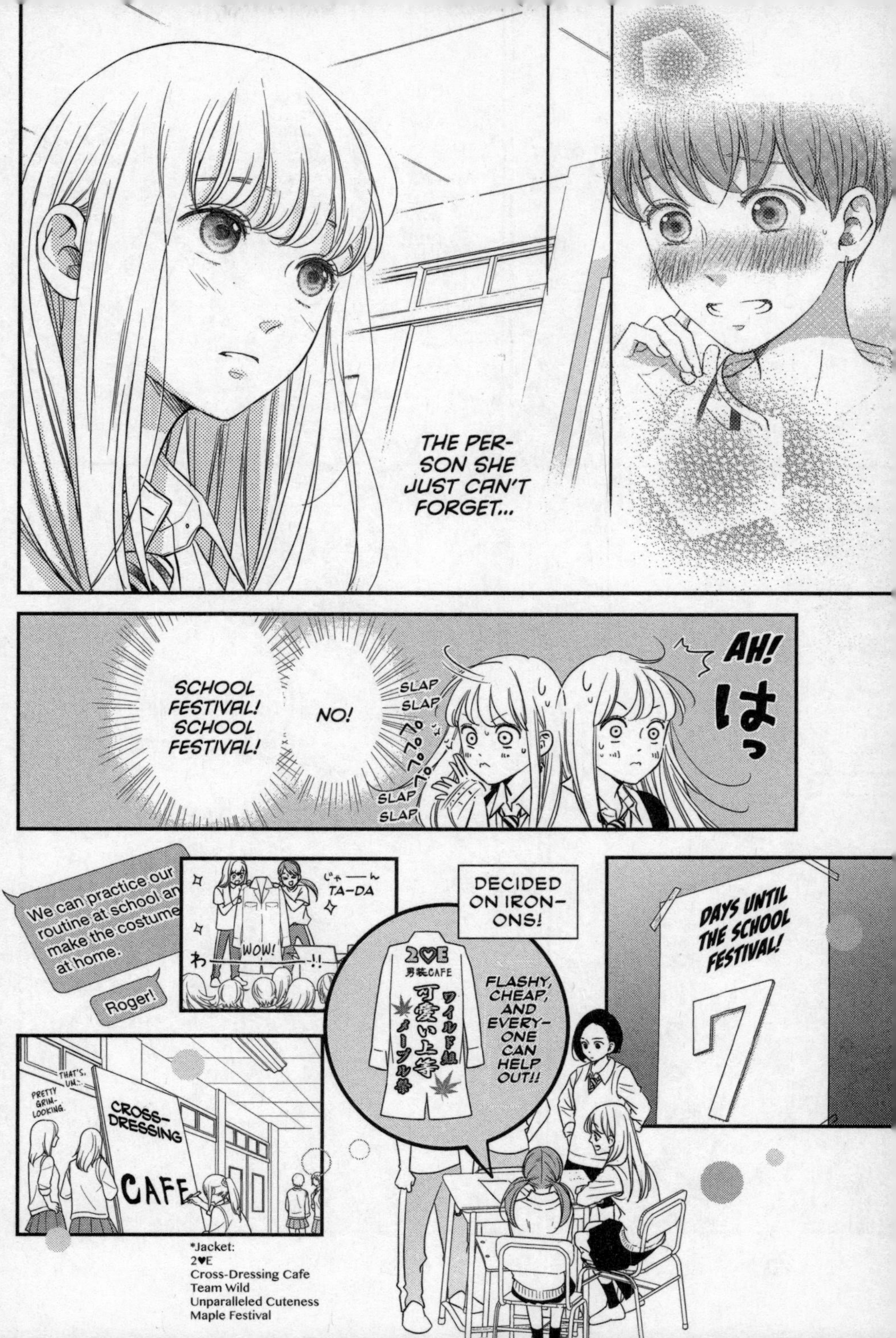
THE PER-SON SHE JUST CAN'T FORGET...
AH!
はっ
SLAP SLAP
ぺぺぺぺ
SLAP SLAP
NO!
SCHOOL FESTIVAL! SCHOOL FESTIVAL!
DAYS UNTIL THE SCHOOL FESTIVAL!
7
DECIDED ON IRON-ONS!
FLASHY, CHEAP, AND EVERY-ONE CAN HELP OUT!!
2♥E
男装CAFE
ワイルド組
可愛い上等
メープル祭
じゃーん
TA-DA
わ
WOW!
-!!
We can practice our routine at school an make the costume at home.
Roger!
THAT'S, UM...
PRETTY GRIM-LOOKING.
CROSS-DRESSING
CAFE

*Jacket:
2♥E
Cross-Dressing Cafe
Team Wild
Unparalleled Cuteness
Maple Festival

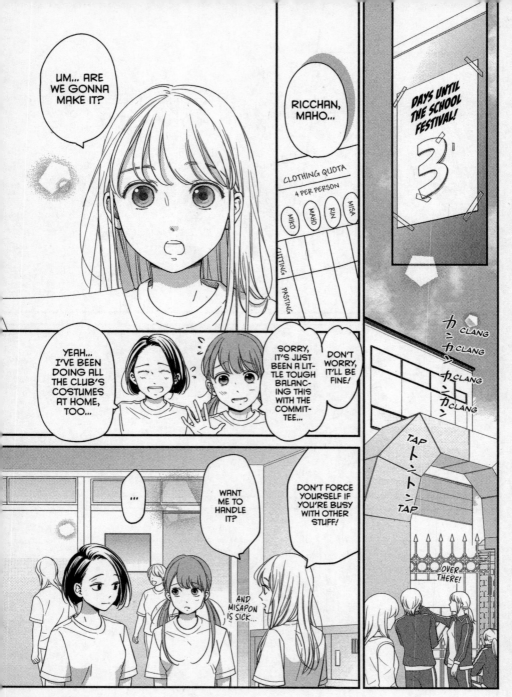

UM... ARE WE GONNA MAKE IT?

RICCHAN, MAHO...

DAYS UNTIL THE SCHOOL FESTIVAL!

3

CLOTHING QUOTA 4 PER PERSON	MICO	MAHO	RIN	MISA
CUTTING				
PASTING				

YEAH... I'VE BEEN DOING ALL THE CLUB'S COSTUMES AT HOME, TOO...

SORRY, IT'S JUST BEEN A LITTLE TOUGH BALANC-ING THIS WITH THE COMMIT-TEE...

DON'T WORRY, IT'LL BE FINE!

CLANG
CLANG
CLANG
CLANG

...

WANT ME TO HANDLE IT?

DON'T FORCE YOURSELF IF YOU'RE BUSY WITH OTHER STUFF!

AND MISAPON IS SICK...

TAP
TAP
TAP

OVER THERE!

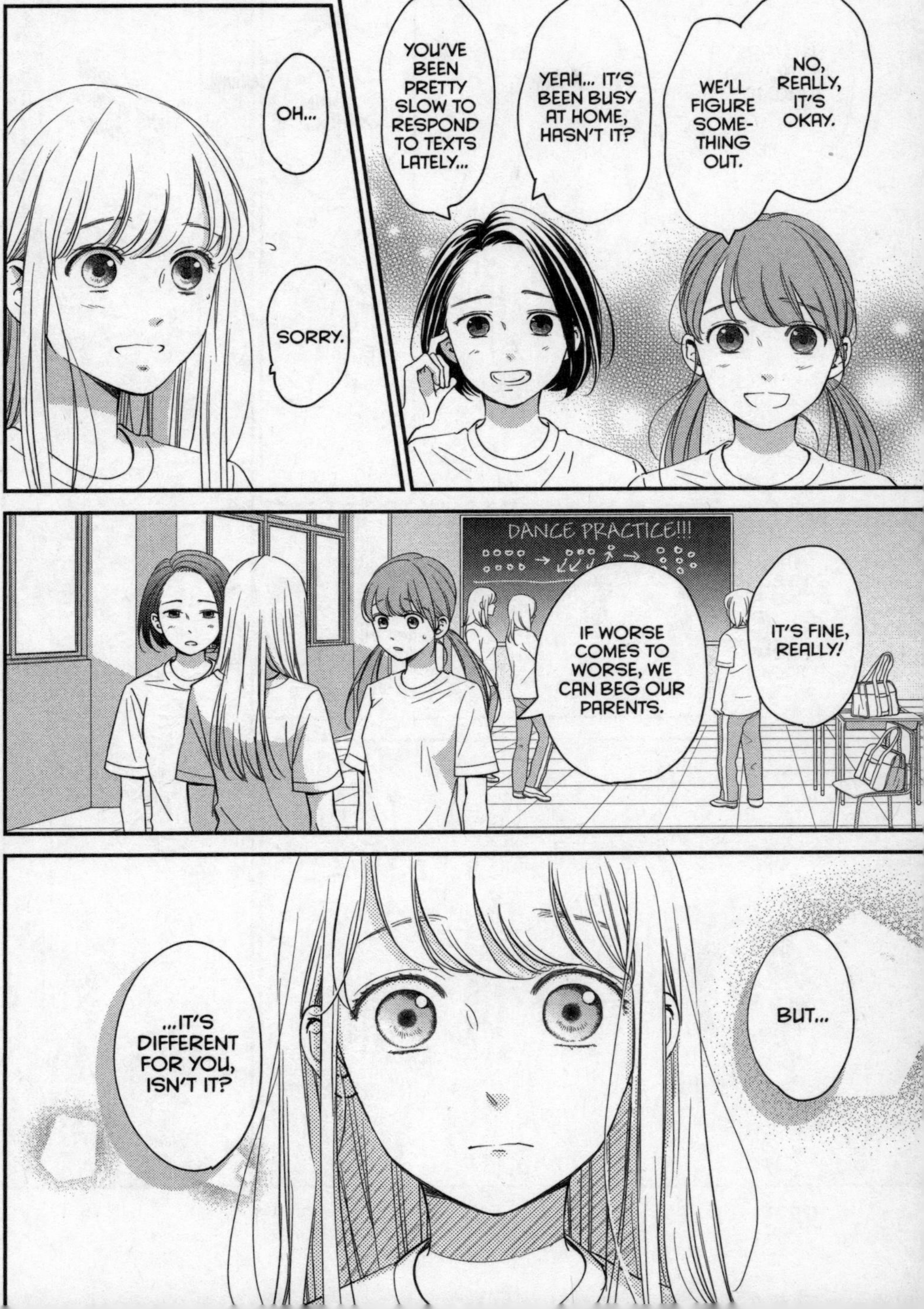
NO, REALLY, IT'S OKAY.
WE'LL FIGURE SOME-THING OUT.
YEAH... IT'S BEEN BUSY AT HOME, HASN'T IT?
YOU'VE BEEN PRETTY SLOW TO RESPOND TO TEXTS LATELY...
OH...
SORRY.
IT'S FINE, REALLY!
DANCE PRACTICE!!!
IF WORSE COMES TO WORSE, WE CAN BEG OUR PARENTS.
BUT...
...IT'S DIFFERENT FOR YOU, ISN'T IT?

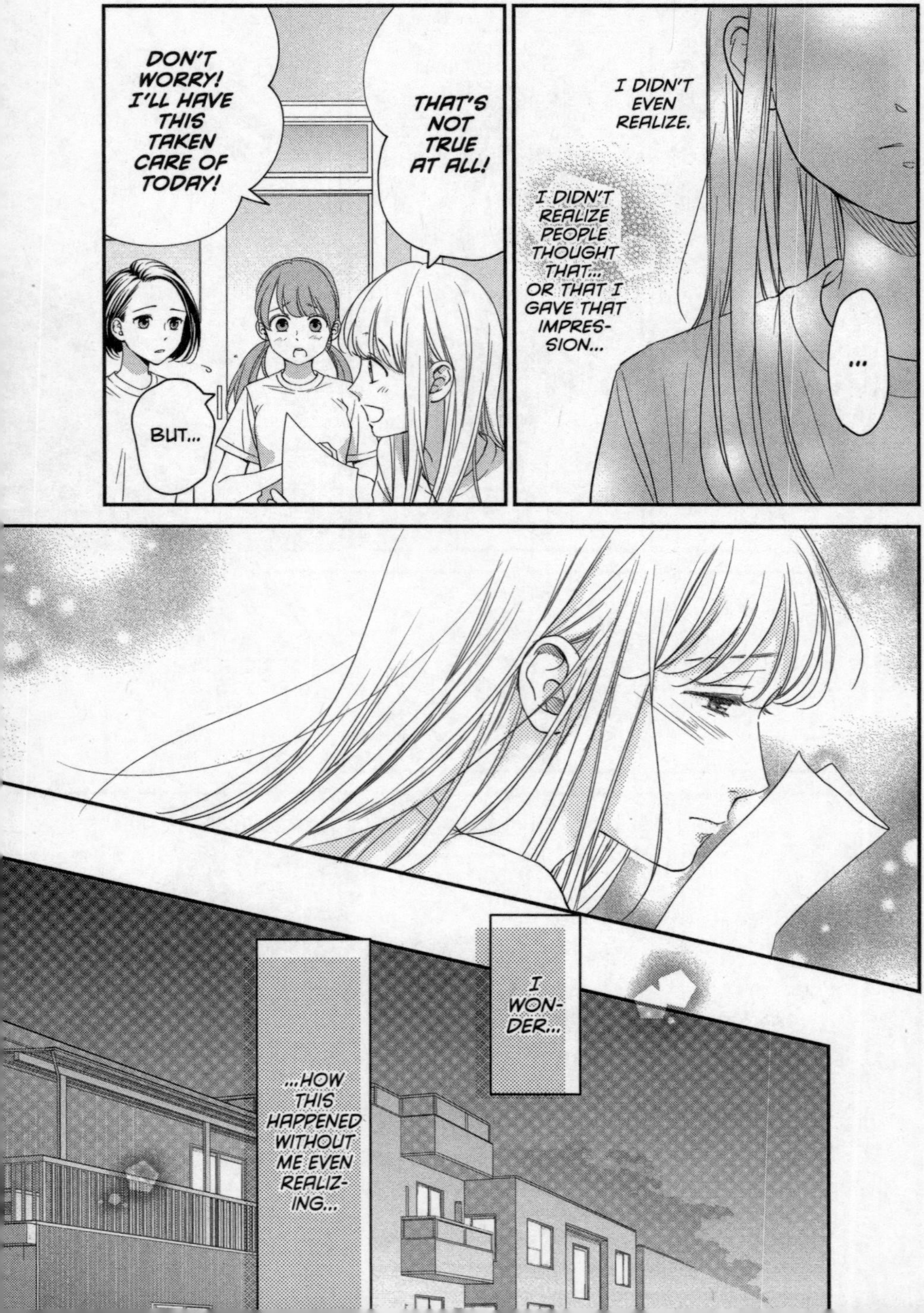
I DIDN'T EVEN REALIZE.
I DIDN'T REALIZE PEOPLE THOUGHT THAT... OR THAT I GAVE THAT IMPRESSION...
...
THAT'S NOT TRUE AT ALL!
DON'T WORRY! I'LL HAVE THIS TAKEN CARE OF TODAY!
BUT...
I WONDER...
...HOW THIS HAPPENED WITHOUT ME EVEN REALIZING...

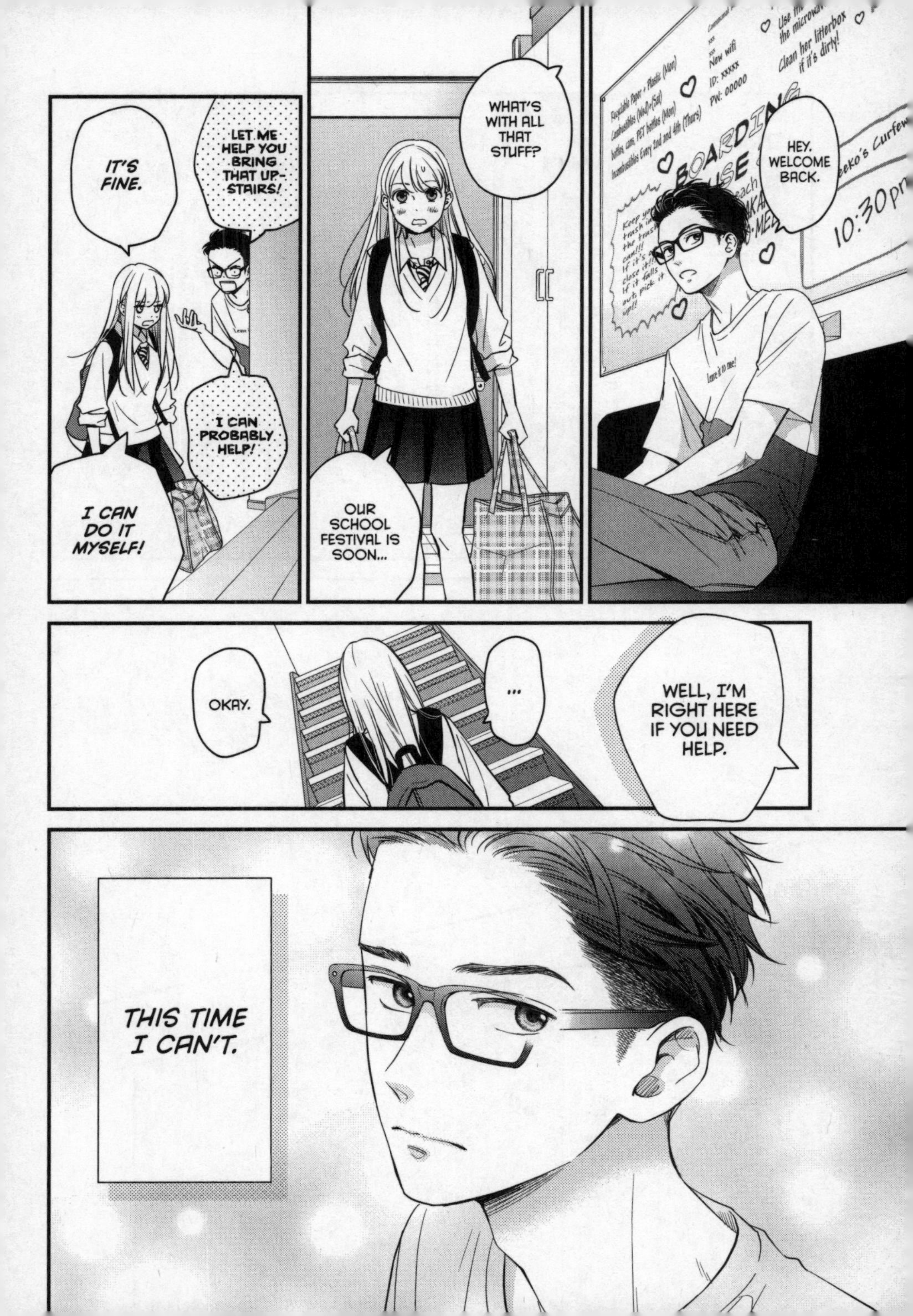
Clean her litterbox if it's dirty!
New wifi
ID: xxxxx
PW: 00000
HEY. WELCOME BACK.
WHAT'S WITH ALL THAT STUFF?
OUR SCHOOL FESTIVAL IS SOON...
LET ME HELP YOU BRING THAT UPSTAIRS!
IT'S FINE.
I CAN PROBABLY HELP!
I CAN DO IT MYSELF!
WELL, I'M RIGHT HERE IF YOU NEED HELP.
...
OKAY.
THIS TIME I CAN'T.

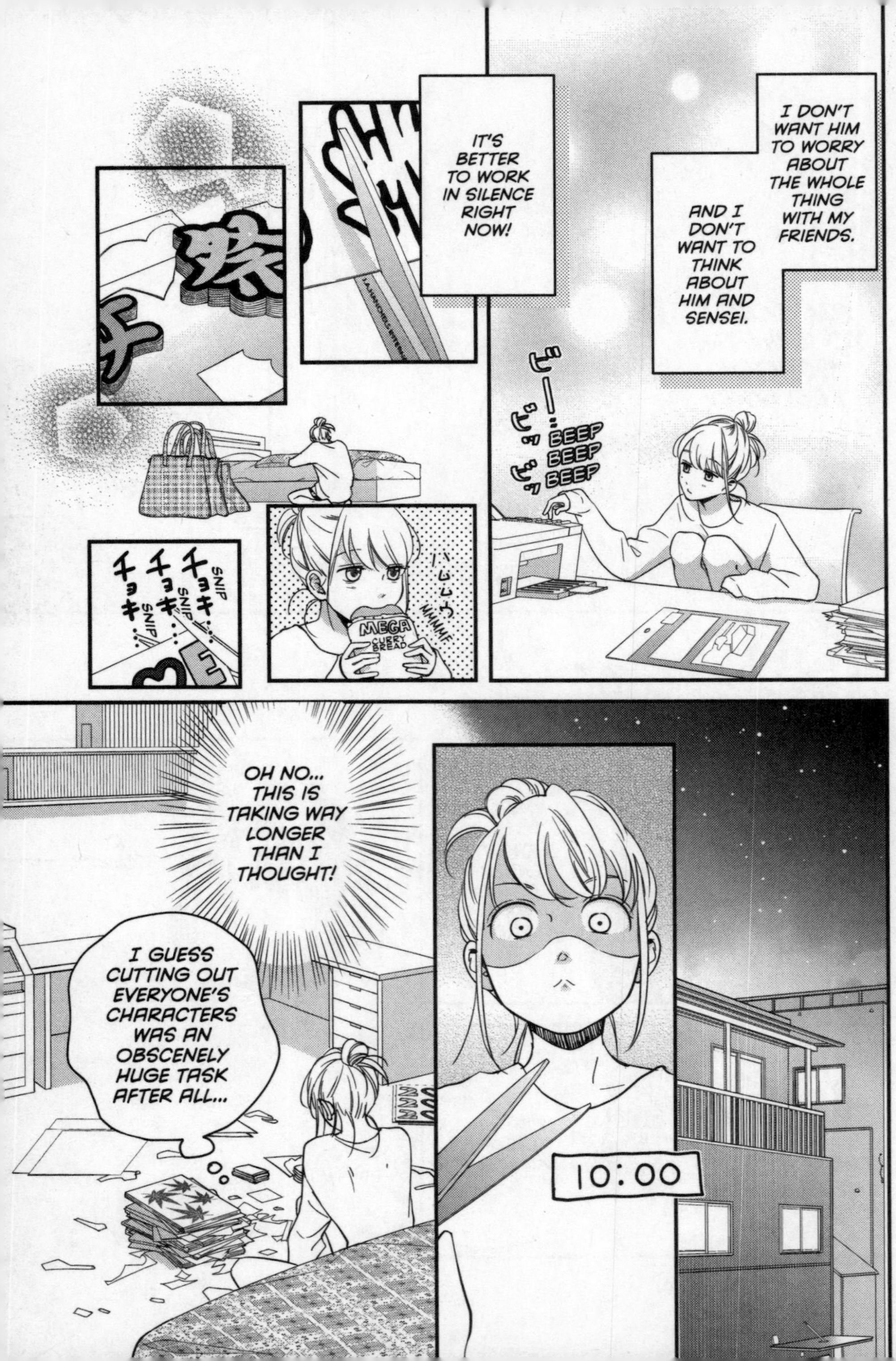
I DON'T WANT HIM TO WORRY ABOUT THE WHOLE THING WITH MY FRIENDS.
AND I DON'T WANT TO THINK ABOUT HIM AND SENSEI.
BEEP BEEP BEEP
IT'S BETTER TO WORK IN SILENCE RIGHT NOW!
MMMMF
MEGA CURRY BREAD
チョキ チョキ チョキ
SNIP SNIP SNIP
10:00
OH NO... THIS IS TAKING WAY LONGER THAN I THOUGHT!
I GUESS CUTTING OUT EVERYONE'S CHARACTERS WAS AN OBSCENELY HUGE TASK AFTER ALL...

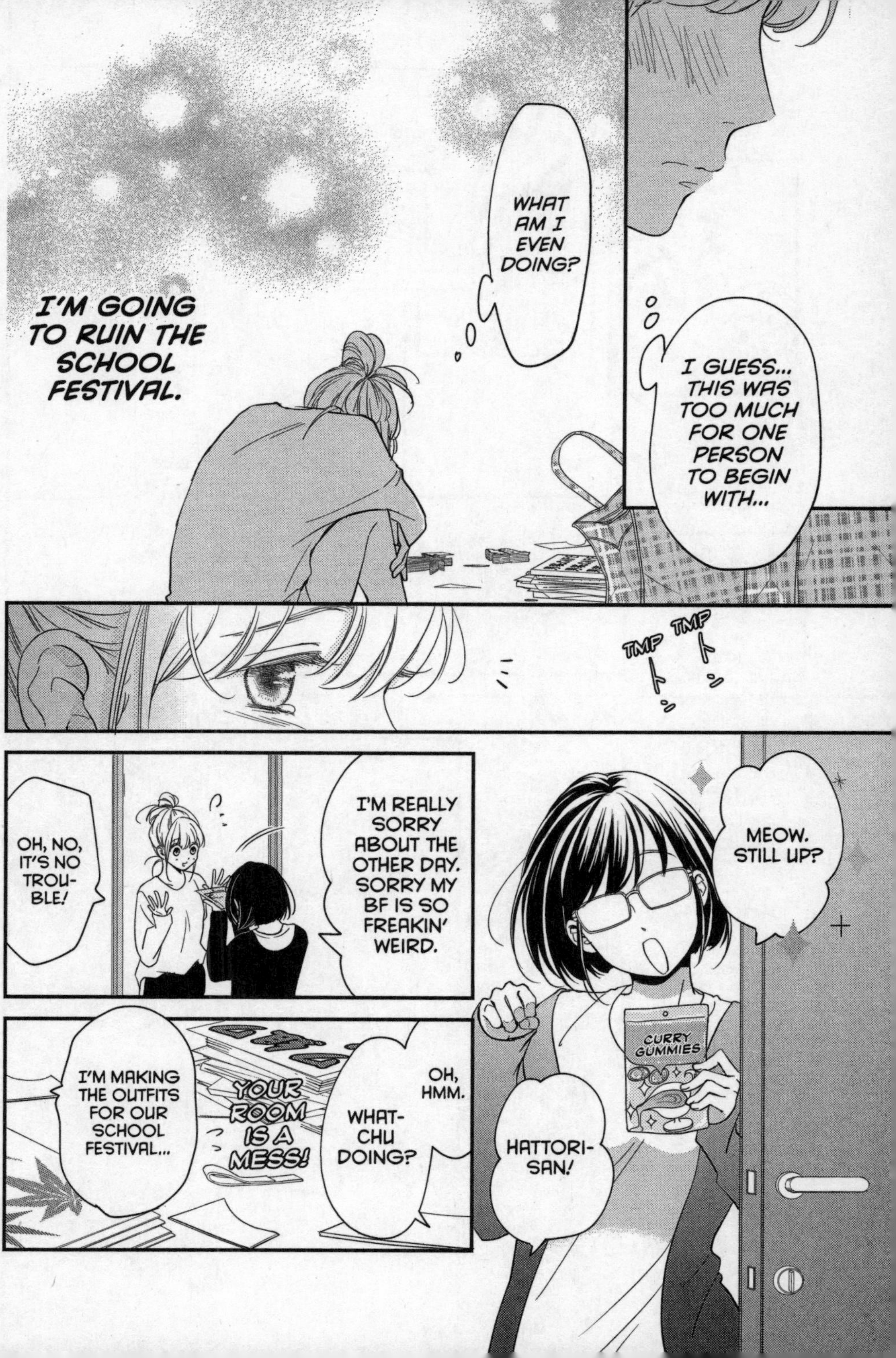
I GUESS... THIS WAS TOO MUCH FOR ONE PERSON TO BEGIN WITH...
WHAT AM I EVEN DOING?
I'M GOING TO RUIN THE SCHOOL FESTIVAL.
TMP TMP
MEOW. STILL UP?
HATTORI-SAN!
I'M REALLY SORRY ABOUT THE OTHER DAY. SORRY MY BF IS SO FREAKIN' WEIRD.
OH, NO, IT'S NO TROUBLE!
OH, HMM.
WHATCHU DOING?
YOUR ROOM IS A MESS!
I'M MAKING THE OUTFITS FOR OUR SCHOOL FESTIVAL...
CURRY GUMMIES

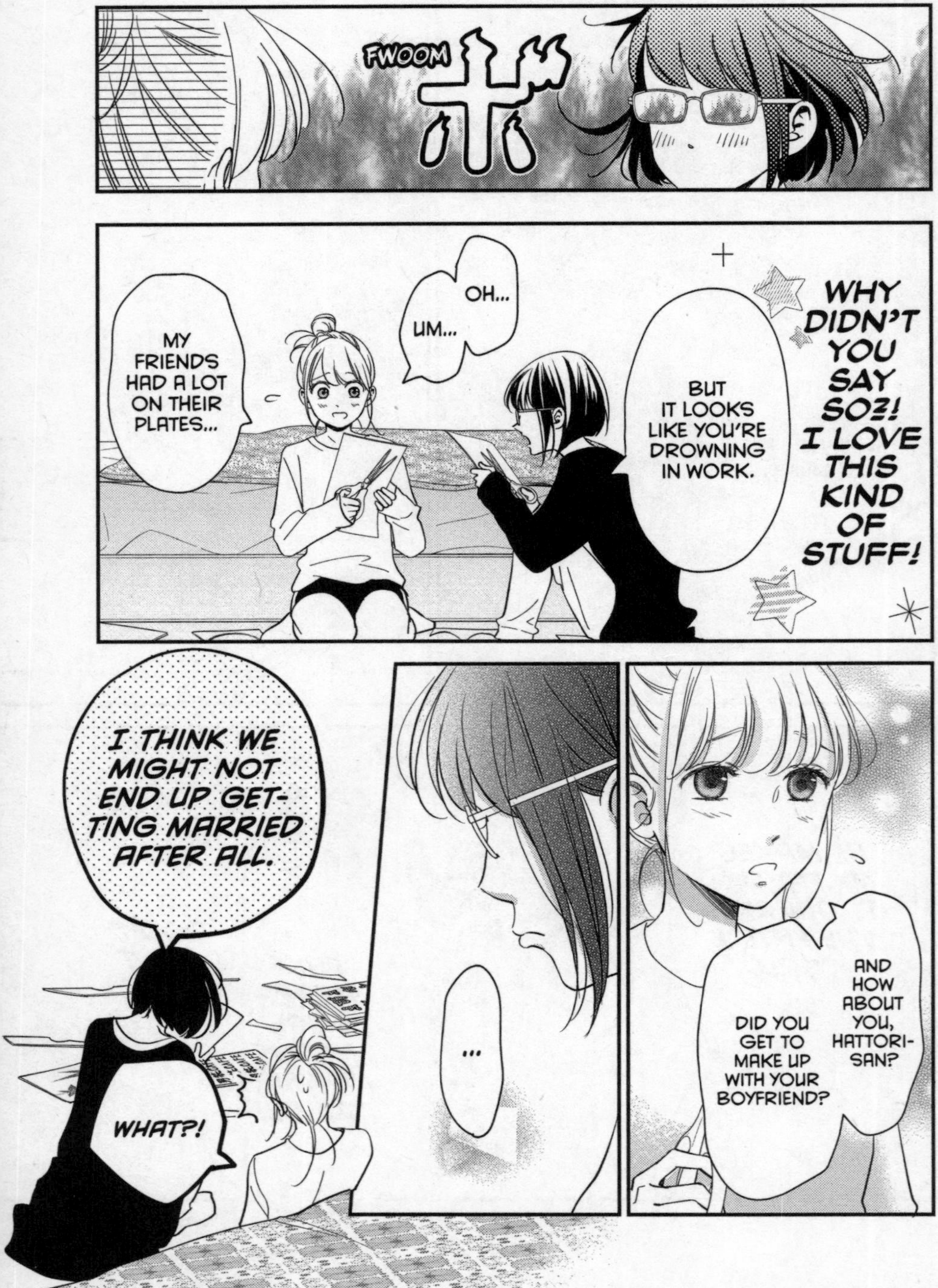
FWOOM
WHY DIDN'T YOU SAY SO?! I LOVE THIS KIND OF STUFF!
BUT IT LOOKS LIKE YOU'RE DROWNING IN WORK.
OH...
UM...
MY FRIENDS HAD A LOT ON THEIR PLATES...
AND HOW ABOUT YOU, HATTORI-SAN?
DID YOU GET TO MAKE UP WITH YOUR BOYFRIEND?
...
I THINK WE MIGHT NOT END UP GET-TING MARRIED AFTER ALL.
WHAT?!

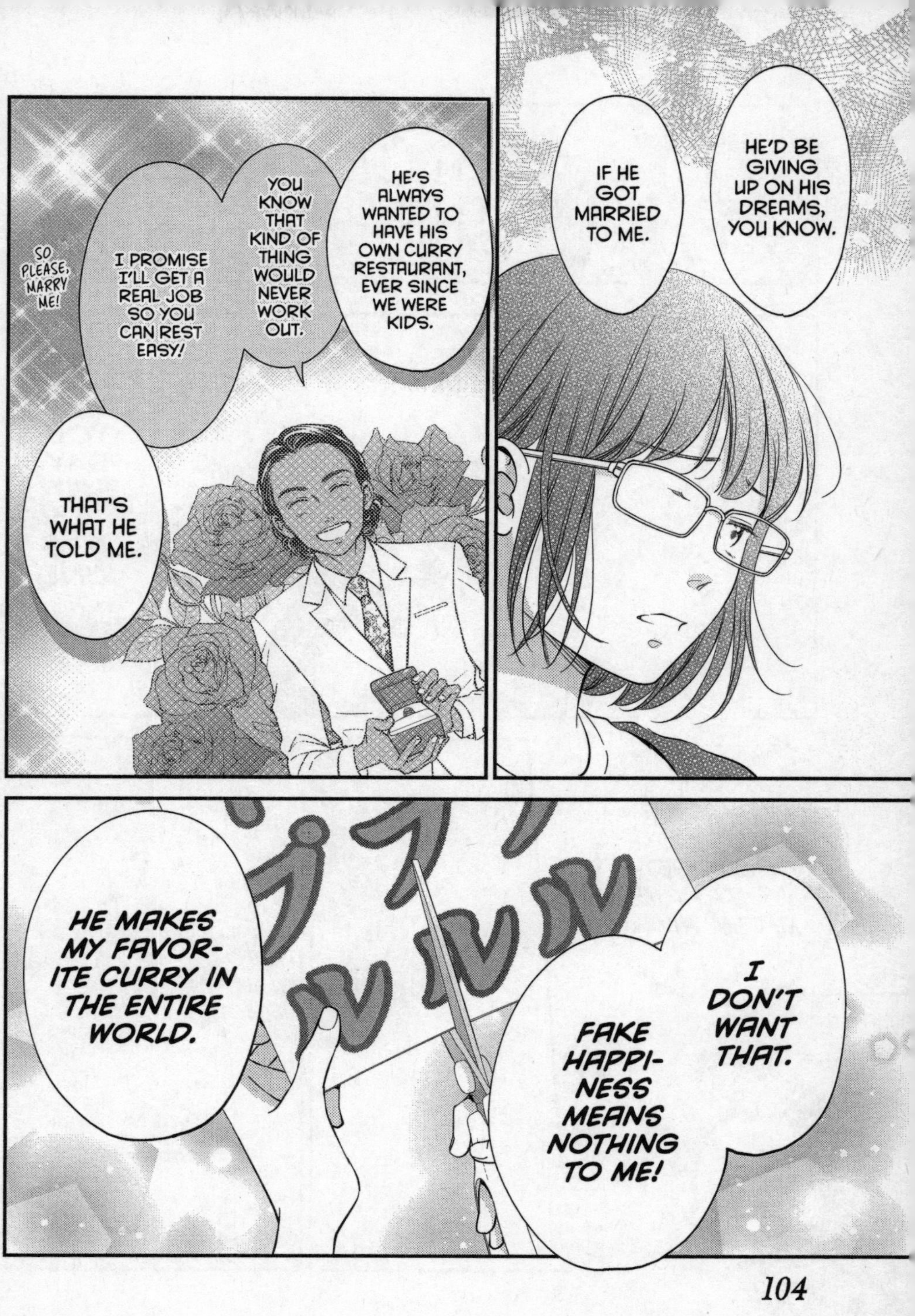
HE'D BE GIVING UP ON HIS DREAMS, YOU KNOW.
IF HE GOT MARRIED TO ME.
HE'S ALWAYS WANTED TO HAVE HIS OWN CURRY RESTAURANT, EVER SINCE WE WERE KIDS.
YOU KNOW THAT KIND OF THING WOULD NEVER WORK OUT.
I PROMISE I'LL GET A REAL JOB SO YOU CAN REST EASY!
SO PLEASE, MARRY ME!
THAT'S WHAT HE TOLD ME.
I DON'T WANT THAT.
FAKE HAPPINESS MEANS NOTHING TO ME!
HE MAKES MY FAVORITE CURRY IN THE ENTIRE WORLD.

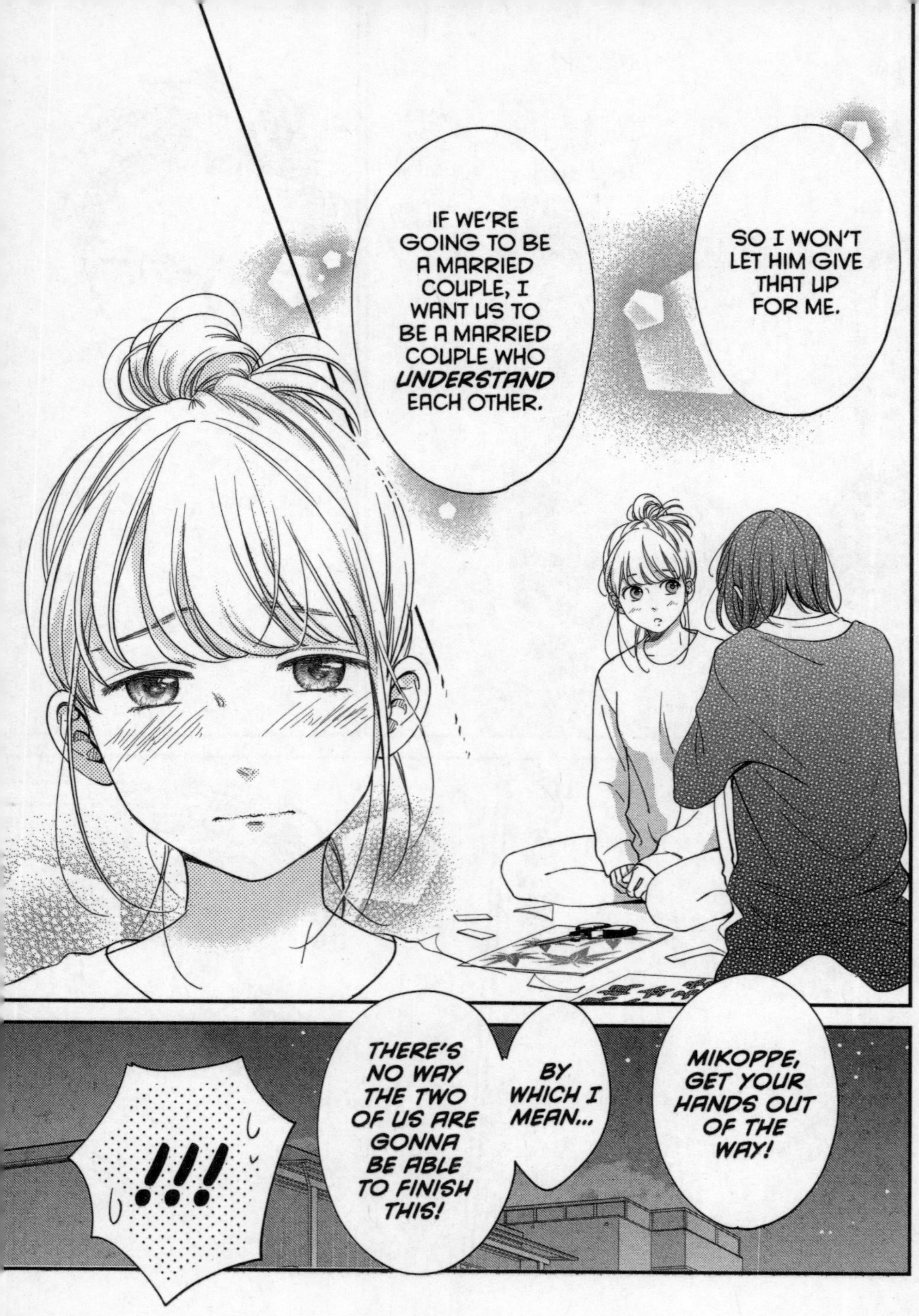
SO I WON'T LET HIM GIVE THAT UP FOR ME.
IF WE'RE GOING TO BE A MARRIED COUPLE, I WANT US TO BE A MARRIED COUPLE WHO UNDERSTAND EACH OTHER.
MIKOPPE, GET YOUR HANDS OUT OF THE WAY!
BY WHICH I MEAN...
THERE'S NO WAY THE TWO OF US ARE GONNA BE ABLE TO FINISH THIS!
!!!

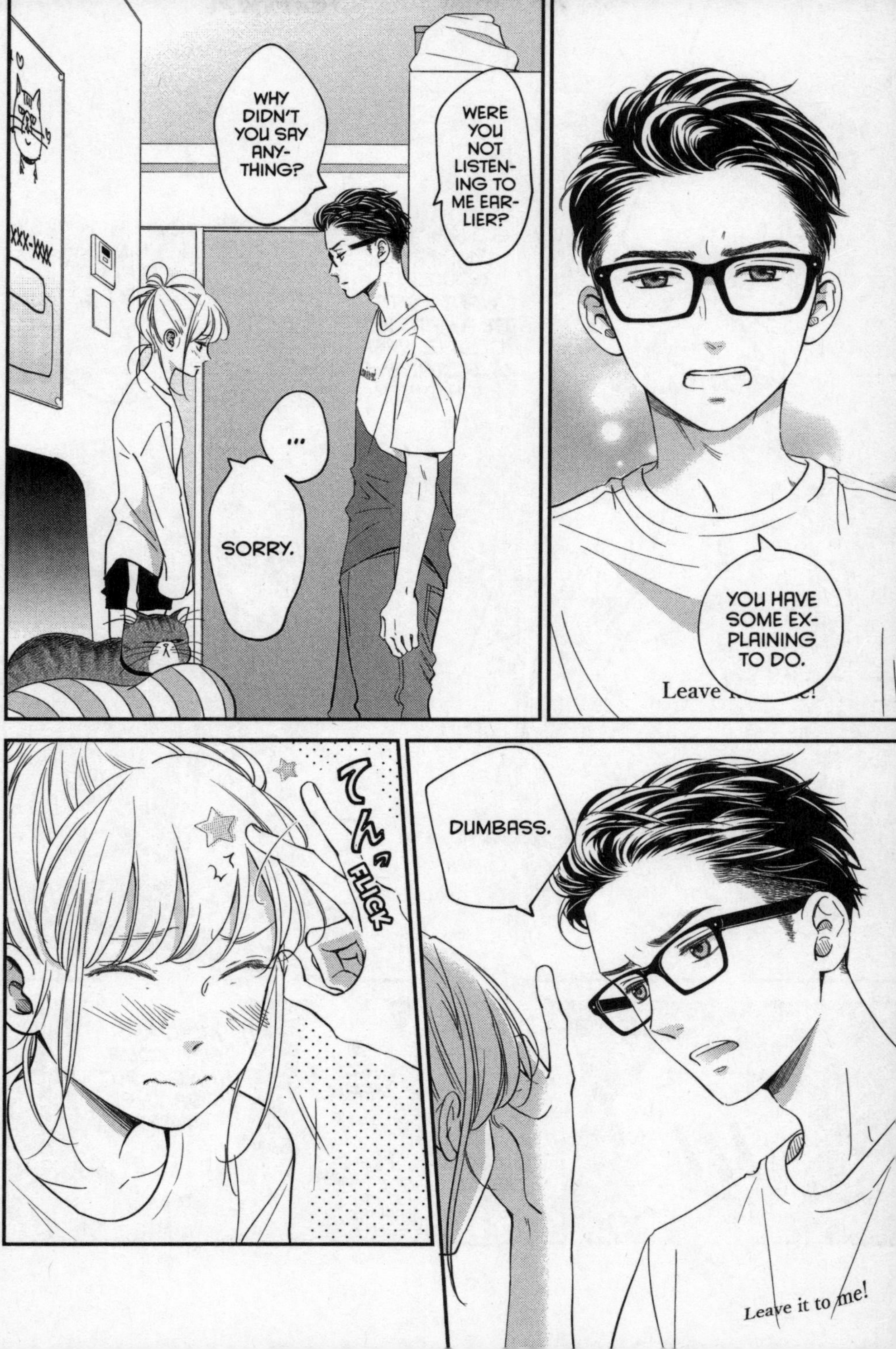
YOU HAVE SOME EXPLAINING TO DO.
WERE YOU NOT LISTENING TO ME EARLIER?
WHY DIDN'T YOU SAY ANYTHING?
...
SORRY.
DUMBASS.
てん
FLICK

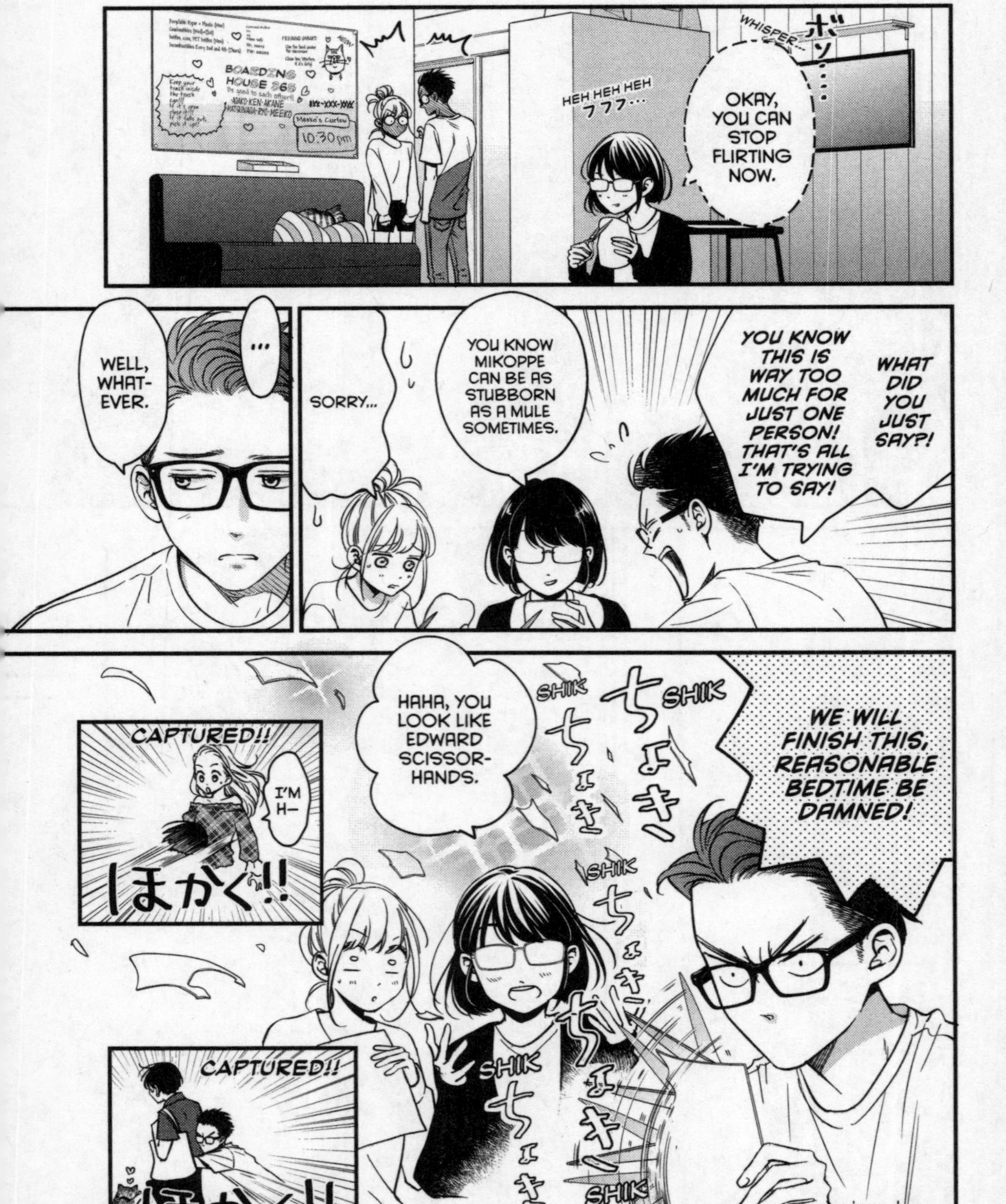
WHISPER... ボソ...
OKAY, YOU CAN STOP FLIRTING NOW.
HEH HEH HEH フフフ...
BOARDING HOUSE 365
Meeko's Curfew
10:30 pm
WHAT DID YOU JUST SAY?!
YOU KNOW THIS IS WAY TOO MUCH FOR JUST ONE PERSON! THAT'S ALL I'M TRYING TO SAY!
YOU KNOW MIKOPPE CAN BE AS STUBBORN AS A MULE SOMETIMES.
SORRY...
...
WELL, WHATEVER.
WE WILL FINISH THIS, REASONABLE BEDTIME BE DAMNED!
SHIK ちょき SHIK ちょき
SHIK ちょき ちょき
SHIK ちょき ちょき SHIK
HAHA, YOU LOOK LIKE EDWARD SCISSORHANDS.
CAPTURED!!
I'M H—
ほかく!!
ive it to me!
CAPTURED!!
ほかく!!

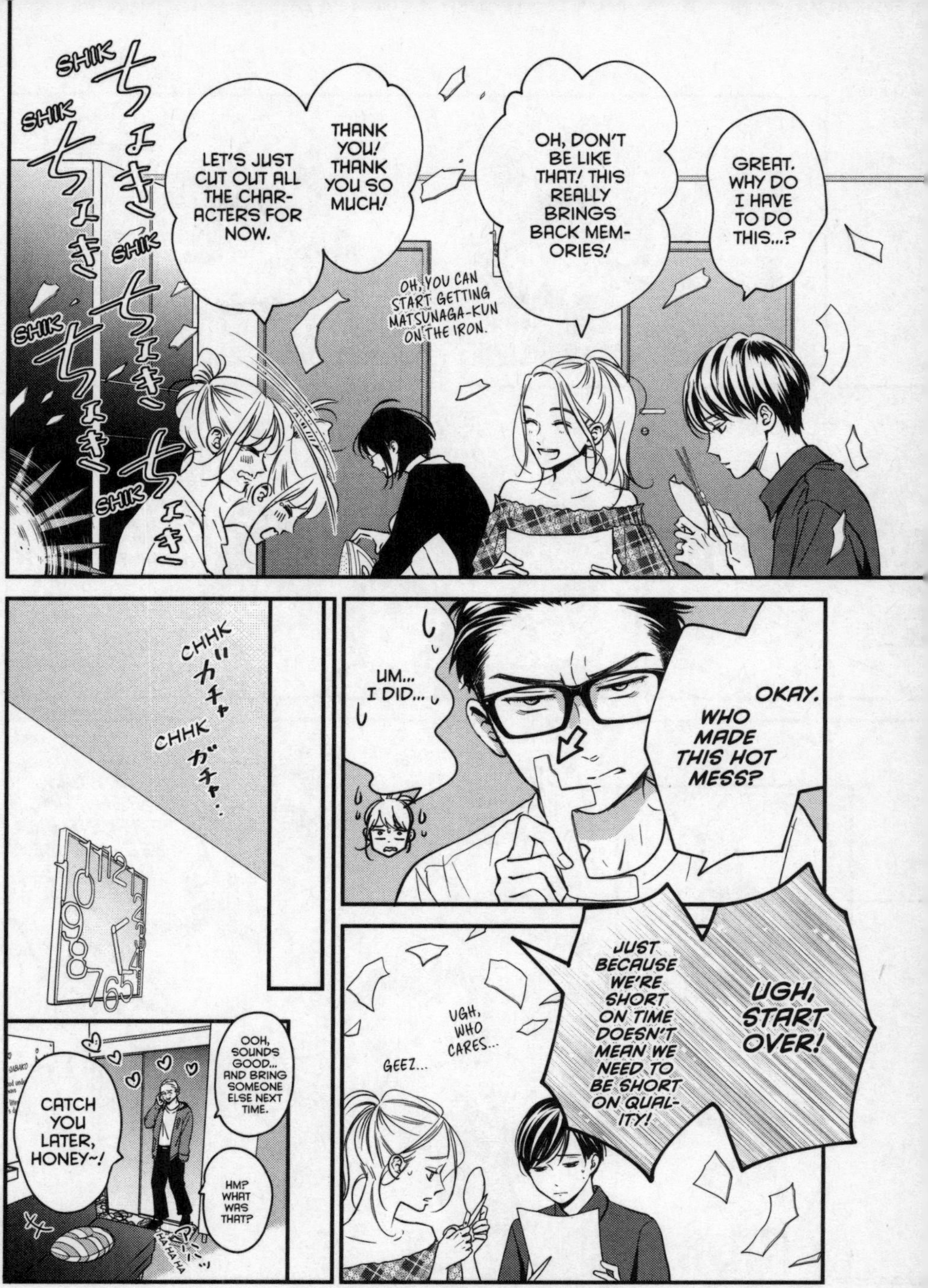
GREAT. WHY DO I HAVE TO DO THIS...?
OH, DON'T BE LIKE THAT! THIS REALLY BRINGS BACK MEMORIES!
OH, YOU CAN START GETTING MATSUNAGA-KUN ON THE IRON.
THANK YOU! THANK YOU SO MUCH!
LET'S JUST CUT OUT ALL THE CHARACTERS FOR NOW.
SHIK ちょき SHIK ちょき SHIK ちょき SHIK ちょき SHIK ちょきー
OKAY. WHO MADE THIS HOT MESS?
UM... I DID...
CHHK ガチャ CHHK ガチャ..
UGH, START OVER!
JUST BECAUSE WE'RE SHORT ON TIME DOESN'T MEAN WE NEED TO BE SHORT ON QUALITY!
UGH, WHO CARES...
GEEZ...
OOH, SOUNDS GOOD... AND BRING SOMEONE ELSE NEXT TIME.
CATCH YOU LATER, HONEY~!
HM? WHAT WAS THAT?
HA HA HA

WHY DO I GET THE FEELING WE WON'T FINISH...?

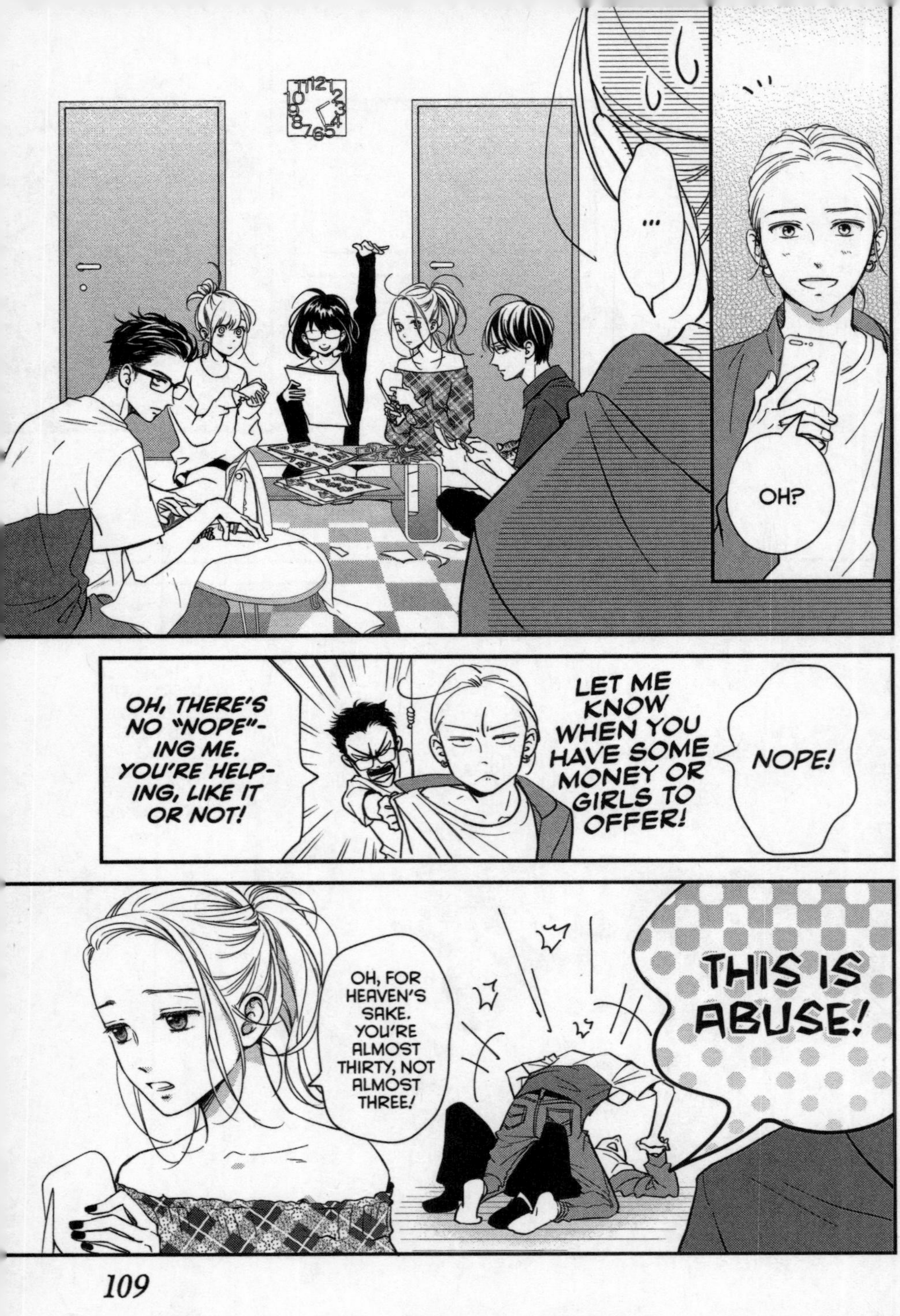
OH?
...
NOPE!
LET ME KNOW WHEN YOU HAVE SOME MONEY OR GIRLS TO OFFER!
OH, THERE'S NO "NOPE"-ING ME. YOU'RE HELPING, LIKE IT OR NOT!
THIS IS ABUSE!
OH, FOR HEAVEN'S SAKE. YOU'RE ALMOST THIRTY, NOT ALMOST THREE!

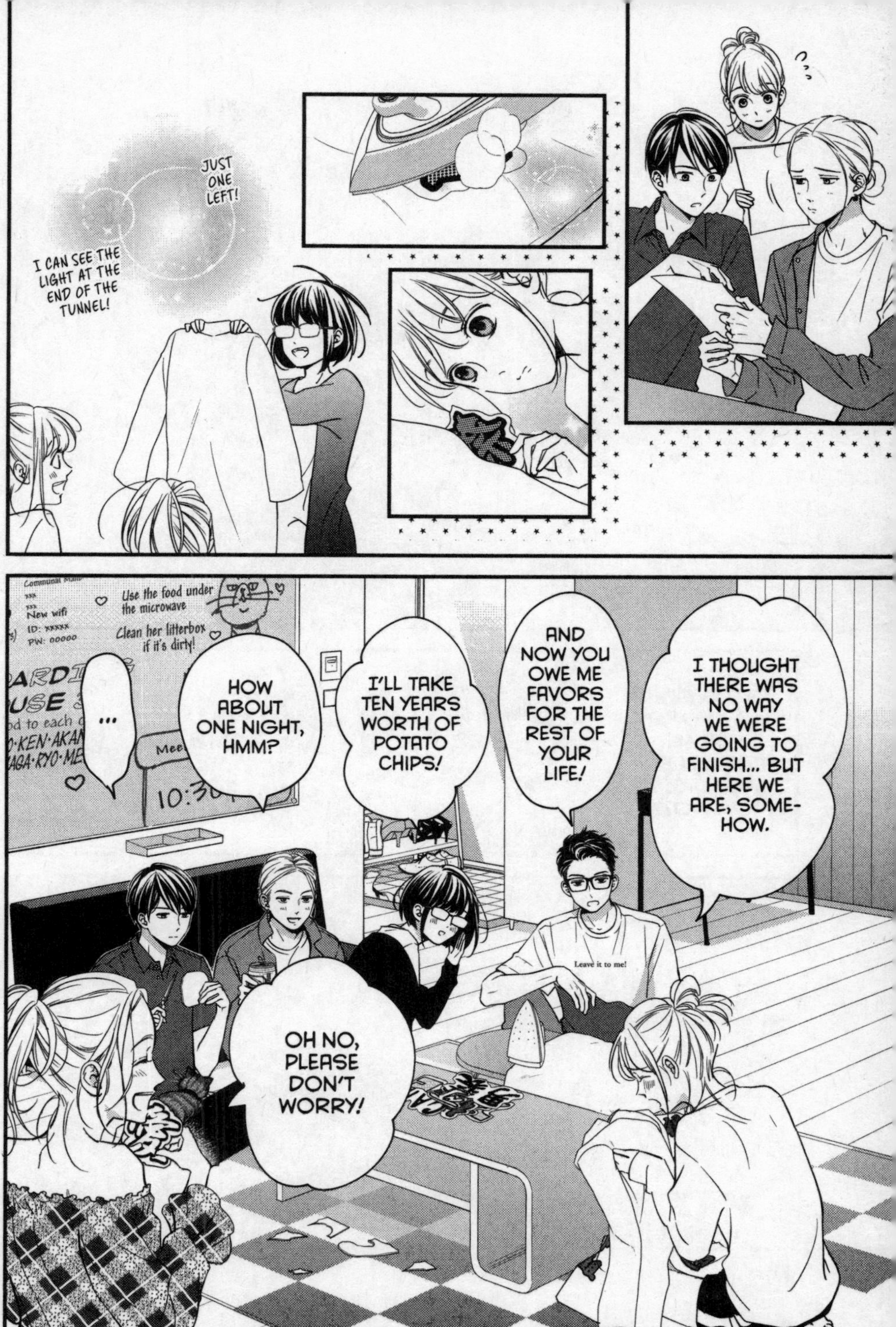
JUST ONE LEFT!
I CAN SEE THE LIGHT AT THE END OF THE TUNNEL!
I THOUGHT THERE WAS NO WAY WE WERE GOING TO FINISH... BUT HERE WE ARE, SOMEHOW.
AND NOW YOU OWE ME FAVORS FOR THE REST OF YOUR LIFE!
I'LL TAKE TEN YEARS WORTH OF POTATO CHIPS!
HOW ABOUT ONE NIGHT, HMM?
...
Use the food under the microwave
Clean her litterbox if it's dirty!
New wifi
ID: xxxxx
PW: 00000
Leave it to me!
OH NO, PLEASE DON'T WORRY!

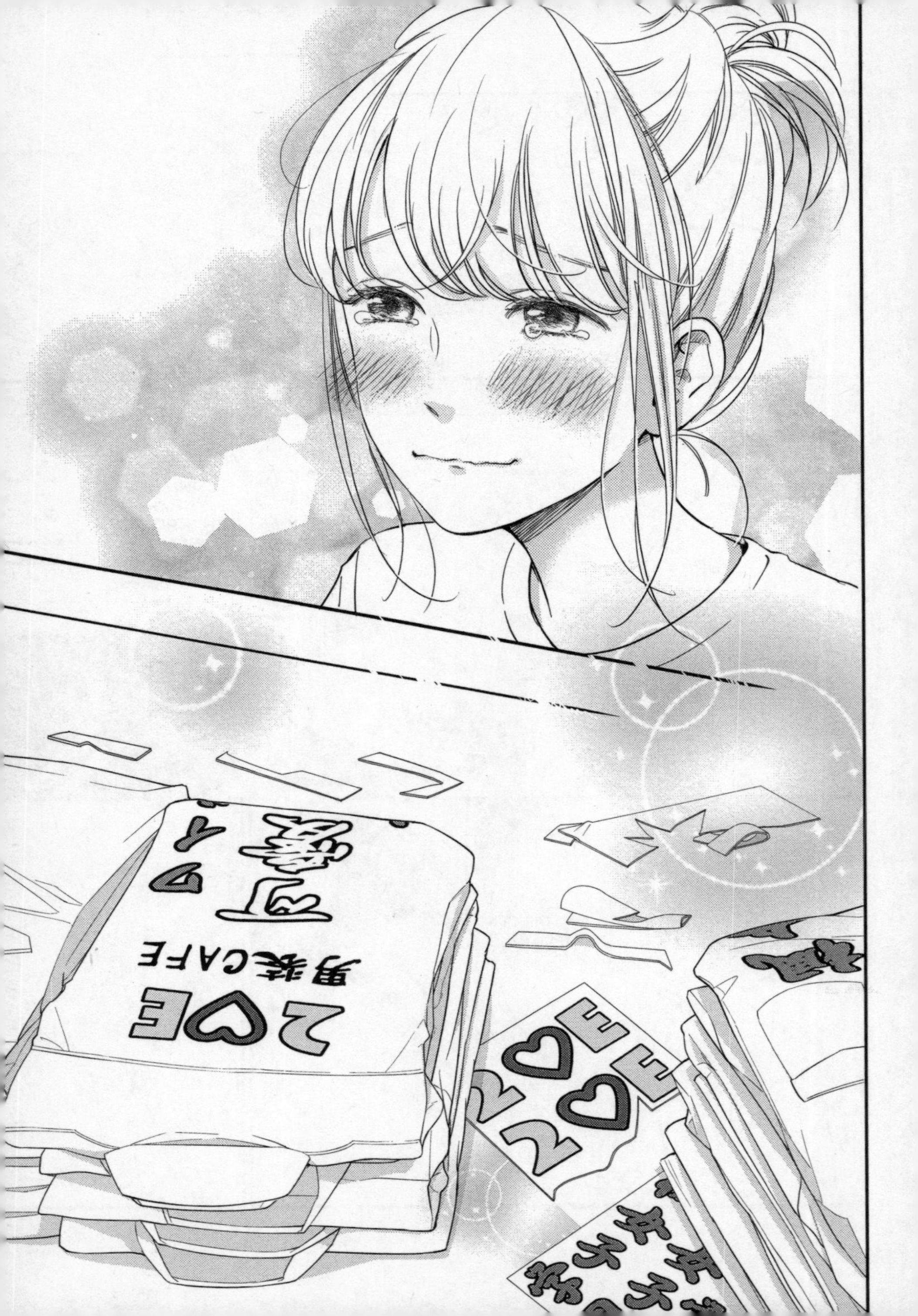
2♡E
男装CAFE
2♡E
2♡E

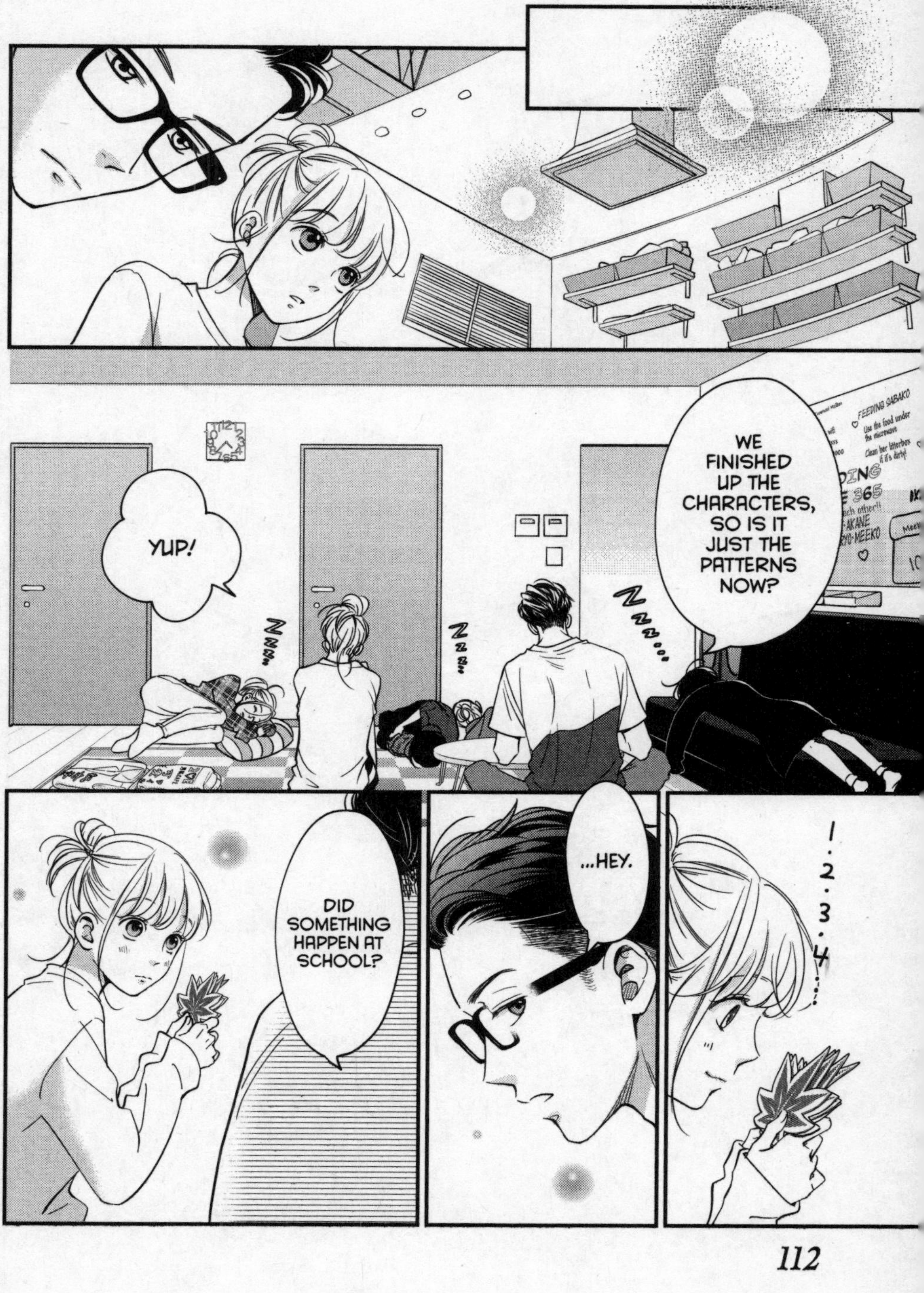
FEEDING SABAKO
Use the food under the microwave
Clean her litterbox if it's dirty!
WE FINISHED UP THE CHARACTERS, SO IS IT JUST THE PATTERNS NOW?
Zzz...
Zzz
Zzz
YUP!
1.2.3.4....
...HEY.
DID SOMETHING HAPPEN AT SCHOOL?

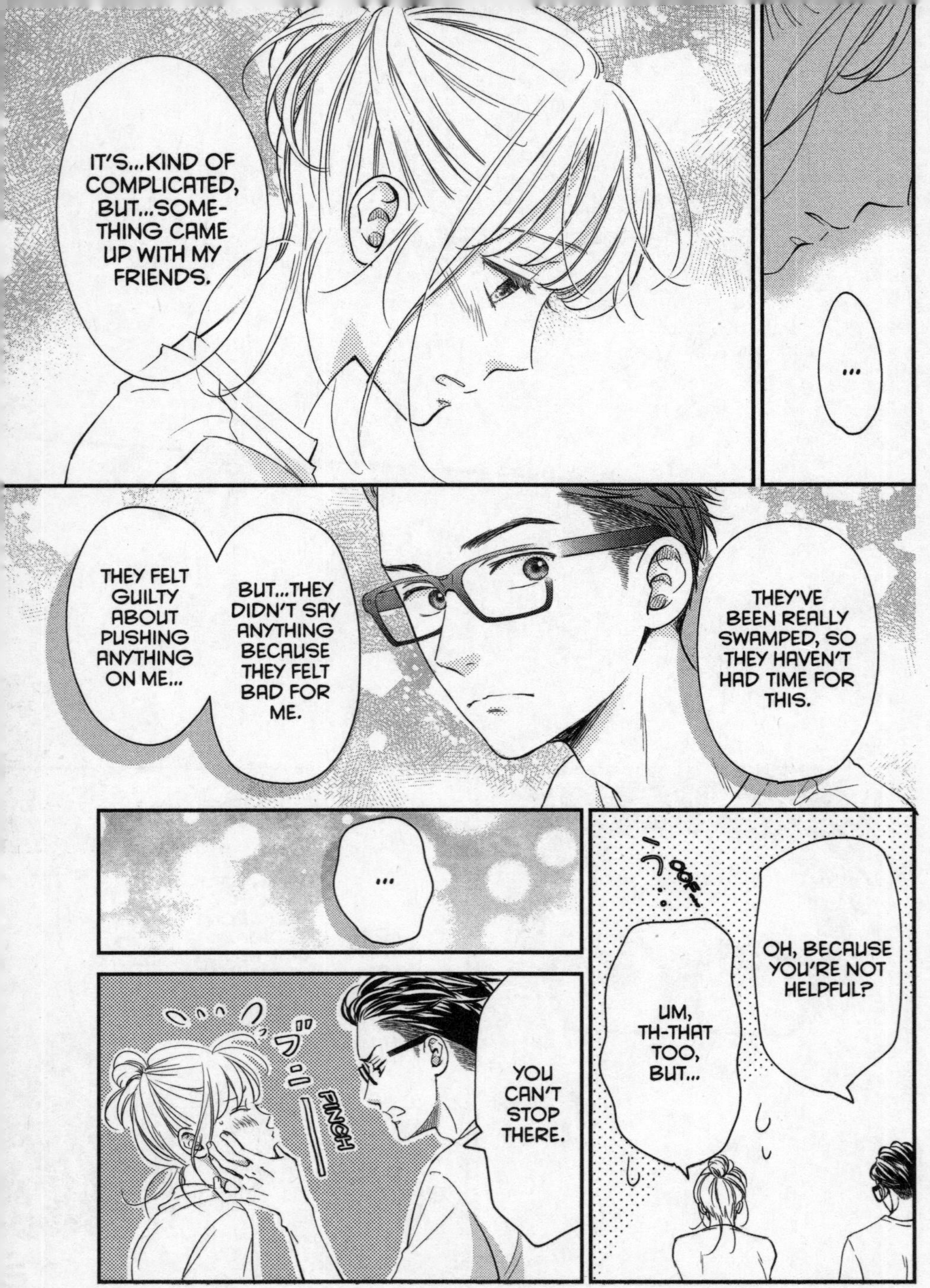
...
IT'S...KIND OF COMPLICATED, BUT...SOME-THING CAME UP WITH MY FRIENDS.
THEY'VE BEEN REALLY SWAMPED, SO THEY HAVEN'T HAD TIME FOR THIS.
THEY FELT GUILTY ABOUT PUSHING ANYTHING ON ME...
BUT...THEY DIDN'T SAY ANYTHING BECAUSE THEY FELT BAD FOR ME.
OH, BECAUSE YOU'RE NOT HELPFUL?
OOF...
UM, TH-THAT TOO, BUT...
...
YOU CAN'T STOP THERE.
PINCH

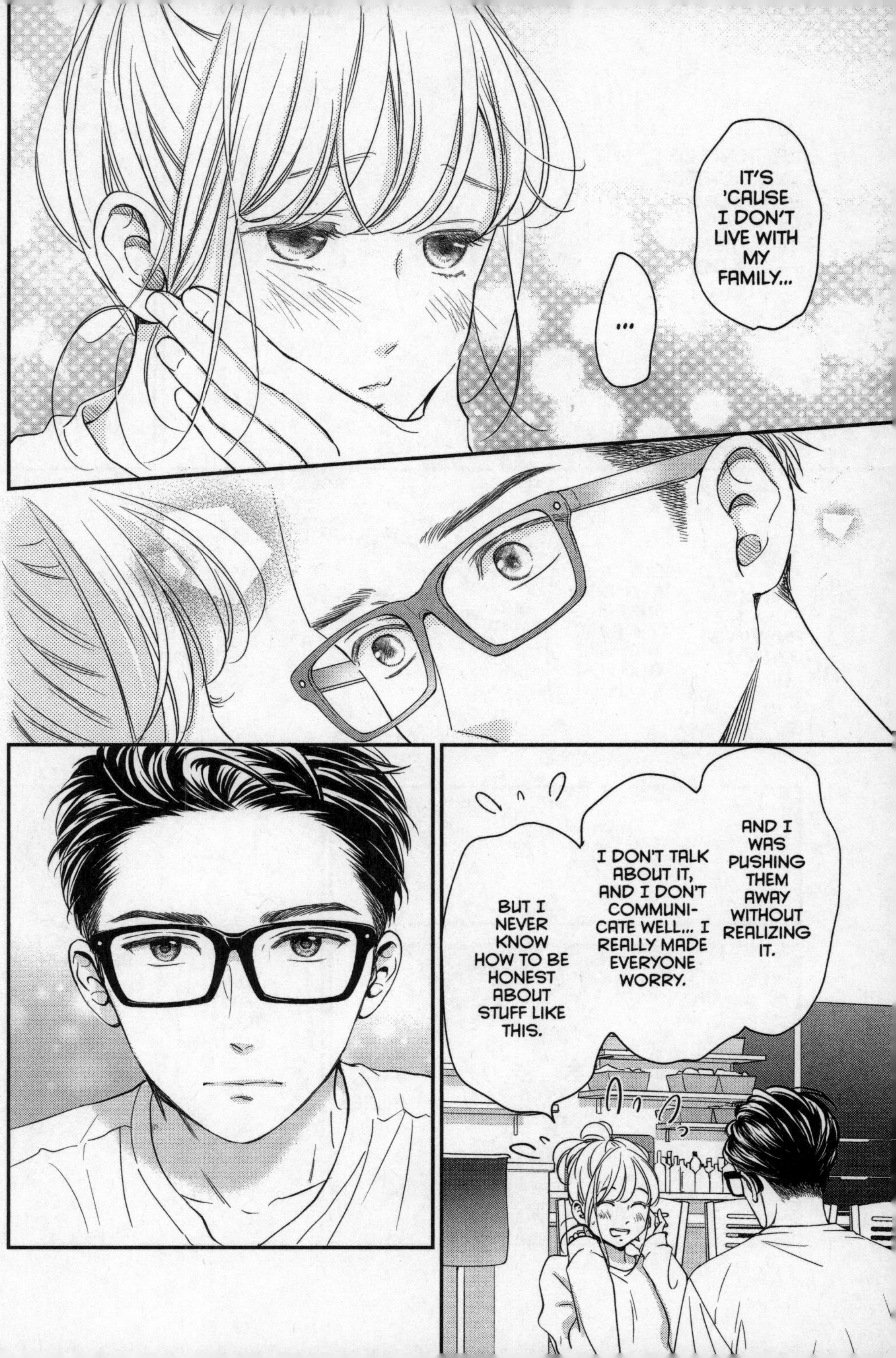
IT'S 'CAUSE I DON'T LIVE WITH MY FAMILY...
...
AND I WAS PUSHING THEM AWAY WITHOUT REALIZING IT.
I DON'T TALK ABOUT IT, AND I DON'T COMMUNI-CATE WELL... I REALLY MADE EVERYONE WORRY.
BUT I NEVER KNOW HOW TO BE HONEST ABOUT STUFF LIKE THIS.

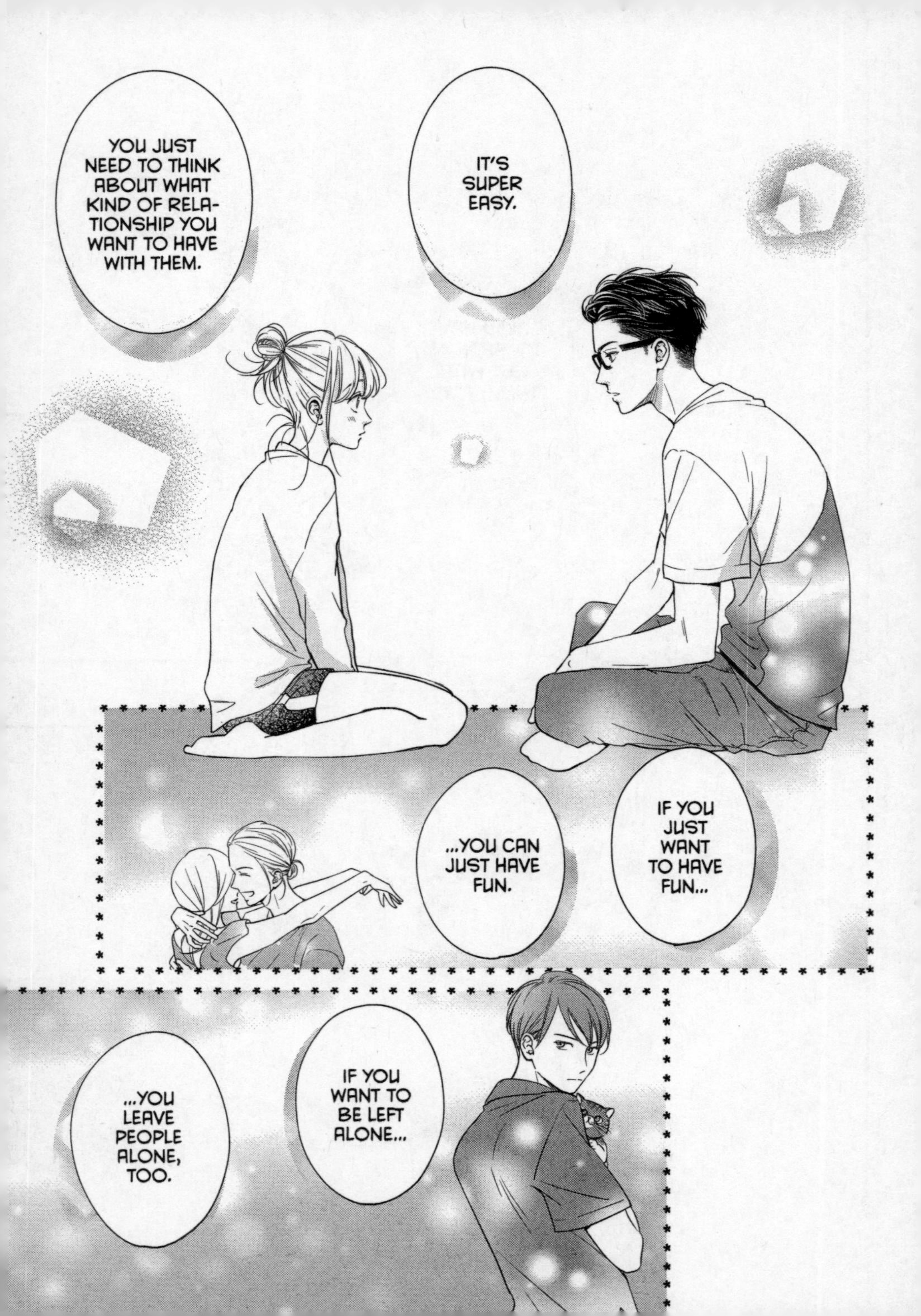
IT'S SUPER EASY.
YOU JUST NEED TO THINK ABOUT WHAT KIND OF RELA-TIONSHIP YOU WANT TO HAVE WITH THEM.
IF YOU JUST WANT TO HAVE FUN...
...YOU CAN JUST HAVE FUN.
IF YOU WANT TO BE LEFT ALONE...
...YOU LEAVE PEOPLE ALONE, TOO.

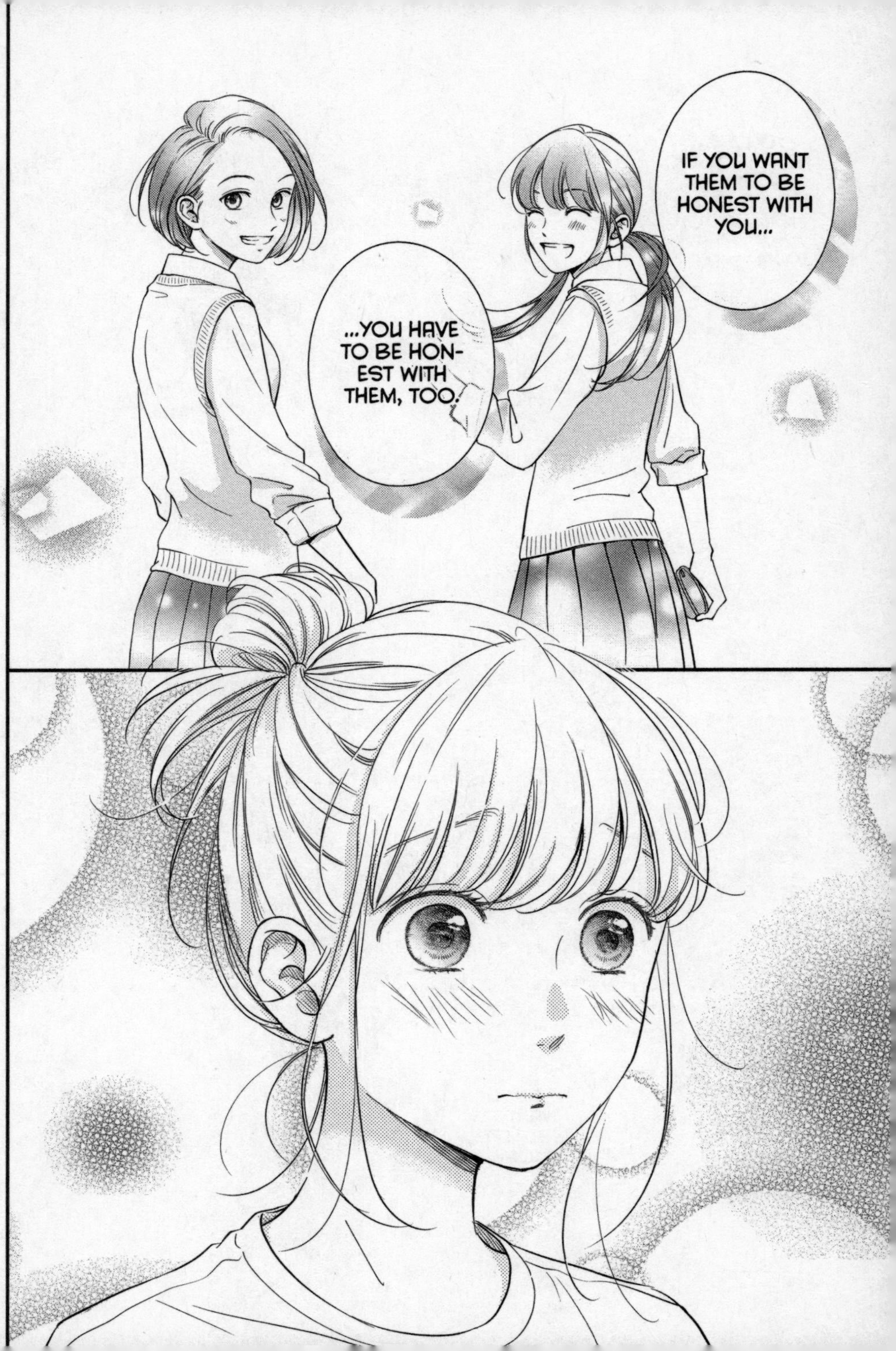
IF YOU WANT THEM TO BE HONEST WITH YOU...
...YOU HAVE TO BE HON-EST WITH THEM, TOO.

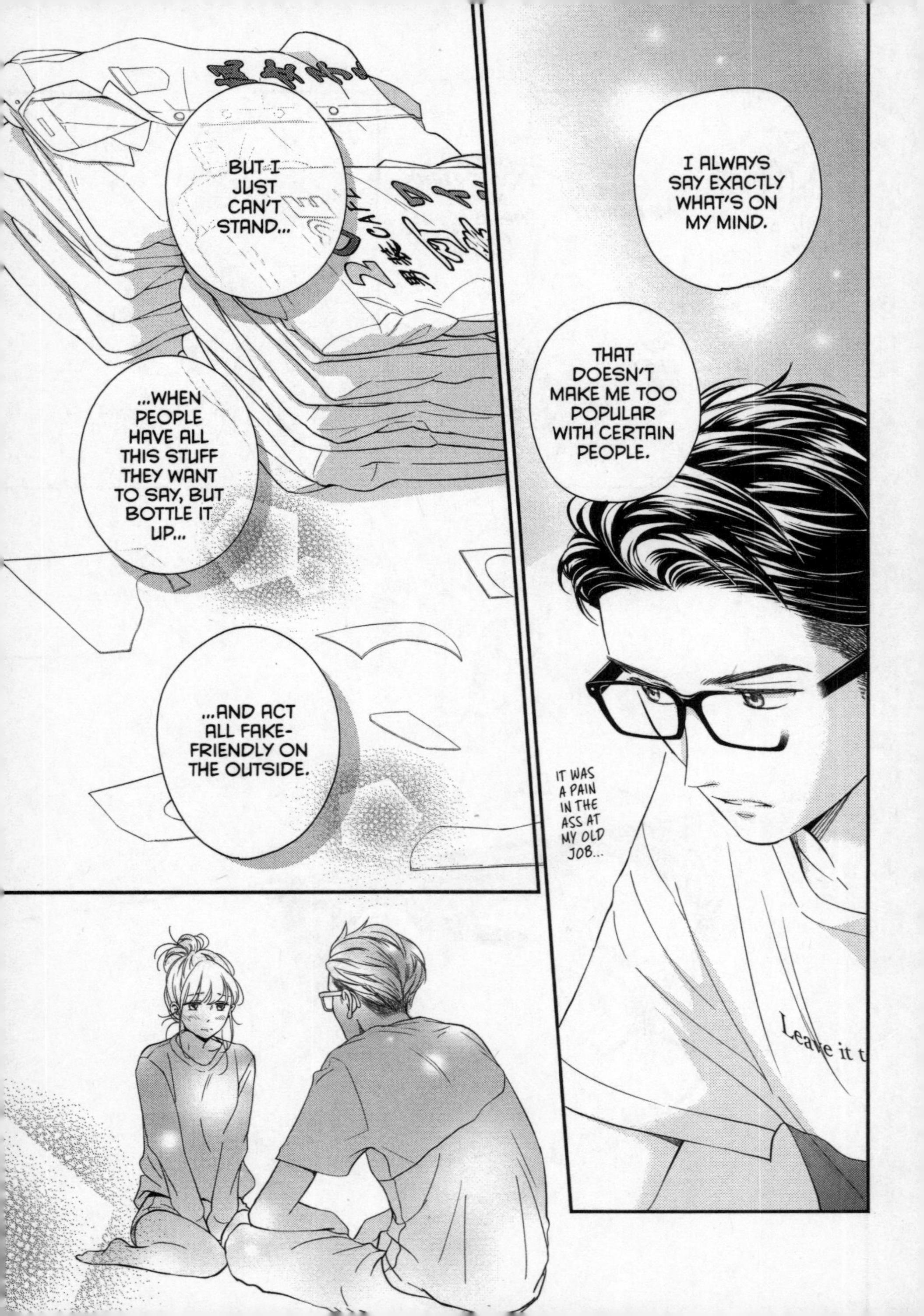
I ALWAYS SAY EXACTLY WHAT'S ON MY MIND.
THAT DOESN'T MAKE ME TOO POPULAR WITH CERTAIN PEOPLE.
IT WAS A PAIN IN THE ASS AT MY OLD JOB...
Leave it t
BUT I JUST CAN'T STAND...
...WHEN PEOPLE HAVE ALL THIS STUFF THEY WANT TO SAY, BUT BOTTLE IT UP...
...AND ACT ALL FAKE-FRIENDLY ON THE OUTSIDE.

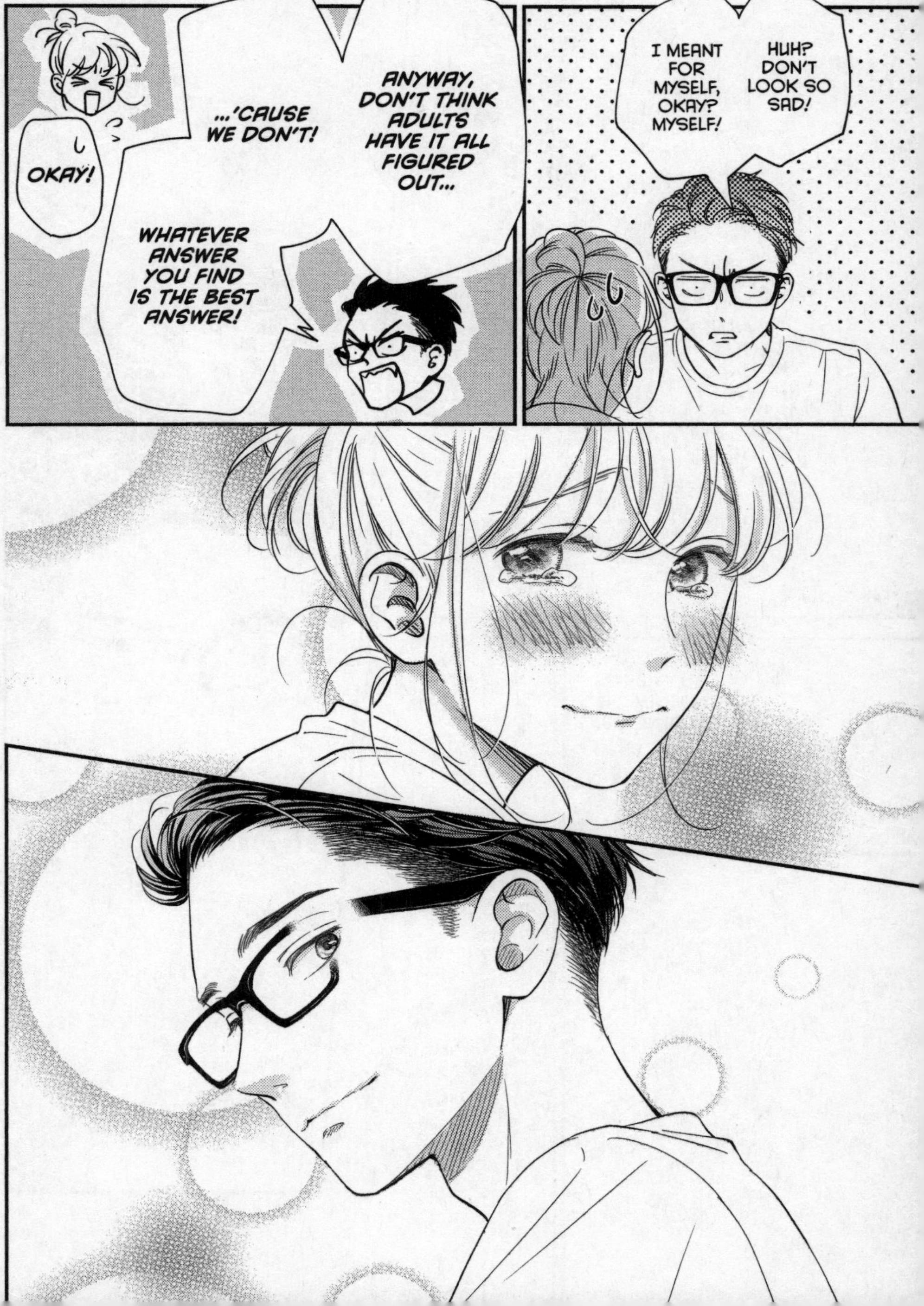
HUH? DON'T LOOK SO SAD!
I MEANT FOR MYSELF, OKAY? MYSELF!
ANYWAY, DON'T THINK ADULTS HAVE IT ALL FIGURED OUT...
...'CAUSE WE DON'T!
WHATEVER ANSWER YOU FIND IS THE BEST ANSWER!
OKAY!

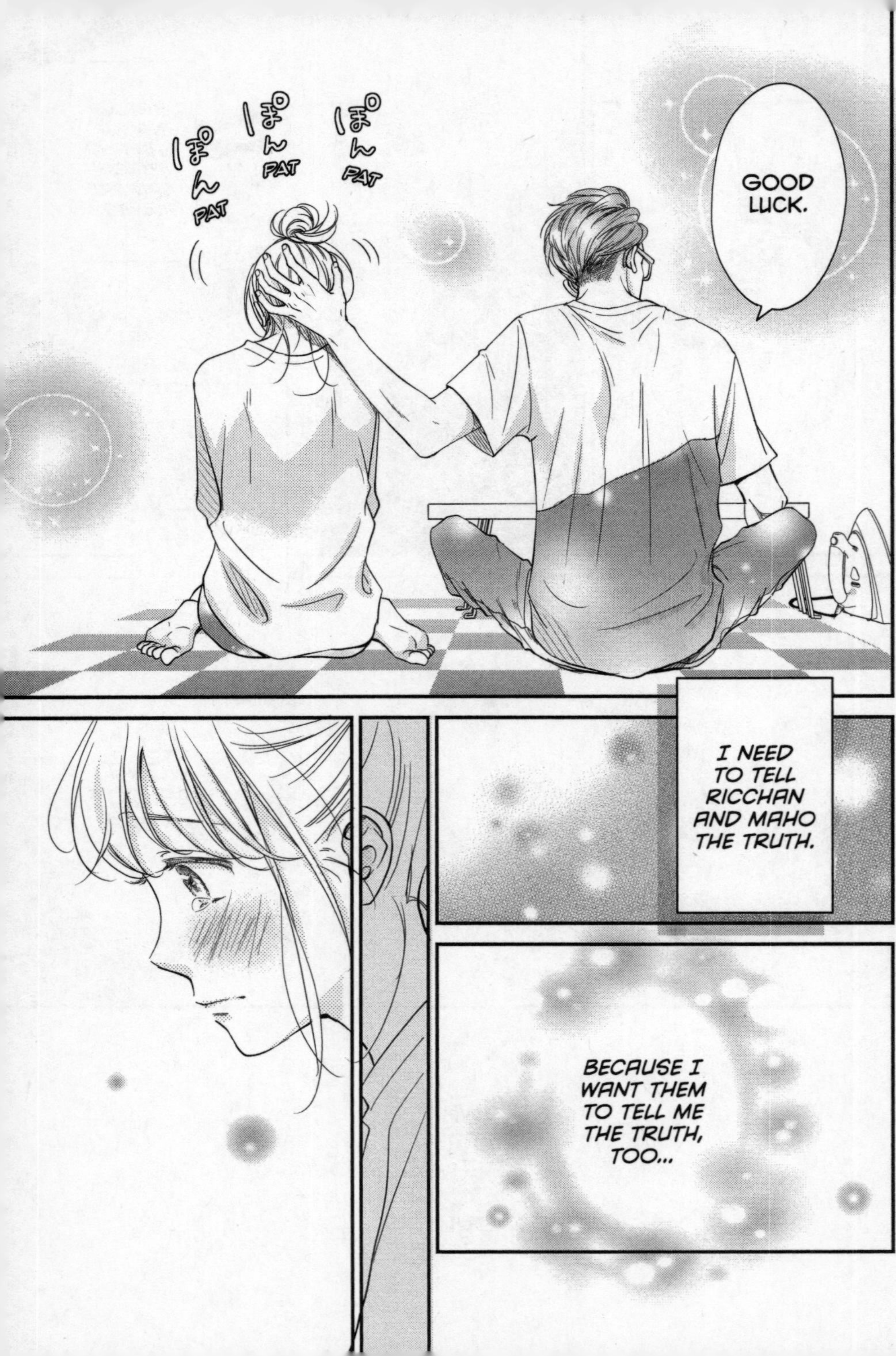
GOOD LUCK.
ぽん PAT
ぽん PAT
ぽん PAT
I NEED TO TELL RICCHAN AND MAHO THE TRUTH.
BECAUSE I WANT THEM TO TELL ME THE TRUTH, TOO...

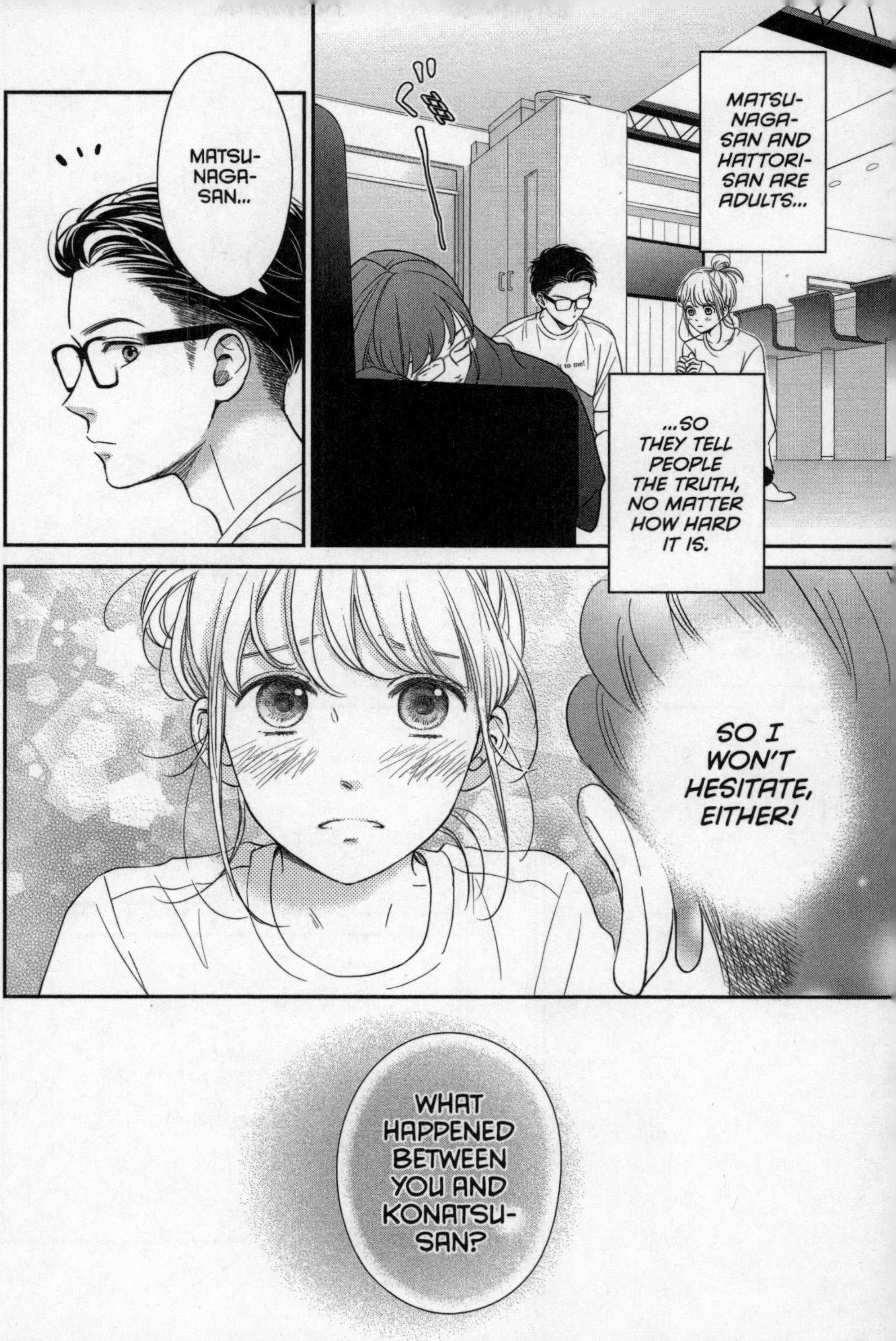
MATSU-NAGA-SAN AND HATTORI-SAN ARE ADULTS...
...SO THEY TELL PEOPLE THE TRUTH, NO MATTER HOW HARD IT IS.
MATSU-NAGA-SAN...
SO I WON'T HESITATE, EITHER!
WHAT HAPPENED BETWEEN YOU AND KONATSU-SAN?

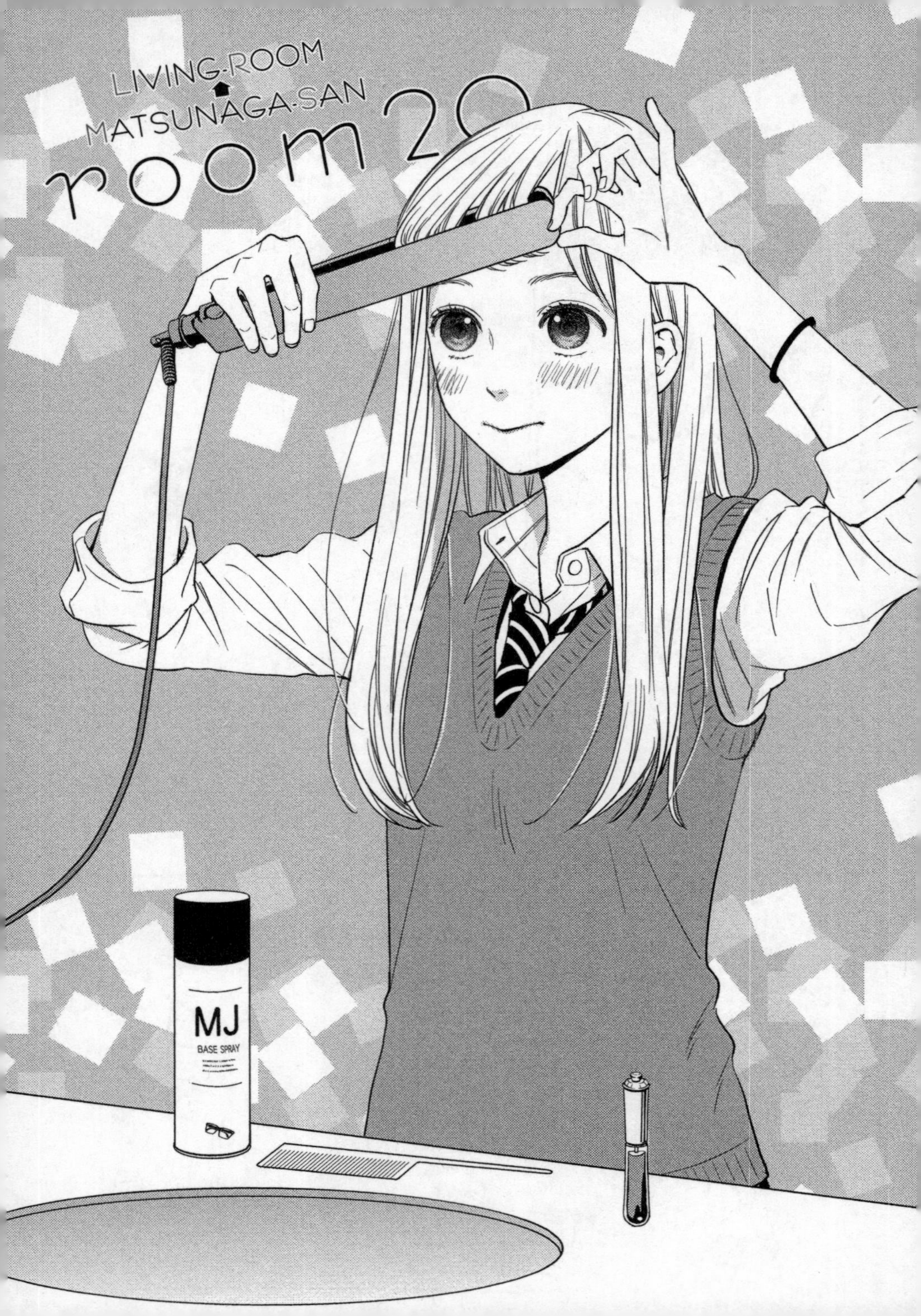
LIVING-ROOM
MATSUNAGA-SAN
room 20
MJ
BASE SPRAY

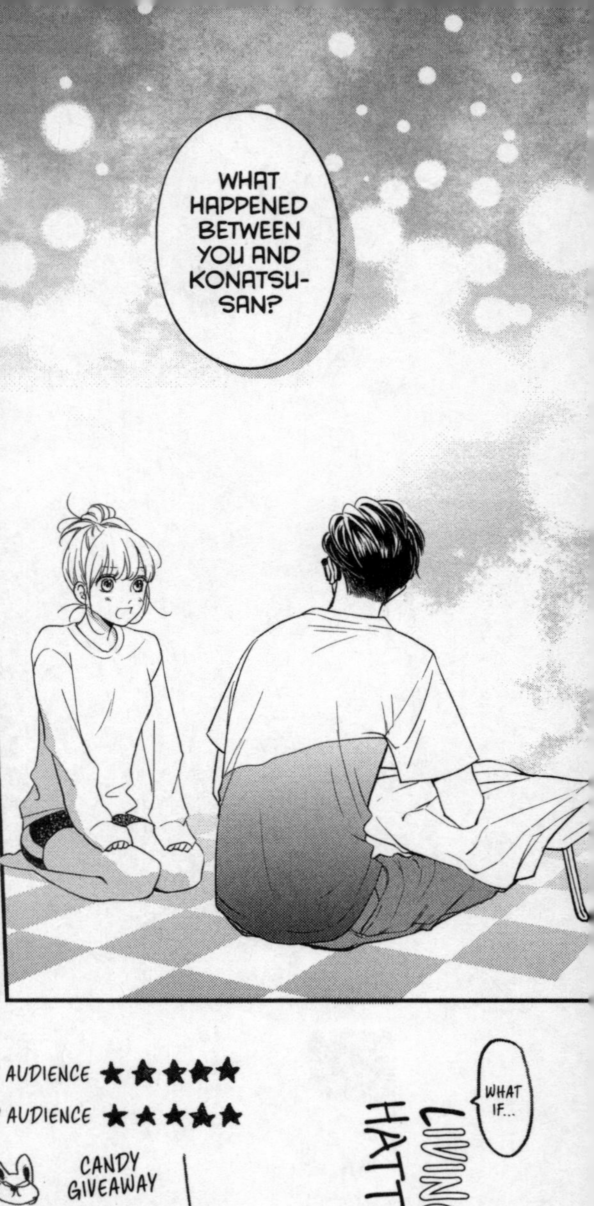
WHAT HAPPENED BETWEEN YOU AND KONATSU-SAN?

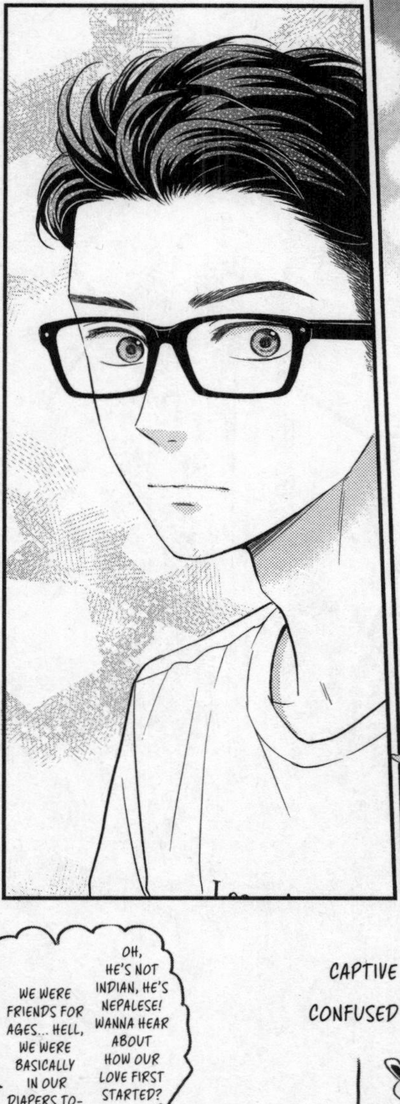

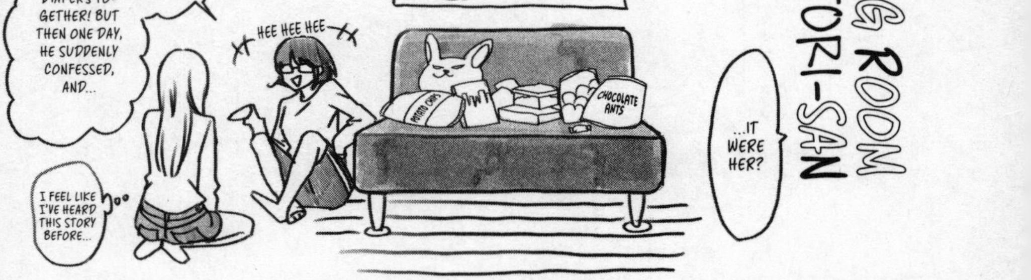
LIVING ROOM HATTORI-SAN
WHAT IF...
...IT WERE HER?
CAPTIVE AUDIENCE ★★★★★
CONFUSED AUDIENCE ★★★★★
CANDY GIVEAWAY
CHOCOLATE ANTS
HEE HEE HEE
OH, HE'S NOT INDIAN, HE'S NEPALESE! WANNA HEAR ABOUT HOW OUR LOVE FIRST STARTED?
WE WERE FRIENDS FOR AGES... HELL, WE WERE BASICALLY IN OUR DIAPERS TOGETHER! BUT THEN ONE DAY, HE SUDDENLY CONFESSED, AND...
I FEEL LIKE I'VE HEARD THIS STORY BEFORE...

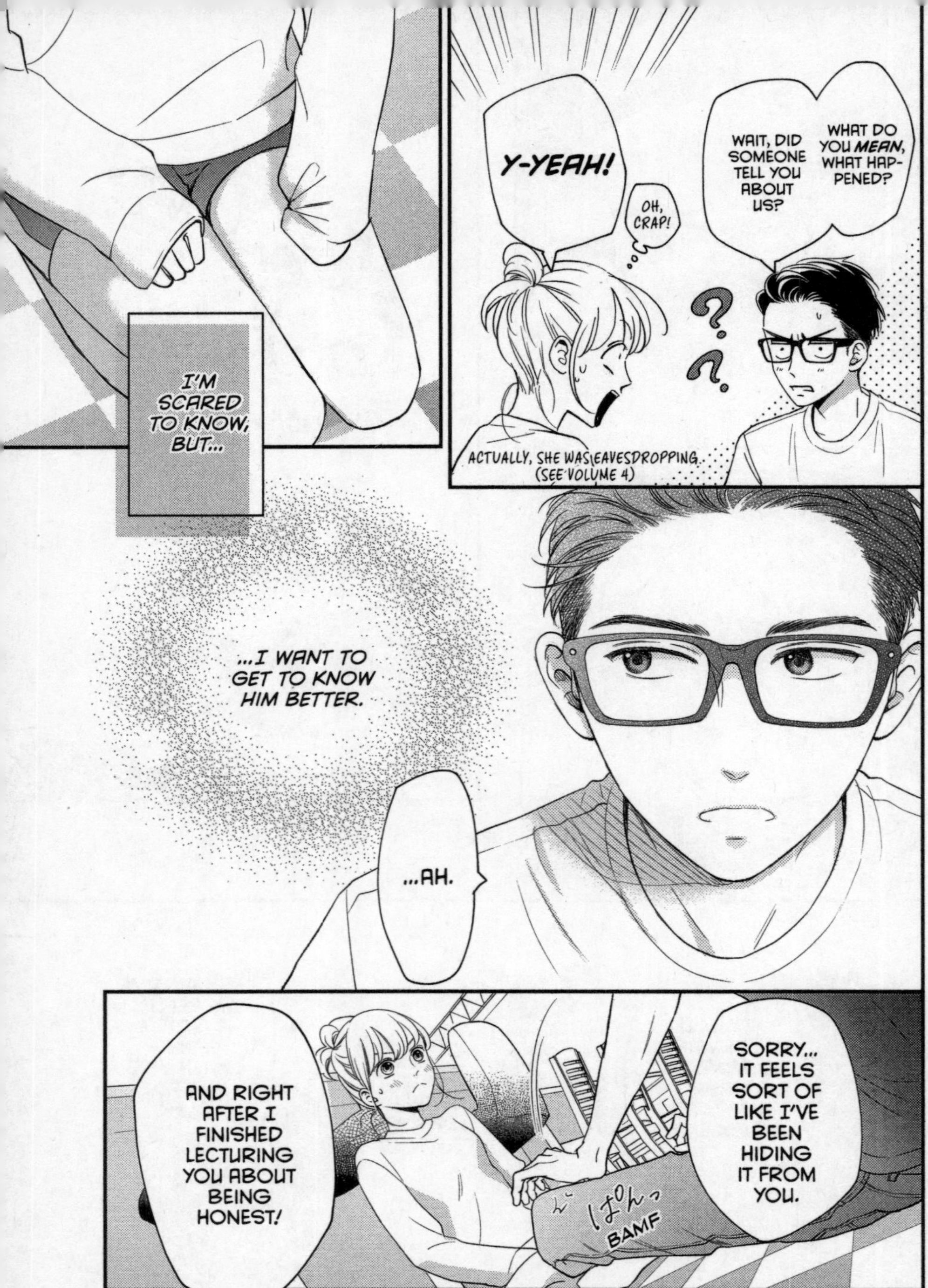
WHAT DO YOU *MEAN*, WHAT HAPPENED?
WAIT, DID SOMEONE TELL YOU ABOUT US?
Y-YEAH!
OH, CRAP!
ACTUALLY, SHE WAS EAVESDROPPING. (SEE VOLUME 4)
I'M SCARED TO KNOW, BUT...
...I WANT TO GET TO KNOW HIM BETTER.
...AH.
SORRY... IT FEELS SORT OF LIKE I'VE BEEN HIDING IT FROM YOU.
ぱんっ
BAMF
AND RIGHT AFTER I FINISHED LECTURING YOU ABOUT BEING HONEST!

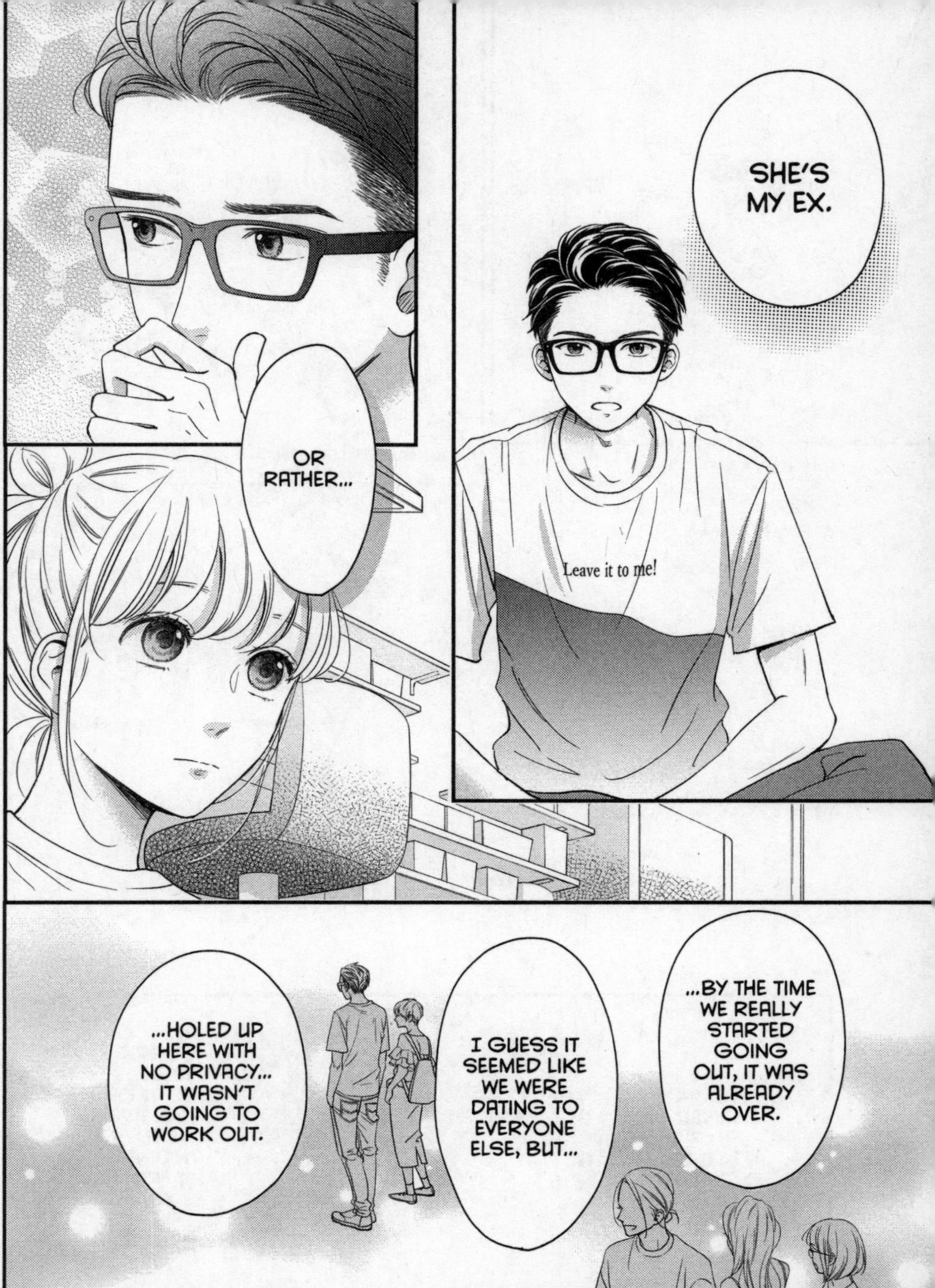
SHE'S MY EX.
Leave it to me!
OR RATHER...
...BY THE TIME WE REALLY STARTED GOING OUT, IT WAS ALREADY OVER.
I GUESS IT SEEMED LIKE WE WERE DATING TO EVERYONE ELSE, BUT...
...HOLED UP HERE WITH NO PRIVACY... IT WASN'T GOING TO WORK OUT.

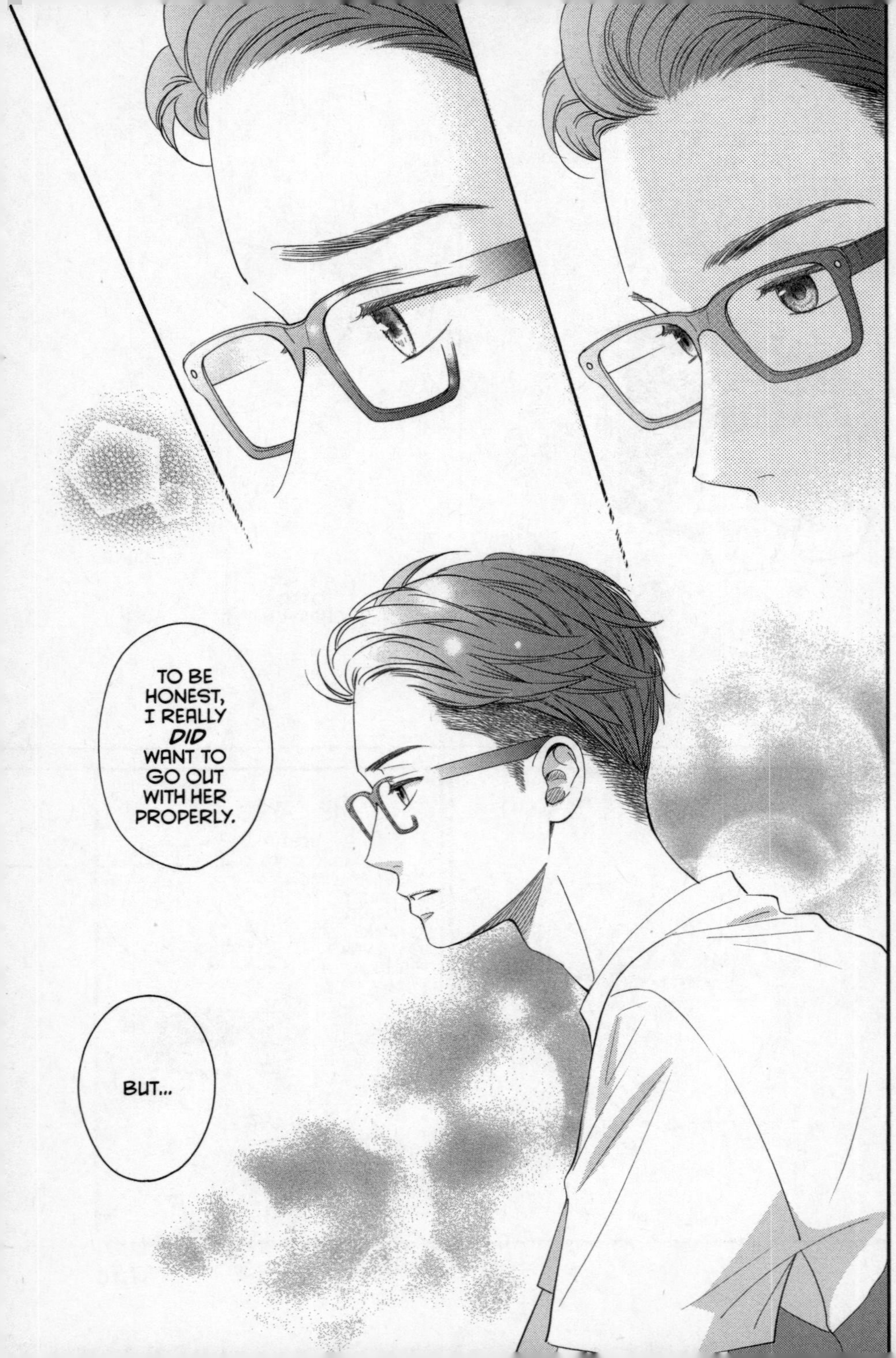
TO BE HONEST, I REALLY *DID* WANT TO GO OUT WITH HER PROPERLY.
BUT...

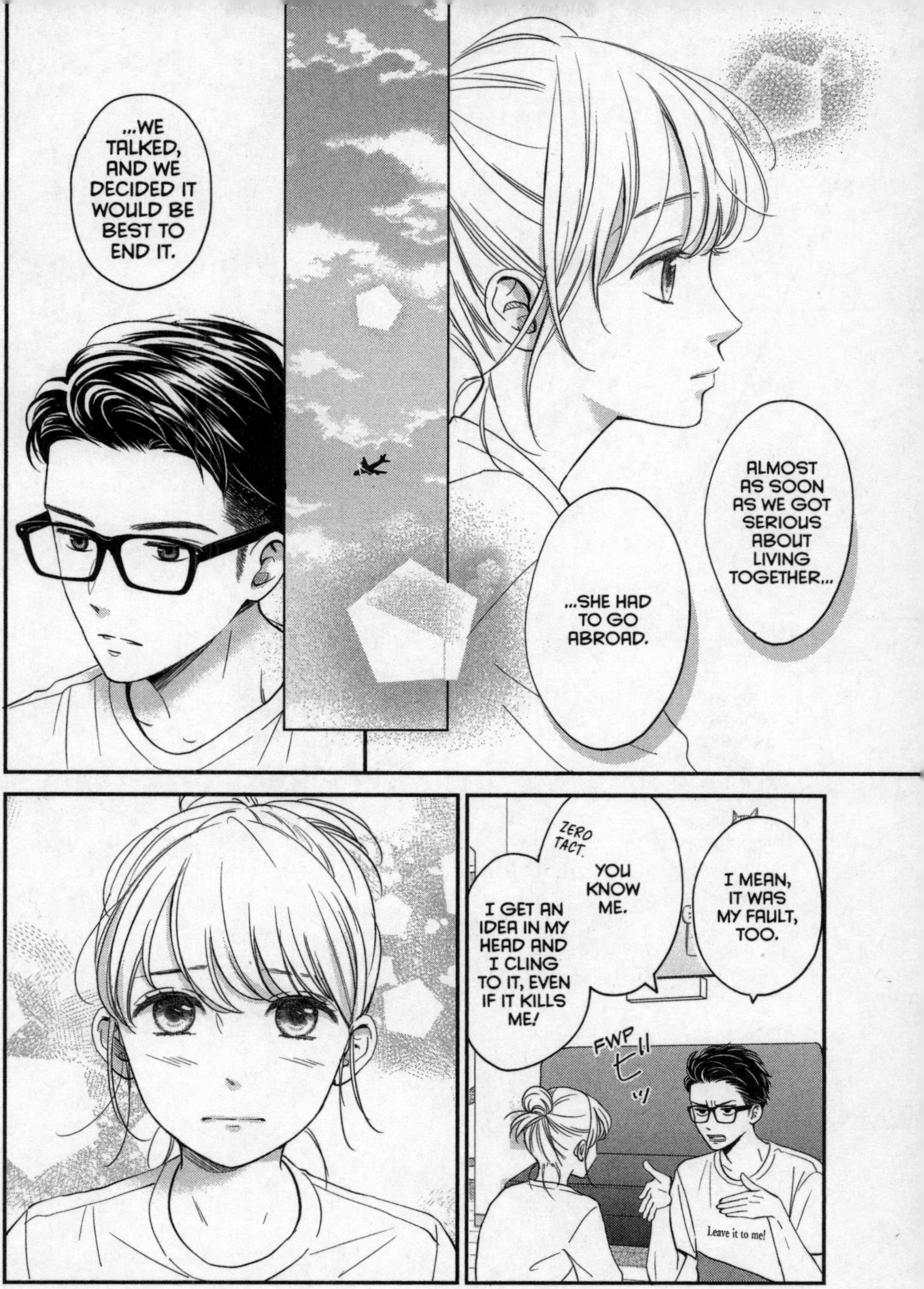
ALMOST AS SOON AS WE GOT SERIOUS ABOUT LIVING TOGETHER...
...SHE HAD TO GO ABROAD.
...WE TALKED, AND WE DECIDED IT WOULD BE BEST TO END IT.
I MEAN, IT WAS MY FAULT, TOO.
YOU KNOW ME.
ZERO TACT.
I GET AN IDEA IN MY HEAD AND I CLING TO IT, EVEN IF IT KILLS ME!
FWP
Leave it to me!

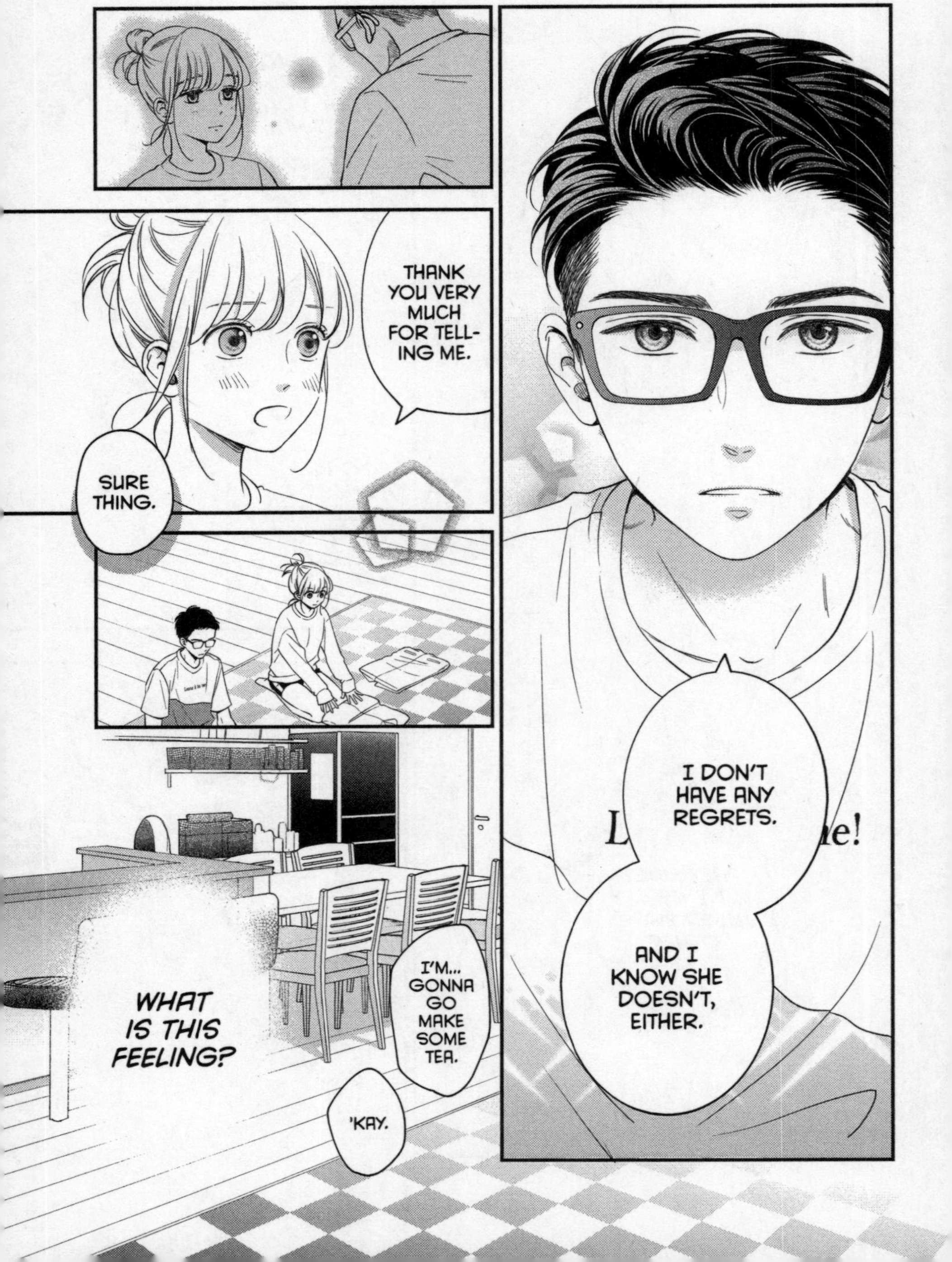
I DON'T HAVE ANY REGRETS.
AND I KNOW SHE DOESN'T, EITHER.
THANK YOU VERY MUCH FOR TELL-ING ME.
SURE THING.
I'M... GONNA GO MAKE SOME TEA.
'KAY.
WHAT IS THIS FEELING?

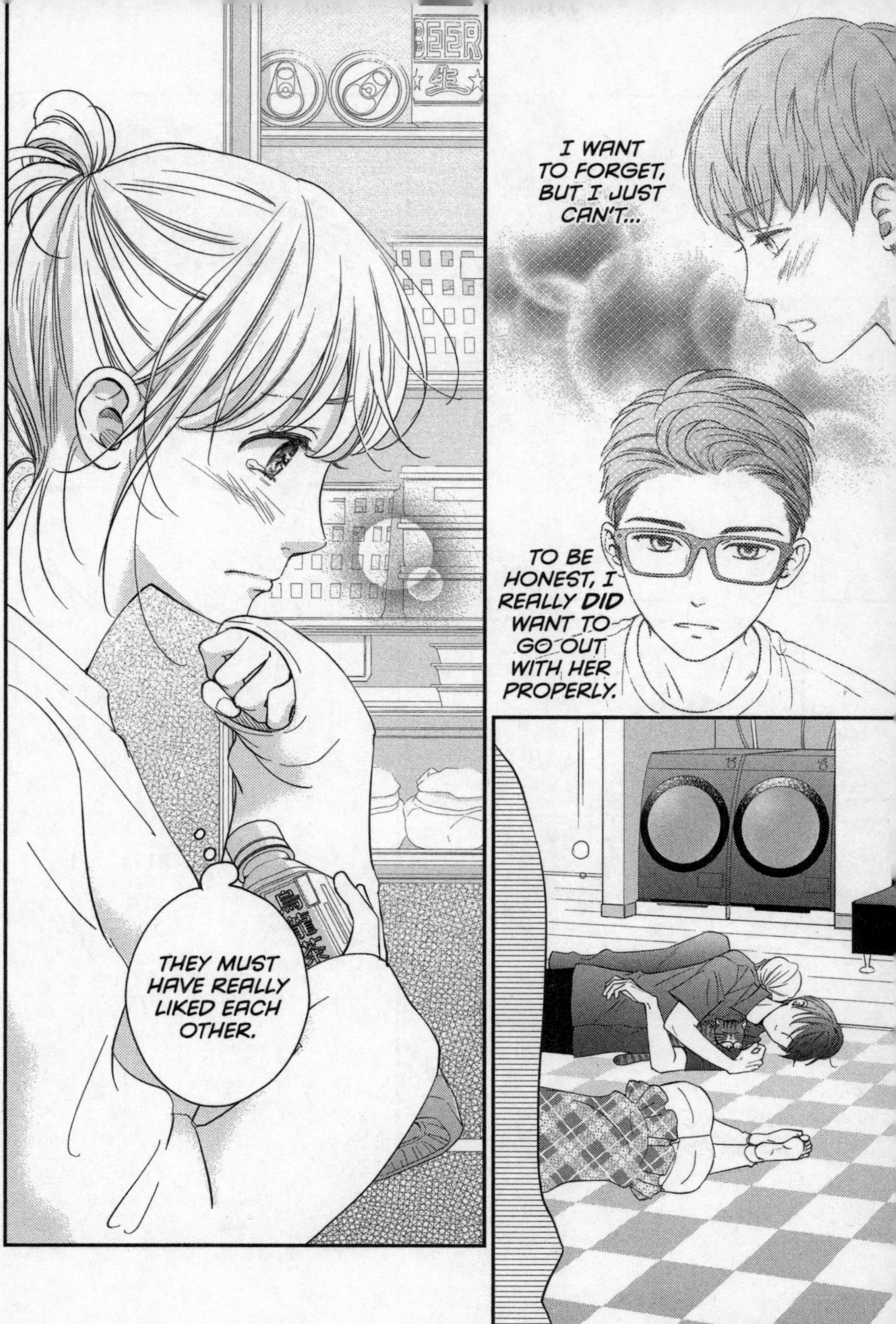
I WANT TO FORGET, BUT I JUST CAN'T...
TO BE HONEST, I REALLY **DID** WANT TO GO OUT WITH HER PROPERLY.
BEER
☆生☆
THEY MUST HAVE REALLY LIKED EACH OTHER.

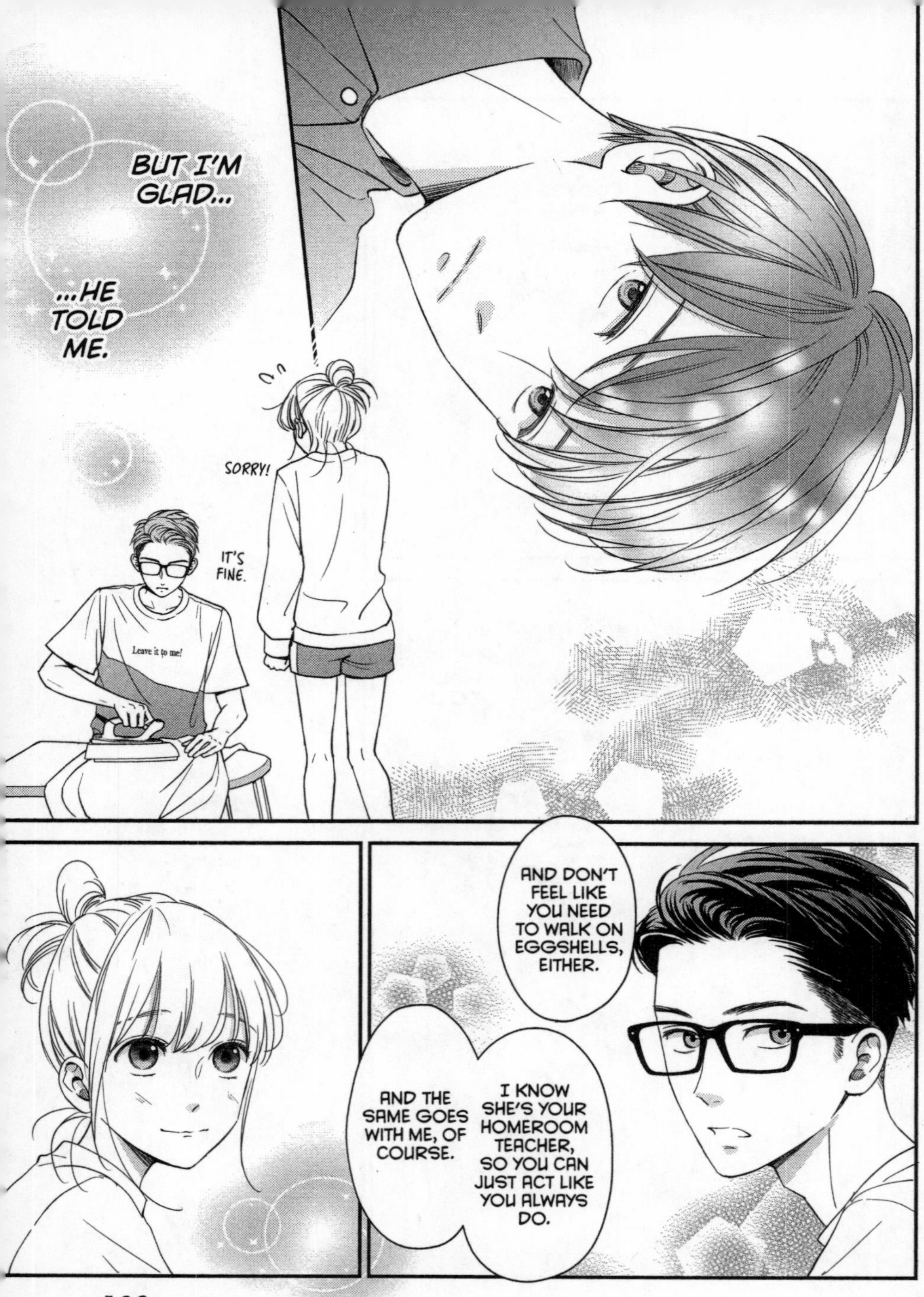
BUT I'M GLAD...
...HE TOLD ME.
SORRY!
IT'S FINE.
Leave it to me!
AND DON'T FEEL LIKE YOU NEED TO WALK ON EGGSHELLS, EITHER.
I KNOW SHE'S YOUR HOMEROOM TEACHER, SO YOU CAN JUST ACT LIKE YOU ALWAYS DO.
AND THE SAME GOES WITH ME, OF COURSE.

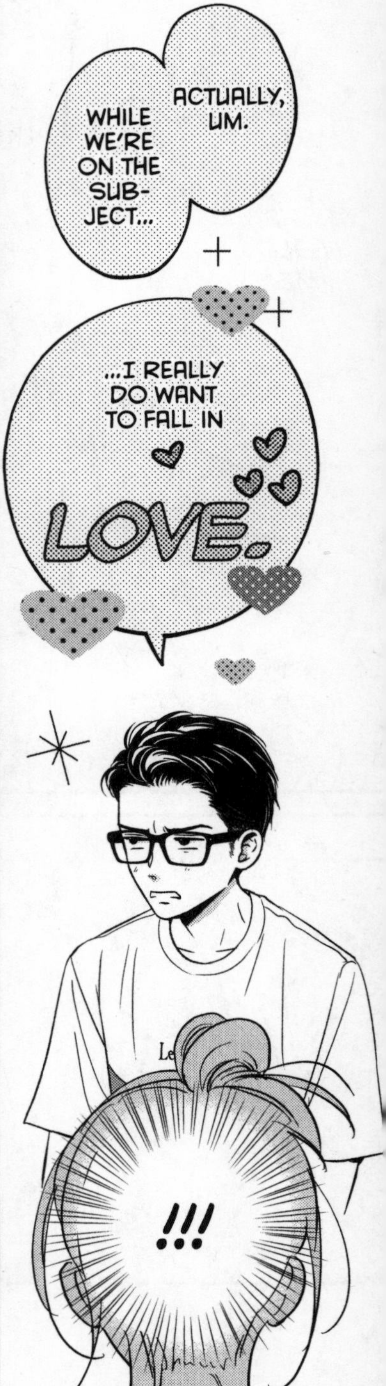
ACTUALLY, UM.
WHILE WE'RE ON THE SUBJECT...
...I REALLY DO WANT TO FALL IN LOVE.
Le
!!!

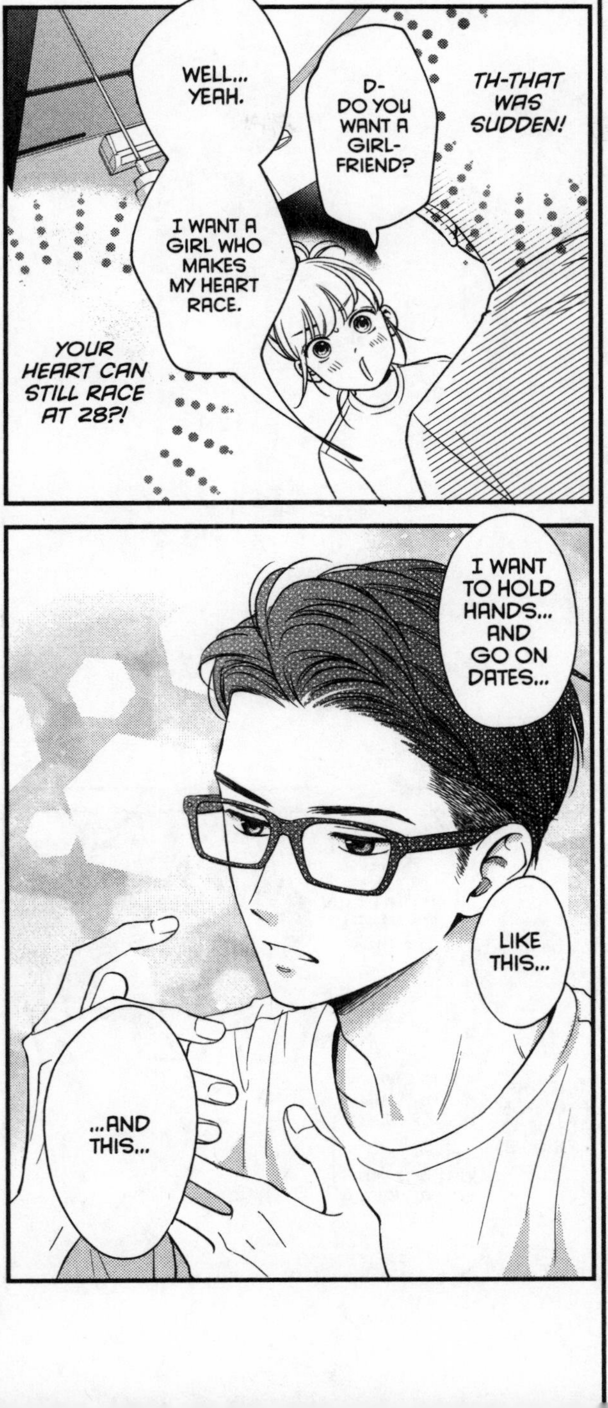
TH-THAT WAS SUDDEN!
D- DO YOU WANT A GIRL-FRIEND?
WELL... YEAH.
I WANT A GIRL WHO MAKES MY HEART RACE.
YOUR HEART CAN STILL RACE AT 28?!
I WANT TO HOLD HANDS... AND GO ON DATES...
LIKE THIS...
...AND THIS...

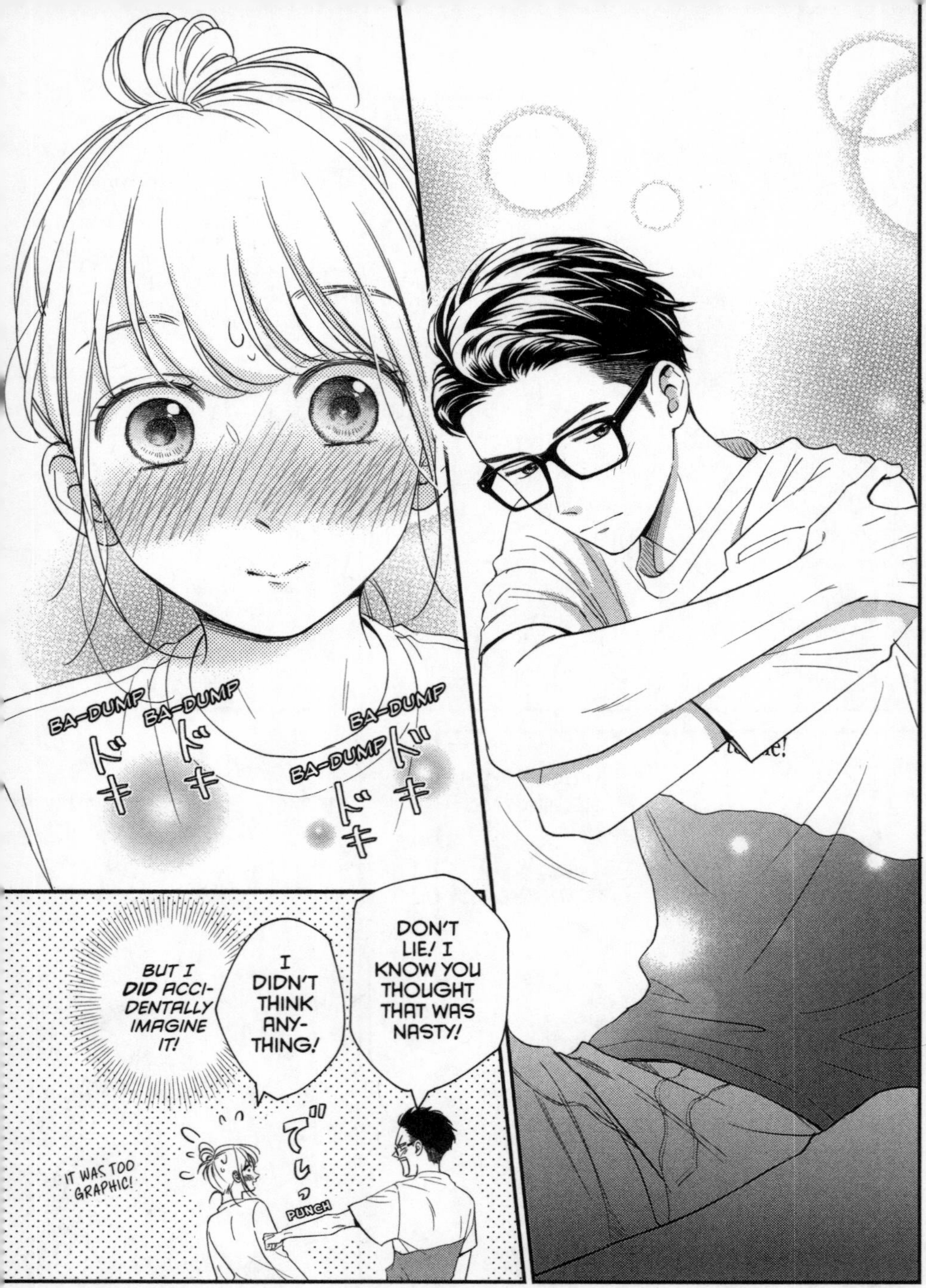
BA-DUMP
BA-DUMP
BA-DUMP
BA-DUMP
ドキ
ドキ
ドキ
ドキ
DON'T LIE! I KNOW YOU THOUGHT THAT WAS NASTY!
I DIDN'T THINK ANY-THING!
BUT I DID ACCI-DENTALLY IMAGINE IT!
PUNCH
IT WAS TOO GRAPHIC!

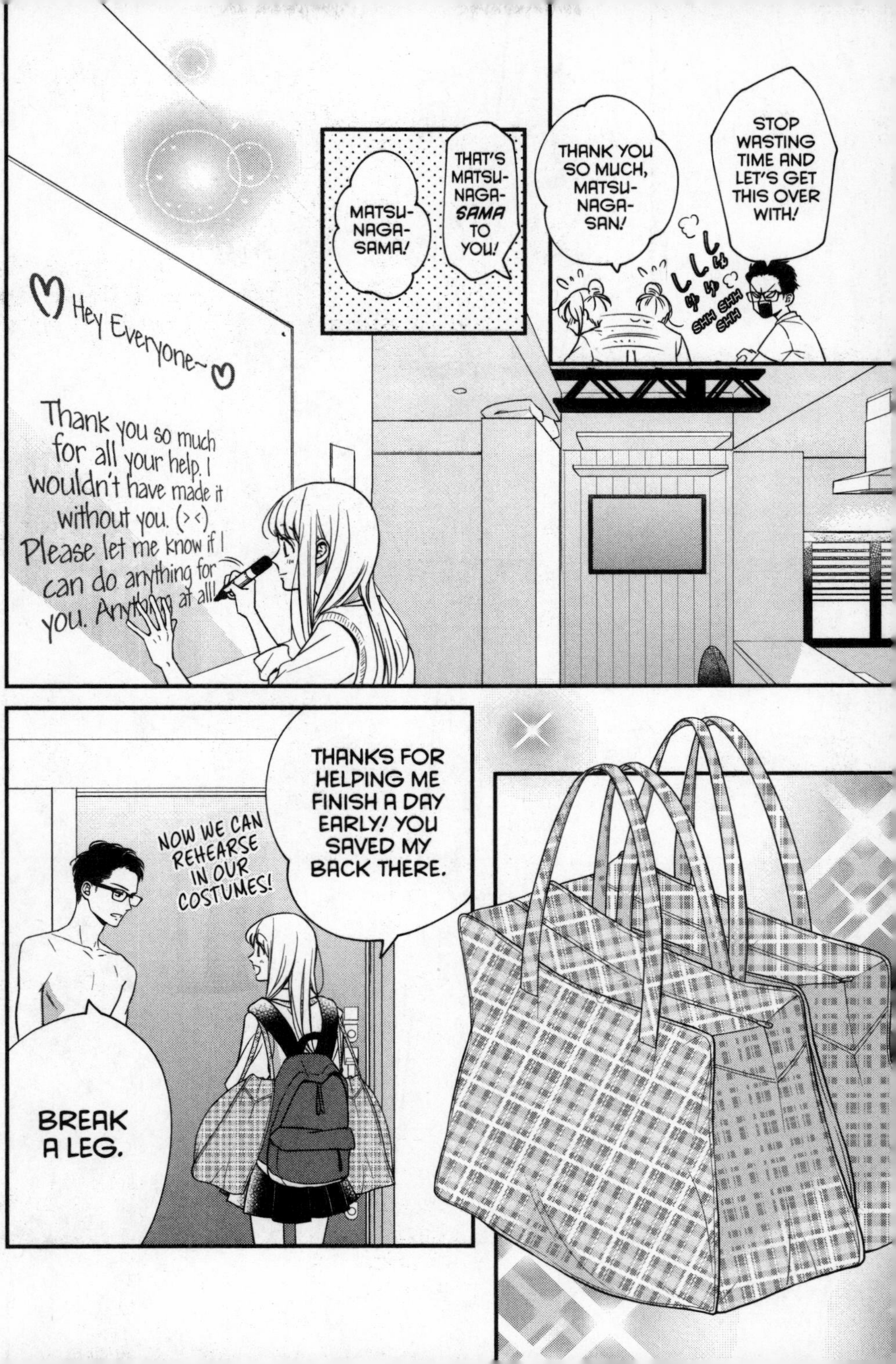
STOP WASTING TIME AND LET'S GET THIS OVER WITH!
THANK YOU SO MUCH, MATSU-NAGA-SAN!
しゅ しゅ しゅ
SHH SHH SHH
THAT'S MATSU-NAGA-SAMA TO YOU!
MATSU-NAGA-SAMA!
Hey Everyone~
Thank you so much for all your help. I wouldn't have made it without you. (><) Please let me know if I can do anything for you.
at all!
THANKS FOR HELPING ME FINISH A DAY EARLY! YOU SAVED MY BACK THERE.
NOW WE CAN REHEARSE IN OUR COSTUMES!
BREAK A LEG.

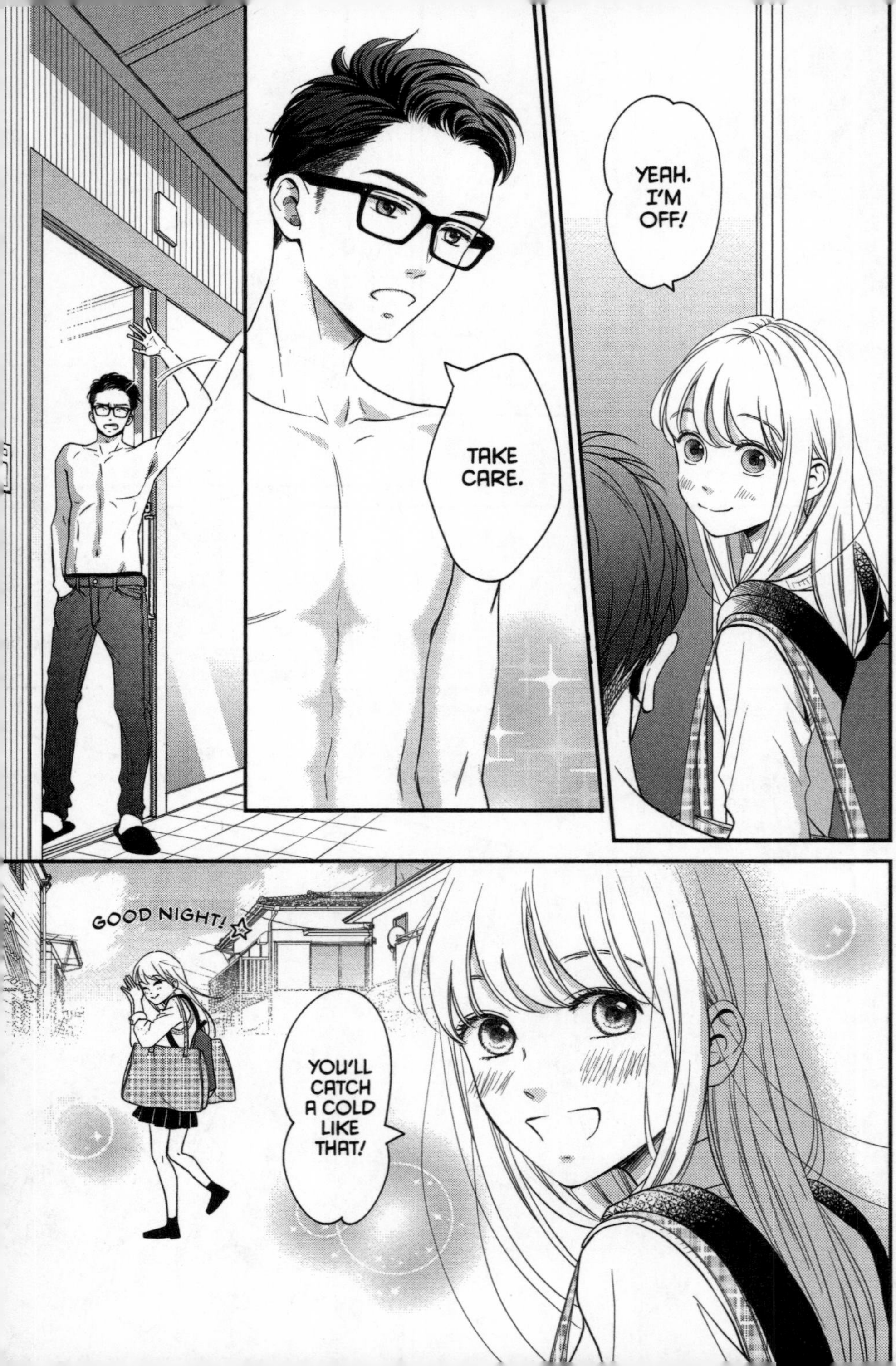

YEAH. I'M OFF!
TAKE CARE.
YOU'LL CATCH A COLD LIKE THAT!
GOOD NIGHT!

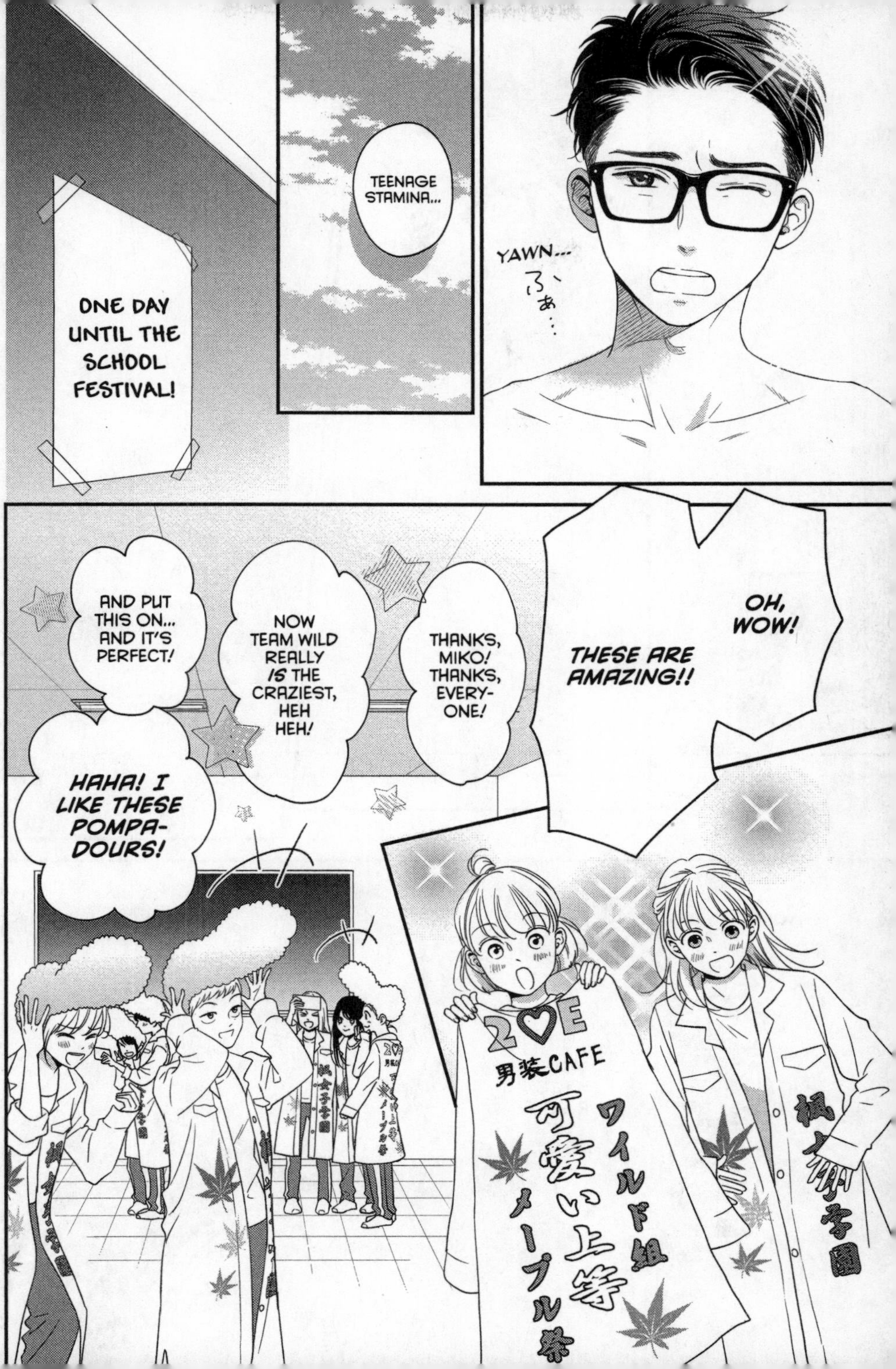
YAWN...
ふぁ...
TEENAGE STAMINA...
ONE DAY UNTIL THE SCHOOL FESTIVAL!
OH, WOW!
THESE ARE AMAZING!!
THANKS, MIKO! THANKS, EVERYONE!
NOW TEAM WILD REALLY *IS* THE CRAZIEST, HEH HEH!
AND PUT THIS ON... AND IT'S PERFECT!
HAHA! I LIKE THESE POMPADOURS!
2♡E
男装CAFE
ワイルド組
可愛い上等
メープル祭

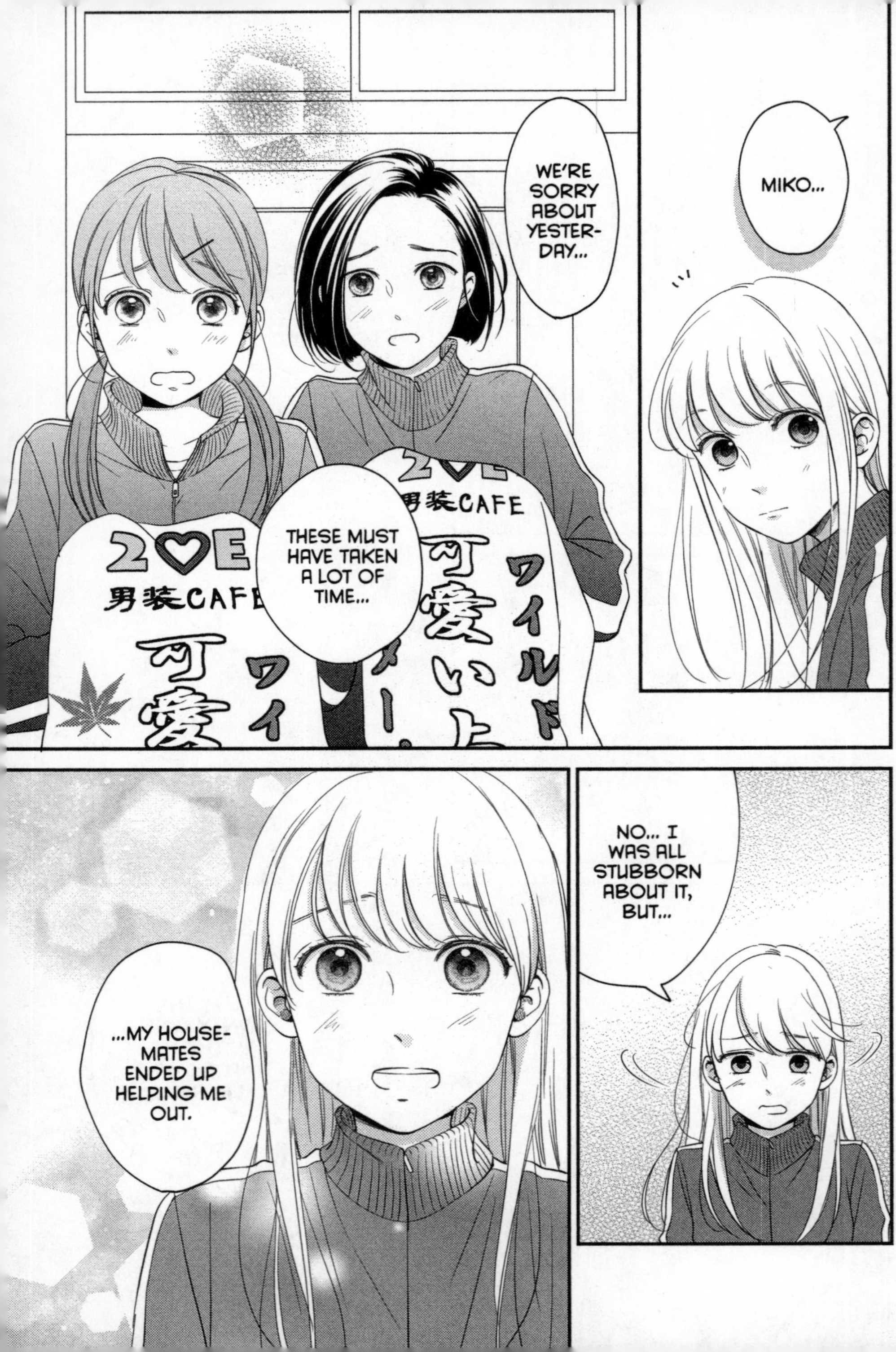
MIKO...
WE'RE SORRY ABOUT YESTER-DAY...
THESE MUST HAVE TAKEN A LOT OF TIME...
2♥E
男装CAFE
2♥E
男装CAFE
NO... I WAS ALL STUBBORN ABOUT IT, BUT...
...MY HOUSE-MATES ENDED UP HELPING ME OUT.

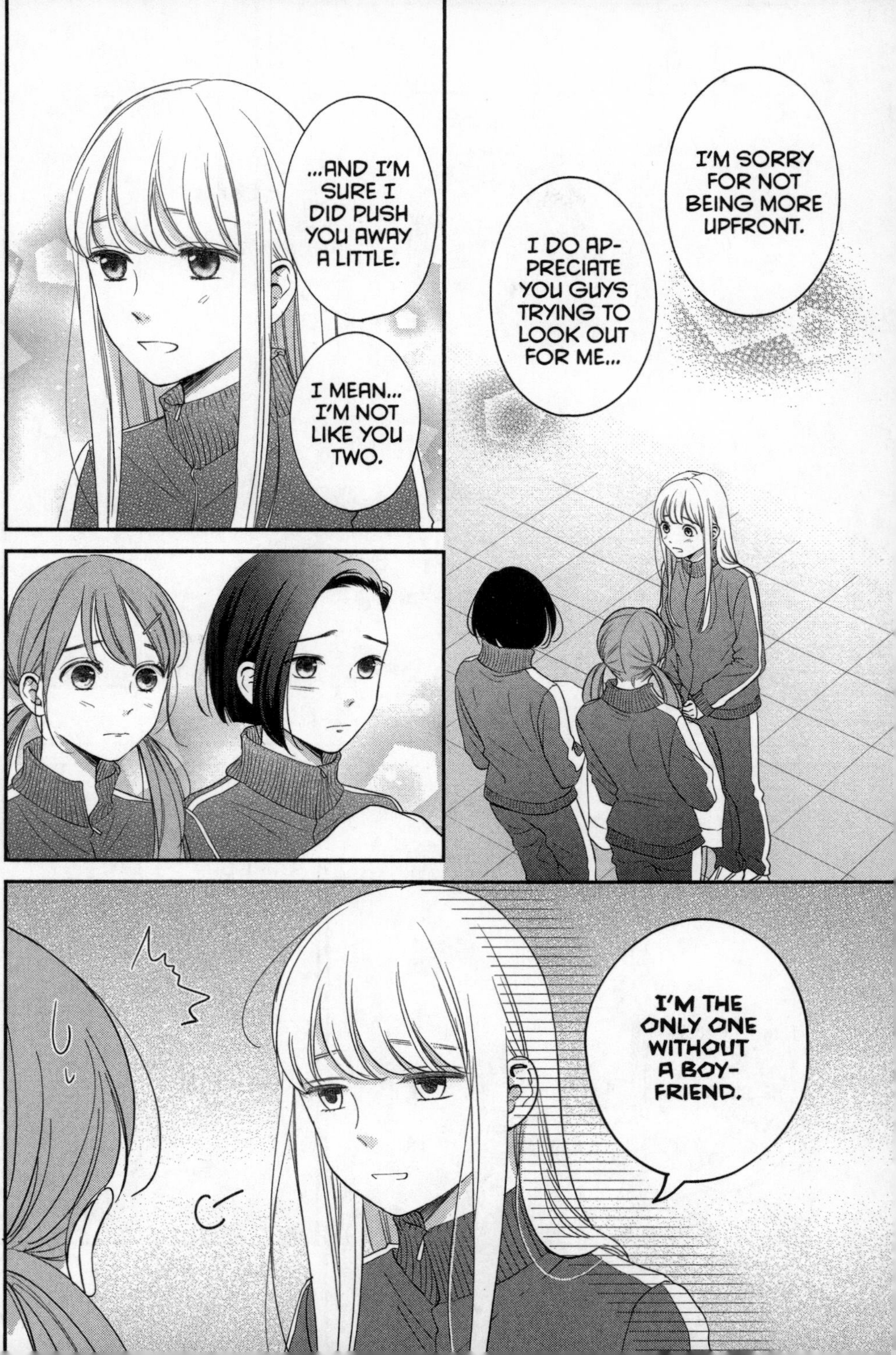
I'M SORRY FOR NOT BEING MORE UPFRONT.
I DO APPRECIATE YOU GUYS TRYING TO LOOK OUT FOR ME...
...AND I'M SURE I DID PUSH YOU AWAY A LITTLE.
I MEAN... I'M NOT LIKE YOU TWO.
I'M THE ONLY ONE WITHOUT A BOYFRIEND.

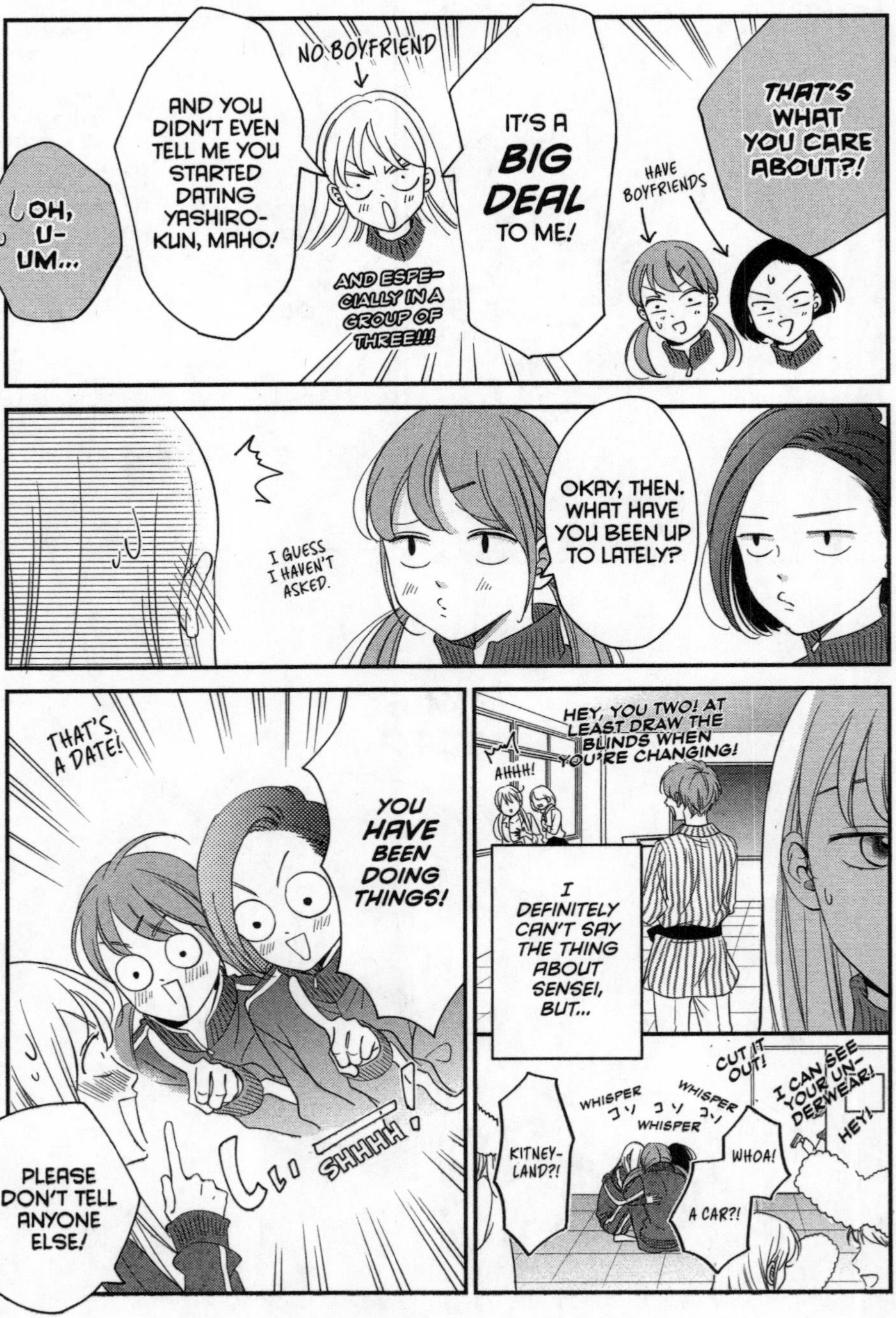
THAT'S WHAT YOU CARE ABOUT?!
HAVE BOYFRIENDS
IT'S A BIG DEAL TO ME!
NO BOYFRIEND
AND YOU DIDN'T EVEN TELL ME YOU STARTED DATING YASHIRO-KUN, MAHO!
AND ESPECIALLY IN A GROUP OF THREE!!!
OH, U-UM...
OKAY, THEN. WHAT HAVE YOU BEEN UP TO LATELY?
I GUESS I HAVEN'T ASKED.
HEY, YOU TWO! AT LEAST DRAW THE BLINDS WHEN YOU'RE CHANGING!
AHHH!
I DEFINITELY CAN'T SAY THE THING ABOUT SENSEI, BUT...
HEY!
I CAN SEE YOUR UNDERWEAR!
CUT IT OUT!
WHISPER
WHISPER
コソ コソ コソ
WHISPER
WHOA!
KITNEY-LAND?!
A CAR?!
YOU HAVE BEEN DOING THINGS!
THAT'S A DATE!
SHHHH!
PLEASE DON'T TELL ANYONE ELSE!

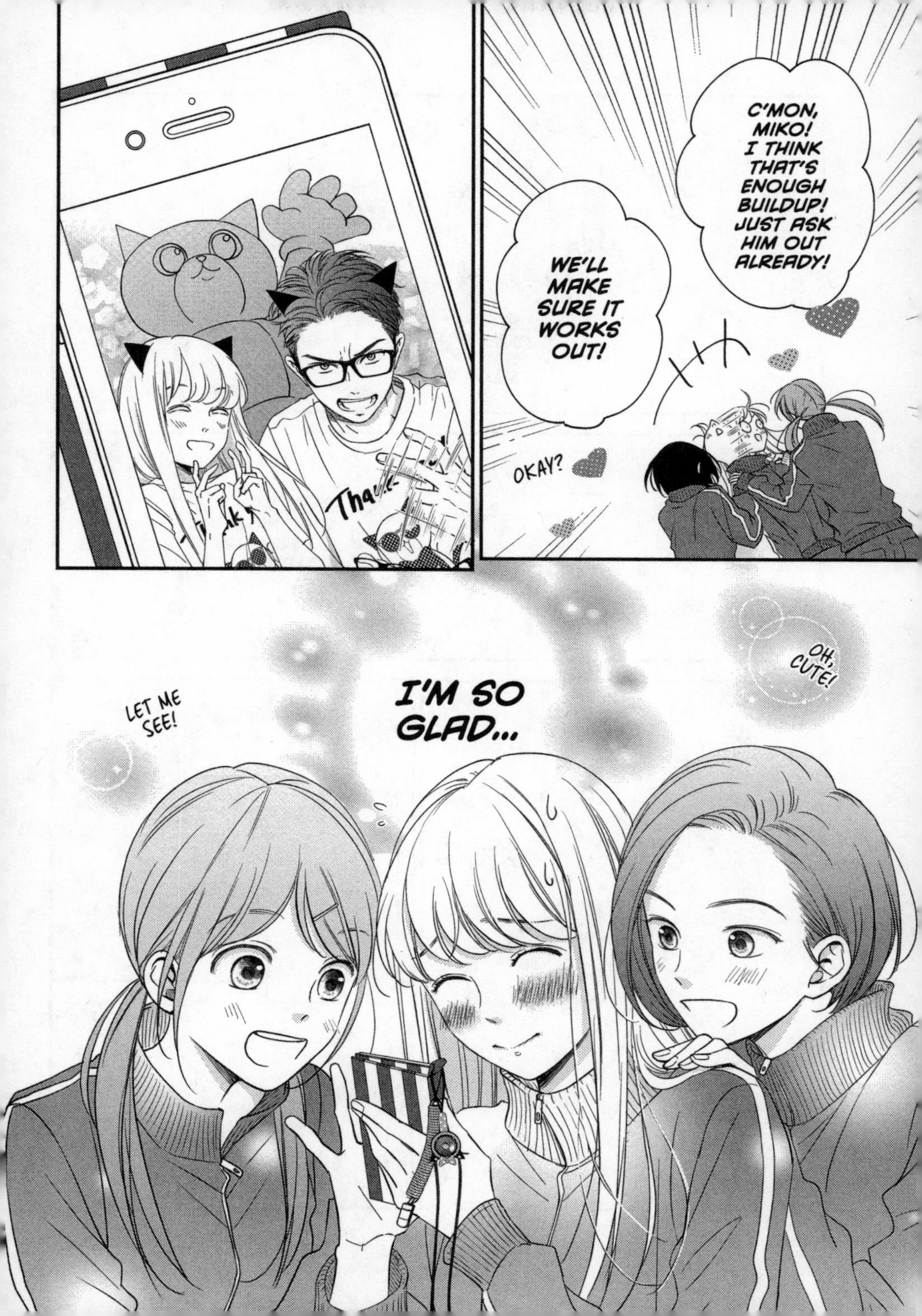
C'MON, MIKO! I THINK THAT'S ENOUGH BUILDUP! JUST ASK HIM OUT ALREADY!
WE'LL MAKE SURE IT WORKS OUT!
OKAY?
OH, CUTE!
I'M SO GLAD...
LET ME SEE!

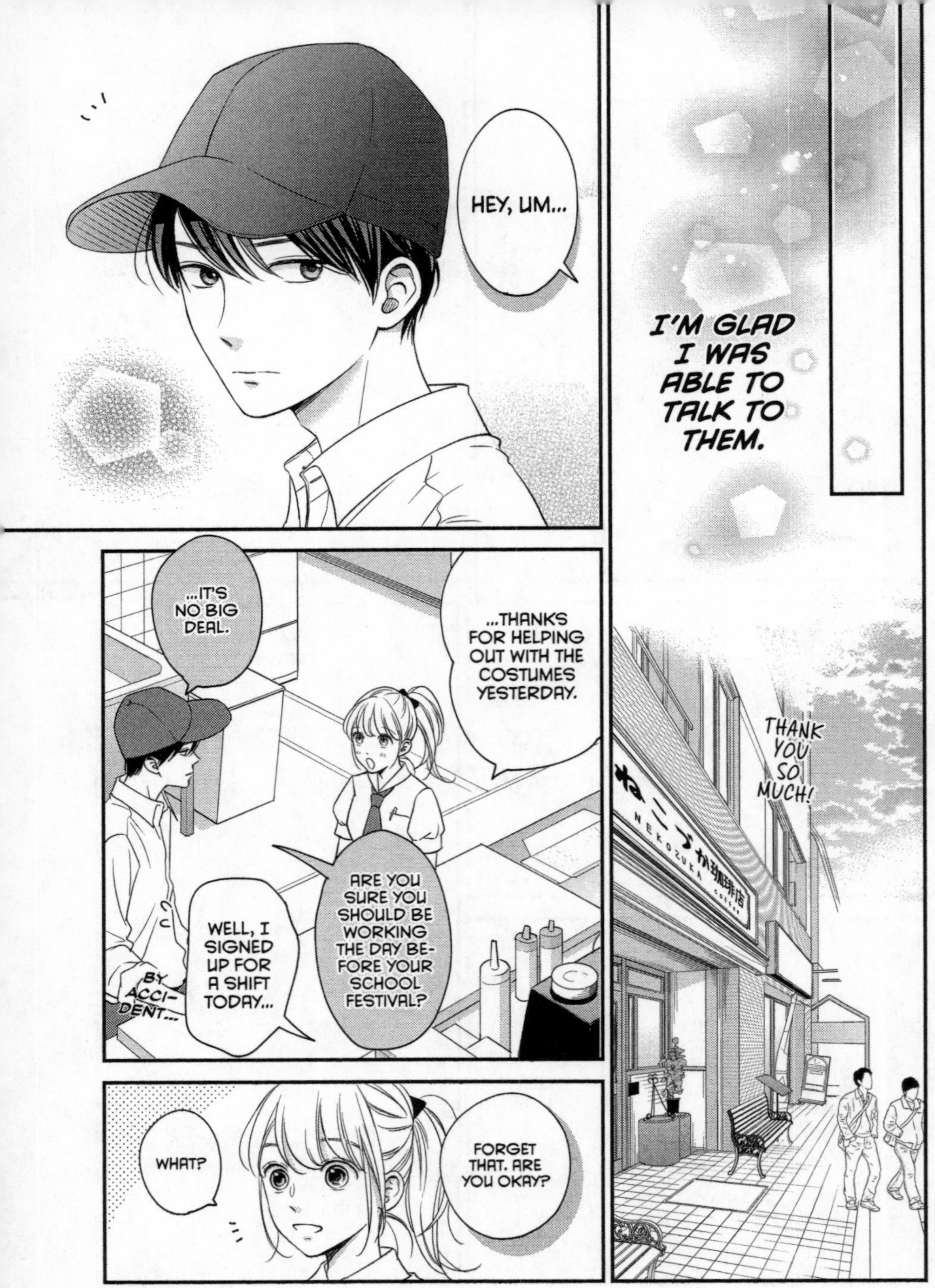
I'M GLAD I WAS ABLE TO TALK TO THEM.
HEY, UM...
THANK YOU SO MUCH!
NEKOZUKA COFFEE
...THANKS FOR HELPING OUT WITH THE COSTUMES YESTERDAY.
...IT'S NO BIG DEAL.
ARE YOU SURE YOU SHOULD BE WORKING THE DAY BE-FORE YOUR SCHOOL FESTIVAL?
WELL, I SIGNED UP FOR A SHIFT TODAY...
BY ACCI-DENT...
FORGET THAT. ARE YOU OKAY?
WHAT?

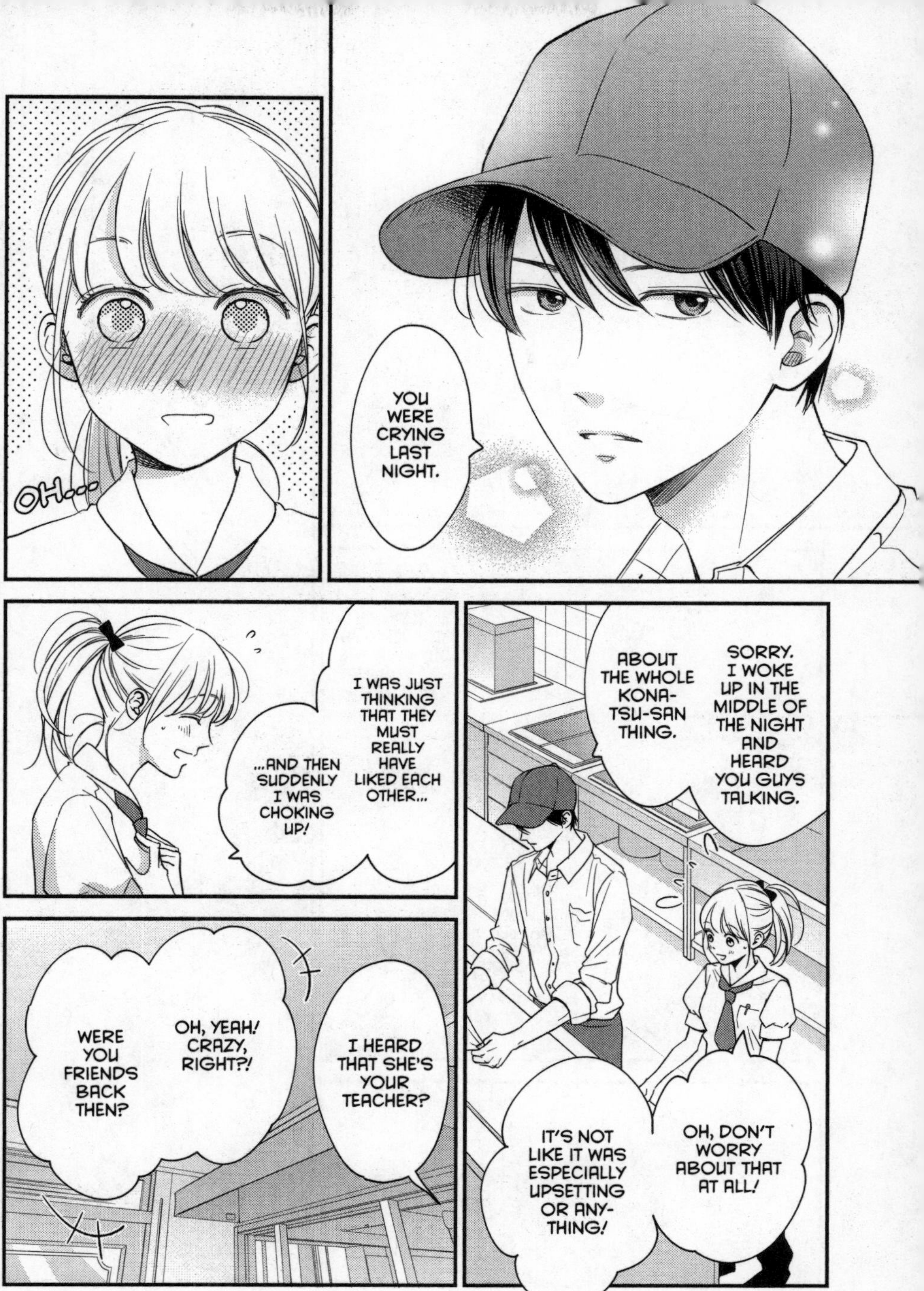
YOU WERE CRYING LAST NIGHT.
OH...
SORRY. I WOKE UP IN THE MIDDLE OF THE NIGHT AND HEARD YOU GUYS TALKING.
ABOUT THE WHOLE KONA-TSU-SAN THING.
OH, DON'T WORRY ABOUT THAT AT ALL!
IT'S NOT LIKE IT WAS ESPECIALLY UPSETTING OR ANY-THING!
I WAS JUST THINKING THAT THEY MUST REALLY HAVE LIKED EACH OTHER...
...AND THEN SUDDENLY I WAS CHOKING UP!
I HEARD THAT SHE'S YOUR TEACHER?
OH, YEAH! CRAZY, RIGHT?!
WERE YOU FRIENDS BACK THEN?

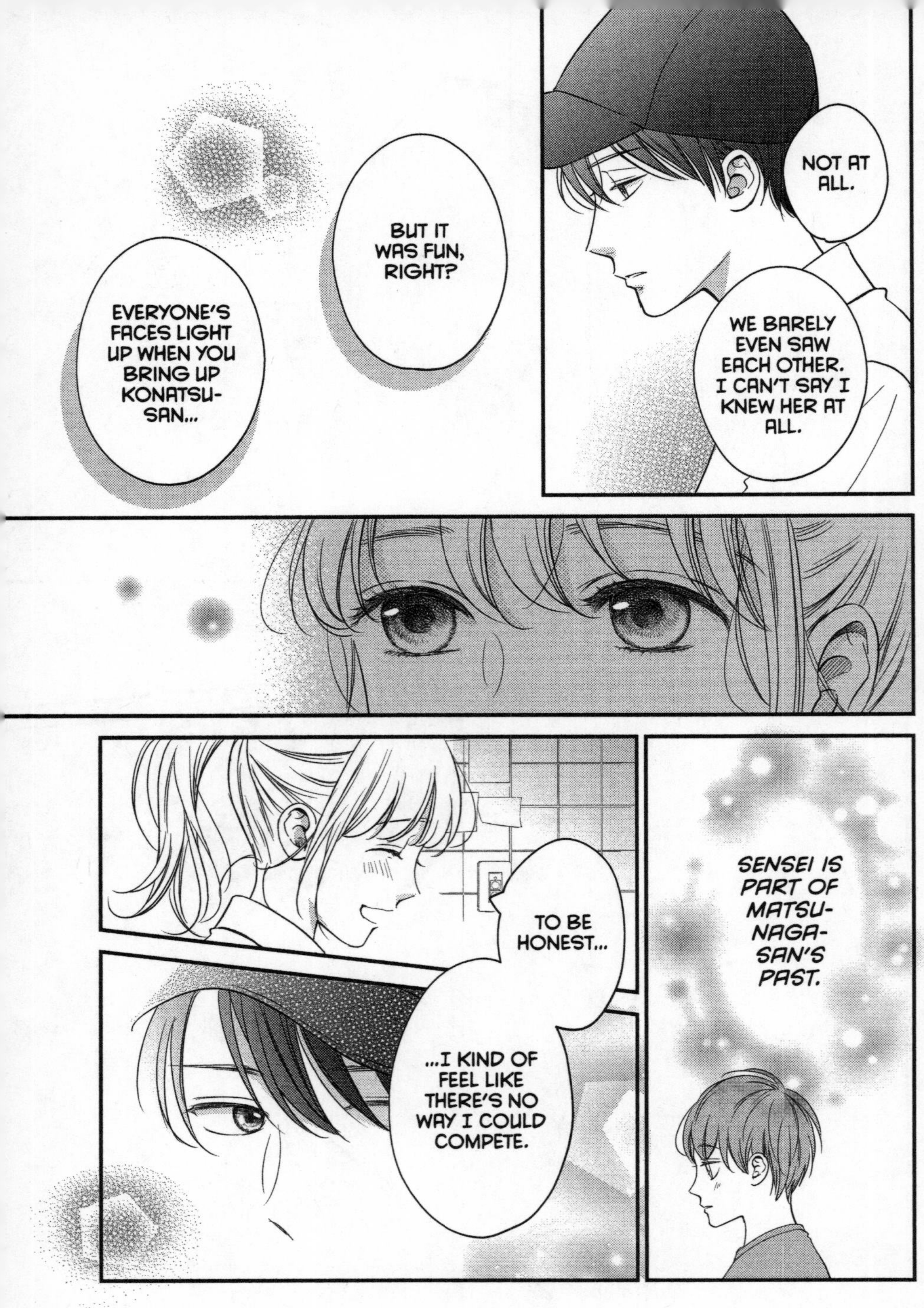
NOT AT ALL.
WE BARELY EVEN SAW EACH OTHER. I CAN'T SAY I KNEW HER AT ALL.
BUT IT WAS FUN, RIGHT?
EVERYONE'S FACES LIGHT UP WHEN YOU BRING UP KONATSU-SAN...
SENSEI IS PART OF MATSU-NAGA-SAN'S PAST.
TO BE HONEST...
...I KIND OF FEEL LIKE THERE'S NO WAY I COULD COMPETE.

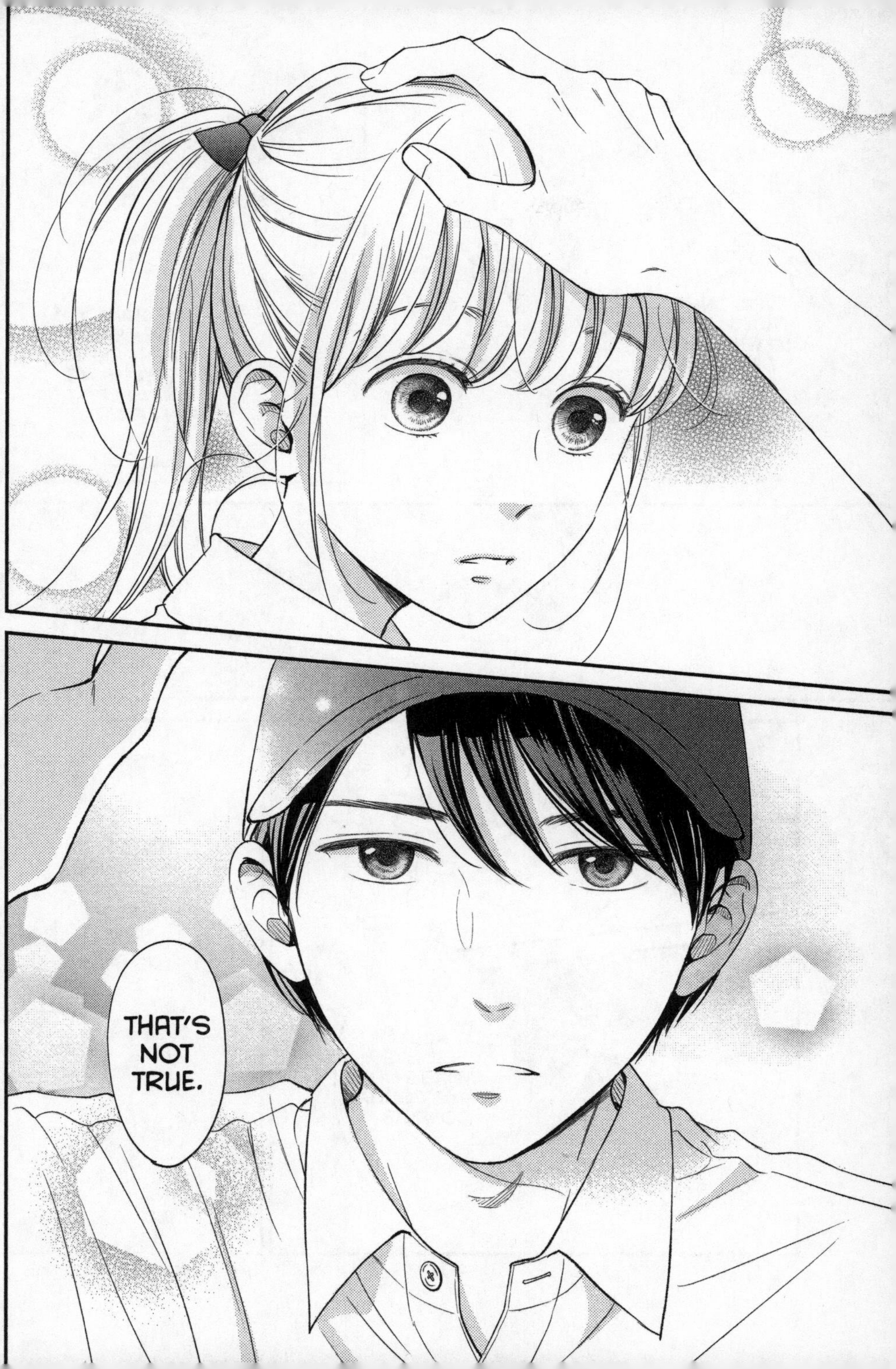
THAT'S NOT TRUE.

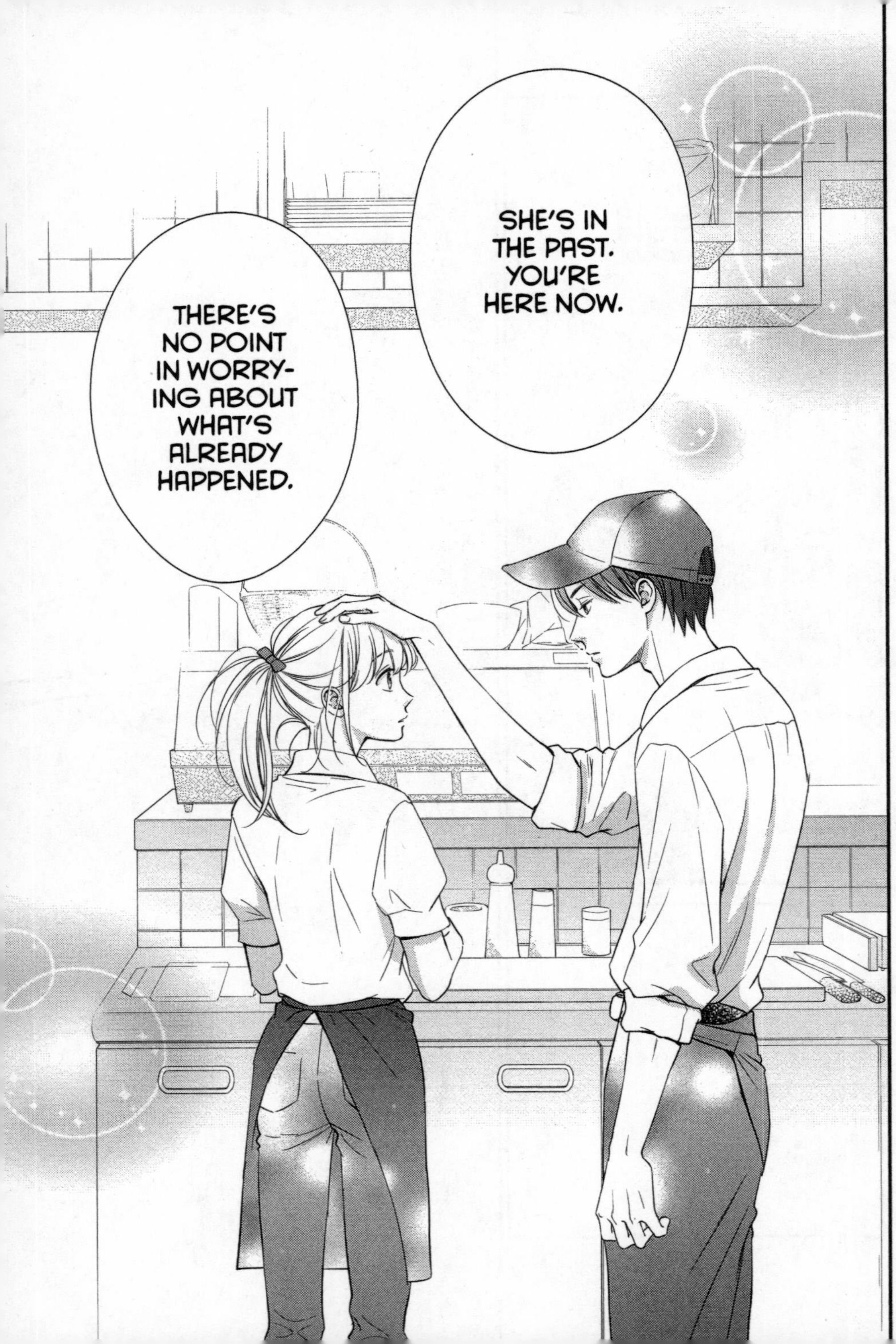
SHE'S IN THE PAST. YOU'RE HERE NOW.
THERE'S NO POINT IN WORRY-ING ABOUT WHAT'S ALREADY HAPPENED.

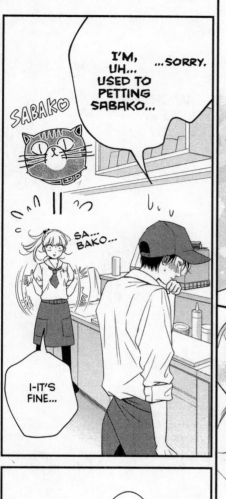

I'M, UH...
USED TO PETTING SABAKO...

...SORRY.

SABAKO

SA... BAKO...

I-IT'S FINE...

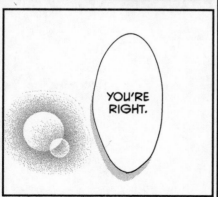

YOU'RE RIGHT.

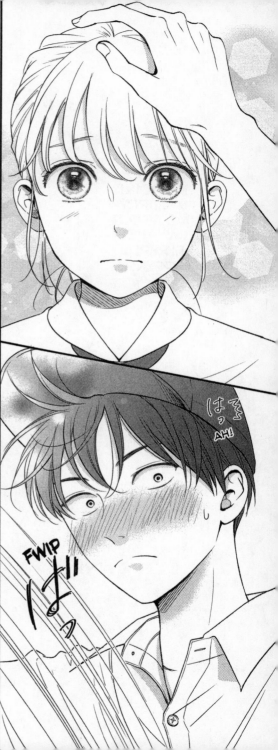

FWIP

AH!

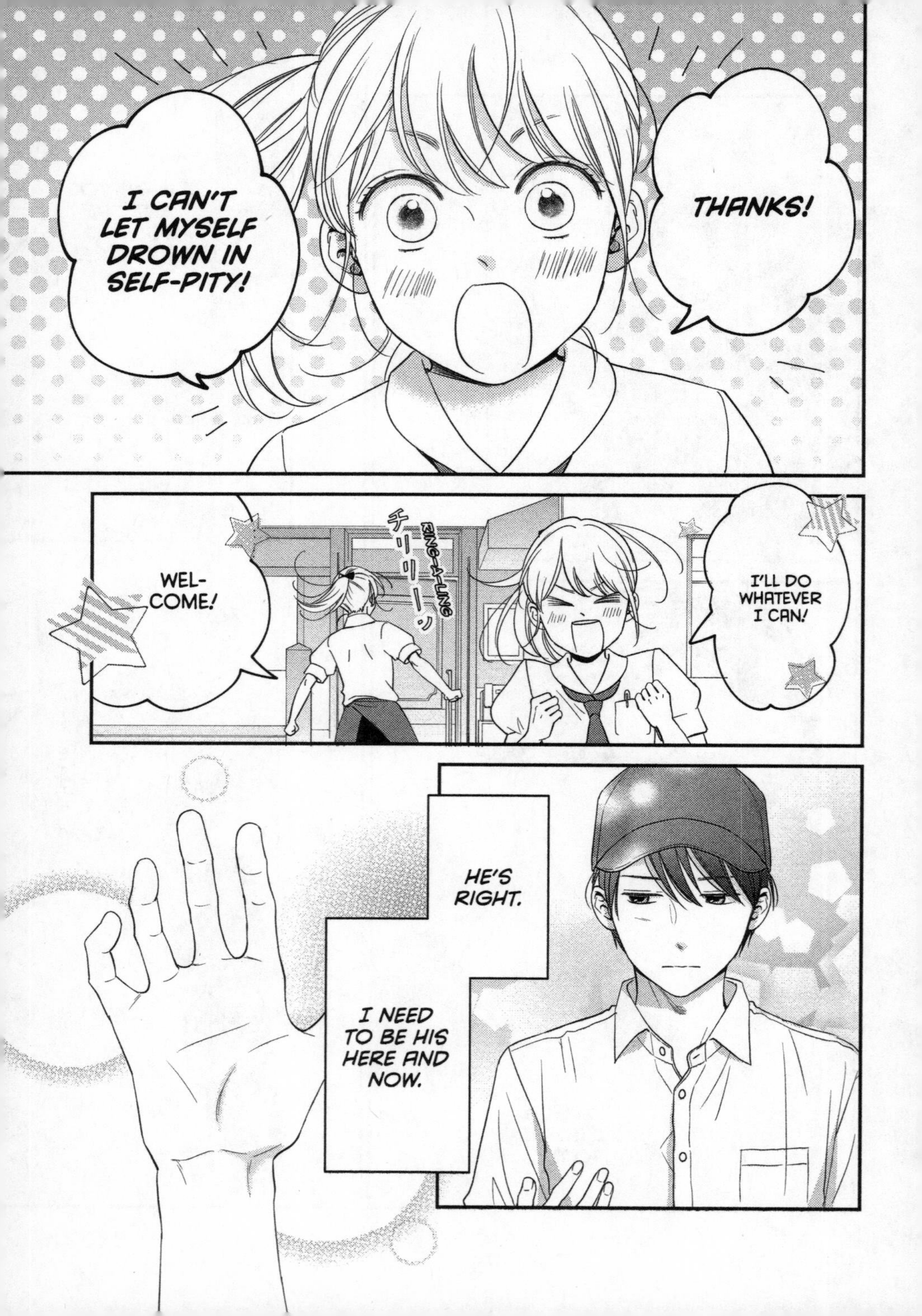
THANKS!
I CAN'T LET MYSELF DROWN IN SELF-PITY!
I'LL DO WHATEVER I CAN!
RING-A-LING
WEL-COME!
HE'S RIGHT.
I NEED TO BE HIS HERE AND NOW.

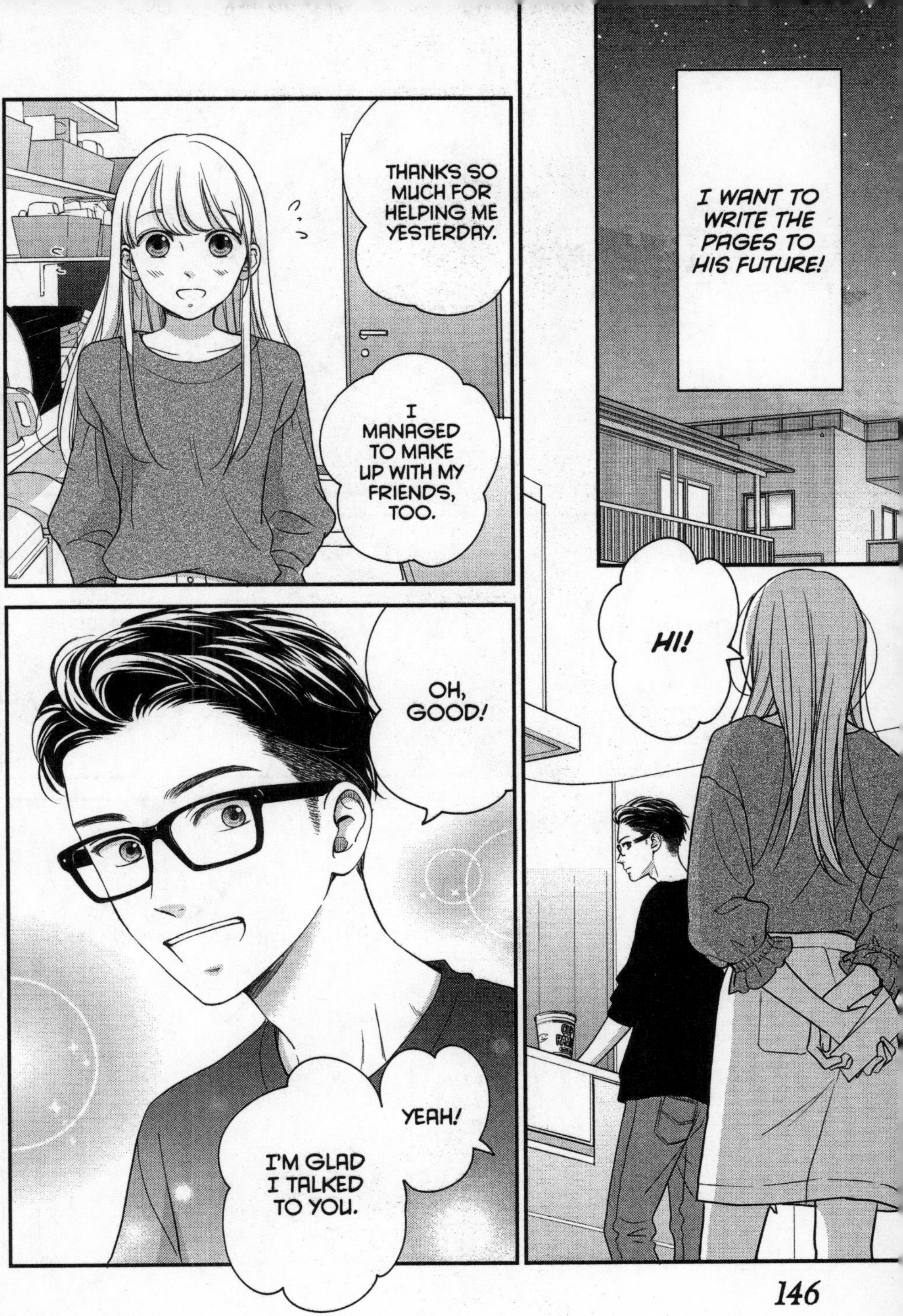
I WANT TO WRITE THE PAGES TO HIS FUTURE!
THANKS SO MUCH FOR HELPING ME YESTERDAY.
I MANAGED TO MAKE UP WITH MY FRIENDS, TOO.
HI!
OH, GOOD!
YEAH!
I'M GLAD I TALKED TO YOU.

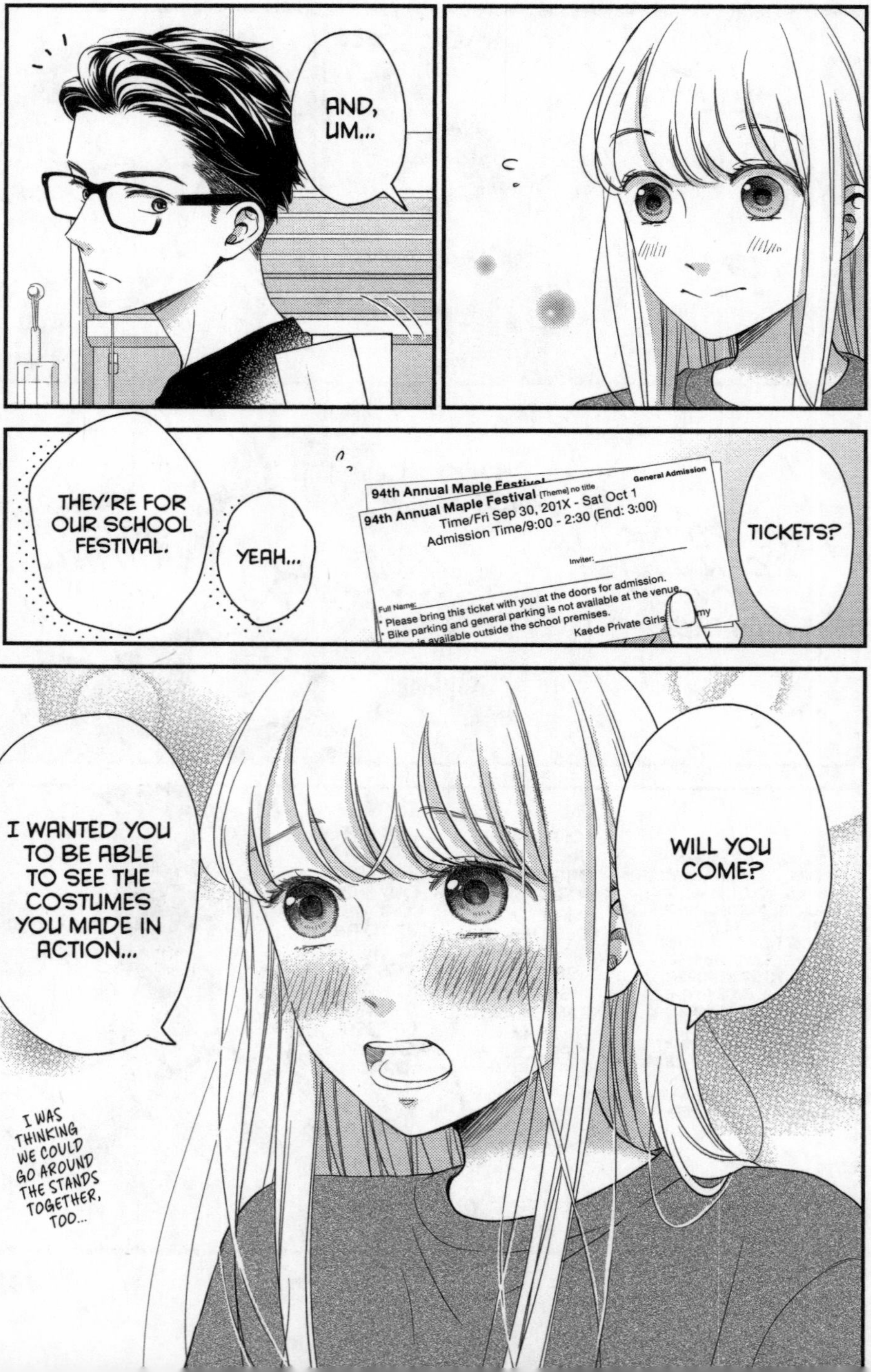
AND, UM...
TICKETS?
General Admission
94th Annual Maple Festival [Theme] no title
94th Annual Maple Festival
Time/Fri Sep 30, 201X - Sat Oct 1
Admission Time/9:00 - 2:30 (End: 3:00)
Inviter:
Full Name:
* Please bring this ticket with you at the doors for admission.
* Bike parking and general parking is not available at the venue.
is available outside the school premises.
Kaede Private Girls
YEAH...
THEY'RE FOR OUR SCHOOL FESTIVAL.
WILL YOU COME?
I WANTED YOU TO BE ABLE TO SEE THE COSTUMES YOU MADE IN ACTION...
I WAS THINKING WE COULD GO AROUND THE STANDS TOGETHER, TOO...

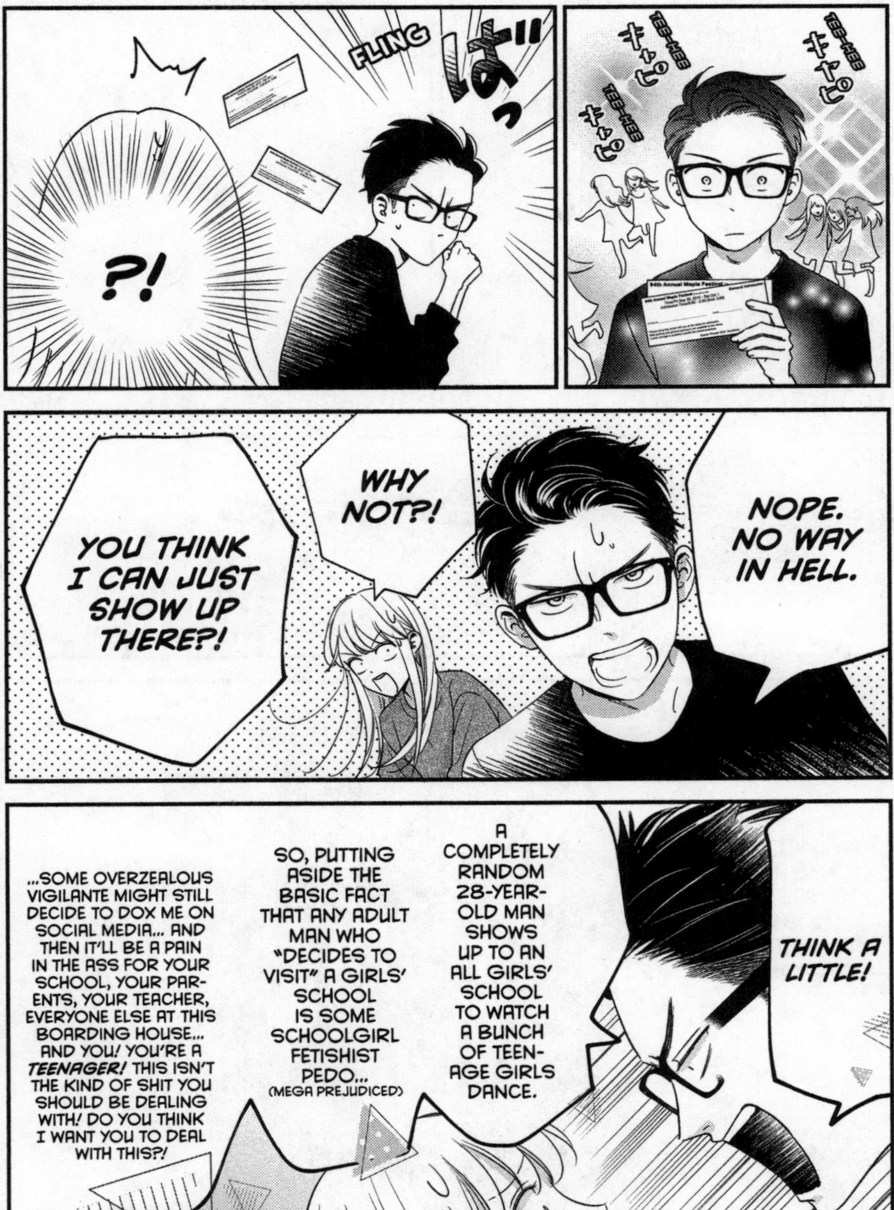
TEE-HEE キャピ
TEE-HEE キャピ
TEE-HEE キャピ
FLING ばっ
?!
NOPE. NO WAY IN HELL.
WHY NOT?!
YOU THINK I CAN JUST SHOW UP THERE?!
THINK A LITTLE!
A COMPLETELY RANDOM 28-YEAR-OLD MAN SHOWS UP TO AN ALL GIRLS' SCHOOL TO WATCH A BUNCH OF TEEN-AGE GIRLS DANCE.
SO, PUTTING ASIDE THE BASIC FACT THAT ANY ADULT MAN WHO "DECIDES TO VISIT" A GIRLS' SCHOOL IS SOME SCHOOLGIRL FETISHIST PEDO...
(MEGA PREJUDICED)
...SOME OVERZEALOUS VIGILANTE MIGHT STILL DECIDE TO DOX ME ON SOCIAL MEDIA... AND THEN IT'LL BE A PAIN IN THE ASS FOR YOUR SCHOOL, YOUR PAR-ENTS, YOUR TEACHER, EVERYONE ELSE AT THIS BOARDING HOUSE... AND YOU! YOU'RE A TEENAGER! THIS ISN'T THE KIND OF SHIT YOU SHOULD BE DEALING WITH! DO YOU THINK I WANT YOU TO DEAL WITH THIS?!

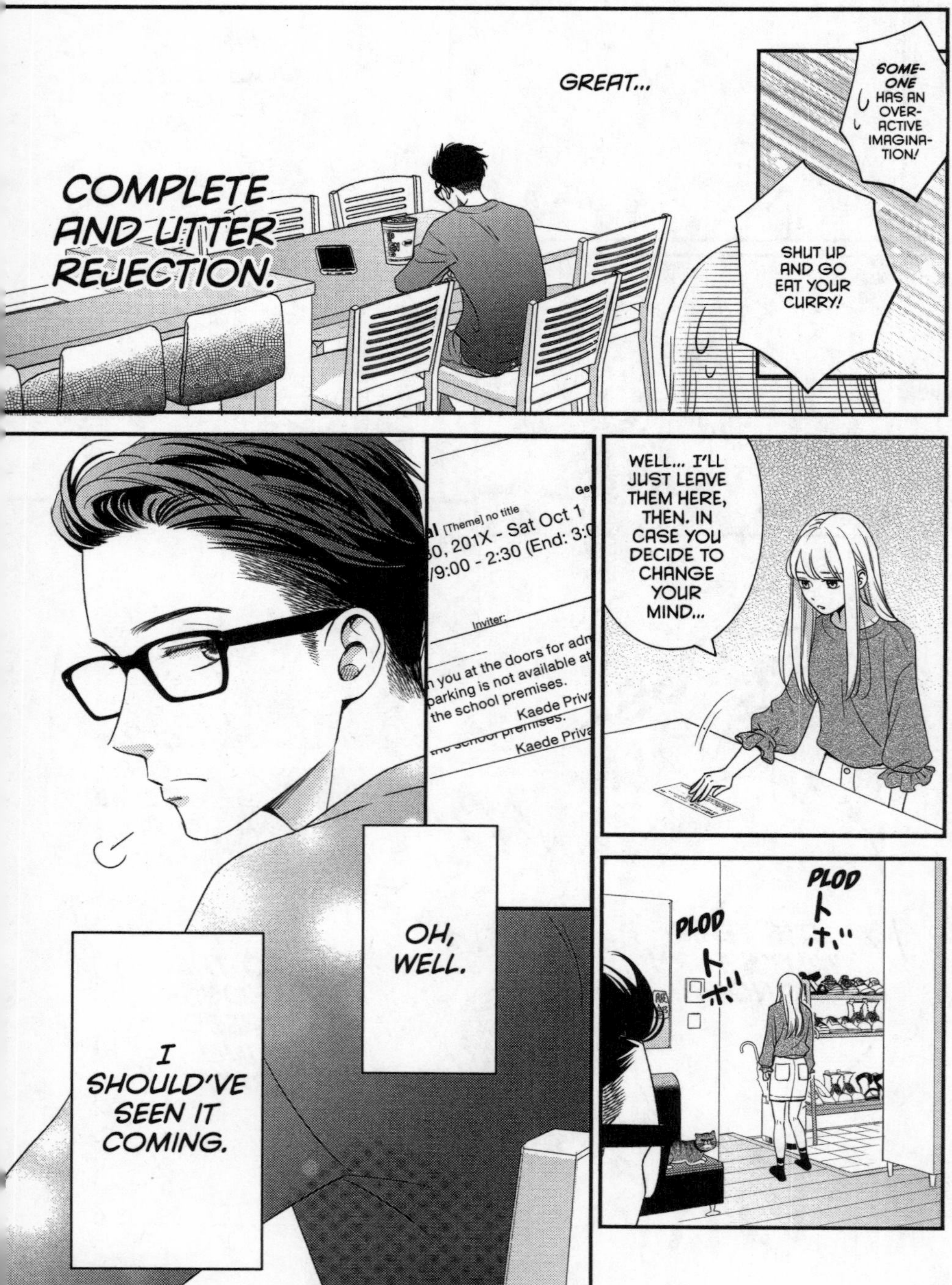
SOME-ONE HAS AN OVER-ACTIVE IMAGINA-TION!
SHUT UP AND GO EAT YOUR CURRY!
GREAT...
COMPLETE AND UTTER REJECTION.
WELL... I'LL JUST LEAVE THEM HERE, THEN. IN CASE YOU DECIDE TO CHANGE YOUR MIND...
PLOD
トボ
PLOD
トボ
[Theme] no title
30, 201X - Sat Oct 1
/9:00 - 2:30 (End: 3:0
Inviter:
n you at the doors for adm
parking is not available at
the school premises.
Kaede Priva
OH, WELL.
I SHOULD'VE SEEN IT COMING.

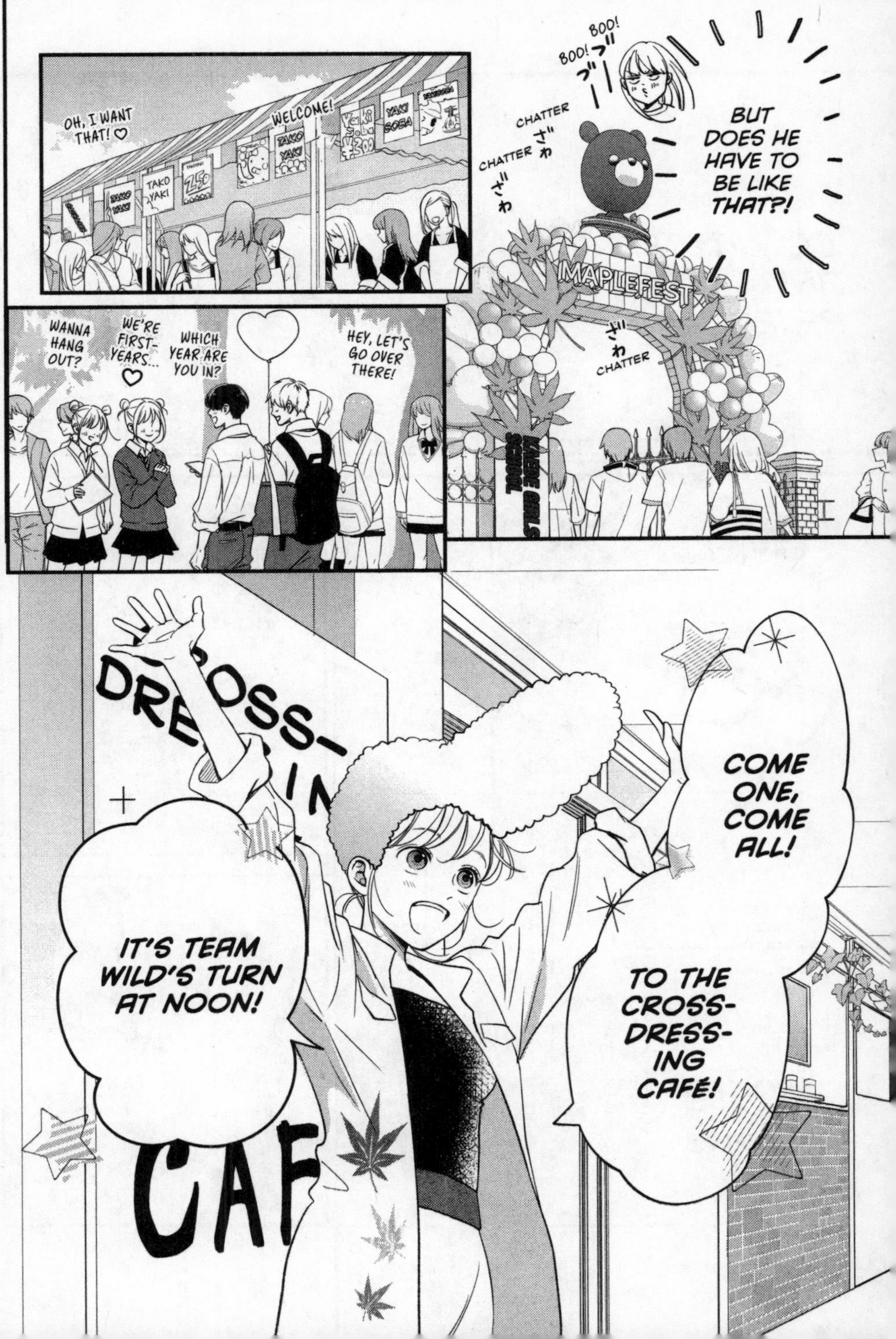
BOO!
BOO!
BUT DOES HE HAVE TO BE LIKE THAT?!
CHATTER
CHATTER
MAPLEFEST
CHATTER
KAEDE GIRLS SCHOOL
WELCOME!
OH, I WANT THAT! ♡
YAKI SOBA
Yaki Soba ¥300
TAKO YAKI
TAKO YAKI
TAKO YAKI
250
HEY, LET'S GO OVER THERE!
WHICH YEAR ARE YOU IN?
WE'RE FIRST-YEARS... ♡
WANNA HANG OUT?
COME ONE, COME ALL!
TO THE CROSS-DRESSING CAFÉ!
CROSS-DRESSIN
CAF
IT'S TEAM WILD'S TURN AT NOON!

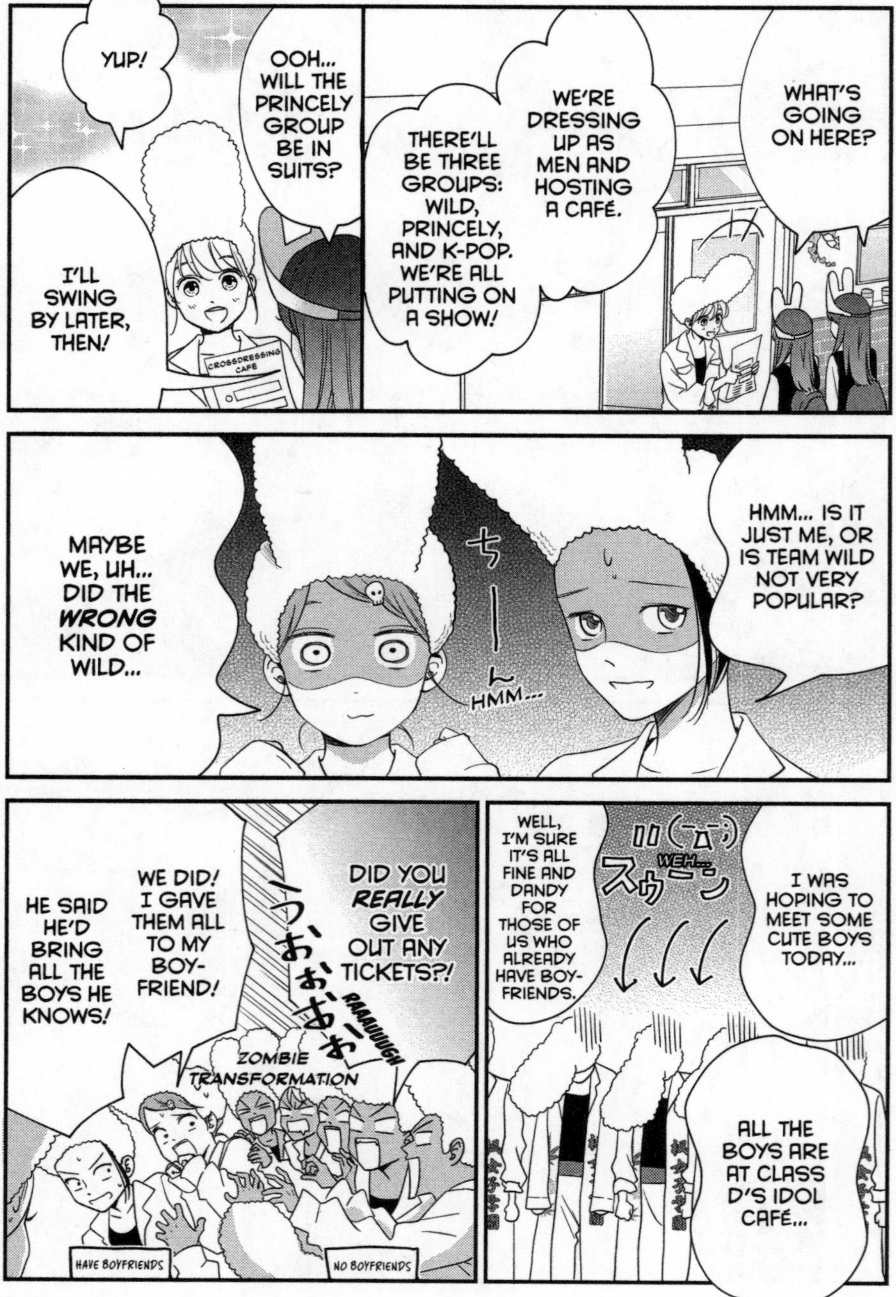
WHAT'S GOING ON HERE?
WE'RE DRESSING UP AS MEN AND HOSTING A CAFÉ.
THERE'LL BE THREE GROUPS: WILD, PRINCELY, AND K-POP. WE'RE ALL PUTTING ON A SHOW!
OOH... WILL THE PRINCELY GROUP BE IN SUITS?
YUP!
I'LL SWING BY LATER, THEN!
CROSSDRESSING CAFE
HMM... IS IT JUST ME, OR IS TEAM WILD NOT VERY POPULAR?
ちーん
HMM...
MAYBE WE, UH... DID THE **WRONG** KIND OF WILD...
I WAS HOPING TO MEET SOME CUTE BOYS TODAY...
スゥーン
WEH...
WELL, I'M SURE IT'S ALL FINE AND DANDY FOR THOSE OF US WHO ALREADY HAVE BOY-FRIENDS.
ALL THE BOYS ARE AT CLASS D'S IDOL CAFÉ...
DID YOU **REALLY** GIVE OUT ANY TICKETS?!
うおおおお
RAAAUUUGH
WE DID! I GAVE THEM ALL TO MY BOY-FRIEND!
HE SAID HE'D BRING ALL THE BOYS HE KNOWS!
ZOMBIE TRANSFORMATION
HAVE BOYFRIENDS
NO BOYFRIENDS

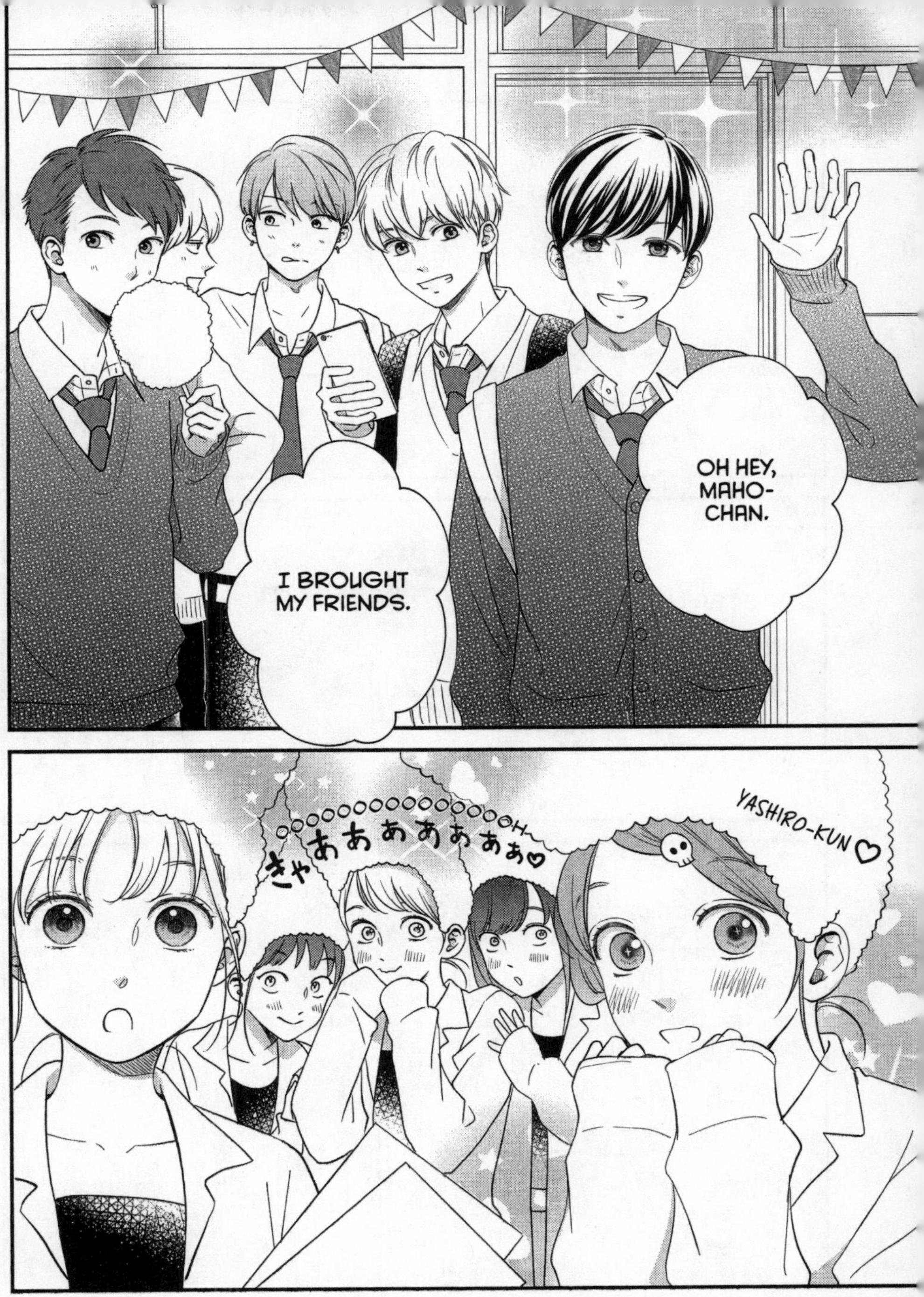
OH HEY, MAHO-CHAN.
I BROUGHT MY FRIENDS.
YASHIRO-KUN♡
きゃあああああああ♡
OOOOOOOOOOOOOOOH-

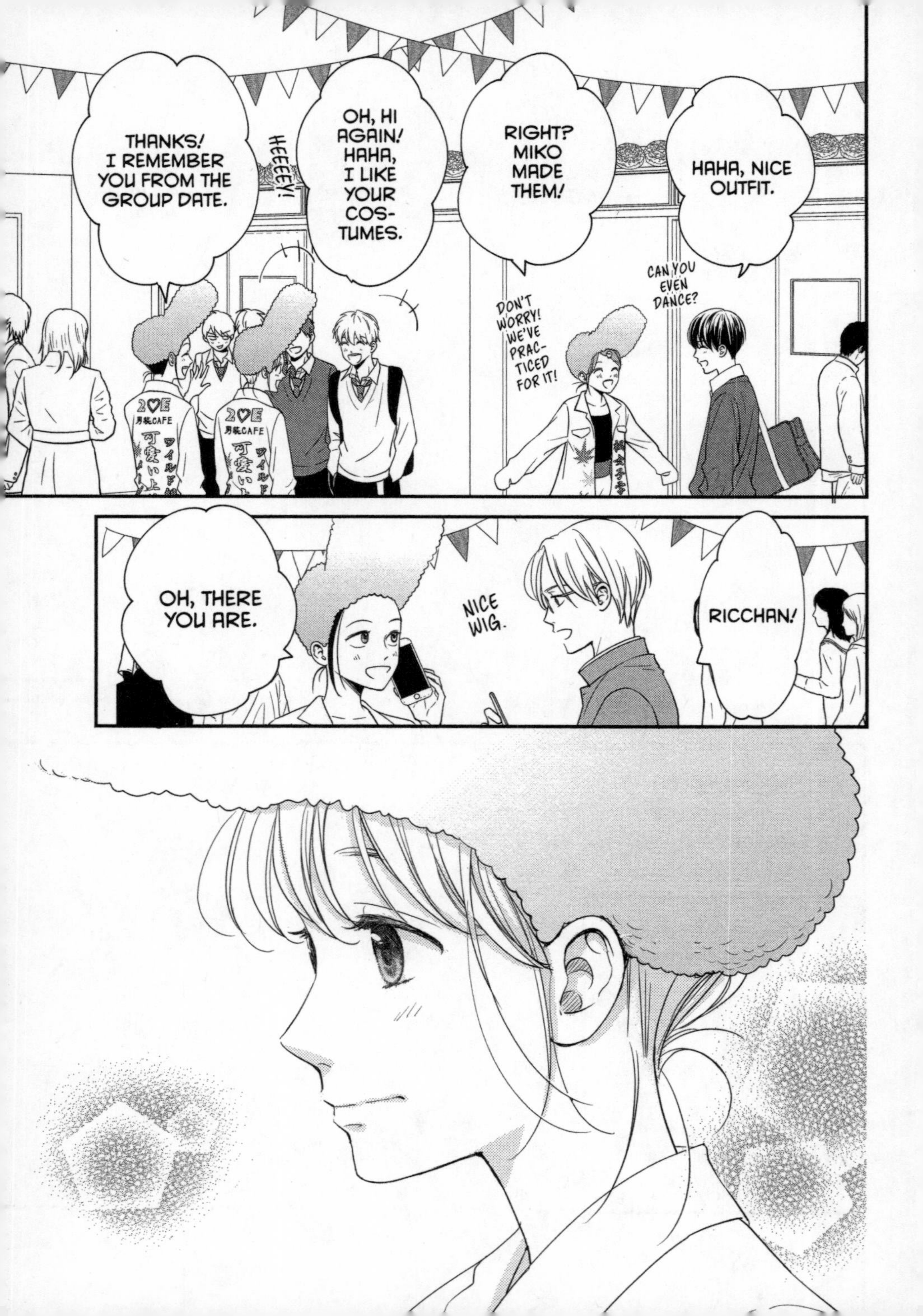
HAHA, NICE OUTFIT.
CAN YOU EVEN DANCE?
RIGHT? MIKO MADE THEM!
DON'T WORRY! WE'VE PRACTICED FOR IT!
OH, HI AGAIN! HAHA, I LIKE YOUR COSTUMES.
HEEEEY!
THANKS! I REMEMBER YOU FROM THE GROUP DATE.
RICCHAN!
NICE WIG.
OH, THERE YOU ARE.

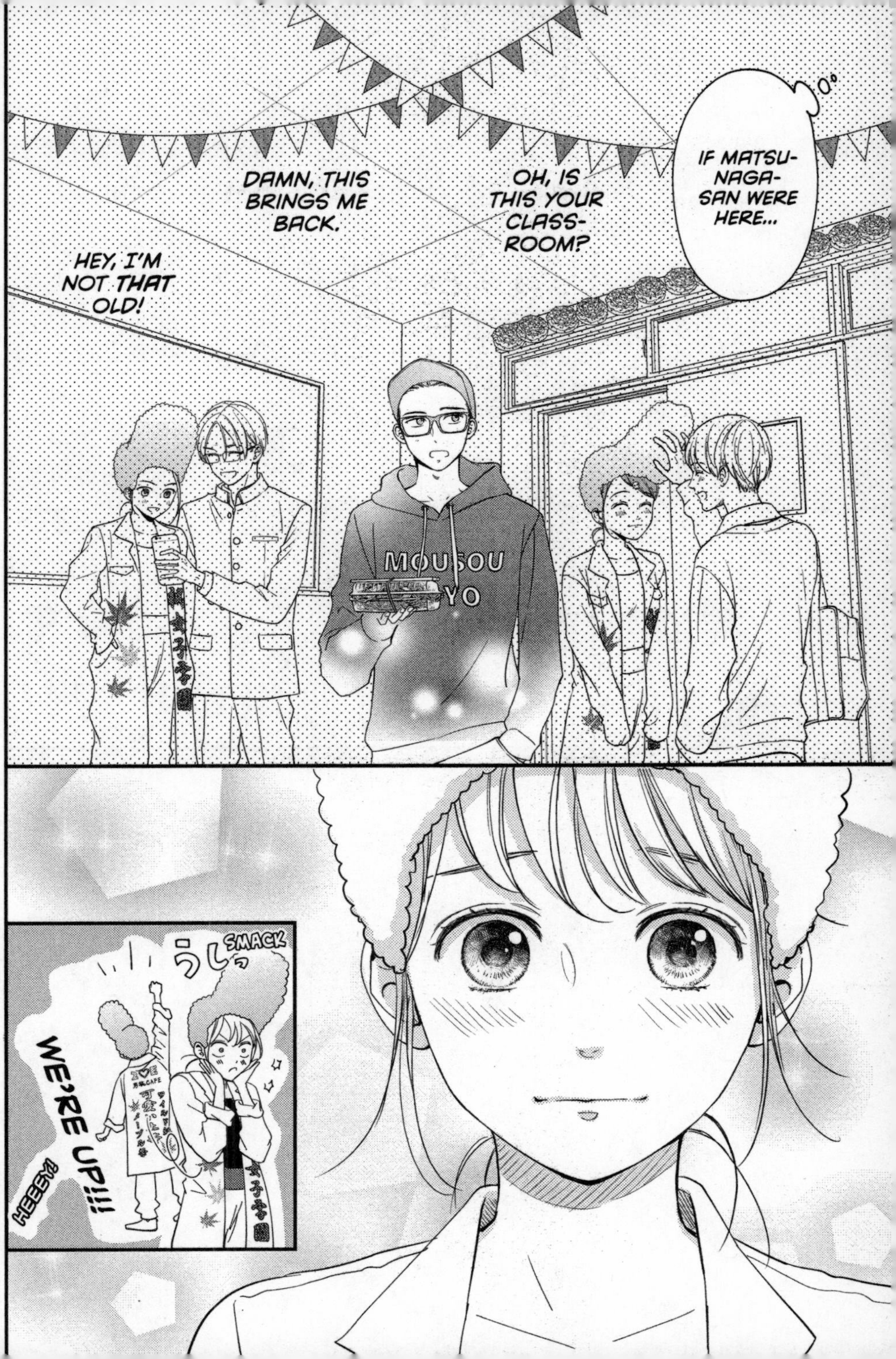
IF MATSU-NAGA-SAN WERE HERE...
OH, IS THIS YOUR CLASS-ROOM?
DAMN, THIS BRINGS ME BACK.
HEY, I'M NOT THAT OLD!
MOUSOU YO
うしっ
SMACK
WE'RE UP!!!
HEEEY!

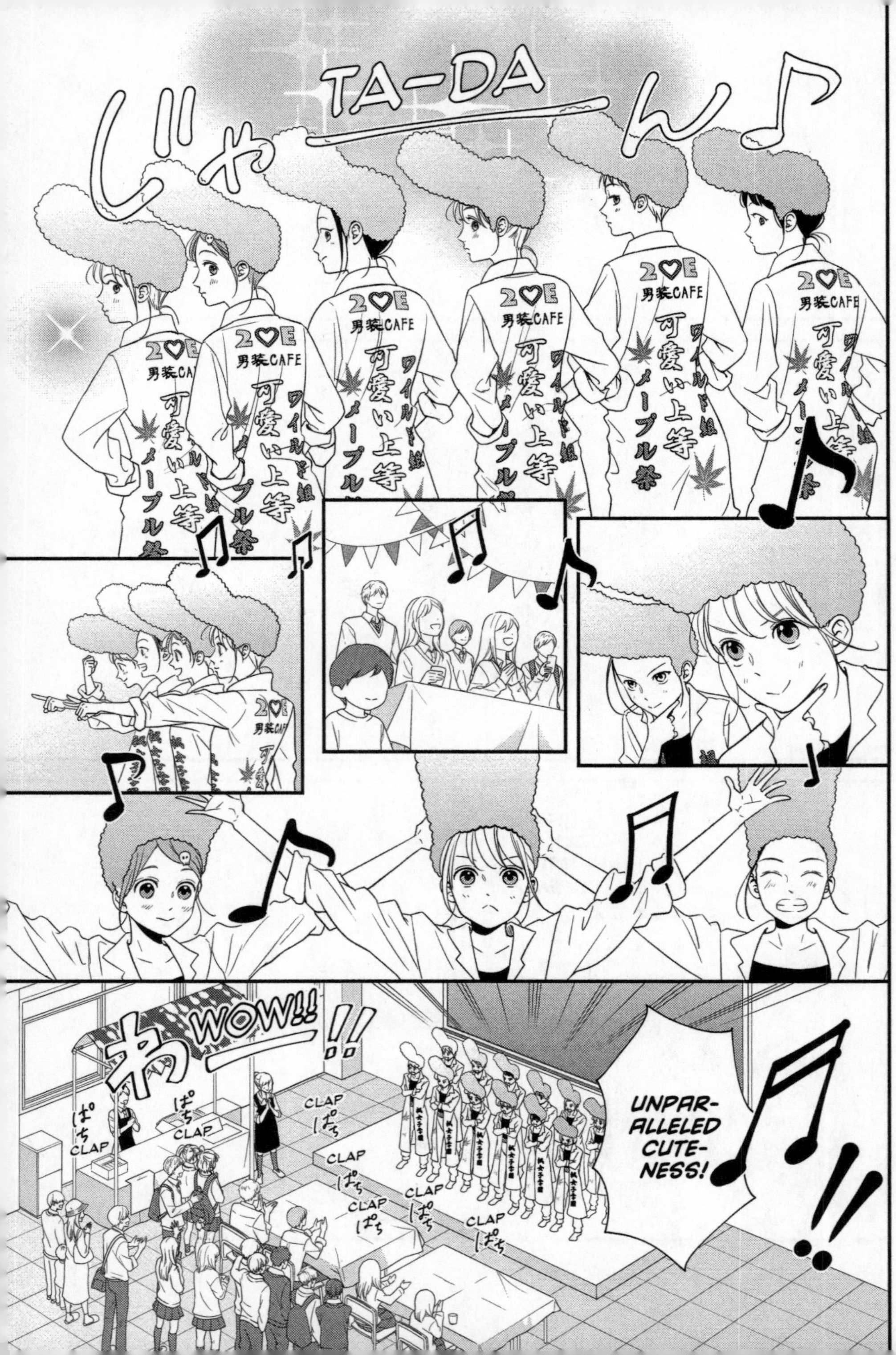

じゃーーん♪
TA-DA
2♡E
男装CAFE
可愛い上等
ワイルド組
メープル祭
UNPAR-
ALLELED
CUTE-
NESS!
CLAP ぱち
CLAP ぱち
CLAP ぱち
CLAP ぱち
CLAP ぱち
ぱち CLAP
ぱち CLAP
わーー!!
WOW!!

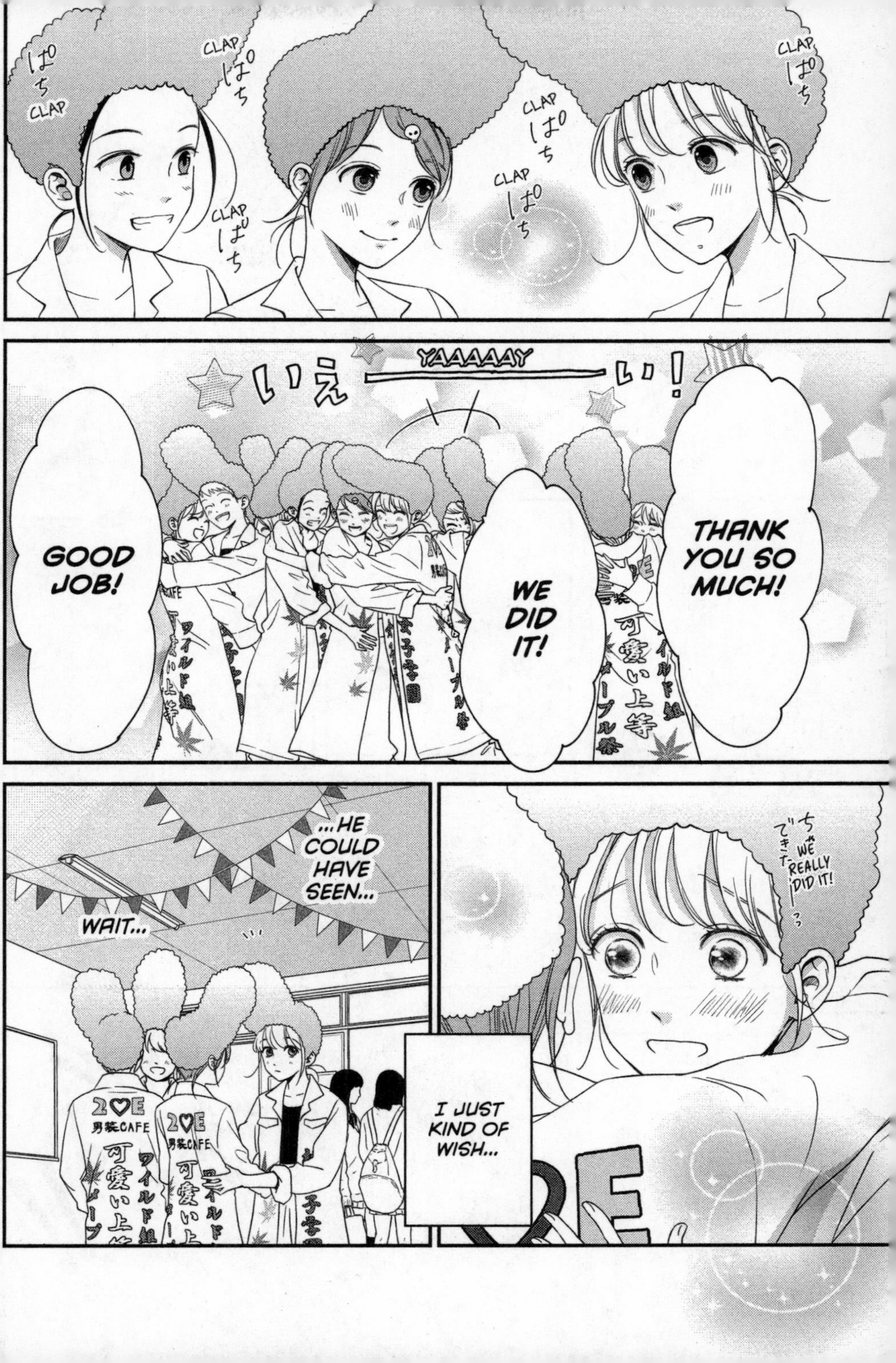
CLAP ぱち
CLAP ぱち
CLAP ぱち
CLAP ぱち
ぱち CLAP
CLAP ぱち
YAAAAAY
いえーい!
THANK YOU SO MUCH!
WE DID IT!
GOOD JOB!
WE REALLY DID IT!
I JUST KIND OF WISH...
...HE COULD HAVE SEEN...
WAIT...

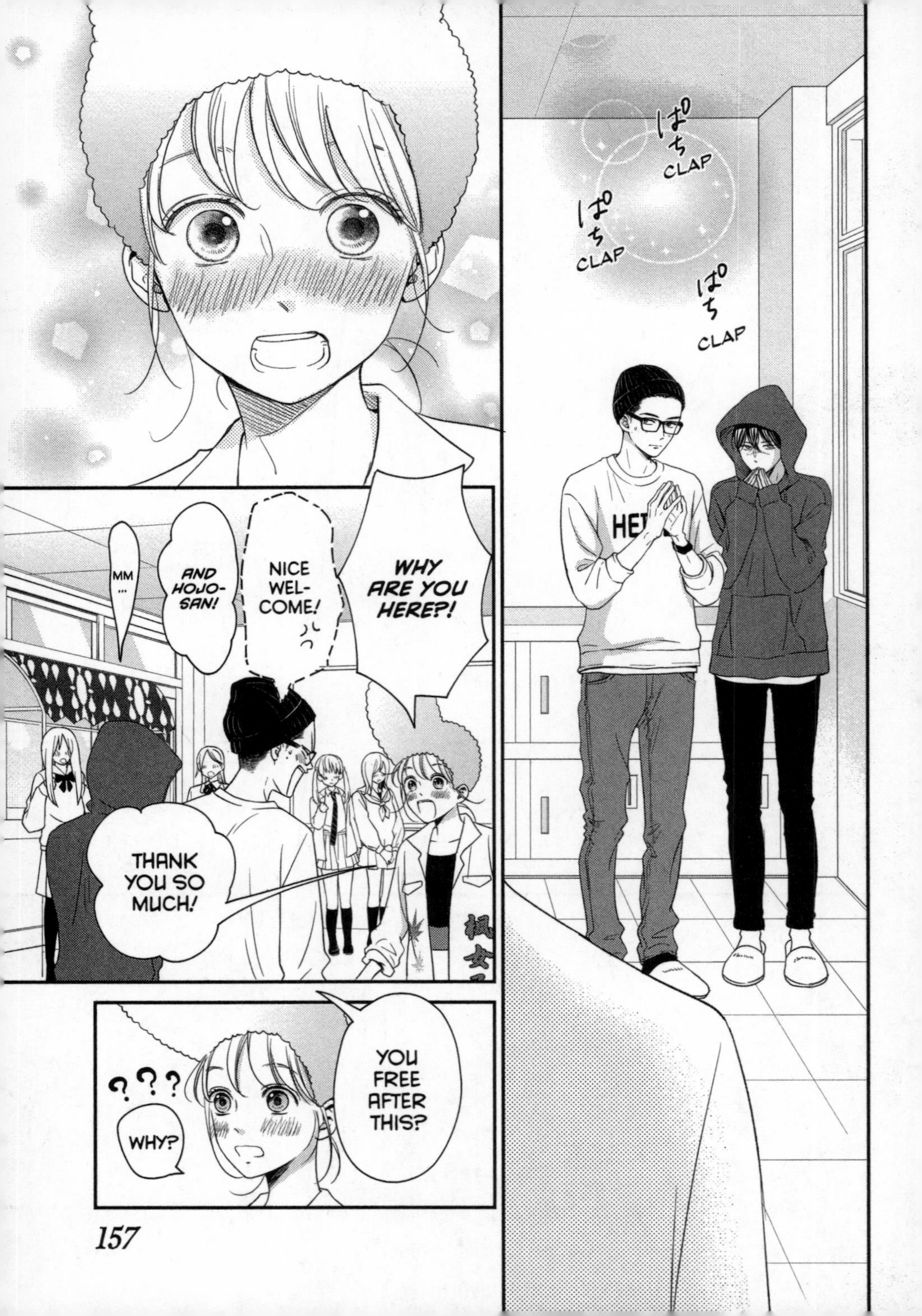

ぱち
CLAP
ぱち
CLAP
ぱち
CLAP
WHY ARE YOU HERE?!
NICE WEL-COME!
AND HOJO-SAN!
MM...
THANK YOU SO MUCH!
YOU FREE AFTER THIS?
???
WHY?

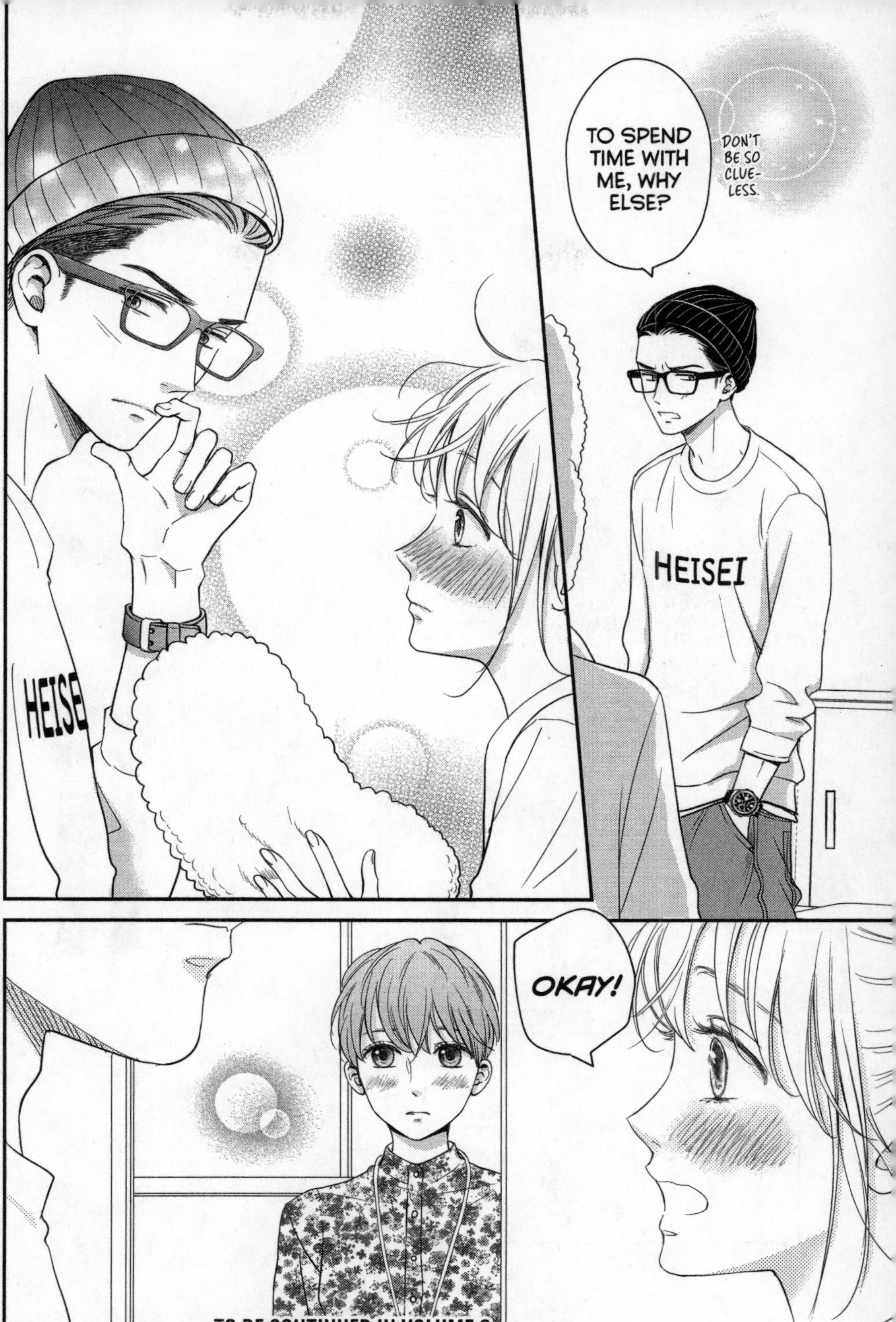
TO SPEND TIME WITH ME, WHY ELSE?
DON'T BE SO CLUE-LESS.
HEISEI
HEISEI
OKAY!
TO BE CONTINUED IN VOLUME 6

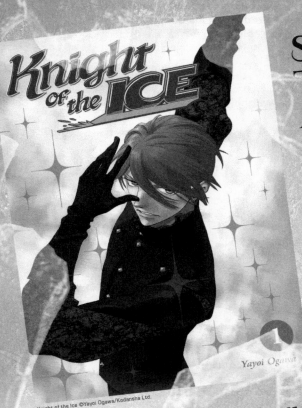

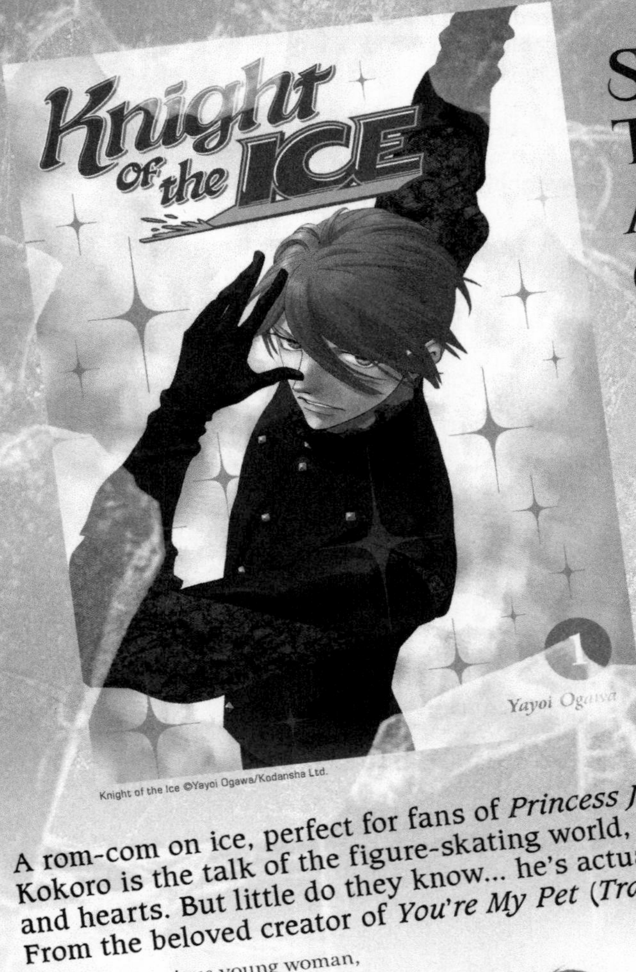

Knight of the Ice ©Yayoi Ogawa/Kodansha Ltd.

Yayoi Ogawa

SKATING THRILLS AND ICY CHILLS WITH THIS NEW TINGLY ROMANCE SERIES!

A rom-com on ice, perfect for fans of *Princess Jellyfish* and *Wotakoi*. Kokoro is the talk of the figure-skating world, winning trophies and hearts. But little do they know... he's actually a huge nerd! From the beloved creator of *You're My Pet* (*Tramps Like Us*).

Chitose is a serious young woman, working for the health magazine *SASSO*. Or at least, she would be, if she wasn't constantly getting distracted by her childhood friend, international figure skating star Kokoro Kijinami! In the public eye and on the ice, Kokoro is a gallant, flawless knight, but behind his glittery costumes and breathtaking spins lies a secret: He's actually a hopelessly romantic otaku, who can only land his quad jumps when Chitose is on hand to recite a spell from his favorite magical girl anime!

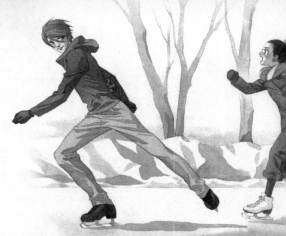

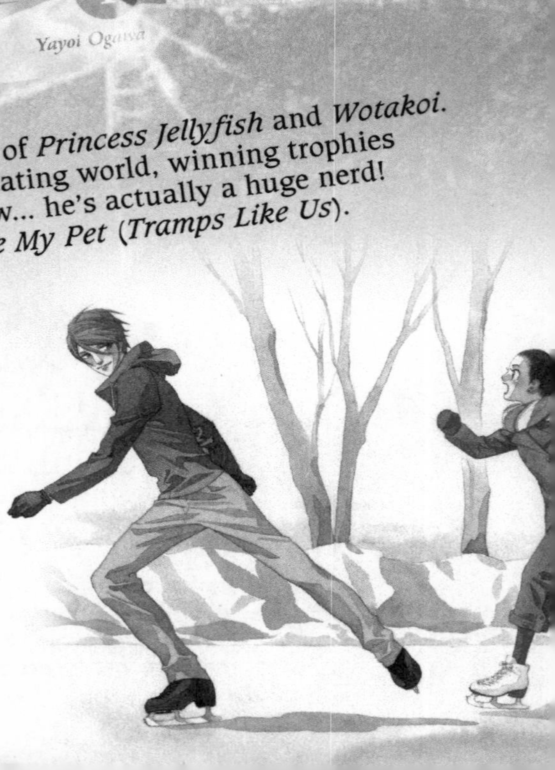

A Kodansha Comics Trade Paperback Original
Living-Room Matsunaga-san 5 copyright © 2018 Keiko Iwashita
English translation copyright © 2020 Keiko Iwashita

Published in the United States by Kodansha Comics, an imprint of
Kodansha USA Publishing, LLC, New York.

Publication rights for this English edition arranged through
Kodansha Ltd., Tokyo.

First published in Japan in 2018 by Kodansha Ltd., Tokyo
as *Living no Matsunaga-san*, volume 5.

ISBN 978-1-64651-054-2

Original cover design by Tomohiro Kusume and Yuu Ikeda (arcoinc)

Printed in the United States of America.

www.kodanshacomics.com

9 8 7 6 5 4 3 2
Translation: Ursula Ku
Lettering: Jan Lan Ivan Concepcion & Ean Scrale
Additional Lettering: Michael Martin
Editing: Thalia Sutton and Tiff Ferentini
Kodansha Comics edition cover design by Phil Balsman

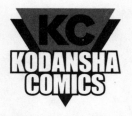

Publisher: Kiichiro Sugawara

Director of publishing services: Ben Applegate
Associate director of operations: Stephen Pakula
Publishing services managing editor: Noelle Webster
Assistant production manager: Emi Lotto, Angela Zurlo